INTERCONNECTED WORLDS
Tourism in Southeast Asia

ADVANCES IN TOURISM RESEARCH SERIES

Series Editor: Professor Stephen J. Page
Scottish Enterprise Forth Valley Chair in Tourism, University of Stirling, UK

Advances in Tourism Research is a new series of monographs and edited volumes which comprise state-of-the-art research findings, written and edited by leading researchers working in the wider field of tourism studies. The series has been designed to provide a cutting edge focus for researchers interested in tourism, particularly the management issues now facing decision-makers, policy analysts and the public sector. The audience is much wider than just academics and each book seeks to make a significant contribution to the literature in the field of study by not only reviewing the state of knowledge relating to each topic but also questioning some of the prevailing assumptions and research paradigms which currently exist in tourism research. The series also aims to provide a platform for further studies in each area by highlighting key research agendas which will stimulate further debate and interest in the expanding area of tourism research. The series is always willing to consider new ideas for innovative and scholarly books and inquiries can be made to the Series Editor.

Published:

ASHWORTH & TUNBRIDGE
The Tourist-Historic City: Retrospect and Prospect of Managing the Heritage City

RYAN & PAGE
Tourism Management: Towards the New Millennium

SONG & WITT
Tourism Demand Modelling and Forecasting: Modern Econometric Approaches

Forthcoming titles include:

BAUM & LUNDTORP
Tourism and Seasonality

PAGE & WILKS
Managing Tourist Health and Safety

Related Elsevier journals

Annals of Tourism Research
Cornell Hotel and Restaurant Administration Quarterly
International Journal of Hospitality Management
International Journal of Intercultural Relations
Tourism Management
World Development

INTERCONNECTED WORLDS
Tourism in Southeast Asia

Edited by

Peggy Teo

T.C. Chang

and

K.C. Ho

2001

PERGAMON

An Imprint of Elsevier Science

Amsterdam-London-New York-Oxford-Paris-Shannon-Tokyo

ELSEVIER SCIENCE Ltd
The Boulevard, Langford Lane
Kidlington, Oxford OX5 1GB, UK

First edition 2001

Library of Congress Cataloging in Publication Data
Interconnected worlds : tourism in Southeast Asia / edited by Peggy Teo, T.C. Chang, and K.C. Ho
    p. cm – (Advances in tourism research series)
    Includes bibliographical references and indexes.
      I. Tourism–Asia, Southeastern. I. Title: Tourism in Southeast Asia. II. Teo, Peggy. III. Chang, T.C.
    IV. Ho, K.C., 1956- V. Series
G155.A743 157 2001
338.4'79159–dc21

British Library Cataloguing in Publication Data
Interconnected worlds : tourism in Southeast Asia.—(Advances in tourism research)
    1.Tourism–Asia, Southeastern
    I.Teo, Peggy II.Chang, T. C. III.Ho, K. C.
338.4'79159

ISBN: 0-08-043695-1

♾ The paper used in this publication meets the requirements of ANSI/NISO Z39.48-1992 (Permanence of Paper).
Printed in The Netherlands.

Contents

vi *Contents*

Preface

In this era of globalisation and increasing interconnections between economies and societies, individuals, corporations, city-states, countries and even whole regions have begun rethinking their fundamental best-practices in areas as diverse as human resource management, industrial planning, migration policies, environmental protection and other critical areas. In the field of tourism, the 1990s has similarly ushered in an era which some have described as "new tourism" (Poon, 1989) and others have termed "post-Fordist tourism" (Urry, 1990) or "postmodern tourism" (Nuryanti, 1996). Despite these semantic differences, these concepts cohesively allude to discernible and significant changes taking place in the way tourists consume places; tourism operators provide services; planners organise policies; and tourism landscapes are configured and developed.

One of the most significant changes in tourism has been the concept of *interconnections* which is evident at various levels of tourism planning. Strategic alliances between rival companies; vertical integration between and across firms; collaborations between public and private sectors; partnerships between countries and regions have indeed become common practice in contemporary tourism and it is the aim of this book to address this theme. Certainly it must be said that this book itself is the fruit of one such interconnection – the alliance between academia and government. The book was first conceived at a conference co-organised by the National University of Singapore (NUS) and the Singapore Tourism Board (STB) offering a platform for academics and practitioners to exchange information and ideas on tourism planning in Southeast Asia. The conference titled *Interconnected Worlds: Southeast Asian Tourism in the 21st Century* held in Singapore (6–7 September 1999) brought together over 200 participants and 48 papers addressing such issues as regional tourism collaboration, ecotourism, heritage tourism, hubs and tourism gateways, and case studies of Southeast Asian locales. Papers dealing specifically with the theme of interconnections – ranging from inter-country collaborations, tourism growth regions, corporate alliances, conceptual discourses on global–local dialectics, and the problems and challenges of regionalisation – were selected for publication after a stringent peer review process. Indeed, this book is proof that the "great divide" between academia and practice that Carson Jenkins (1999) speaks of can certainly be bridged.

Our focus on Southeast Asia in this book is strategic in different respects. At an academic level, there has been little attention devoted to the study of inter- and intra-regional connections in Southeast Asian tourism even though tourism research on the region itself has ballooned in recent years. Notwithstanding the achievements by Richter (1989), Hitchcock *et al.* (1993), Picard and Wood (1997), and Hall and Page (2000), this book is born from the Editors' personal conviction that it is no longer enough just to investigate tourism in Southeast Asian countries on a case to case basis. Rather the focus should be on how individual countries have coalesced (or have attempted to coalesce) with each other and the 'outside' world under the banner of regionalism and globalisation. Already, ASEANTA (ASEAN Tourism Association) is promoting the region as ASEAN 10 and countries like Thailand, Brunei and Singapore are marketing themselves to the world as regional gateways. We hope that, by researching and initiating dialogues on regional and global inter-connections, this book will contribute to what the late Stephen Britton has termed "critical geography of tourism" (Britton, 1991) – an academic understanding of tourism that adds value to current research and debates in economic geography, geopolitics, cultural politics, globalisation and the financial and environmental crises in Southeast Asia. By projecting the voice of tourism researchers in these critical areas of study, we also hope that tourism research will be better appreciated and acknowledged.

On an institutional and personal level, this book on Southeast Asia is an explicit attempt to anchor the Centre for Advanced Studies (at NUS) as a resource centre of Asian research and knowledge. Just as it is no longer enough to develop and market one's country as a tourism destination isolated from the larger regional canvas, as academics and researchers it is also no longer enough to confine our research lens to the local (although this remains critical) but to engage also in local–regional–global affairs. Just as the CAS is committed to high-quality research investigating issues of relevance to East, South and Southeast Asia, the three Editors of this book, as researchers and teachers at NUS, also share a commitment to study, write and teach of an interconnected world especially as it pertains to our home region. Increasingly as the boundaries between nation-states and region-states blur (Ohmae, 1995) it is unhelpful and certainly a disservice to our students and fellow academics to continue talking of cities and countries as if they are (or ever were!) sharply delineated entities either impregnable by external forces or willy-nilly vulner-able to such pressures. Engaging in sensitively nuanced research that probes the grey areas of glocalisation, the global–local nexus, hybridity, new regionalism – *cliché* terms they may be – is thus a personal agenda we are engaged in and to which this book is ultimately devoted.

In this venture, the Editors would like to take the opportunity to thank the Centre for Advanced Studies, Faculty of Arts and Social Sciences and the National University of Singapore for the academic vigour, conducive research environment and financial resources that have enabled this work to come into being. We also appreciate the financial and other support given by the Singapore Tourism Board; it is indeed a privilege to be able to work so well with the Board. Special mention must be made of the efforts of Patrick Lau whose wide experience at the Board was freely shared with us and who was able to provide insights from an industry point of view. Indeed this book and the conference from which it originated are outputs from a Memorandum of Understanding signed by NUS and STB in 1996, establishing a mutual and highly productive dialogue between academics and policy makers for which we are truly thankful. We are also most appreciative of the support lent to us by Lily Kong (Acting Dean, Faculty of Arts and Social Sciences, NUS) and Tong Chee Kiong (former Dean, Faculty of Arts and Social Sciences, NUS) who encour-aged this book project from the very start, and Stephen Page (Co-editor, *Tourism Management*) for his invaluable and wise advice pertaining to our myriad editorial queries. We also thank Lee Li Kheng for rendering her superb map-drawing expertise; Chang Siew Ngoh who turned the multiple manuscript formats into a uniform one and paid attention to edits that we missed; Valerie, Yati and Selvi at CAS for the long hours that went into the conference; Shirlena Huang for lending us her expertise and a good ear; and Victor R. Savage and Brenda Yeoh for pushing us on. Last but not least, we acknowledge the support and faith that each of our families has in us.

T.C. Chang
Department of Geography, National University of Singapore

References

Britton, S. (1990) 'Tourism, capital, and place: Towards a critical geography of tourism'. *Environment and Planning D: Society and Space*, 9(4), 451–78.

Hall, C.M. and Page, S. (eds.) (2000) *Tourism in South and Southeast Asia: Issues and Cases*. Oxford: Butterworth-Heinemann.

Hitchcock, M., King, V.T. and Parnwell, M.J. (eds.) (1993) *Tourism in Southeast Asia*. London and New York: Routledge.

Jenkins, C. (1999) 'Tourism academics and tourism practitioners: Bridging the great divide', in D.G. Pearce and R.W. Butler (eds.) *Contemporary Issues in Tourism Development*. London and New York: Routledge, 52–64.

Nuryanti, W. (1996) 'Heritage and postmodern tourism'. *Annals of Tourism Research*, 23(2), 249–60.

Ohmae, K. (1995) *The End of the Nation State. The Rise of Regional Economies*. New York: The Free Press.

Picard, M. and Wood, R.E. (eds.) (1997) *Tourism, Ethnicity, and the State in Asian and Pacific Societies*. Honolulu: University of Hawai'i Press.

Poon, A. (1989) 'Competitive strategies for a "new tourism"', in C.P. Cooper (ed.) *Progress in Tourism, Recreation and Hospitality Management*, Vol. 1. London: Belhaven Press, 91–102.

Richter, L. (1989) *The Politics of Tourism in Asia*. Honolulu: University of Hawai'i Press.

Urry, J. (1990) *The Tourist Gaze. Leisure and Travel in Contemporary Societies*. London: Sage Publications.

The Contributors

Kathleen M. Adams, Department of Sociology and Anthropology, Loyola University Chicago, 6525 N. Sheridan Avenue, Chicago, IC 60626, USA

Heather Black, School of Urban and Regional Planning, Faculty of Environmental Studies, University of Waterloo, Waterloo, Ontario N2L 3G1, Canada

Peter Burns, School of Services Management, University of Brighton, Darley Road, Eastbourne BN20 7UR, UK

Carolyn Cartier, Department of Geography, University of Southern California, Los Angeles CA 90089-0255, USA

T. C. Chang, Department of Geography, National University of Singapore, 1 Arts Link, Singapore 117570

Erik Cohen, Department of Sociology and Anthropology, The Hebrew University of Jerusalem, Mount Scopus, Jerusalem 91905, Israel

Carl Grundy-Warr, Department of Geography, National University of Singapore, 1 Arts Link, Singapore 117570

C. Michael Hall, Centre for Tourism, University of Otago, PO Box 56, Dunedin, New Zealand

K. C. Ho, Department of Sociology, National University of Singapore, 10 Kent Ridge Crescent, Singapore 119260

Kevin Markwell, Department of Leisure and Tourism Studies, University of Newcastle, Callaghan NSW 2038, Australia

Wiendu Nuryanti, Department of Architecture, Gadjah Mada University, Jl. Lingkar Utara 34, Yogyakarta, Indonesia

Can-Seng Ooi, Department of International Business and Economics, Copenhagen Business School, Howitzvej 60, DK-2000 Frederiksberg, Denmark

Stephen Page, Department of Marketing, University of Stirling, Stirling FK9 4LA, UK

Michael J. G. Parnwell, Centre for Southeast Asian Studies, Department of Politics and Asian Studies, University of Hull, Hull HU6 7RX, UK

Douglas G. Pearce, School of Business and Public Management, Victoria University of Wellington, PB 600, Wellington, New Zealand

Martin Perry, Department of Geography, National University of Singapore, 1 Arts Link, Singapore 117570

K. Raguraman, Department of Geography, National University of Singapore, 1 Arts Link, Singapore 117570

Trevor H. B. Sofield, Department of Sociology, Social Work and Tourism, University of Tasmania, Locked Bag 1-340G, Launceston; Tasmania 7250, Australia

Peggy Teo, Department of Geography, National University of Singapore, 1 Arts Link, Singapore 117570

Geoffrey Wall, Department of Geography, Faculty of Environmental Studies, University of Waterloo, Waterloo, Ontario N2L 3G1, Canada

Wong P. P., Department of Geography, National University of Singapore, 1 Arts Link, Singapore 117570

Brenda S. A. Yeoh, Department of Geography, National University of Singapore, 1 Arts Link, Singapore 117570

List of tables

List of figures

1

Introduction: Globalisation and Interconnectedness in Southeast Asian Tourism

Peggy Teo, T. C. Chang and K. C. Ho

Introduction

Globalisation involves the interplay of powerful market forces with local situations whereby the webs of connections are complex and, when investigated more carefully, display an interweaving of the external with local conditions and circumstances. While this description more aptly portrays the reality (see e.g. Dicken *et al*, 1997; Kelly, 1999), there continues to be a preoccupation with globalisation as an all-encompassing unilateral and hegemonic force that has a momentum of its own which, according to Kelly and Olds (1999:1), is emblematic of our time with national leaders and private entrepreneurs harping its rhetoric in order to justify sweeping policy and corporate changes that affect society and economy in significant ways. In a time where people, goods and information move so rapidly in tandem with technology, time–space compression is felt in all arenas of life – including politics, economics, and the social, cultural, religious and moral aspects of our daily activities. Interactions between the local, national, regional and global arenas have thrust multiple structures and agents together so that an understanding of the processes underpinning globalisation must be examined *across* rather than within scales (Cox, 1997), an endeavour this book attempts in its focus on *inter*connections.

Tourism is undoubtedly part of the macro global forces described in much of the literature on globalisation, especially by cultural theorists (Ritzer, 1993; Bhabba, 1994; Bryman, 1995; Appadurai, 1996) who describe hydridisation, syncretism and homogenisation across the globe. Since the time of Turner and Ash's (1975) apt description of tourists as the 'golden hordes', the tide of leisure has not abated and has in fact increased with higher levels of affluence and more free time. It seems timely at this point to revisit the impacts of tourism, less as a study of physical, economic and socio-cultural impacts as described in the classic work of Mathieson and Wall (1982). Rather, this book tries to show that the effects of tourism are better understood as outcomes of global processes in which the nature, intensity and extent of social interaction involving people, commodities, capital and information are intertwined. The multitudinous connections which bind nations together are acknowledged as inevitable although not necessary outcomes (see Kelly, 1999 for an argument on inevitability *vis-à-vis* necessity), and it is argued that the implications for destination countries should be studied less as negative versus positive effects (see also, Wood, 1993) and more as part of a process which is dynamic, contingent and contested. As much as tourism is part of globalisation that impinges, it is itself impinged upon by individual actors and social groups beyond the overpowering structures of the economy (Giddens, 1996). These delicate relationships are discussed in the specific context of the Southeast Asian region, which is selected for two reasons. First, as part of the East Asia/Pacific macro-region, the World Tourism Organisation (WTO) (cited in Go, 1997:5) describes it as having the most dramatic growth in tourist arrivals in the 1980s and 1990s. Second, unified state action to promote development has a track record in Southeast Asia (Hall and Page, 2000: 17–23; Mittelman, 2000:112–114), and tourism has been used as an expedient and convenient instrument to reach development targets at a faster rate, making it all the more important to investigate its implications for the region.

Southeast Asian tourism connections

The emergence of Japan, the rise of the newly industrialised economies, the practice of 'open regionalism' and ASEAN's integration as a region with the economies of North America and Europe account for much of the shift of the tourism (and other investment) trade to Asia and the Pacific (Go, 1997:3–4). Following the WTO's definition of East Asia and the Pacific, it is said that the region accounted for 11 per cent of total international visitor arrivals or 16 per cent of the world's market in 1990, up from 3 per cent in 1960 (Mak and White, 1992:14). The subset Southeast Asia (comprising Brunei, Indonesia, Cambodia, Laos, Malaysia, Myanmar, the Philippines, Vietnam, Thailand and Singapore) (Figure 1.1) has experienced a similar trend whereby the number of international visitor arrivals has increased (Table 1.1). Southeast Asia recorded a growth rate of 15.7 per cent compared to the world's average of 9.3 per cent (WTO, 1997:6) between 1980 and 1995. In 1995 alone, the region received 29.1 million visitors. This went up to 33.9 million in 1999 (Pacific Asia Travel Association (PATA), 1999). Another noteworthy trend is the high amount of intra-regional travel arising from the increased affluence of the people in the region (WTO, 2000).

According to Hall and Page (2000:5–7), Southeast Asia as a region emerged only in the post-war period. Citing references from Fisher (1964) and Dixon and Drakakis-Smith (1997), they argue that diversity in religion, language, culture, natural endowments and historical backgrounds were impediments to a regional identity, and that it was only after decolonisation and the need to develop that nations were thrown into joint action. From "scarcely a geographical expression" (Fryer, 1970:1) to a "paragon of development" (Rigg, 1997:3), Southeast Asia as part of the

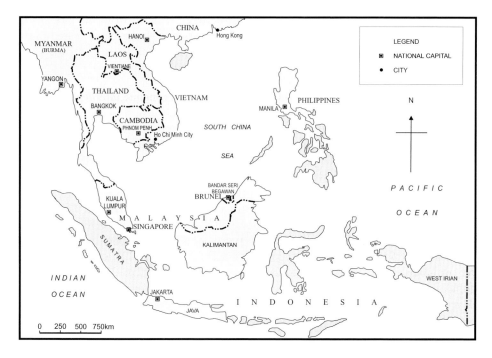

Figure 1.1 Southeast Asia

Table 1.1: International tourism arrivals and receipts for Southeast Asia, 1993–1999

	1993 arrivals	1999 arrivals	Percentage which is intra-regional (1999)	1998 international tourism receipts (US$m)	1998 GNP (US$m)
Brunei	-	636,606	89.9	-	7,150[a]
Cambodia	118,183	262,907	18.6	166	3,001
Indonesia	3,403,138	4,727,520	38.8	4,045	138,501
Lao PDR	-	614,278	72.7	80	1,641
Malaysia	6,503,860	7,931,149	75.0	2,456	79,848
Myanmar	48,425	198,211	16.5	35	-
Philippines	1,372,097	2,170,514	6.5	2,413	78,896
Singapore	6,425,778	6,958,196	31.8	5,162	95,095
Thailand	5,760,533	8,651,260	21.5	5,934	134,433
Vietnam	669,862	1,781,754	-	-	25,617

Source: Compiled from PATA (1999); World Tourism Organisation (1999; 2000)
[a] 1995 figure.

Asian Miracle has founded its success on a "combination of sound, market-based, foreign investment-friendly, export-oriented...policies" (Rigg, 1997:3). The transborder approach, its openness and the fluid interaction and interconnections with the world do not necessarily imply a 'definitive' region subject to exogenous forces decided by Wall Street (Kelly and Olds, 1999:2). Rather, the region is used as a convenient construct to examine the *linkages* between scales – from the global, the regional, the state, the city, the firm and even the personal – all are implicated in the spread of tourism across the globe.

Far from a black ship: charting a global–local nexus of economic interdependence

Raz (1999:12) muses that globalisation has too long been imagined as a black ship – a travelling armada spreading economic and cultural homogeneity and consent, and bearing an asymmetric perspective of development which divides core from periphery (Wallerstein, 1974) and metropole from satellite (Frank, 1967). As a source of social change, globalisation is often neglected as a reflexive phenomenon in which local actors contribute as much to its character and nature as it itself tries to influence and shape cosmopolitan citizens. 'Globalisation from below', in which globalisation is depicted not as an 'out there' but 'in here' phenomenon which involves "transformations in everyday lives" (Giddens, 1999:12), offers a perspective which is very relevant to tourism. As Yeung (1998:296–303) argues, even global markets are socially regulated, and nation-states continue to be the key players in such regulation. Territoriality remains an important organising principle as the state's role is to guarantee the rights of capital, create the conditions necessary for the global expansion of domestic capital, regulate the global economy 'within' and outside its jurisdiction, and perform a key role in the internationalisation of capital.

At a very concrete level, governments in Southeast Asia have recognised that tourism can be strategically harnessed to meet the demands of a very volatile world market. The 'new institutionalism' as described by Amin and Thrift (1994) is encapsulated in the heterogeneous institutions that have gelled together into a framework for activating regional economic governance of tourism in Southeast Asia. The four key constitutive elements which they describe are present in Southeast Asia, *viz*:

- a strong institutional presence (firms, financial institutions, chambers of commerce, government offices etc.);
- a high degree of interaction between the above so that networking, cooperation and information exchange can take place;
- well-defined structures of domination, coalition-building and collective representation of order; and
- presence of a cognitive mapping of place to the extent that members recognise a common agenda for collective representation (Amin and Thrift, 1994 cited in Jones and MacLeod, 1999:299).

In investigating the interconnectedness of Southeast Asia, a few levels of cooperation are evident: foreign direct investments in tourism; government-to-government initiatives; and regional bloc collaborations. Chang and Raguraman in this book describe the Singapore Tourism Board (STB) as a strong subscriber of regional interconnections. Their chapter outlines the Board's efforts to formalise its regional focus, establishing joint ventures and investments, government-to-government collaborations, information and expertise sharing, and collective representation in the marketplace. Singapore's connections to its Asian hinterland are worked through networks of competition *and* cooperation. While it encourages 'win–win' relationships with its ASEAN partners, it also recognises the competition for position as a regional hub for both air and cruise traffic. Similarly, the chapters by Pearce and Page reflect on the competition for hub position, and suggest room for a complementary hierarchy of hubs with Singapore and Bangkok leading the competition for regional hub status and supported by vital links established in second-tier hubs such as Kuala Lumpur, Jakarta and Manila and smaller hubs such as Kuching, Bali and Chiangmai. Page even suggests that the network of links already established and being built upon in many of the extended metropolitan regions (EMRs) of Southeast Asia is critical for the spatial reconfiguration of economic activities and the increase of the region's competitiveness in the global marketplace.

To be successful, interconnections must be presented as a cognitive unit. In this regard, Grundy-Warr and Perry's chapter on the Indonesia–Malaysia–Singapore Growth Triangle as well as Parnwell's discussion of the Greater Mekong Subregion (or Jewels of the Mekong) discuss how the regions are jointly promoted and indicate the collaborative planning that takes place. Under the rubric of 'new tourism' (Poon, 1989), various countries have come together to overcome problems of inaccessibility, high cost of development and limited attractions or infrastructure. Each of the strategies described shows how important the regional scale is for convening economic life. Even so, Pearce's chapter argues that a clear understanding of the complex interconnections that underlie the region's collaborative efforts is critical to its continued viability. It is one thing to define a region (either cognitively or for the sake of popularity) and to justify its coming into existence, but quite another to outline the exact functions to be performed by each node (as a source of origin, as a hub, as a gateway, as a destination in its own right) and how these functions are to be complemented. Worse, it is a challenge to decipher empirical measures that will assist the operational fulfilment of the regional structure that is emplaced in 'new tourism'. In spite of these difficulties, cross-border cooperation is viewed as advantageous for the mutual strengthening of tourism projects and economic interdependence is a preferred path in Southeast Asia for developing tourism.

In the same genre that questions the notion of a truly borderless world (Leyshon, 1997; Yeung, 1998), Hall argues in his chapter that the interconnections that exist in Southeast Asia for tourism are not necessarily spontaneous outcomes of the forces of globalisation but are instead *cultivated* by governments and must have political backing and support. The economic interdependence of regional blocs arises because nation-states *choose* to become transnational players. It is from the cooperative efforts of many nations that the Asia-Pacific Economic Cooperation (APEC) has come up with a Tourism Charter to back the tourism endeavours of the regional partners and to strengthen both horizontal and vertical integration of the industry players in Asia-Pacific, including Southeast Asia. Without the support of local governance, collaborative efforts to propel tourism will come to naught.

Reinventing tradition in an interconnected world

Hollinshead (1998) proposes that the *raison d'être* for tourism is difference. In particular he discusses this statement in the light of cultural tourism and supports MacCannell's (1976) and Urry's (1990:9–11) thesis that the tourist likes to gaze on something out of the routine and the ordinary onto something that is pleasurable. Through the imagineering industry such as Disney, concoctions that are 'unique' but stereotypical and idealised places capture the attention of the leisure consumer and the tourist. Tourism promoters claim to have captured the essence of a location but essentially what is portrayed is a contrived authenticity, a figment of the imagination which the industry players think will bring in the tourist dollar. From theme parks discussed in Teo and Yeoh's chapter to contrived events in Cohen's chapter on Thailand, the message rings true that the economic motive behind tourism drives the very image of a country. Markwell's discussion of Borneo's natural attractions has a history that dates back to colonial times and is a Western-imposed image of an 'exotic' tropic which is challenging yet safe. Similarly Black and Wall, in their investigation of three World Heritage sites, namely Ayutthaya (Thailand), Borobudur and Prambanan (Indonesia), reveal that local values attached to these ancient sites are ignored by the authorities who have the international backing of UNESCO. Local opinions are hardly sought in the conservation of these historic sites, leading to conflicts as 'classical'/high culture is preserved over vernacular/low culture (Butlin, 1987:37).

The appropriation of images in this global network is not, however, exclusive and should not be viewed as a Disneyisation (Bryman, 1995) or McDonaldisation (Ritzer, 1993) process without recourse. Like Sofield, Teo and Yeoh argue that local cultures are persistent in their resistance to homogenisation and do contribute to place-making. Theme parks, which are the landscapes most vulnerable to Disneyisation, do assert their localness by celebrating their local nationalistic identity either in the actual attractions offered, in the mascots they use, or in the programme of activities they run (e.g. festivities). While Cohen is more pessimistic about the 'touristic transition' of Pattaya in Thailand, he accedes that tradition which is reinvented for the sake of tourism can in fact become 'naturalised' as a local event and celebrated by the locals as if it were their own invention. Viewed in this way, sometimes also known as 'glocalisation', culture is conceived as dynamic, and globalisation as manifested in tourism both influences and is influenced by local conditions. It is this intersection of global–local processes that is not fully appreciated and tourism, suggests Sofield, offers one of the best investigations of the commingling of global trends with local nuances.

Cultural connections are obviously multiscalar and can draw upon a number of dimensions in the presentation of a cogent image which is attractive to tourists. To the 'outsider' who knows little about Southeast Asia (e.g. the German, American or French tourist), the reference to a pan-Asian identity as well as a Southeast Asian identity seems to make sense. Ooi shows how Singapore's National Museum draws on national, regional and pan-Asian identities to present an artistic heritage which is exciting for tourists and contributes to nation-building. This flexibility is emblematic of the looseness with which claims can be made about pasts and presents in an increasingly fluid space. Cartier's chapter on the imaging of Melaka in Malaysia also reinvents or reinscribes history to position the city more effectively to compete in the global tourist market. By focusing on Melaka's global role as a maritime port with historic links to cosmopolitan cultures and communities the world over, Melaka's heritage goes beyond just the 'local' and the 'regional'.

One world: an interconnected environment

Besides economic interdependence, global governance, internationalisation of knowledge and mass communication, Robertson (1992:8) also identified civil rights and the regulation of the environment as key features of globalisation. In Southeast Asia where ecotourism is fast becoming a major attraction, joint efforts at safe-guarding the environment are critical. Wong, for example, points to the many regional collaborative efforts under ASEAN's Sub-regional Environment Programme (ASEP) to protect the environment. They cover haze, marine resources, forest etc. International linkages have also been established with the USA, Canada, Germany and the European Union to monitor the region's rich ecological resources.

While we attempt to 'put right' globalisation's place in making changes in the world, there is also a case to be made for harnessing and encouraging globalisation processes. Civil society movements represent the most sanguine of the potential benefits of globalisation. Mittelman (2000:29) asserts that "politics beyond the parameters of the state is more fluid than it is within the state. Civil society transcending the state is emerging as a major site of contestation where diverse groups seek to recast politics, including its time-space dimensions". The idea that civil society is imported into the politics of globalisation is never so clear as in the environmental problems that plague the late twentieth century. Because of the state's unwillingness or inability to respond to environmental problems, civil society has become the watchdog and the voicebox of environmental problems. Other arenas where civil society is globalised include human rights, labour exploitation, women's and indigenous peoples' groups (Marden, 1997).

Parnwell's chapter raises the issue of civil society in two areas which are directly related to tourism: environment and indigenous population groups. He describes the efforts of an NGO group (TERRA or Towards Ecological Recovery and Regional Alliance) to monitor environmental problems associated with tourism development in the region which it publicises in its magazine *New Frontiers*, which goes out to an international audience. The 'human zoo' debacle involving the Paduang and the Karen peoples is exemplary of the human rights protection efforts of TERRA. Hall identifies a similar process in Myanmar, where human rights violations have received international attention because of the opening of Myanmar to tourism. Grundy-Warr and Perry also highlight the dilemmas faced by displaced villagers affected by resort development in the Indonesia–Malaysia–Singapore Growth Triangle.

Problems and potentials

The term 'interconnectedness' describes a key component of globalisation and itself suggests that many possibilities exist in its interpretation. Adams, in her incisive analysis of danger zone tourism, offers a good example of unexplored connections opened up by tourism. In their bid to experience the unconventional, danger zone tourists have caught on to a niche area which by itself is hard to sustain but if presented as a basket of attractions in a region, each with its own inherent political/social/religious disjunctures, is capable of catching the imagination of a larger group of leisure seekers.

However, connections can also present problems. It is apparent that globalisation is rooted in material processes of qualitative change whereby social relations across space are being integrated in more intensive as well as extensive ways (see Kelly, 1999:395). Rethinking global futures can therefore be fraught with pitfalls. In Burns' chapter on Vietnam where *Doi Moi* reform has essentially opened up the country to tourism, at the local level, people are uncertain about the implications of tourism. Micro-enterprises have sprung up like flowers in bloom and women and children have offered their services to the industry. Burns also shows that the national agenda does not translate well at the local government level, so that in this aspect the connections of tourism do not gel well and create a problem for Vietnam's tourism development.

Jumping onto a bandwagon without understanding the potential dangers is also a problem faced by Indonesia. Nuryanti's assessment of the Indonesian plan to use Bali and Jakarta as gateways into tourism 'regions' within Indonesia may not yield the intended results that planners forsee. It is not possible to 'will' into existence something which scientific investigations (in this case using gravity model and input–output analysis) show to be faulty. Nevertheless, money is poured into infrastructures that are viewed as having potential in developing national interconnections in tourism.

Indeed, Wall's reference to tourism as both a homogenising and differentiating global phenomenon aptly describes the range of possible consequences for the interconnections that already exist in Southeast Asia. As an open region which receives as well as sends tourists, it is best not to view the global and the local as a dyad in need of reconciliation but as a dialectical *process*. The interconnections, whether at the national, regional or global scales, are an inherent part of globalisation and the relativity of scales only adds to the problematisation of globalisation, as what can occur as a local phenomenon can simultaneously occur as a regional or global event elsewhere. How the interconnections are manifested, how states play one against the other, how they cooperate, will determine to a large extent the role tourism plays in changing the social and economic landscape of Southeast Asia.

Organisation of the book

As a guide to discussing the above issues, we would like to explain the organisation of the book. As global interdependency becomes more apparent, it is necessary to dwell on the political contexts of tourism. Part 1 provides the background, explaining the political discourse behind tourism and bringing to light some systematic questions regarding the tensions associated with the interconnections.

Part 2 focuses on deterritorialisation and the development of new regionalisms, paying specific attention to collaborative efforts in tourism development and to fostering greater movement within and in and out of the region.

Part 3 presents the sociocultural implications associated with tourism as a globalising phenomenon, but the dialogue does not only cover global–local tensions but also 'regional identities' and 'pan-Asian' heritage, especially as portrayed to outsiders.

Part 4 pulls together ecological and community concerns under the umbrella of ecotourism, which is an important aspect of the tourism potential of the region. The chapters examine the way nature is interpreted and promoted, the collaborative efforts to develop sustainable tourism as well as the joint monitoring systems of the environment.

Part 5 itemises potentials and problems when Southeast Asia latches onto the new spatial structures of economic interaction. The challenges of global interdependency are re-examined as vulnerabilities and volatilities linked with tourism interconnections become more apparent. As Southeast Asia works out its place in this highly connected world, the role of tourism in shaping change, whether in a spontaneous or planned fashion, should be better investigated as we attempt to do in this book.

References

Amin, A. and Thrift, N. (1994) 'Living in the global', in A. Amin and N. Thrift (eds.) *Globalisation, Institutions and Regional Development in Europe*. Oxford: Oxford University Press, 1–22.

Appadurai, A. (1996) *Modernity at Large: Cultural Dimensions of Globalisation*. Minneapolis: University of Minnesota Press.

Bhabha, H. (1994) *The Location of Culture*. London: Routledge.

Bryman, A. (1995) *Disney and His Worlds*. London and New York: Routledge.

Butlin, R.A. (1987) 'Theory and methodology in historical geography', in M. Pacione (ed.), *Historical Geography: Progress and Prospect*. London: Croom Helm, 16–45.

Cox, K. (ed.) (1997) *Spaces of Globalisation: Reasserting the Power of the Local*. New York: Guilford Press.

Dicken, P., Peck, J. and Tickell, A. (1997) 'Unpacking the global', in R. Lee and J. Wills (eds.) *Geographies of Economies*. London: Arnold, 158–66.

Dixon, C. and Drakakis-Smith, D. (1997) *Uneven Development in Southeast Asia*. Aldershot: Ashgate.

Fisher, C.A. (1964) *Southeast Asia*. London: Methuen.

Frank, A.G. (1967) *Capitalism and Development in Latin America*. New York and London: Monthly Review Press.

Fryer, D. (1970) *Emergent Southeast Asia: A Study in Growth and Stagnation*. London: Philip.

Giddens, A. (1996) 'Affluence, poverty and the idea of a post-scarcity society'. *Development and Change*, 27, 365–77.

Giddens, A. (1999) *Runaway World: How Globalisation is Reshaping our Lives*. London: Profile Books.

Go, F. (1997) 'Asian and Australasian dimensions of global tourism development', in F. Go and C.L. Jenkins (eds.) *Tourism and Economic Development in Asia and Australasia*. London: Pinter, 3–34.

Hall, C.M. and Page, S. (2000) 'Introduction: Tourism in South and Southeast Asia – region and context', in C.M. Hall and S. Page (eds.) *Tourism in South and Southeast Asia: Issues and Cases*. Oxford: Butterworth-Heinemann, 3–28.

Hollinshead, K. (1998) 'Tourism, hybridity and ambiguity: The relevance of Bhabha's "third space" cultures'. *Journal of Leisure Research*, 30(1), 121–56.

Jones, M. and McLeod, G. (1999) 'Towards a regional renaissance? Reconfiguring and rescaling England's economic governance'. *Transactions of the Institute of British Geographers*, 24(3), 295–313.

Kelly, P.F. (1999) 'The geographies and politics of globalisation'. *Progress in Human Geography*, 23(3), 379–400.

Kelly, P.F. and Olds, K. (1999) 'Questions in a crisis: The contested meanings of globalisation in the Asia-Pacific', in K.Olds, P. Dicken, P.F. Kelly, L. Kong and H.W.C. Yeung (eds.) *Globalisation and the Asia-Pacific: Contested Territories*. London and New York: Routledge, 1–16.

Leyshon, A. (1997) 'True stories? Global dreams, global nightmares, and writing globalisation', in R. Lee and J. Wills (eds.) *Geography of Economies*. London: Arnold, 133–46.

MacCannell, D. (1976) *The Tourist: A New Theory of the Leisure Class*. London: Macmillan.

Mak, J. and White, K. (1992) 'Comparative tourism development in Asia and the Pacific'. *Journal of Travel Research,* 30(2), 14–23.

Marden, P. (1997) 'Geographies of dissent: Globalisation, identity and the nation'. *Political Geography*, 16, 37–64.

Mathieson, A. and Wall, G. (1982) *Tourism: Economic, Physical and Social Impacts*. London: Longman.

Mittelman, J.H. (2000) *The Globalization Syndrome: Transformation and Resistance*. Princeton, New Jersey: Princeton University Press.

Pacific Asia Travel Association (PATA) (1999) *Annual Statistical Report 1999*. Bangkok: PATA.

Poon, A. (1989) 'Competitive strategies for a "new tourism"', in C.P. Cooper (ed.) *Progress in Tourism, Recreation and Hospitality Management*, Vol.1. New York and London: Belhaven Press, 91–102.

Raz, A.E. (1999) *Riding the Black Ship: Japan and Tokyo Disneyland*. Cambridge, Massachusetts and London: Harvard University Asia Center.

Rigg, J. (1997) *Southeast Asia: The Human Landscape of Modernisation and Development*. London and New York: Routledge.

Ritzer, G. (1993) *The McDonaldisation of Society*. Thousand Oaks: Pine Forge.

Robertson, R. (1992) *Globalisation: Social Theory and Global Change*. London: Sage Publications.

Turner, L. and Ash, J. (1975) *The Golden Hordes: International Tourism and the Pleasure Periphery*. New York: St. Martin Press.

Urry, J. (1990) *The Tourist Gaze: Leisure and Tourists in Contemporary Society*. London: Sage Publications.

Wallerstein, I. (1974) *The Modern World System*. New York: Academic Press.

Wood, R. (1993) 'Tourism, culture and sociology of development', in M. Hitchcock, V. King and M. Parnwell (eds.) *Tourism in Southeast Asia*. London and New York: Routledge, 48–79.

World Tourism Organisation (WTO) (1997) *Yearbook of Tourism Statistics*. Madrid: WTO.

WTO (1999) *Yearbook of Tourism Statistics*. Madrid: WTO.

WTO (2000) *Compendium of Tourism Statistics 1994-1998*. Madrid: WTO.

Yeung, H.W.C. (1998) 'Capital, state and space: Contesting the borderless world'. *Transactions of the Institute of British Geographers*, 23, 291–309.

Part One

Regional Context

2

Tourism and Political Relationships in Southeast Asia

C. Michael Hall

Introduction

The relationships between tourism and politics in Southeast Asia are probably more important now than they have ever been before. The impacts of the Asian financial crisis have served to heighten the interconnectedness of the Asian economies through the increased mobility of capital, information, investment, labour, tourists and, consequently, their political relationships as well. Tourism is a very significant part of these relationships. Tourism, for long one of the mainstays of the region's economy – accounting for 10.3 per cent of Asia's gross domestic product (GDP) (*AsiaWeek*, 6 November 1998) – has now become an even more important source of economic development, foreign exchange, and employment generation. Indeed, the extent to which the Asian financial crises and political crises are related illustrates the way in which a better understanding of the political dimensions of tourism may assist government and industry in developing appropriate policy settings. Such an observation reflects the comment of Richter and Waugh (1986:231):

...tourism may decline precipitously when political conditions appear unsettled. Tourists simply choose alternative destinations. Unfortunately, many national leaders and planners either do not understand or will not accept the fact that political serenity, not scenic or cultural attractions, constitute the first and central requirement of tourism.

After years of not so 'benign neglect' (Richter, 1983), the political dimensions of tourism are starting to receive considerable attention in the research literature (e.g. Richter, 1989; Hall, 1994; Hall and Jenkins, 1995; Pizam and Mansfield, 1996). An appreciation of the political context of tourism is critical to an understanding of the complex nature of tourism, particularly in Southeast Asia where politics has had a dramatic effect on tourism flows, investment, development and policy decisions. As Hall (1994:195) noted, "[t]ourism is...very much part of the competition for and consumption of scarce resources, the seeking of which *must* surely lead one to the essential elements of the politics of tourism: *Politics is about power, who gets what, where, how and why*". Issues of political stability and political relations within and between states are extremely important in determining the image of destinations in tourist generating regions and, of course, the real and perceived safety of tourists (e.g. Brackenbury, 1995; Pizam and Mansfield, 1996). Moreover, tourism is increasingly becoming a component of international trade agreements in the region (e.g. Tham, 1999) and is therefore a component of international trade diplomacy. In addition, it can potentially contribute to the development of international understanding and, possibly, the development of an Asian identity (Ministry of Foreign Affairs (MOFA), 1999). Indeed, an appreciation of the political dimensions of tourism can be regarded as a prerequisite to understanding tourism's wider role in the processes and implications of globalisation. As S. Jayakumar, Singapore's Minister for Foreign Affairs, stated at the 1999 East Asia–Latin America Forum:

The post Cold War has seen two contradictory trends. The ever closer integration of the global economy has not created greater international cohesion. On the contrary, globalisation has meant an ever greater disconnection between economic geography, political geography, financial geography and social and cultural geographies. Economic space no longer coincides neatly with political boundaries or even continental boundaries. To deal with this new reality requires a total change of entrenched mindsets.

(*The Straits Times*, 3 September 1999).

This chapter analyses some of the ways in which tourism is part of the new political geography of globalisation and of Asia in particular. It first discusses the changing role of the state in the global political environment and the manner in which tourism is part of the process of regionalisation. The chapter then goes on to examine the role of the state in relation to tourism policy. The third major section discusses the function that political stability plays in tourism development and tourist flows, and utilises the ethical questions raised in examining how tourism is used as a tool of development to highlight broader ethical questions in the politics of tourism. The final section suggests certain key themes and issues that require further research and analysis if the role that tourism plays in the region is to be understood.

Tourism and globalisation

Globalisation is "a concept with consequences" (Hirst, 1997:424). Globalisation has had the effect of changing the 'rules of the game' in the struggle for competitive advantage among firms, destinations and places within, as well as between, countries and regions (Hall, 1997; Higgott, 1999). Globalisation is a complex, chaotic, multi-scalar, multi-temporal and multi-centric series of processes operating in specific structural and spatial contexts (Jessop, 1999). Global interdependence typically results from processes which operate at various spatial scales, in different functional sub-systems, and involve complex and tangled causal hierarchies rather than a simple, unilinear, bottom-up or top-down movement (Jessop, 1999). However, the discourse of globalisation is more than a description of contemporary social change, it has the power to influence policy formulation and implementation (Kelly and Olds, 1999). Globalisation has constructed a view of geographical space that implies the deferral of political options from the national to the supranational and global scales, and from the local to the national. In effect, globalisation "has become a political force, helping to create the institutional realities it purportedly merely describes" (Piven, 1995:108). In addition to this 'structural context' of globalisation, authors such as Ohmae (1995), Higgott (1999) and Jessop (1999) point to a more strategic interpretation of globalisation, which refers to individual and institutional actors' attempts to promote the global coordination of activities within different functional systems. For example, inter-firm alliances, the creation of international and supra-national regimes to govern particular fields of action, and the development of inter-national and supranational systems of governance.

Tourism is therefore enmeshed in the processes of economic globalisation in a number of forms. First, the formation of regional economic and trading blocs, e.g. Asia-Pacific Economic Cooperation (APEC), and the development of formal links between those blocs (e.g. the Asia–Europe Meetings) (Hall and Page, 2000). Second, the growth of 'local internationalisation' or 'virtual regions' through the develop-ment of economic ties between contiguous, e.g. 'border regions' or non-contiguous local and regional state authorities, e.g. growth regions and triangles in different national economies which often bypass the level of the nation-state but which still retain support at the national level (Hall, in press a). Third, the widening and deepening of international and supranational regimes which cover economic and economically relevant issues and which may also provide for regional institutiona-lised governance (Hall, 2000). Fourth, the internationalisation of national economic spaces through greater inward and outward flows of goods, services, communica-tions and mobility. Fifth, the extension and deepening of multinationalisation by multinational firms, including tourism corporations. Finally, the "emergence of glo-balisation proper through the introduction and acceptance of global norms and standards, the development of globally integrated markets together with globally oriented strategies, and 'deracinated' firms with no evident national operational base" (Jessop, 1999:23).

Given the availability of space, the following discussion examines the first two examples of economic globalisation noted above. Tourism is often a significant component in the establishment of regional economic unions and the establishment of free trade agreements which aim to enhance the flow of goods and services and provide for increased mobility of investment and people. However, while increased personal mobility between countries is regarded as important for leisure travel, it is important to note that other considerations include improving accessibility for busi-ness travellers and providing for regional labour mobility. For example, the Japanese MOFA (1999:n.p.) *Report of the Mission for Revitalisation of Asian Economy* speci-fically recommended the promotion of two-way interaction between people in Japan and Asian countries and called for the formulation and implementation of "long-term, large-scale programmes for human exchange" through relaxing the constraints on human exchange, particularly through improved international air links and inter-national airport hub development, and "simplification and acceleration of immigra-tion, quarantine, and customs procedures".

In the case of Asia, three sets of inter-related factors underpinned the extension of production networks which provided much of the region's economic growth in the early 1990s but which also left it vulnerable to the problems of the Asian financial crisis in the late 1990s (Hall, in press a). The first set of factors was the change in relative factor costs within the region. For companies in north-east Asia (Japan, Korea and Taiwan) seeking to increase their production of relatively mature products, the costs of undertaking the investment necessary to increase domestic capacity were far in excess of those of establishing new facilities elsewhere in the region where labour, infrastructural and land costs were much lower (Garnaut, 1990).

The second group of factors was political. The original tensions over trade imbalances and market access between Japan and the USA, and later Japan and Europe and Australasia, were extended to Korea and Taiwan in the late 1980s. International tensions in turn generated domestic political forces that interacted with and reinforced underlying economic change. In tourism terms, it is notable that Japan utilised outbound tourism as a means of improving trade relations and providing its trading nations with a source of funds to purchase Japanese manufactured goods (Hall, 2000). Indeed, economic interdependence between Japan and Asia has been deepening steadily since the mid 1980s when the first wave in Japanese offshore investment began. As a result, Asia now has an extremely high degree of intraregional trade and investment interdependence (Japan External Trade Organisation (JETRO), 1999). Trade interdependence within the region – including Japan and the nine East Asian countries, the four newly-industrialised economies (NIEs), the four major economies of the Association of Southeast Asian Nations (ASEAN) and China – has risen as high as 52 per cent. This is almost on a par with intraregional interdependence in the European Union, which is 61 per cent and exceeds that of the North American Free Trade Area (NAFTA) at 48 per cent (Arai, 1998). Around 40 per cent of Japan's trade is now with Asia, which is also the destination for around 30 per cent of Japanese total investments (Yosano, 1998).

The third set of factors is related to changes in the production process which have facilitated flexible production techniques through the advent of the microelectronics and communications revolution. These, in turn, decreased the significance of economies of scale, thereby opening up markets for a whole range of non-standardised products. Smaller companies have therefore been able to gain a footing in increasingly regionalised production chains. Many areas of the Asian regional economy now consist of clusters of inter-related industrial sectors that are better described as networks rather than as unconnected 'industries', the basic organisational 'unit' being the interaction between firms linked together in chains of production, exchange and distribution. Such network relations have been facilitated by the willingness of government to encourage overseas investment, often in partnership with local industry, and by the development of policy settings which have sought to reinforce freer trade and investment in the region, including supranational developments such as Asia-Pacific Economic Cooperation (APEC).

Although not formally classified as a regional economic union (JETRO, 1996), APEC is a major force for free trade in the Pacific Rim and in creating improved dialogue and relations between the major economic powers in the region. APEC has no charter which forces contractual obligations on its members, instead it works by a consensus driven approach (Hall and Samways, 1997). APEC was established in 1989 to provide a forum for the management of the effects of the growing inter-dependence of the Pacific Rim and to help promote economic growth. As part of the APEC framework, 10 working groups have been established, covering broad areas of economic, educational and environmental cooperation, including tourism "on the basis that the tourism industry is of growing importance in promoting economic growth and social development in the Asia-Pacific region" (APEC Tourism Working Group (ATWG), 1995:n.p.).

During its two meetings held in 1999 (Manzanilo, Mexico and Lima, Peru), the ATWG's work programme included activities in the areas of trade and investment liberalisation and facilitation, and economic and technical cooperation, including the development of an APEC Tourism Charter (ATWG, 1999; Hall, in press a). A tourism task force, comprising Brunei Darussalam, Korea, Mexico, New Zealand and Singapore, with inputs from peak industry organisations, the Pacific Asia Travel Association (PATA) and the World Travel and Tourism Council (WTTC), identified four main APEC Tourism Charter goals. These are:

- sustainable management of tourism impacts and outcomes – environmental, economic, social and cultural;
- increase mobility of visitors and demand for tourism goods and services in the APEC region;
- remove impediments to tourism business and investment; and
- enhance recognition and understanding of tourism as a vehicle for social and economic development – harmonisation and sharing of tourism information, expanding the knowledge base (ATWG, 2000).

In principle, the APEC Tourism Charter, proposed for adoption by APEC Tourism Ministers in June 2000, is to include measures that will

- contribute to the minimisation of the regulatory impediments to tourism;
- promote environmentally and socially sustainable tourism;
- reduce congestion and improve passenger processing facilitation;
- identify emerging issues in tourism;
- improve the understanding of tourism; and
- enhance visitor services and tourism infrastructure (ATWG, 2000).

Undoubtedly, the actions of a group such as the ATWG are not spectacular in terms of the amount of media coverage which they receive. However, they are extremely influential in terms of the direction of tourism development, and serve to strengthen the horizontal and vertical integration of the tourism industry within the Asia-Pacific region. In addition, it should be noted that organisations such as APEC, while seeking greater freedom of trade and investment in the Asia-Pacific, are part of a hierarchy of organisations which are seeking to develop new regimes of international tourism trade (Hall, 2000). Such organisations serve to integrate the supranational, national and regional interests of institutional and political actors in the Asia-Pacific with respect to the role and value of tourism for foreign exchange, regional economic development, and employment generation. For example, at the sub-national level, a major development in the world trade system in the 1990s has been the emergence of regional networks of production. Such growth triangles or polygons (depending on the number of national actors involved) have been a substantial driving force for growth in a number of regional economies throughout the 1990s although in the Asian context, much of the initial driving force for such integration has come from the private sector rather than government (Toh and Low, 1993). In East Asia, a number of subregional growth areas have been established to maximise cross-border movements of goods, services, investment and human resources, including tourism, and to exploit comparative advantages of geographical areas divided by political boundaries (Hall and Samways, 1997). However, although models of public policy and international relations are well developed to deal with the activities of nation-states, the growth of supranational and sub-governmental institutions as international actors provides significant challenges to our understanding of economic globalisation and its spatial and policy implications. In an era of economic globalisation, the rise of 'new' supranational policy issues such as the environment, tourism and labour mobility are profoundly different in scope from traditional strategic and security issues. New policy issues involving tourism may be described as 'intermestic' in nature, that is they are simultaneously both domestic and international policy issues which, while being of substantial domestic concern, cross international boundaries thereby creating international interest in the setting of policy (Cohn and Smith, 1996). Therefore, any understanding of the international dimensions of tourism also requires analysis of the domestic influences on policy settings.

Tourism and the state

Despite suggestions that the state is dead in the age of globalisation (e.g. Ohmae, 1995), such pronouncements are unnecessarily premature. The nation-state still serves as an important 'container' within which tourism is regulated and controlled. Even the development of institutional arrangements at the supranational level remains dependent on the decisions of state parties. The state therefore continues to play an important role even though the nature of that role may be changing.

One of the most significant actions of the state with respect to tourism is the setting of the regulatory environment within which the industry operates. The movements of people within and between countries are set by governments. Such policies may be utilised to achieve a variety of political aims. For example, the lack of direct transport links between China and Taiwan reflects the diplomatic impasse that exists between the two nations. Similarly, access of tourists to Tibet is also closely regulated and monitored by the Chinese authorities who seek to cast their occupation of the territory in a positive light to Western tourists and media (Hall and Page, 2000).

Governments also have substantial influence on the location of tourist facilities, often through national, regional and local tourism plans which designate what areas can be developed as resorts. For example, the large-scale development of tourism at Nusa Dua in Bali occurred because of the development of a master tourism plan for the island in conjunction with overseas advisors (Economist Intelligence Unit, 1991). However, the centralised tourism planning of the past is facing increased opposition by local groups who often feel that they are ignored in the tourism planning process and/or are not adequately compensated for the loss of their land, which is often compulsorily purchased. In addition, development-specific reports, such as environmental and social impact statements or environmental and social statements, may provide extremely brief overviews of development impacts or have little impact on the planning process, if they are called for at all (Hall and Page, 2000). While governments in Southeast Asia are signatories to relevant international conventions, often within the ASEAN context, and while most countries also have a set of national planning laws, such conventions and laws often have little impact on the ground and can be easily overridden by national and regional development agencies working in conjunction with industry partners. Such a situation reflects wider uncertainty about the effective implementation of planning laws as well as the relatively weak role of participatory democracy in planning regulations. Furthermore, the desperate need of some areas to attract investment, employment and economic development, as well as political corruption in some instances, also affects the policy and planning process. Countries such as Indonesia and Thailand, as well as the developing countries of Cambodia, Myanmar and Vietnam, all face substantial difficulties in the implementation of effective planning laws which would give local people the ability to say "no" to tourism projects (e.g. AMPO (AMPO derives its name from the *Nichi-bei Anzen Hosho Joyaku* (US–Japan Security Treaty)), 1991).

National tourism policies and plans are usually a deliberate tool of regional development strategies and/or broader trade policies. For example, the Japanese government has invested substantial funds into the development of resorts for the domestic market. According to McCormack (1991), so many local government authorities were seeking 'resort area' designation under the Resort Act in the 1990s that 19.2 per cent of the country's land area was involved. Many of the resort projects under the Act are large-scale integrated resort developments which include marinas and golf courses (Rimmer, 1992). Given the size of many of the projects under the Resort Act, the scheme served to benefit large corporations such as construction companies, banks, real estate developers and trading companies (Fujiwara, 1991). Furthermore, considerable opposition emerged to some of the projects on environmental grounds and because of lack of community support in some instances (AMPO, 1991). Indeed, the new Resort Law relaxed environmental regulations and removed many of the restrictions on conversion of agricultural land to other uses. However, tourism development is still being encouraged in many rural and semi-rural areas because many communities are experiencing some of the same effects of economic restructuring and deindustrialisation as their Western counterparts, particularly after the collapse of the Japanese bubble economy. As Graburn (1995:57) noted, "It is the policy of the national and regional governments as well as business to hold the line on population loss by replacing the declining industries – forestry, farming and fishing – with rural tourism." More recently, Japan has also included tourism as one of the components in its package of measures following the Asian economic crisis.

In April 1998, the largest-ever package of emergency economic measures (¥16 trillion or US$119 billion) was adopted, with a supplementary budget passed in June of that year. These measures, with implementation of the FY 1998 budget, were underpinned by new corporate and income tax cuts worth well over ¥6 trillion or

US$44 billion. In addition, a second supplementary budget of more than ¥10 trillion (US$74 billion) was formulated in an effort to revive domestic demand. According to Minister Yosano (1998:n.p.), "this domestic demand-led economic recovery will help to restore the Asian economy by providing Asian economies with the stable market indispensable for Asian economic growth." As part of these measures, Japan designed a programme to improve the business environment and create new industries known as the "Program for the 15 New and Growing Fields" (MITI, 1999). Tourism expansion is explicitly envisaged within the field entitled "culture and living" and there is a call for "the development of sophistication of leisure-related industries such as tourism" (MITI, 1999:n.p.). Such domestic measures will also be integrated with international tourism services through the growth of international airport hubs and the deregulation of the domestic aviation market (MITI, 1999). The Japanese government predicts that employment in these sectors will expand from approximately 10.6 million people in 1995 to about 18 million in 2010, and the market scale from about ¥200 trillion in 1995 to about ¥500 trillion in 2010, with as many as 100,000 businesses starting during this period (Yosano, 1998; MITI, 1999). However, Japanese tourism policies are different from those of other countries in the Asia-Pacific in the international sphere, with the possible exception of Taiwan, in that Japan overtly seeks to encourage outbound tourism in order to meet trade and cultural policy goals (Go and Jenkins, 1997). Travel-related expenditures are the third largest import category in Japan, behind mineral fuels and machinery and equipment. In 1990, the number of Japanese travelling abroad reached 11 million travellers, ensuring that the plan to increase overseas travel known as the 'Ten Million Programme', launched in 1987, reached its target a year ahead of schedule. In 1989, Japan had the highest deficit travel account balance in the world, ahead of Germany, and in 1990, the travel trade balance of payments (balance of total travel and passenger fares) was in deficit by US$21.34 billion, a figure equivalent to one-third of the total trade surplus (US$63.5 billion). By 1996, the travel deficit was almost US$33 billion and payments from tourism were almost 10 times those of the receipts, although there has been a subsequent lessening in the travel trade gap in 1997 and 1998 following the impacts of the Asian financial crisis and domestic recession (Hall, in press b). Such figures may seem surprising for a nation which has had an export-led economic development strategy for most of the post-war period. However, it is precisely because of the aggressive export orientation of Japanese industry that tourism has become a significant tool of Japan's trade policy as tourism serves to act as a balance to the export of goods and services from Japan.

Tourism may also be utilised to achieve other political goals. For example, in the case of Singapore, in "projecting Singapore as a multiethnic destination to the world, the state was... making a public statement on local society and culture while fulfilling the political goal of nation building. Tourists' fascination with the country's ethnic composition would foster a sense of civic pride, which in turn would help knit the ethnically diverse people together" (Chang, 1997:552). Following their stay in Singapore, tourists often compliment the island for its cleanliness, efficiency and remarkable achievements. As the local state-owned media points out, these comments by tourists confirm that Singapore ranks amongst the best in the world. This privileged position, moreover, is due wholly to the capable leadership of the ruling

People's Action Party (PAP). Tourism may therefore be interpreted as having taken on a potential propaganda role by showcasing Singapore to foreigners for the purposes of instilling pride and loyalty amongst Singaporeans. Through tourism, a political climate favourable to the PAP may be created, ensuring that any challenge to its supremacy is unlikely to succeed (Hall and Oehlers, 2000).

However, the relationship between tourism and politics is by no means unidirectional. Indeed, perceptions of political stability are vital to tourism in terms of presenting a safe destination for tourists and an appropriate destination for investment. For example, following the protests against the Suharto regime in Indonesia in 1997 and attacks against ethnic Chinese which received widespread media coverage in tourist-generating countries, the Balinese tourism industry took immediate steps to attempt to distinguish between Bali and the rest of Indonesia, and Jakarta in particular, in the marketplace. The head of the Bali Tourism Office, Luther Barrung, sent out a message to all Bali hotels and foreign consulates based in Bali:

Bali remains peaceful and calm. Any demonstrations that have occurred to-date have taken the form of dialogues which been orderly and confined to the campus area in the centre of Denpasar. These dialogues have been characterised by a free exchange of opinions with participants from all walks of Balinese society...Without exception, these dialogues have focused on the issue of political reform and at no time have any of Bali's many tourists and visitors been the focus of any protest...All hotels, tourist attractions and tours continue to operate in Bali as usual with no interruptions or disturbances in services provided to our valued tourism visitors.

(*TravelAsia*, 1998a:n.p.)

In addition, Bali launched a "Two years in Bali" campaign in June which provided for cheap flights from key European and Asian markets and a certificate guaranteeing guests three extra room nights, which they could use either to extend their stay or during a return visit anytime before December 1999 (*TravelAsia*, 1998b). At the national level, the Indonesian Tourism Promotion Board launched a "Let's Go Indonesia!" campaign to attempt to attract visitors back to the country. However, the campaign only received marginal support from Bali, which sought to pursue a 'Bali first' policy and differentiate itself in the marketplace from the rest of Indonesia (Hall and Page, 2000).

The Balinese example also illustrates the manner in which the media plays an influential role in affecting tourist perceptions of a destination. Therefore, media influence is sought not only by governments but by a range of political actors at all institutional levels. The relationship between tourism, media and image is one that is difficult to control by any single actor. Advances in communications technology mean that images and text can be transferred almost instantaneously around the world. It is becoming increasingly difficult for state actors to control external images unless they are willing to restrict all access to places, with such restrictions thereby creating potentially negative images in their own right. However, the extent to which place images and therefore tourist flows may be affected by negative images is becoming an increasingly fraught issue for many governments. In the globalised economy, intermestic issues such as human rights, which are highlighted by the media, raise ethical concerns with respect to tourism that challenge not only governments but also interested tourists as to the political consequences of their actions, and it is to these concerns that we will now turn.

Tourism and human rights

Because tourism represents the mobility of people across borders, governments may seek to encourage tourism not only because of the potential economic benefits it may bring but also because of the contribution it may make in creating a favourable impression of a regime in the international media. For example, the Philippines under the Marcos government openly encouraged tourism in order to try to promote a positive image of the country in the United States (Richter, 1989). Similarly, during the apartheid years, the government of South Africa also used tourism to try to create favourable impressions for nationals from countries which may potentially impose trade sanctions on South Africa (Pizam and Mansfield, 1996). However, the use of tourism as a political tool by governments and its very visibility means that tourism may be an easy target for political opposition which may sometimes turn violent. Indeed, tourists and tourism facilities have been the target of terrorist attacks because of such visibility (Richter and Waugh, 1986). Nevertheless, tourism may also be the subject of more peaceful means of protest by which pressure groups may attempt to encourage tourists not to travel to a region because of the legitimacy it may bestow on a regime. In Asia, such measures have occurred at various times in recent years with respect to travel to China, Tibet and Myanmar (Hall and Page, 2000).

In the case of Myanmar, one of the main deterrents to tourism development is the poor image that the country faces through its abject human rights record. As many as 10,000 people were thought to have been killed by the army in the 1988 pro-democracy demonstrations. In 1990, the National League for Democracy (NLD), led by Aung San Suu Kyi, won 82 per cent of the seats in the election. The junta simply imprisoned those who tried to establish the government. In January 1995, the BBC reported that slave labour was being used to build roads and other infrastructure needed to support the tourism industry. This claim was further documented by John Pilger in a documentary "Inside Burma: Land Of Fear" screened in June 1996 (*The Sydney Morning Herald*, 1 June 1996). The documentary showed children and chain gangs being used as slave labour to build roads, bridges, airports, railways, the imperial palace in Mandalay and other tourist attractions. In 1990, 4,000 people living in Pagan, one of the last wonders of the ancient world, equivalent to Angkor Wat in Cambodia, were forced to leave their homes as the city was being opened up for tourism development. Only guides and the staff of a planned strip of hotels were permitted to stay. In 1996, the International Confederation of Free Trade Unions reported that a million people had been forced from their homes in Rangoon alone, in preparation for tourism and foreign investment (*The Sydney Morning Herald*, 1 June 1996). According to Oo and Perez (1996), some 2 million Myanmese including women and children have been used as slave labourers in the beautification campaign for Visit Myanmar Year. Human rights groups, such as Amnesty International, also charged that forced and prison labour were being used to develop

Myanmar's infrastructure and people were being forced to relocate from slum areas so that tourists do not see them (Campbell, 1996). The Director-General of Myanmar's Directorate of Hotels and Tourism, categorically denied such allegations, calling those advancing such notions as "against the government" and "out of touch with what is really happening in Myanmar" (cited in Campbell, 1996:n.p.).

Myanmar's opposition leader, or more appropriately, legitimately elected leader, Aung San Suu Kyi, joined human rights groups in calling on tourists to boycott the country in protest against the use of forced labour and other human and political rights abuses (Oo and Perez, 1996). In the 1996 documentary interview with John Pilger, Aung San Suu Kyi declared, "...They (tourists) should stay away until we are a democracy. Look at the forced labour that is going on all over the country. A lot of it is aimed at the tourist trade. It's very painful. Roads and bridges are built at the expense of the people. If you cannot provide one labourer you are fined. If you cannot afford the fine, the children are forced to labour."

The actions of the Myanmar government and the campaign of the opposition raise fundamental questions with respect to the relationship between tourism and politics and the actions that governments should take on tourism issues as well as the tourism industry. As *TravelAsia* (1996:n.p.) editorialised, "It is clear political events have an impact on tourism – from how consumers perceive the country (safe or unsafe) to whether they feel they should support a regime which does not fall in line with their own beliefs." Nevertheless, Oo and Perez (1996:n.p.) posed the issue more bluntly:

The State Law and Order Council (SLORC) government is well known for its track record in human rights violations. For over 7 years now (it seized power through a bloody coup in 1988), it has been arresting, detaining, torturing, killing and conscripting into slave labour the Myanmese people. But it is desperate to make 'Visit Myanmar Year' a success. It hopes to generate enough income to boost a failed economy from the tourists and foreign investors who have poured in $1 billion to hotel construction. And more importantly, it hopes to project a 'good image' internationally...PATA delegates have generally praised Burmese efforts in opening up the once hermit nation. They praised Burmese authorities for improving customs and immigration procedures, constructing quality hotels and opening up large areas of the country once off-limits to foreigners. And of course, not a single word was spoken on the social costs and impact of 'Visit Myanmar Year'. For them, money is more important than human rights.

The attitude of *TravelAsia* (1996:n.p.) represented a substantial point of difference to that of human rights groups: "As travel business professionals, we have to keep a clear head and not take sides. Indeed, the only side we should be on is our customers'! The only questions we should ask are, does Myanmar have the products, the infrastructure and the will to become one of Asia's great destinations?" There are no easy answers in trying to determine the most appropriate course of action with respect to tourism in Myanmar. Each government, corporation and individual will have a perspective on this vexed question depending on their economic and social interests. Within Asia, fellow ASEAN countries such as Thailand and Singapore have invested substantially in Myanmar's tourism industry, whereas the United States and Australia have avoided such actions. Asian countries may claim that a constructive engagement through economic and diplomatic relations may be the best means to bring Myanmar within the realm of international human rights regimes. In contrast, Western countries and human rights groups believe that sanctions including encouraging tourists to boycott Myanmar pose the best policy choice in encouraging appropriate behaviour from the Myanmar regime. Either way, it is readily apparent that the growth of intermestic policy issues such as tourism require a far more sophisticated approach to the politics of tourism in an interconnected world than has hitherto been the case.

Conclusions: the new realities of tourism

This chapter has provided only a brief introduction to the interconnections between tourism and politics in Southeast Asia. It has highlighted such relations with respect to globalisation and economic regionalisation, the role of the state and human rights issues. Such understandings are significant from a range of policy and industry perspectives including a more relevant contribution of tourism research to international and domestic tourism issues; improved risk analysis for tourism destinations; and improved tourism policy analysis, decision-making, planning and implementation, especially with respect to the way in which tourism policy is integrated with other policy fields. As Singapore Minister for Foreign Affairs S. Jayakumar stated at the 1999 East Asia–Latin America Forum:

> The new realities of a globalised world cannot be artificially fragmented into neat distinct slices. In the global economy, trade, culture, education, politics, finance and a host of other issues and areas act and interact with each other in a seamless web of influences. It is no longer possible to comprehend the parts without understanding the whole. This prescribes a new logic. We believe grasping this new reality as a whole is the key in dealing with the new kind of world that we all find ourselves in. Only by changing our mindsets and making a paradigm shift in the way we conceptualise our relationships, can we take full advantage of the potential that exists and mitigate the downside.
>
> (*The Straits Times*, 3 September 1999).

Tourism is an important component of the new reality of a globalised world and an increasingly interconnected Southeast Asia. Moreover, it indicates that tourism is not just a passive receptor of politics but that tourism influences political perspectives. As this chapter has argued, tourism needs to be recognised as a significant intermestic policy issue which is relevant to national and supranational actors as well as sub-national actors such as provinces, regions and cities which respond to an increasingly globalised business environment and seek to attract investment, employment and tourists. Moreover, the role of tourism in establishing regional images through place-marketing processes may see it being given closer attention as a factor in supranational policy development. Such an understanding lies substantially outside the traditional realms of international relations and tourism policy analysis. An appreciation of the policy and territorial dimensions of tourism's functions in economic integration remains a poorly developed though potentially highly significant subject of study. Indeed, the desire of tourism organisations and politicians to deliver 'good news' or 'positive images' with respect to tourism may even actively work against political analysis which may be critical of policy settings. Nevertheless, without an appropriate understanding of the political dimensions of tourism our picture of tourism in Southeast Asia will remain sadly incomplete.

References

AMPO (1991) *AMPO, Japan-Asia Quarterly Review: Special Issue on Resort Development*, 22(4).

Arai, H. (1998) 'A Scenario for Dynamic Recovery from the Asian Economic Crisis', *Speech by Hisamitsu Arai, Vice-Minister for International Affairs, Ministry of Trade and Industry (MITI), 21 August, Thai-Japanese Association and JETRO, Bangkok, Thailand*. Tokyo: MITI, n.p.

Asia-Pacific Economic Cooperation (APEC) Tourism Working Group (1995) *Asia-Pacific Economic Cooperation (APEC) Tourism Working Group*. Singapore: APEC Secretariat/Singapore Trade Development Board.

APEC Tourism Working Group (ATWG) (1999) 'Terms of Reference'. Online. Available HTTP:http://apec-tourism.org/terms-of-reference/ (3 December 1999).

ATWG (2000) 'Activities by Groups: Tourism'. Online. Available HTTP: http://www.apecsec.org.sg/workgroup/tourism_upd.html (9 February 2000).

AsiaWeek (1998) 'The perfect vacation', 6 November, 48–52.

Brackenbury, M. (1995) *Managing the Perceptions and Realities of Physical Safety and Security in Tourism Destinations*, PATA Occasional Papers Series No.13. San Francisco: Pacific Asia Travel Association.

Campbell, D. (1996) *Myanmar Tourism Under Fire*. Online. Available HTTP:http://web3.asia1.com.sg/timesnet/data/tna/docs/tna2949.html (10 July 2000).

Chang, T.C. (1997) 'From "Instant Asia" to "Multi-faceted Jewel": Urban imaging strategies and tourism development in Singapore'. *Urban Geography*, 18(6), 542–62.

Cohn, T.H. and Smith, P.J. (1996) 'Subnational governments as international actors: Constituent diplomacy in British Columbia and the Pacific Northwest'. *BC Studies: The British Columbian Quarterly*, 110 (Summer), 25–59.

Economist Intelligence Unit (1991) 'Indonesia'. *EIU International Tourism Reports*, 3, 23–40.

Fujiwara, M. (1991) 'Resort Act: Panacea for the construction industry'. *AMPO: Japan-Asia Quarterly Review*, 22(4), 37–40.

Garnaut, R. (1990) *Australia and the Northeast Asian Ascendancy*. Canberra: Australian Government Publishing Service.

Go, F. and Jenkins, C. (eds.) (1997) *Tourism and Economic Development in Asia and Australasia*. London: Cassell.

Graburn, N.H.H. (1995) 'The past in the present Japan: Nostalgia and neo-traditionalism in contemporary Japanese domestic tourism', in R.W. Butler and D.G. Pearce (eds.) *Change in Tourism: People, Places, Processes*. London: Routledge, 47–70.

Hall, C.M. (1994) *Tourism and Politics: Policy, Power and Place*. Chichester: Wiley.

Hall, C.M. (1997) 'Geography, marketing and the selling of places'. *Journal of Travel and Tourism Marketing*, 6 (3/4), 61–84.

Hall, C.M. (2000) *Tourism Planning*. Harlow: Prentice Hall.

Hall, C.M. (in press a), 'Territorial economic integration and globalisation', in C. Cooper and S. Wahab (eds.) *Tourism and Globalisation*. London: Routledge.

Hall, C.M. (in press b) 'Japan and tourism in the Pacific Rim: Locating a sphere of influence in the global economy', in D. Harrison (ed.) *Tourism in the Less Developed Countries*. Wallingford: CAB International.

Hall, C.M. and Jenkins, J. (1995) *Tourism and Public Policy*. London: Routledge.

Hall, C.M. and Oehlers, A.L. (2000) 'Tourism and politics in South and Southeast Asia: Political instability and policy', in C.M. Hall and S. Page (eds.) *Tourism in South and South-East Asia*. Oxford: Butterworth-Heinemann, 77–93.

Hall, C.M. and Page, S. (eds.) (2000) *Tourism in South and South-East Asia*. Oxford: Butterworth-Heinemann.

Hall, C.M. and Samways, R. (1997) 'Tourism and regionalism in the Pacific Rim: An overview', in M. Oppermann (ed.) *Pacific Rim Tourism*. Wallingford: CAB International, 31–44.

Higgott, R. (1999) 'The political economy of globalisation in East Asia: The salience of "region building"', in K. Olds, P. Dicken, P.F. Kelly, L. Kong and H.W. Yeung (eds.) *Globalisation and the Asia-Pacific: Contested Territories*. London: Routledge, 91–106.

Hirst, P. (1997) 'The global economy – myths and realities'. *International Affairs,* 73(3), 409–25.

Japan External Trade Organisation (JETRO) (1996) *White Paper on International Trade 1996*. Tokyo: JETRO.

JETRO (1999) *JETRO White paper on International Trade Fall in Prices Causes Slowdown in World Trade (Summary)*. Tokyo: JETRO.

Jessop, B. (1999) 'Reflections on globalisation and its (il)logic(s)', in K. Olds, P. Dicken, P.F. Kelly, L. Kong and H.W. Yeung (eds.) *Globalisation and the Asia-Pacific: Contested Territories*. London: Routledge, 19–38.

Kelly, P.F. and Olds, K. (1999) 'Questions in a crisis: The contested meanings of globalisation in the Asia-Pacific', in K. Olds, P. Dicken, P.F. Kelly, L. Kong and H.W. Yeung (eds.) *Globalisation and the Asia-Pacific: Contested Territories*. London: Routledge, 1–15.

McCormack, G. (1991) 'The price of affluence: The political economy of Japanese leisure'. *New Left Review*, 188 (July-August), 121–34.

Ministry of Foreign Affairs (MOFA) (1999) *Report of the Mission for Revitalization of the Asian Economy: Living in Harmony with Asia in the Twenty-first Century*. Tokyo: MOFA.

Ministry of International Trade and Industry (MITI) (1999) *Strategy for Revitalising Industry*. Tokyo: MITI.

Ohmae, K. (1995) *The End of the Nation State: The Rise of Regional Economies*. New York: Harper Collins and The Free Press.

Oo, A.N. and Perez, M. (1996) *Behind the Smiling Faces*. Online. Available HTTP:http:/www.comlink.ap-c.org/fic/newslett/eng/28/page_36.htm (25 September 1996).

Piven, F. (1995) 'Is it global economics or neo-laissez-faire?'. *New Left Review* 213, 107–14.

Pizam, A. and Mansfield, Y. (eds.) (1996) *Tourism, Crime and International Security Issues*. Chichester: Wiley.

Richter, L.K. (1983) 'Tourism politics and political science: A case of not so benign neglect'. *Annals of Tourism Research*, 10, 313–35.

Richter, L.K. (1989) *The Politics of Tourism in Asia*. Honolulu: University of Hawaii Press.

Richter, L.K. and Waugh, W.L., Jr. (1986) 'Terrorism and tourism as logical companions'. *Tourism Management*, December: 230–38.

Rimmer, P. (1992) 'Japan's "resort archipelago": Creating regions of fun, pleasure,relaxation, and recreation'. *Environment and Planning A*, 24, 1599–625.

Straits Times, The (1999), 'Buffet of projects served at forum', 3 September, Singapore.

Sydney Morning Herald, The (1996) 'The land of fear', 1 June, Sydney.

Tham, E. (1999) 'Regionalisation as a strategy for Singapore's tourism development', paper presented at *Interconnected Worlds: Southeast Asian Tourism in the 21st Century*, 6–7 September, Singapore.

Toh, M.H. and Low, L. (eds.) (1993) *Regional Cooperation and Growth Triangles in ASEAN*. Singapore: Times Academic Press.

TravelAsia (1996) 'Our say: Balancing politics and tourism'. Online. Available HTTP: http.://www.travelasia.com (26 July 1996).

TravelAsia (1998a) 'Bali travel trade acts'. Online. Available HTTP: http.://www.travelasia.com (22 May 1998).

TravelAsia (1998b) '"Two years in Bali" campaign launched'. Online. Available HTTP: http.://www.travelasia.com (12 June 1998).

Yosano, K. (1998) 'Revitalizing Japanese and ASEAN Economies', *Speech by Kaoru Yosano, Minister of International Trade and Industry, 23 September, Singapore*. Tokyo: MITI, n.p.

3

Towards a Regional Analysis of Tourism in Southeast Asia

Douglas G. Pearce

Introduction

The past decade has seen a growing awareness of the need to take a more integrated approach to tourism in Southeast Asia, to recognise the increasing interdependency between different parts of the region and the interconnectedness between the region and other parts of the globe. This concern with regional interactions and interconnectedness is particularly evident in the plans and policies that have been developed in Southeast Asia during the 1990s. The recent tourism masterplans for Sarawak and Sabah, for example, highlight the broader regional context of tourism in the two states (Pearce, 1995a; Institute for Development Studies/Tourism Resource Consultants, 1996); in Singapore, the state has embarked on a programme of tourism regionalisation (Chang, 1998); and in the Greater Mekong Subregion (GMS), an integrated approach to tourism is being developed (Thailand Institute of Scientific and Technological Research, 1998). These plans and developments underline the need to go beyond the largely descriptive accounts of tourism in particular countries or regions which have characterised much of tourism research in this and other regions to date. They indicate clearly the necessity to develop a more functionally-oriented and conceptually-based approach that stresses the roles of different places and their linkages and interactions with other nodes in a regional network.

The need for an improved understanding of tourism through the development and application of such an approach will increase as the effects of globalisation impact further upon the region. The growth in long-haul and intra-regional traffic, for instance, will see increased competition between destinations within Southeast Asia and meeting this competition will require effective positioning strategies within the regional context. Developing a better understanding of the functional structure of the region and the nature of the interconnections which exist or might be developed will contribute not only to more effective planning and policy-making but also enhance work in related areas, such as marketing and impact assessment (Yuan and Christensen, 1994).

While some very useful initiatives exploring issues of interconnectedness have been taken in the planning and policy arena, this work is rather fragmented, pragmatic in orientation and key ideas, assumptions and approaches are often not very explicit. It is in this context that this chapter seeks to develop a more systematic approach to the regional analysis of tourism in Southeast Asia by elucidating key concepts and out-lining methodological considerations. It does not attempt to provide a comprehen-sive analysis of tourism in the region but instead presents a five-step approach by which such a task might progressively be accomplished.

Characterisation of the regional context

Planning, policy-making and other tasks should not be done in a spatial vacuum and the analysis of the spatial structure of tourism needs to be set against the broader national or regional space economy (Rognant, 1990; Pearce and Priestley, 1998). An essential first step is to set the scene for the regional analysis by clearly and concisely establishing the fundamental contextual features of the region to aid the elaboration and interpretation of the subsequent steps. This might be done from several perspec-tives: physiographic elements, economic or cultural conditions, tourism attributes, core-periphery terms, etc. From all of these perspectives, Southeast Asia can be seen as a region of great complexity. O'Connor (1995:270), for example, notes that "the region's physiography, a complex mix of mountain ranges, rivers, coastline and islands, has limited the development of long-distance road and rail links, so that that air transport is the only effective means of intercity links". This has important implications for the forms of tourism that will exist, the types of linkages to be explored, and the functions of cities to be examined. Thus, distinctive features of Asian tourism noted by Go (1997:15) include the prominence of air travel and the role of major cities. Similarly, Teo and Chang (1998:121) observe that "[c]lassifying the region as a single destination area belies the fact that its member countries are at different stages of the tourism development cycle". They then identify three broad categories: countries with highly developed tourism industries and sophisticated infrastructure, countries where tourism is emerging as a potential source for devel-opment, and countries where there have been few efforts in tourism promotion. Inequalities within countries such as Indonesia and the Philippines are also noted. The existence of regional cores and peripheries (however these might be defined) and the extent to which the region itself is peripheral to core global markets or economies are other key features to be taken into account, as Zurick (1992) demonstrates in the case of Nepal.

Conceptualisation of nodal functions

Within the regional context, the spatial structure of tourism might be considered as a network of interacting nodes. What is required here is to identify the functions of the different nodes or places before examining the relationships between them. Places are no longer seen in terms of their proper names but rather in terms of the functions that they fulfil within the network. Elements of such an approach are already found in tourism plans within the region. For instance, outlining the complementary destination clusters in the Philippines Tourism Master Plan, Reider (1997:228) notes: "[e]ach *cluster* would have at least one *international gateway centre*...near which would be located at least one or two *mass-market beach resort destinations.* *Satellite destinations* within the clusters were to concentrate on niche or mass-market development..." (my emphasis). Similarly, the GMS North–South Tourism Flows Strategy is presented in three stages focusing respectively on the gateway, hubs and sub-hubs and the GMS Tourism Circuit (Thailand Institute of Scientific and Technological Research, 1998).

These and other terms are not used consistently from one study or discipline to another and often are not explicitly defined at all, let alone be conceptually based. Moreover, nodes, especially major cities, frequently have more than a single function which complicates any analysis (Pearce, 1981; 1995b). Additional complexity also arises as different forms of tourism are to be found throughout a region such as Southeast Asia – some 'destinations' will cater to those seeking a beach holiday, others for segments such as ecotourists or adventure tourists, while cities may constitute another set of destinations. Scope exists, therefore, for a more systematic conceptualisation of key terms before they are used to characterise particular places.

Most models of tourist space and tourist travel are based on an underlying origin–linkage–destination system (Pearce, 1995b). This system can be used to elaborate key functions. The end components – the origins and destinations – are rarely explicated at any length and are relatively straightforward. The linkage component, on the other hand, is a critical one in any regional analysis and the associated nodal functions require more elaboration.

Origins

Origins are the markets or source areas of visitors to and within the region. The latter is an important qualification as visitors generated within the region may be a significant component of total demand but one which is often overlooked as attention is commonly focused solely on incoming tourists. As a result, the generating function of cities and other areas is often neglected in regional analyses and an incomplete picture is consequently presented. In contrast, use of a range of demand data can reveal major market functions for places otherwise thought of primarily as destinations; such is the case with Madrid as Pearce and Priestley (1998) demonstrate in their analysis of the spatial structure of tourism in Spain. Similarly, major Southeast Asian metropolitan areas such as Bangkok, Kuala Lumpur and Singapore act as significant generators of domestic and intra-regional tourist traffic.

Various models classify the flows of tourists emanating from origins in terms of volume, duration of trip and distance travelled so that a series of concentric rings of decreasing travel intensity may be identified (Pearce, 1995b). In the real world, these theoretically regular concentric rings are extended by positive deformations (e.g. low cost of living and favourable climate) and compressed by negative factors (e.g. political conditions). Origins, however, need to be considered not just in terms of the actual or potential pool of tourists who live there and the resultant flows, but also with reference to the market-based sectors of the tourist industry: retail travel agents, tour wholesalers, airlines, information offices of foreign national tourist organisations, etc.

Destinations

'Destination' is a widely used term, so much so that its sense is taken for granted and it is rarely defined. Transport analysts speak of 'true destinations' as the endpoint of the trip (Fleming and Hayuth, 1994) though it should be noted that in some cases, travel itself may be the prime activity, for example, on touring holidays (Pearce, 1995b). In general, tourist destinations might be thought of as the places which constitute the object of the trip where all or a major part of the visit is played out. From this perspective, the functions of destinations need to be explored in terms of what they offer visitors, a question that can be considered in terms of both demand (motivations, benefits) and supply (resources and attractions). As people travel for a variety of reasons, clearly a variety of destination types might be identified in this way. Destinations might also be differentiated according to the extent to which tourism is the dominant function (as in resorts) or just one of several activities in a multifunctional area (e.g. in cities or rural villages). Distinctions might also be made according to the extent to which destinations are spatially concentrated (as in cities and resorts) or dispersed (as may be the case with sites visited by ecotourists or adventure tourists), and the degree to which they are incorporated into the local space-economy (Zurick, 1992) or isolated within it (Britton, 1982). Of these types, resort enclaves have been the most explicitly conceptualised, being seen *inter alia* as "islands of affluence within the country, walled in and separate from the rest of the population" (Goonatilake, 1978:7), that is, an enclave is not just a physical entity but also a social and economic structure (Jenkins, 1982).

Gateways

In the tourism literature, gateways in a general sense are seen as major entry/exit points for travellers into or out of a national or regional system (Pearce, 1995b). Understanding the role of gateways is critical to any regional analysis of tourism, for gateways not only link other nodes within the regional network but they also serve to link one network to another (Burghardt, 1971). Further elaboration of the concept is therefore needed.

Burghardt's seminal paper in the broader geographical literature outlines the key features of the gateway in contrast to the prevailing emphasis on central places. For Burghardt (1971:269): "The word 'gateway' gives a fairly clear image of the unique positional characteristic of a gateway city. It is an entrance into (and necessarily an exit out of) some area". He also notes the following attributes of gateway cities:

- they are "in command of the connections between the tributary area and the outside world" and develop "in positions which possess the potentiality of controlling the flows of goods and people" (Burghardt, 1971:282);

- they often develop in the contact zones between differing intensities or types of production;
- although local ties are obviously important, gateways are characterised best by long distance trade connections; and
- they are heavily committed to transportation and wholesaling.

For van Klink and van den Berg (1998:1) "[g]ateways are nodal points, where intercontinental transport flows are being trans-shipped onto continental axes and *vice-versa*" but as Zurick (1992) observes, gateways can exist at a variety of scales, not just the intercontinental. Van Klink and van den Berg draw on Fleming and Hayuth (1994:4) who consider the role of gateways and other transportation hubs in terms of centrality and intermediacy, the latter term being used to describe "locations between important origins and destinations – locations that are chosen as waystops, route junctions, break-in-bulk points, gateways, etc.". They also argue that "[i]ntermediacy is...a port's most expected situational characteristic and one which most ports are striving to enhance" (Fleming and Hayuth, 1994:6). Proximity – the attribute of being close to a market or set of productive resources – is another factor included by Fleming and Hayuth, according to whom one of the clearest examples is gateway proximity to tourist attractions. O'Connor (1995) uses these ideas of centrality, intermediacy and proximity to examine changes in airport development in Southeast Asia.

The notion of intermediacy is inherent in Pearce's (1981) model of the multiple functions of large cities, the gateway function being augmented by an associated staging-post role whereby visitors are sent onwards to other centres or resorts. These functions may be especially significant in cases such as New Zealand where circuit tourism predominates (Forer and Pearce, 1984) or where adventure tourism in more remote locales is the dominant form (Zurick, 1992; Yuan and Christensen, 1994; Ewert, 1996). The latter writers use the term 'portal community', defined by Ewert (1996:60) as "organised social groups such as towns that are adjacent to remote natural landscapes such as National Parks or Forests" that "act as 'staging areas' or portals for adventure-based activities such as mountaineering and expeditioning". But even in resort-oriented regions or destinations, the intermediate role of gateways remains important. Britton (1982:342) describes the latter situation in small Pacific islands in these terms:

Tourist arrival points in the periphery are typically the primary urban centres of ex-colonies, now functioning as political and economic centres of independent countries. Within these towns are located the national headquarters of foreign and local tourism companies and retail outlets of travel, tour, accommodation, airline, bank and shopping enterprises.

In many respects, some tourism gateway services such as those provided by major tour operators (inbound or outbound), parallel the wholesale function described by Burghardt (1971) in a different context.

Broadening out the range of tourism services beyond the transportation sector emphasised by transport analysts is an essential development in terms of understanding tourism gateways. Underlining its entry/exit functions in the context of a tourism plan for Belize, Pearce (1984:298) described a gateway in these terms:

...the place plays a key role in the tourist system of a country. The tourist has his first direct contact with a country at the gateway. It is important that first impressions are favourable because they often affect enjoyment for the remainder of the stay. In this respect entry procedures...should be simple and straightforward. The appearance of a gateway centre should also help create a favourable impression. A gateway should be a node in the transportation system that channels visitors to other parts of the country. Additional information about the country should be provided at these centres. This service is especially important for independent travellers...

As the case of Belize showed, immigration and information will be critical features at smaller entry/exit points, such as secondary overland border-crossings where many of the other features of major gateways may be absent.

Recent Asian studies also highlight the need to extend gateway functions beyond transportation services. Efficient gateway immigration and customs services were recognised by the GMS project as being essential to opening up multi-country visits through Bangkok into a region in which international travel had previously been severely constrained (Thailand Institute of Scientific and Technological Research, 1998). Writing without reference to this wider literature, Low and Toh (1997:246) stress that a gateway should offer a range of services and facilities: "infrastructure, including communications and telecommunication facilities, accommodation, entertainment and recreation and others, such as its manpower support and conducive socio-political support for foreign visitors". In the case of Singapore, their specific focus, Low and Toh also identify a second set of conditions, notably "how the neighbouring countries in Southeast Asia are willing to accept Singapore as a gateway...This is a matter of economic cooperation and political goodwill, and also other destinations not seeing Singapore as an unnecessary middleman".

Hubs

The concept of hubs derives largely from the work of transport geographers and other transport specialists. Traditionally used in a fairly general sense to mean a place which functions as a crossroads (Thompson, 1995; Li and Zhang, 1997) or any large airport or airline operating base, the term has come to assume a more technical meaning as the result of recent changes in airline operating practices (Dennis, 1994). Hubs are now seen more specifically in terms of their transfer functions within a wider network. O'Kelly and Miller 1994:31) note that: "[h]ubs...allow the construction of a network where direct connections between all origin and destination pairs can be replaced with fewer indirect connections". They define a hub as "a major sorting or switching centre in a many-to-many distribution system...the key idea is that the flow between a set of origin–destination cities passes through one or more hubs en route to the final destination". Later, O'Kelly (1998:171) suggests that hubs are "special nodes that are part of a network, located in such a way as to facilitate connectivity between interacting places". For Dennis (1994:221), the term is associated with "an integrated interchange point where one or two specific airlines operate waves of flights". Hubbing thus involves "scheduling alternating banks of arriving and departing flights...in order to allow the interchange of passengers and bags" (Caves and Gosling, 1999:94).

O'Kelly (1998:171) asserts that "[h]ubs are geographical in that they serve a specific regional area and they often confer benefits on the region in which they are located. Hubs are usually a catalyst for agglomeration and scale economies". Dennis (1994) identifies three critical factors in developing an effective airline hub operation:

- a central geographical location in relation to the markets so as to minimise flying time and costs;
- good airport facilities; and
- coordination of schedules to mimimise the time spent on the ground.

While transport linkages are an important component of any regional tourism system, the broader tourism implications of hubs and hubbing remain largely unexplored. As an illustration of the agglomeration effects of hubs, O'Kelly (1998:174) suggests that a hub increases a city's ability to attract conventions and business meetings, but little empirical evidence of this is available. It is also recognised that whereas hubbing may produce benefits for the airlines concerned through the increased load efficiencies that the practice brings compared to point-to-point services, such scheduling generally results in more indirect travel for passengers (Caves and Gosling, 1999). However, in the absence of any detailed research, the impact (if any) of hubbing on tourist visitation patterns, particularly where circuit travel is concerned, is essentially unknown. The various stopover packages offered by airlines would indicate it is having some effect.

Multiple functions and synthesis

That places may have multiple and overlapping functions is seen clearly in the use of such terms as *gateway hubs* which Caves and Gosling (1999) use to refer to gateways on the periphery of Europe which provide onward services to secondary centres and in observations such as "[s]trong originating demand at the hub airport helps underpin a wide range of services from that location" (Dennis, 1994:221). Explicit recognition of these multiple functions in the terms set out here is important in developing a fuller understanding of any regional network.

The development concepts prepared for the Sarawak and Sabah tourism masterplans (Figures 3.1 and 3.2) provide practical illustrations of the ways in which the multiple functions of different places can be brought together for a particular purpose (Pearce, 1995a; Institute for Development Studies/Tourism Resource Consultants, 1996). These development concepts are based on substantial and wide-ranging research and reflect policy considerations and development strategies. Three broad zones of varying tourism potential and intensity have been recognised in each state. Within each zone, places are identified in terms of one or more functions, the zones and places also having a variety of linkages, both internal and external. Kuching, for instance, was identified as a gateway and destination in its own right, with linkages outwards to the hubs of Singapore and Kuala Lumpur and inwards to the northern regional hub of Miri and to more dispersed locations. It is also a source of local tourism. In addition to their functions as international hubs and gateways, Singapore and Kuala Lumpur also serve as significant generators of short-haul tourist traffic. Kota Kinabalu plays a similar role in Sabah, although due to its

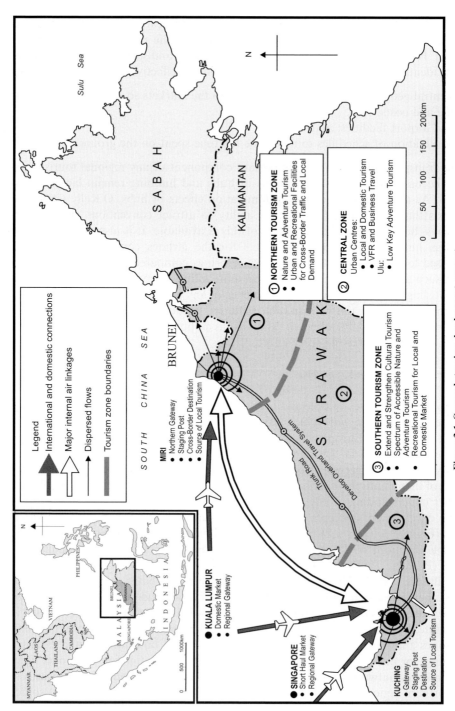

Figure 3.1 Sarawak tourism development concept
Source: After Second Sarawak Tourism Masterplan

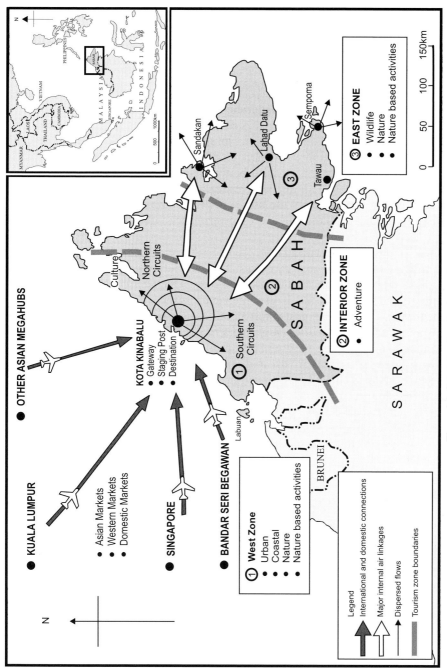

Figure 3.2 Sabah tourism development concept
Source: After Sabah Tourism Masterplan

geographical location and the different markets served, air links have also been developed with other Asian hubs such as Hong Kong. The diffused character of the nature and wildlife-oriented tourism in Sabah's eastern zone is also reflected in the travel patterns away from secondary nodes such as Sandakan and Lahad Datu.

Empirical measures of nodes and relationships

The conceptualisation of nodal functions in a regional network needs to be complemented by the systematic derivation of practical empirical measures of these functions and of the inter-relationships between nodes. Methodologically, developing and implementing a comprehensive regional approach is challenging and resource-intensive as it requires the use of multiple data sources, the development of a range of indicators and the use of diverse techniques (Pearce and Priestley, 1998).

In their analysis of the world city system, Smith and Timberlake (1995) identify two dominant methodological strategies: the attributional strategy based on the attributes of cities; and the linkage-based strategy which employs data that directly link cities to one another or to a larger entity such as the world system. They indicate that the former has been the most common but argue that attributional data are only circumstantial when the theories employed stress relationships among places. Smith and Timberlake found the lack of appropriate data to be a major limitation in applying a linkage-based approach and ended up using air travel data to analyse the network of world cities. Interestingly, on this measure, Singapore ranked among the most interconnected global cities.

The distinction between the attributional and linkage-based strategies, although not necessarily mutually exclusive, is a potentially very useful one in terms of the regional analysis of tourism. Given the paucity of information presently available, both have something to offer in developing a more comprehensive understanding of the structure of tourism in Southeast Asia. The former will enable a more detailed picture of the functions of particular places to be built up, the latter will provide greater understanding of the interconnections between nodes in the regional system and how Southeast Asia is linked into global markets.

A fundamental issue with the attributional approach is the selection of the attributes to be examined. This will depend largely on the specific goal of the research as well as on what information can be obtained. In the analysis of competitive destinations for Sarawak, this author included the following factors: context, markets, air access, attractions, accommodation, prices and development processes (Pearce, 1997a). Air access (measured by the number of direct international flight connections) is, in Smith and Timberlake's (1995) terms, a relational measure. The information was obtained from short field visits and secondary statistical sources and analysed by means of a comparative matrix. In this case, the analysis was limited to eight destinations deemed to be competitors of Sarawak. The approach could be extended to the rest of the region to build up a fully comprehensive picture of tourism in Southeast Asia but significant resources would be required to accomplish this. Other data might also be added to assess more closely the functions of different places. The destination function, for instance, might be explored not only in absolute terms, such as accommodation capacity and bednights, but also by the use of relative measures such as the proportion of tourism-related employment or revenue in the local or regional economy.

Other more specific relational measures are employed by Caves and Gosling (1999) in their comparative analysis of European hub performance, notably measures of transfers, connectivity, direct links and daily frequency. Such measures might be also be applied to determine hubbing functions in Southeast Asia. Fleming and Hayuth (1994) use true origin–destination data and indicators of mid-journey traffic as measures of centrality and intermediacy but warn that these "are overlapping concepts, which makes statistical precision unlikely". Likewise O'Connor (1995) draws on total passenger numbers and airport flight connections in his analysis of the development of airports in Southeast Asia.

As the examples show, and as Smith and Timberlake (1995) found, air traffic statistics are amongst the most readily available comparative data. For the purposes of tourism analysis, they constitute an important component but by no means provide the total picture. In particular, aggregate flight, capacity or passenger data do not allow the actual travel patterns of tourists to be easily determined. More specific tourist flow data are needed to elaborate on the functions of places and the strength and nature of the links between them. If available, standard arrival figures can provide a first level of analysis for individual gateways, as has been shown in the case of Indonesia (Pearce, 1995b). However, more detailed survey data, usually collected by entry or exit surveys, are needed in order to undertake analyses of tourist travel patterns and to establish the relative roles of individual places (Oppermann, 1992; Pearce, 1994; 1995b; 1997b).

Various measures can be employed here. A first concern may be with establishing the extent to which a given country or place is visited as a sole destination or as part of a larger circuit. Circuit travel can then be analysed in terms of the size and nature of the circuits concerned and the relative role of individual nodes within the larger circuit. The latter can be examined in terms of the Trip Index which relates the proportion of nights spent in any one place to the total length of the trip (Pearce and Elliott, 1983). Survey data reveal a clear distinction between short-haul Singaporean short-break tourists making Sarawak the sole focus of their trip and long-haul visitors for whom the state was but a relatively short stop on a longer circuit (Pearce, 1997b). For a significant number of the latter group, Singapore acted as a regional gateway. Establishing the sequence in which places are visited enables gateway and other functions to be determined in more detail. Such analysis can be carried out in terms both of country-to-country flows and intra-national travel patterns, that is, analysing where visitors go between arriving in a country and subsequently departing from it. Oppermann (1992), for example, found that pleasure travellers in Malaysia 'overnighted', on average, in only two localities and that flows were concentrated along the west coast of the peninsula. Much more work of this sort is needed.

Research is also required into the nature of the channels of distribution for tourism in Southeast Asia, of the ways in which these are structured and the effects this has in turn on structuring tourism in the region and influencing the role of particular nodes in the network. Different perspectives on these issues might usefully be combined into a more systematic regional analysis. Again, both attributional and relational approaches might be developed. Establishing the location and structure of wholesalers, retailers, tour operators and other tourism partners within a country or throughout the region would enable the broad picture of the channels of distribution to be developed. This might be complemented by more detailed analysis of key relationships, particularly with a spatial emphasis. For example, the early work by Britton (1982) on the structure of tourism in small Pacific islands could be augmented by more recent marketing and managerial oriented approaches. March (1997) examined buyer–supplier relationships in Australia and found varying levels of dependence between Cairns and the Gold Coast, part of this variation being a consequence of the proportion of ex-Japanese flights into the Cairns gateway and the higher proportion of Japanese guests in Cairns hotels. Pursuit of such issues requires collection of detailed primary data.

Scale considerations and notions of hierarchies

The macro-region of Southeast Asia is the focal scale of analysis being dealt with here. However, varying levels of interconnectedness can be found and research at other scales is also valid. The explicit incorporation of scale and hierarchies is an integral part of such analyses for both practical and conceptual reasons. Given the issues and data requirements outlined above, developing a macro-regional picture will be very resource demanding. Progressively building up such a picture through a series of regional or national analyses may therefore be a more practical option, especially if a consistent comparative approach can be developed. Furthermore, the responsibility for tourism, or for particular aspects of it, can vary from the local to the regional, national and macro-regional scales. As a result the practical implementation of recommendations arising from any analysis will likewise vary from one scale to another (Pearce, 1995a; 1997b). Joint international activities such as marketing within the region of the Association of Southeast Asian Nations (ASEAN) or the development of an integrated strategy for the Greater Mekong Subregion do take place, but little activity actually occurs at the level of Southeast Asia *per se*. Rather, it is at the level of individual countries, regions and localities, or some grouping of these, that planning, policy-making and operational decision-making generally takes place. Nevertheless, activities at these scales will benefit considerably from a better understanding of the macro-regional network and of the roles of individual nodes, at whatever other scale, within it.

The notion of scale and of hierarchies of functions is also critical conceptually, a point developed by several writers previously mentioned in terms of the functions they have discussed. Burghardt (1971:284), for example, notes: "[j]ust as there is a hierarchy of central places, so one may speak of a corresponding hierarchy of gateways. Such hierarchies will occur in sequence with distance, in zones of gradually declining productivity". Thus he speaks of a gateway as the link between two matrices of interconnections. The gateway roles of Singapore and Bangkok might usefully be conceived of in this way with regard to Southeast Asia and its links to other macro-regions. Zurick's (1992) core-periphery model of adventure tourism in Nepal provides a more direct tourism application of this notion. He writes (1992:619–20):

...adventure travel proceeds from the Western generating areas through intervening international gateways, national and regional staging areas. Hence, a more complicated hierarchy of tourism gateways may result. The intervening gateway, located by the model in the semi-periphery of the world economy, is often an important world travel link, such as Bangkok.

At a global scale, Zurick (1992:621) sees Nepal as occupying a peripheral position, with adventure tourism occurring in the "frontier regions of Nepal's space-economy".

Likewise, in their discussion of hubs, Fleming and Hayuth (1994:18) observe:

Centrality needs to be redefined with changes in scale...Intermediacy needs even more frequent redefinition with changes in scale, changes in transport technology, changes in government policy and, especially, changes in the transportation carriers' individual corporate choices. Intermediacy can, therefore, be quite transitory...

The dynamic nature of hubs and changes in their scale of operations are also highlighted by O'Connor (1995:274):

Given the intercontinental non-stop services that are common today, the international hub stage creates a new dimension of intermediacy: the hub provides an intermediate stop now at an inter-continental scale. This effect is illustrated in the way that Qantas currently uses Singapore airport.

Explanation

To move beyond a purely descriptive regional account and provide explanation for the structure and functioning of the network of tourism in Southeast Asia, key factors influencing its development and operation must be identified and examined. As tourism in the region itself has been scarcely analysed in the terms set out in preceding sections, it is not surprising that relatively little work of this nature has been undertaken. Nevertheless, valuable insights into the factors at work and approaches to be developed can be obtained by considering specific sectors or examples from more limited parts of the region.

Transport studies again provide a useful lead, with much research having been carried out on factors influencing the evolution of air transport networks, both in Southeast Asia and elsewhere. Much of this work has been policy oriented and centred on the analysis of air service agreements (ASAs) and corresponding changes in routes and services. Not only is this a key policy area between governments but it is also one where the ASAs and official airline guides constitute tangible and accessible sources of data permitting the analysis of change over time and a focus for explanatory investigation.

Inter-related factors influencing airline development in Southeast Asia mentioned by O'Connor (1995) include: changing aircraft technology (notably the development in long-haul planes which overcame the need for intermediate stops), regional economic development (which boosted the role of places such as Bangkok as destinations in their own right) and changing airline operating practices (e.g. the introduction of hubbing). In this latter regard, he notes that the development of feeder services to international hubs such as Singapore (see also Low and Toh, 1997) may be constrained by political and economic considerations:

> In this stage of development there is a shadow effect cast from the large place. The strength of this shadow is limited by the desire of each national government to have its own carrier provide the international service, but that desire cannot always counter the pressure of the market, which makes the feeder services so attractive.
>
> (O'Connor, 1995:272)

Bowen (1997:136) also underlines the impact of such considerations in his comprehensive review of the prospects for multilateral airline liberalisation in the Asia-Pacific region. As an example of restrictive bilateral structures, he cites the case of air access to Sarawak: "... eleven possible flight combinations for a traveller to Kuching from New York [are listed], all but two of them pass through Kuala Lumpur despite the fact that a routing through Manila, Taipei or Hong Kong would be more direct". At the same time some bilateral reform and the development of a more liberal environment has increased the intensity of the airline network in Southeast Asia. Bowen shows a significant growth in transborder air services from 1979 to 1996 and notes that over the same period, non-stop international flights to Bali increased from 11 a week to 100, with seat capacity increasing tenfold to 25,000 per week.

Diverse factors have led to these changes and influenced the regulatory regime in which airlines operate. These include:

- sustained economic growth and the development of more externally oriented economies;
- the emergence of new international airlines, privatisation of carriers and multiple designation in ASAs; and
- political support (or lack of) for new carriers and services.

Bowen (1997:133) asserts:

> In most of the NIEs, the state remains a pervasive force over the industry: the state retains a large, often controlling, share in flag carriers and competition from new entrants is constrained...The prevalence of vested interests in the established regulatory regime helps to explain the continued reluctance of policy-makers to unleash competition in the industry. Perhaps the most important reason why the state has not liberalised the airline industry further and faster is that the industry still has a very high profile role in national economic development strategies.

Bowen also suggests that in the face of variable progress at the broader regional level, sub-regional initiatives may serve as a way forward and cites the priority given to air transport in the East ASEAN Growth Area (EAGA).

While tourism will not necessarily be subjected in the same way or to the same extent to these external factors, the approach adopted in these airline studies shows what might be done. A more direct tourism illustration of these issues is provided by

Chang's (1998) account of regionalism and tourism in Singapore. Chang concludes (1998:91–92) that:

In an interdependent world, globalism and regionalism are viable avenues for economic expansion and tourism can capitalise on these strategies. Singapore's tourism experience illustrates that regionalisation can help expand the scope of the local tourism industry. At the same time, involvement in regional tourism can also secure additional growth and diversification in the country's economic development.

At a different scale, Pearce (1997b) considered some of the interplay and tourism marketing implications arising out of the different responsibilities of federal and state tourism agencies in Malaysia. These analyses of official policy developments can usefully be extended to consider the actions of all players in the process, including the motivation and behaviour of the different sectors of the tourist industry, the tourists themselves and the local populations (Pearce, 1995a). Much more work of this kind is needed to understand fully the nature and structure of tourism in Southeast Asia.

Conclusion

Southeast Asia is a complex region. Tourism has many dimensions and multiple strands of interconnectedness are to be found there. As a result, considerable scope exists for a much more systematic and rigorous analysis of tourism in the region. This chapter has outlined five inter-related steps by which such an analysis might be undertaken:

- characterisation of the regional context;
- conceptualisation of nodal functions;
- derivation of empirical measures of nodes and relationships;
- consideration of scale and notions of hierarchies; and
- explanation.

Such an approach is resource-intensive and calls for the use of multiple data sources. The emphasis on interconnectedness generates a need for the development of better relational measures. The implications of this are that a comprehensive analysis of tourism in Southeast Asia is a major undertaking, perhaps best carried out in stages and with input from multidisciplinary teams. The Sarawak and Sabah examples have illustrated some of the applications of the approach advocated and shown what can be achieved at a smaller spatial scale. Progressive application of this approach at a range of scales within Southeast Asia would lead to a much improved understanding of how the tourism sector functions throughout the region and provide a firmer basis for planning, marketing and policy-making.

References

Bowen, J. (1997) 'The Asia Pacific airline industry: Prospects for multilateral liberalisation', in C. Findlay, L.S. Chia and K. Singh (eds.) *Asia Pacific Air Transport*. Singapore: Institute of Southeast Asian Studies, 123–53.

Britton, S.G. (1982) 'The political economy of tourism in the Third World'. *Annals of Tourism Research*, 9(3), 144–65.

Burghardt, A.F. (1971) 'A hypothesis about gateway cities'. *Annals of the Association of American Geographers*, 61(2), 269–85.

Caves R.E and Gosling, G.D. (1999) *Strategic Airport Planning*. Oxford: Pergamon.

Chang, T.C. (1998) 'Regionalism and tourism: Exploring integral links in Singapore'. *Asia Pacific Viewpoint*, 39(1), 73–94.

Dennis, N. (1994) 'Airline hub operations in Europe'. *Journal of Transport Geography*, 2(4), 219–33.

Ewert, A.W. (1996) 'Gateways to adventure tourism: The economic impacts of mountaineering on one portal community'. *Tourism Analysis*, 1(1), 59–63.

Fleming, D. K. and Hayuth, Y. (1994) 'Spatial characteristics of transportation hubs: Centrality and intermediacy'. *Journal of Transport Geography*, 2(1), 3–18.

Forer, P.C. and Pearce, D.G. (1984) 'Spatial patterns of package tourism in New Zealand'. *New Zealand Geographer*, 40(1), 34–42.

Go, F.M. (1997) 'Asian and Australasian dimensions of global tourism development', in F.M. Go and C.L. Jenkins (eds.) *Tourism and Economic Development in Asia and Australasia*. London: Cassell, 3–34.

Goonatilake, S. (1978) *Tourism in Sri Lanka: The Mapping of International Inequalities and their Internal Structural Effects*, Working Paper No. 19, Centre for Developing Area Studies. Montreal: McGill University.

Institute for Development Studies/Tourism Resources Consultants (1996), *Sabah Tourism Masterplan*. Kota Kinabalu: State Government of Sabah.

Jenkins, C.L. (1982) 'The effects of scale in tourism development projects in developing countries'. *Annals of Tourism Research*, 9(4), 499–521.

Li, L. and Zhang, W. (1997) 'Thailand: The dynamic growth of Thai tourism', in F.M. Go and C.L. Jenkins (eds.) *Tourism and Economic development in Asia and Australasia*. London: Cassell, 286–303.

Low, L. and Toh, M.H. (1997) 'Singapore: Development of gateway tourism', in F.M. Go and C.L. Jenkins (eds.) *Tourism and Economic Development in Asia and Australasia*. London: Cassell, 237–54.

March, R. (1997) 'An exploratory study of buyer-supplier relationships in international tourism: The case of Japanese wholesalers and Australian suppliers'. *Journal of Travel and Tourism Marketing*, 6(1),55–68.

O'Connor, K. (1995) 'Airport development in Southeast Asia'. *Journal of Transport Geography*, 3(4), 269–79.

O'Kelly, M.E. (1998) 'A geographer's analysis of hub-and-spoke networks'. *Journal of Transport Geography*, 6(3), 171–86.

O'Kelly, M.E. and Miller, H.J. (1994) 'The hub network design problem: A review and synthesis'. *Journal of Transport Geography*, 2(1), 31–40.

Oppermann, M. (1992) 'Intranational tourist flows in Malaysia'. *Annals of Tourism Research*, 19(3), 482–500.

Pearce, D.G. (1981) 'L'espace touristique de la grande ville: Éléments de synthèse et application à Christchurch (Nouvelle-Zélande)'. *L'Espace Géographique*, 10(3), 207–13.

Pearce, D.G. (1984) 'Planning for tourism in Belize'. *Geographical Review*, 74(3), 291–303.

Pearce, D.G. (1994) 'Circuit tourism in Asia and the Pacific', in *Proceedings, 17th New Zealand Geographical Society Conference*. Wellington: New Zealand Geographical Society, 546–51.

Pearce, D.G. (1995a) 'Planning for tourism in the 1990s: An integrated, dynamic multiscale approach', in R.W. Butler and D.G. Pearce (eds.) *Change in Tourism: People, Places, Processes*. London: Routledge, 229–44.

Pearce, D.G. (1995b) *Tourism Today: A Geographical Analysis*, 2nd edition. Harlow: Longman.

Pearce, D.G. (1997a) 'Competitive destination analysis in Southeast Asia'. *Journal of Travel Research*, 35(4), 16–24.

Pearce, D.G. (1997b) 'Tourism markets and marketing in Sarawak, Malaysia'. *Journal of Travel and Tourism Marketing*, 6(3/4), 85–102.

Pearce, D.G and Elliott, J.M.C. (1983) 'The Trip Index'. *Journal of Travel Research*, 22(1), 37–50.

Pearce, D.G. and Priestley, G.K. (1998) 'Tourism in Spain: A spatial analysis and synthesis'. *Tourism Analysis*, 2(3/4), 185–205.

Reider, L.G. (1997) 'Philippines: The development of Philippines tourism in the post-Marcos era', in F.M. Go and C.L. Jenkins (eds.) *Tourism and Economic Development in Asia and Australasia*. London: Cassell, 222–36.

Rognant, L. (1990) *Un Géo-Système Touristique National: l'Italie, essai systemique*. Aix-en Provence: Centre des Hautes Études Touristiques.

Smith, D.A and Timberlake, M. (1995) Conceptualising and mapping the structure of the world system's city system'. *Urban Studies*, 32(2), 287–302.

Teo, P. and Chang, T.C. (1998) 'Critical issues in a critical era: tourism in Southeast Asia'. *Singapore Journal of Tropical Geography*, 19(2), 119–29.

Thailand Institute of Scientific and Technological Research (1998) *Brief Summary of the GMS North-South Tourism Flows*. Bangkok: Tourism Authority of Thailand.

Thompson, I.B. (1995) 'High-speed transport hubs and Eurocity status: The case of Lyon'. *Journal of Transport Geography*, 3(1), 29–37.

van Klink, H.A. and van den Berg, G.C. (1998) 'Gateways and intermodalism'. *Journal of Transport Geography*, 6(1), 1–9.

Yuan, M.S. and Christensen, N.A. (1994) 'Wildland-influenced economic impacts of nonresident travel on portal communities: The case of Missoula, Montana'. *Journal of Travel Research*, 32(4), 26–31.

Zurick, D.N. (1992) 'Adventure travel and sustainable tourism in the peripheral economy of Nepal'. *Annals of the Association of American Geographers*, 82(4), 608–28.

Part Two

Deterritorialisation and New Regionalisms

4

Singapore Tourism: Capital Ambitions and Regional Connections

T. C. Chang and K. Raguraman

Introduction

In the new millennium, the Singapore Tourism Board (STB) envisions Singapore as a 'tourism capital' playing a trinity of roles as a world-class tourist *destination*; a vibrant tourism *business centre*; and a tourism *hub/gateway* to Asia. Released in 1996, *Tourism 21: Vision of a Tourism Capital* (STB, 1996a) is the most ambitious tourism master plan to date, departing radically from earlier plans which focused on local agendas and emphasising instead regional and global ambitions. As a tourism capital, Singapore aspires to be a leader by providing a place where tourism entrepreneurs and enterprises can converge and where concepts and innovations in tourism are born.

This chapter explores the challenges and achievements in Singapore's quest to be a tourism capital using questionnaire data collected from business travellers and tourism companies, as well as in-depth interview data of leading entrepreneurs based in the country. We argue that much of Singapore's ambition to be a tourism capital is predicated on regional connections between the city-state and its neighbouring countries. For Singapore to prosper as a tourism capital, it has to be sustained by critical *interconnections* with the Asia-Pacific region, particularly Southeast Asia. These connections, we contend, tie Singapore to its Asian hinterland through networks of *competition* and *cooperation*.

The chapter is structured in three sections. The first section opens our discussion by explaining the concept of 'tourism capital' and the contributing role of regional interconnections. We will show specifically that capital cities are sustained by the connections they enjoy with their hinterland through the flows of people, investments and ideas. The second section of the chapter discusses three avenues through which Singapore's capital ambitions may be fulfilled. These avenues include connections that tie Singapore to the rest of Asia through the movements of business travellers, tourist enterprises and tourism-related innovations into and out of the country. Singapore's role as a business tourist destination, tourism business centre and tourism hub/gateway will also be explored. The concluding section summarises our main findings.

Capital connections: concepts

The STB envisions Singapore as a 'tourism capital' of the twenty-first century, acclaimed for its leadership in tourism product and service development. The STB explains: "[a]ll great cities of the world acquire the status of capital – not in terms of being a seat of government, but rather in acknowledgement of the pivotal role they play in a given field" (STB, 1996a:3). London and New York are acknowledged financial capitals and Rome, Jerusalem and Mecca are renowned religious cities. Singapore aspires to be a capital "at the forefront of tourism developments", enjoying the "distinction and excitement of being a tourism metropolis" while generating opportunities and spin-offs for visitors, residents and tourism enterprises (STB, 1996a:21)

As a tourism capital, Singapore has three roles to play: (i) a *destination* of "world-class status with broad appeal"; (ii) a *business centre* with a vibrant concentration of tourism, leisure and lifestyle enterprises; and (iii) a tourism *hub* or gateway for visitors, companies and information trends entering the region (STB, 1996a:24). In short, Singapore aspires to be a 'Total Tourism City'. This section of the chapter explains key concepts relevant to our argument. Specifically we explore: (i) the notion of regional collusion and competition; (ii) the idea of capital cities and regional connectivities; and (iii) the principles of regional tourism.

Regional collusion and competition

While Singapore's tourism capital ambitions are acknowledged by academics, policy-makers and practitioners, the contributing role of regional interconnectivity is far from sufficiently analysed. We argue in this chapter that Singapore's capital ambitions are underpinned by a strong network of regional connections. These connections may be either collusive in nature or competitive. Low and Toh (1997) observe, for example, that Singapore's gateway function is implicit on neighbouring countries acknowledging its ambitions and colluding with it to funnel their visitors through the city-state. Notwithstanding this contention, regional connectivities are not always problem-free. Indeed, *Tourism 21* recognises the advantages *and* challenges facing Singapore's tourism. Being "in the heart of one of the world's most exciting and fast-growing tourism and economic regions" encourages win–win partnerships between Singapore and its neighbours (STB, 1996a:25). On the other hand, Singapore will also encounter challenges of having to compete with the "rousing 'tigers' in the region, which are very attractive destinations in their own right" (STB, 1996a:24). To be a capital, therefore, Singapore will have to compete with its neighbours in certain respects while colluding with them in other aspects of tourism development.

For the purpose of this chapter, we define regional interconnections broadly to mean linkages between Singapore and other Asian countries, tying them together through networks of cooperation and competition. These links are broadly conceptualised to mean different things. Examples of *collusive* or *cooperative* links include:

- endorsement of Singapore as a business tourist destination (especially by regional tourists);
- choice of Singapore as a regional headquarters base for companies with subsidiaries in Asia (e.g. Club Med Hotels and Resorts);
- joint cooperation projects that align Singapore's tourism agenda with that of other countries and governments (e.g. the Growth Triangle); and
- export of Singapore tourism expertise to neighbouring countries (e.g. Vietnam and India).

Equally important are *competitive* links such as:

- choice of Singapore by tourism enterprises as an investment centre (as opposed to say Hong Kong or Kuala Lumpur);
- competition between different cities to be a tourism gateway (e.g. the rivalry between Singapore and Bangkok); and
- strengths and weaknesses of Singapore *vis-à-vis* regional urban rivals.

These collusive and competitive ties will become more apparent when we substantiate our discussion with examples from business tourists and tourism enterprises.

Capital cities and regional connectivities

In general, capital cities are characterised by their intense connections to other cities and towns within national boundaries as well as at an international level. Such intra-urban connections are evident in the networks of people, capital, goods and information flows tying cities together. Paris, for example, is a renowned fashion capital with extensive links to the rest of the world. These links are exemplified by people flocking to watch the fashion runways of Paris; the agglomeration of fashion companies here to service global markets and to increase their international visibility; the diffusion of Parisian trends through the media to the 'outside' world; and the drawing of foreign influences and trends by couturiers in their design of 'French' fashion.

A similar example of interconnectivity is evident in the case of cultural capitals. New York City, for instance, draws its allure not only from local influences but international support and connections. The presence of cultural tourists from around the world, as well as investments in the arts by international galleries and cultural institutions guarantee the city's reputation as the world's leading cultural centre. Similarly the concept of 'European City of Culture' recognises the importance of global factors in the promotion of cultural hubs. Cities like Glasgow, Barcelona, Athens and Florence have benefited from improvements in their urban infrastructure, artistic performances from around the world, large numbers of international visitors, and investments in civic projects (Bianchini *et al.* 1988; Bianchini, 1991). Yet it must be noted that the choice of which city has the title of 'European

City of Culture bestowed upon it is highly competitive. Cities pit themselves against each other based on their infrastructure and services. Furthermore, tourists and investors opting to visit/locate in a particular city often forgo another city in their quest to stretch their dollar further.

The notion of competition and collusion is also exemplified by the concept of political capitals. Morris (1994) argues that the newly united Europe necessitates a new capital city. Important criteria in the designation of a European capital include agglomeration of transnational corporations (TNCs), infrastructure, technology, number of engineers and technicians, airport traffic, industrial activity and quality of life (Morris, 1994:231). Top contenders include London and Paris among the first tier of cities, and Berlin, Belgium and Amsterdam in the second tier. Apart from conducive local conditions, continental interconnectivities are also critical. For example, the designated city must attract large numbers of tourists and migrants, have a concentration of leading financial houses, and be unilaterally recognised as exemplifying the European ideal of unity, modernity and tradition.

Paris' urban plans in the 1990s have been undertaken with an eye "to make Paris an example for Europe", with its design motifs and urban scale "based on a noble reinterpretation of the concept of the European city" (Morris, 1994:257). The modernisation of the Grand Louvre with its distinctly postmodern-international style is interpreted as a forward look to the future rather than "falling back on the prestigious historic remains of the past" (Morris, 1994:247). Similarly, Berlin's quest to restructure itself rests heavily on its ability to tap the European consciousness of diversity while down-playing its communist past. The race to capital status thus draws heavily on a bedrock of communal sentiments and shared experiences, but the race is also competitive because cities are compared with each other based on their relative strengths and capabilities.

Regional tourism

As with fashion, religion, cultural or political capitals, how well Singapore performs as a tourism capital also depends on regional and international factors, apart from the purely local. The acceptance by other countries of Singapore's capital ambitions; the choice of Singapore as a headquarters base for footloose multinational companies; and the ease of Singapore companies seeking market opportunities in the region are crucial factors in determining its tourism welfare. *Tourism 21* recognises Singapore will never gain capital status by merely improving its local infrastructure and business conditions. Instead, a 'Tourism Unlimited' approach is required to break free from "traditional thinking which limits our tourism activities to the resources we possess... adopting a transborder approach in going beyond [Singapore's] physical boundaries, to participate in the growth of the Asia Pacific region" (STB, 1996a:16). Realising this transborder vision entails regional collaboration as well as meeting the inevitable challenges emanating from the region.

'Regionalism' and 'regionalisation' in tourism policy have been endorsed by many small countries since the late 1980s as a way to overcome resource and space constraints. Smith (1989:162) explains that tourism regions "do not exist in themselves; they are created for, and only for, some larger purpose". These purposes include joint promotion and marketing, and collaborative planning. In Asia alone, a number of tourism regions have emerged particularly in the form of collaborations between proximate countries in promoting and developing single destination areas. These include the Growth Triangle (Indonesia, Malaysia and Singapore); Northern Growth Triangle (Penang, Medan and Phuket and surrounding environs); Pearl River Delta (Hong Kong, Macau and Guangdong); BIMP–EAGA (Brunei, Indonesia, Malaysia, Philippines–East Association of Southeast Asian Nations (ASEAN) Growth Area); and the Jewels of the Mekong (Cambodia, China, Laos, Myanmar, Thailand and Vietnam) (Rimmer, 1994). These triangles espouse the principle of win–win partnerships and exemplify Poon's (1989) notion of "new tourism" in which individual countries regard each other as collaborators rather than competitors. Regional planning also helps overcome local problems of inaccessibility, competition from neighbours and wasteful duplication of tourist infrastructure (Chang, 1998).

Regional tourism is also predicated on the notion of collective attractiveness. Rather than go it alone, individual countries collaborate to create a more attractive single destination area than each is able to achieve on its own. This principle of collective attractiveness is endorsed by the STB through its practice of *Shakkei*, the Japanese landscaping strategy of "borrowed attractiveness", in which "scenery from one's garden is made more beautiful by incorporating the scenery from afar..." (STB, 1996a:16). The STB explains that *Shakkei* offers "a new way for Singapore to look at itself, as well as the world.... In particular, it calls for greater partnership with our neighbouring countries, working in a borderless manner, and creating new economic space for everyone through leveraging resources regionally and globally to overcome each individual country's natural limitations" (STB, 1996a:16). For small countries, *Shakkei* helps to overcome severe constraints of land, resources and scenic attractions, making it an attractive development option for places like Hong Kong, Macau, Brunei and Singapore.

Notwithstanding the importance of collaboration, it must be noted that regional tourism also opens countries to tensions and competition that would not otherwise emerge. These problems are an inevitable aspect of regional development arising from different political ideologies, cultural mindsets and working styles. For example, it has been argued that greater regional ties in Indo-China have led to increased border crossings of illegal migrants into cities as well as the proliferation of diseases such as HIV-AIDS in rural areas (Parnwell, 1998). In the Northern Triangle, it has also been documented that Malaysian, Indonesian and Thai authorities often conflict over border disputes, issues of piracy and the role of each government in tourism infrastructure development. The BIMP–EAGA has also faced problems because of marked differences in target tourist markets of member countries, with the Philippines and Indonesia preferring coastal resort tourists and Brunei opting for smaller numbers of premium-paying visitors (Baum and Conlin, 1997). Negotiating national differences thus becomes a necessary element in ensuring successful regional development.

Competition also exists between different tourism triangles. For example, in Southeast Asia alone, there are four tourism triangles (mentioned above) competing for the same tourist market (a combination of cruise, cultural and eco-tourists). The

Northern Triangle, for example, poses a direct competition to the Indonesia–Malaysia Singapore Growth Triangle because of their geographic proximity and similarity in resources. Tourism hubs in each of the triangles also compete with each other to achieve tourism capital status. Hence Hong Kong, Bangkok and Singapore compete as investment locations for tourism enterprises, air transport hubs, convention cities and centres of tourism expertise and knowledge. It is thus important to acknowledge, as this chapter does, that regional tourism is characterised by both competition and collaboration, tying cities, countries and tourist regions together through complex networks of collusion and rivalry.

Methodology

Fieldwork involving business travellers and tourism enterprises in Singapore was conducted to generate the data used in this chapter. A questionnaire survey of 1,132 business tourists visiting Singapore was conducted in 1997 to elicit views on business conditions and infrastructure. The empirical data uncovered the strengths and weaknesses of Singapore as a 'business tourist destination' *vis-à-vis* other regional and international cities. The business tourists were intercepted through random unsolicited airport surveys over a period of three weeks with the help of student assistants. A questionnaire survey of 30 tourism/leisure companies based in Singapore was also conducted in 1998, followed by in-depth interviews with 24 selected entrepreneurs in 1999. The STB publications *Lifestyle and Leisure* (STB, 1996b) and *Singapore: Global City for the Arts* (STB, 1995) were used to identify a list of possible interview informants. The STB also provided invaluable assistance in contacting selected informants. A mix of foreign and locally-owned tourism enterprises were selected for interviews. This second leg of research provided information on Singapore's role as a 'tourism business centre' and a 'tourism hub/gateway' to the region.

Capital ambitions, regional connections

As a tourism capital, Singapore's success or failure is dependent on the many ties it has with the rest of Asia. Here we discuss three areas of regional interconnectivity, namely the connections brought about by the movements of *people, investments* and *information flows* tying Singapore to its regional hinterland. Our discussion will also systematically cover the three roles of Singapore as a tourist *destination, business centre* and *hub*.

People connections: Singapore as a business tourist destination

Singapore aspires to be a tourist destination attracting business and leisure travellers from around the world. In this section, we look at Singapore's connections to the world of business travel in two ways: the source countries from which business tourists come, and the strengths/weaknesses of Singapore as a business destination *vis-à-vis* regional and international cities.

Table 4.1: Singapore's competitiveness as a business tourist destination

	1996 (n = 40)		1997 (n = 40)	
Criteria	Singapore's rank	Top city	Singapore's rank	Top city
Looks and visual impression	7	Vancouver	8	Paris
Cleanliness and lack of pollution	4	Auckland	1	Singapore
Ease of doing business	5	Sydney	1	Singapore
Ease of getting around (signposting)	4	Vancouver	1	Singapore
Prices	27	Bangkok	24	Rangoon
Interesting sightseeing	32	Rome	27	Rome
Quality of night life	21	New York	21	Bangkok
Eating out	6	New York	4	Hong Kong
Quality of shopping	6	New York	5	Hong Kong
Ease of getting taxis	3	Auckland	NA	NA
Road traffic	5	Auckland	NA	NA
Friendliness to foreign visitors	12	Sydney	NA	NA
Overall Rank	4	Sydney	4	Vancouver

Source: *Business Traveller Asia-Pacific* (1996; 1997a)
Note: 40 cities are compared in this poll. A number "1" ranking means the best of 40 cities.

Although Singapore is reputed to be an international business destination, the lion's share of its business travel market actually comes from Asia. In 1998, out of the total of 1.03 million business tourists to the country, 63.7 per cent originated from Asia compared to 15.7 per cent from Europe, 11.8 per cent from the Americas and 7.6 per cent from Oceania (STB, 1999:32). Our survey sample of 1,132 business tourists revealed a comparable ratio of 48.8 per cent Asians, 26.1 per cent Europeans, 11.5 per cent Americans and 10.9 per cent from Oceania. These proportions have remained constant over the years and are expected to remain so in years to come. Of these numbers, a disproportionately large share is represented by ASEAN business travellers. In 1998, Southeast Asian countries constituted 29.6 per cent of the entire business market, followed by 11.6 per cent of Japanese, 10.8 per cent from the USA and 6.5 per cent from the Hong Kong SAR (STB, 1999:32).

The high proportion of Asians is matched by their higher than average endorsement of Singapore as a conducive business locale. In our survey, 96.2 per cent of Asian respondents agreed that Singapore is a 'conducive place to undertake business' compared to the average of 95.7 per cent of all respondents and the comparatively lower proportion of 84.0 per cent of African tourists. Many Asian travellers praised Singapore's political stability, efficient airport and public transport and graft-free environment as a welcome departure from other countries in the region. Many Western tourists also praised Singapore for its efficient infrastructure, although they also criticised its overly strict and regulated business environment.

Table 4.2: Attributes that make Singapore "Best in the world" (per cent)

Attributes in Singapore which are "best in the world"	Per cent agree (%)	Per cent disagree (%)	Total number of respondents
Place to do business	87.8	12.2	963
Airport	86.4	13.6	1,069
Access from airport to city	85.0	15.0	993
Transportation system	78.3	21.7	939
Capable and courteous staff	76.7	23.3	926
Convention facilities	71.6	28.4	546
Shopping	49.8	50.2	886
Value for money	42.9	57.1	893
Attractions and scenery	40.6	59.4	818

Source: Field data
Note: Total number of respondents for each attribute varies because it includes only those who agree or disagree with the statement. It excludes those with a "neutral" or "unsure" reply.

The figures above indicate that Singapore features prominently as a business centre for Asian travellers. With its sophisticated airport, hotels, convention venues and business services, many Asian visitors consider Singapore the best business destination in the region. Singapore is also the homebase for many mega-events and exhibitions with a predominantly Asian clientele such as the Pacific Asia Travel Association (PATA) Travel Mart and Edutech Asia. With its central location and comprehensive transport links, many exhibition organisers also target Singapore as a base, funnelling Asian (as opposed to Western) clienteles to the country. Messe Dusseldorf Asia, for example, holds most of its Asia-based exhibitions in Singapore including the recently concluded Star Trek world tour. Managing Director Richard Tan explains the choice of Singapore: its large Asian catchment; superior infrastructure; availability of skilled manpower; and proactive government agencies. Tan, however, notes that Singapore is less attractive to Western markets and exhibitors because of its high venue charges, hotel costs and business overheads. In fact, Singapore is an even more expensive exhibition location than London, Berlin or Munich. Singapore's popularity as a business tourist destination is therefore best explained by its support and endorsement from a primarily Asian market.

A second way of understanding spatial connections is to examine tourist perceptions of Singapore *vis-à-vis* regional and international cities. Table 4.1 provides results from a *Business Traveller Asia-Pacific* (1996; 1997a) poll, listing the criteria by which business cities are compared. Singapore competes extremely well in cleanliness, ease of doing business and accessibility, but fares less well in 'software' touches such as interesting nightlife and tourist attractions. Overall, Singapore was ranked fourth most conducive business city in 1996 and 1997, and second after Hong Kong in 1998.

Singapore's pre-eminence as a tourism business destination, however, is contingent on the performance of other cities. Bearing in mind that many business travellers forgo one business site if they visit another (in our sample, for example, 68.5 per cent of respondents chose Singapore as their sole option compared to 28.3 per cent who were

Table 4.3: Competitor cities to Singapore

Attribute	Ranking of cities	Per cent
Best airport	1. Amsterdam	25.5
(n = 145)	2. London	13.1
	3. Frankfurt	8.3
	4. Chicago	6.2
	5. Tokyo	4.8
	5. Zurich	4.8
Best access from airport to city	1. London	16.1
(n = 149)	2. Amsterdam	10.1
	3. Frankfurt	8.1
	3. Hong Kong	8.1
	5. Tokyo	4.7
Best transportation system	1. London	11.3
(n = 204)	2. Tokyo	10.3
	3. Hong Kong	5.9
	4. Paris	4.9
	5. Amsterdam	3.4
Best value for money	1. Hong Kong	11.6
(n = 510)	2. Kuala Lumpur	9.4
	3. Bangkok	5.7
	4. Jakarta	2.7
	5. London	2.5
Best convention facilities	1. Hong Kong	7.1
(n = 155)	2. New York	4.5
	3. London	3.2
	4. Melbourne	2.6
	5. Washington D.C.	1.9
Most capable and courteous staff	1. Tokyo	8.8
(n = 216)	2. Bangkok	6.0
	3. Jakarta	3.7
	3. Hong Kong	3.7
	5. London	3.0
Best shopping	1. Hong Kong	23.4
(n = 445)	2. London	3.1
	3. Bangkok	2.9
	3. Paris	2.9
	5. New York	2.5
	5. Jakarta	2.5
Best attractions and scenery	1. Paris	5.8
(n = 486)	2. Sydney	5.1
	3. London	4.5
	4. Hong Kong	2.9
	5. Tokyo	2.7
Most efficient place to conduct business	1. Hong Kong	16.1
(n = 118)	2. New York	7.6
	2. Sydney	7.6
	4. Frankfurt	3.4
	4. Amsterdam	3.4

Source: Field data

Note: The "n" figure varies in each case because it refers to the total number of respondents who were able to think of a competitor city to Singapore for each stated attribute. Some cities share the same rank.

Table 4.4: Entrepreneurs' response to the statement "Singapore is the best location base for your company, but future competition may attract your company to invest elsewhere" (per cent).

Response	Foreign Company	Local Company
Yes	56.3% (9)	28.6% (4)
No	25.0% (4)	35.7% (5)
Neutral	18.8% (3)	35.7% (5)
Total	100.0% (16)	100.0% (14)

Source: Field data
Note: Total number in brackets

visiting more than one business site), the strengths of a particular city *vis-à-vis* other cities are critical in ensuring its competitiveness. Table 4.2 provides a list of criteria by which business travellers considered Singapore as 'best in the world'. As one can see, Singapore was ranked 'best' by at least half the respondents in six categories. Singapore performed less well in shopping, value for money and scenic attractions.

Table 4.3 provides further details of competitor cities in all nine categories. Clearly, Singapore's main competitors are other global cities such as London, Hong Kong, Amsterdam and Tokyo in terms of 'hardware' business infrastructure such as airport, transport and convention facilities. In terms of 'software' such as value for money, courteous people and shopping, its rivals are Asian cities like Bangkok, Kuala Lumpur and Jakarta. As cities constantly evolve and change their infrastructure, how well Singapore fares overall as a tourist destination depends on how well other cities perform relative to it. In this way, cities are inevitably connected to each other through networks of competition and rivalry.

To summarise, Singapore's pre-eminence as a business destination has been sustained by the support and presence of Asian business travellers, many of whom recognise the city as offering the best business facilities in the region. However, how well it continues to perform in the future also depends on competition posed by regional and international cities rivalling Singapore as potential business hubs. Collusion and competition play critical roles in determining Singapore's tourism business climate.

Investment connections: Singapore as a tourism business centre

Singapore's capital ambition is also dependent on its role as a tourism business centre, attracting world-class tourism/lifestyle/leisure enterprises to be based here. The investment connections that tie Singapore to the region are both competitive and collusive. Competitively, Singapore markets itself as the best investment site in Asia, providing enterprises with a conducive environment in which to test products, market themselves and locate their headquarters. In this regard Singapore competes with Bangkok, Kuala Lumpur and Hong Kong, which also aggressively promote themselves as business capitals. At the same time, Singapore's tourism business environment is also dependent on the collusion and support provided by neighbouring countries. In select areas such as cruise and auction facilities, some regional countries acknowledge Singapore's superiority and collude with it in mutually cooperative ventures that benefit both Singapore and themselves.

Let us start by looking at the competitive relationship between cities. In a questionnaire survey we conducted with 30 leisure enterprises in Singapore, many companies considered Singapore a conducive investment site, while also stating that competition from regional cities may lure them away in the future. Table 4.4 indicates that local (Singapore-owned) companies are more prone to relocate than foreign firms, citing reasons such as escalating overheads, strict government rules, shrinking local market opportunities and more attractive options in foreign cities. The highly competitive relationship between cities is echoed by many respondents during our interviews with them. Colin Au, President and Chief Executive of Star Cruises, which uses Singapore as its marketing centre and where most of its ships are based, spoke of Bangkok and Hong Kong as potential cruise hubs. Cruise companies monitor the inflow of air-bound tourists into a country and the number of air connections an airport enjoys, since cruise visitors often enter/depart a cruise hub by air. Improvements in Bangkok's airport and the opening of new airports in Hong Kong and Kuala Lumpur have obviously affected Singapore's competitiveness as a cruise business location.

Nevertheless Singapore has many competitive strengths over its regional rivals. Our survey of business companies reveals that 'political stability', 'transport and communications infrastructure', 'language environment' and 'business and financial services' are its primary strengths. In choosing where to locate a regional headquarters, companies compare cities according to strict criteria. Cirque du Soleil, a Canadian entertainment company, chose Singapore as its Asia-Pacific base in 1998 after considering Tokyo, Kuala Lumpur and Hong Kong. Sharon Tan, Deputy Managing Director (Asia-Pacific), elaborated that government assistance was the tipping factor in Singapore's favour:

I believe that we have looked at different cities and especially at Hong Kong because we have performed in Hong Kong before...so it could be a natural step to go to Hong Kong. But we decided to come to Singapore for various reasons. I think we have mentioned this so many times before. The stability here, infrastructure, and geographical factors because we are performing in the Asia-Pacific. So, it's really quite neat to be in the centre and also the manpower as well. I think we have a good staff strength here and most of all, support from the government. I think STB played a big part in the decision...Hong Kong we looked at, and Kuala Lumpur we looked at too because it would have been much cheaper in Kuala Lumpur! In terms of distance it's not out of our track. Like I said, the tipping point was the very proactive approach by the government agencies and the relative facilities available if you put the two together.

(Personal interview, 23 June 1999)

Cirque du Soleil Producer and Co-President Daniel Gauthier similarly explained, "We realised we had great acceptance in Asia after the circus did a Hong Kong tour...But Hong Kong is too Chinese and Tokyo, too Japanese. The quality of English-speaking Singapore staff and the place being bang centre in the territory we would be covering convinced us to come here." (*The Straits Times*, 1 June 1998).

Some tourism companies have also relocated their headquarters from rival cities to Singapore. For example, both Club Med Hotels and Resorts and Aman Hotels and Resorts relocated from Hong Kong to Singapore in 1992 and 1999 respectively. Herve Cacheur, Director of Administration and Finance (Club Med, Asia-Pacific), explains the choice of Singapore as a pragmatic one based on urban competitiveness:

Well, it was not such a clear-cut decision. It was in the early nineties when we decided to pull the different offices together. It was very different at that time; the most competitive city apart from cost was Hong Kong. The most competitive in cost was KL. But then if you take in the scoring in all the different areas we are looking at that time, than it was Singapore.

(Personal interview, 20 July 1999)

Club Med reviews its investment options every five years, so it should be noted that securing tourism investments is no guarantee of a lifelong investment commitment.

Business environments compete not only in cost, infrastructure and location alone. The living conditions of a place and its aesthetic appeal are also critical in providing an appropriate homebase for high-skilled employees. In this regard, some arts companies felt Singapore would never become a cultural business centre. The government's stringent control of entertainment events and strict censorship laws are considered hostile to arts practitioners. On the other hand, however, others also expressed the view that Singapore's strict enforcement of rules makes it a secure place for expatriates. Michael Bruner, Vice-President of Operations at Planet Hollywood, whose Asian headquarters is based in Singapore, spoke of 'ease of living' as a main consideration:

I think the lifestyle environment in which the key expatriate staff live is very important for the quality work they can produce in a job like this. I think Singapore has, in my experience, the best environment in Asia. The shopping, the transportation, the lack of pollution...There is also the language [factor]; English being the first language is very important for the people in this company. And because of all these factors, it's easy to work from the business point of view. It is quite easy to run an office here; we don't have a big problem with the language, things are pretty easy to locate.

(Personal interview, 12 May 1998)

Competition aside, Singapore's tourism business conditions are also contingent on the cooperation offered by other countries. In the area of cruise development, for example, Singapore's elaborate facilities (cruise and ferry terminals, an international airport and wide range of hotels) make it the undisputed cruise hub in the Growth Triangle (comprising Indonesia, Malaysia and Singapore). Cruise companies such as Star Cruise, Renaissance Cruise and Mitsui OSK Lines thus deploy Singapore as a marketing base while using different sites in Indonesia and Malaysia as destination sites, repair centres, refuelling stops and so forth. Places like Port Kelang, Phuket and Bintan thus serve as secondary destinations to Singapore's primary role as cruise gateway and business headquarters site. There is seldom any dispute of Singapore's key role because of the latter's ability to funnel large numbers of tourists to them and the recognition that Singapore's buoyant cruise industry would benefit them as well (Low and Toh, 1997). The converse is also true. As the primary cruise centre of the region, Singapore is also highly dependent on its hinterland of subsidiary cities because without them there is little impetus for cruise visitors to visit the region in the first place.

The art auctioneering industry also provides support to this theme of regional cooperation. Sotheby's established a headquarters in Singapore in 1985 as a base in Southeast Asia. According to its Managing Director (Singapore), Quek Chin Yeow, Singapore serves as the main marketing and auction site while regional cities like Manila, Kuala Lumpur and Bangkok serve as sales representative offices. This regional division of labour is based on collusion rather than competition. With an expansive airport and stable political climate, clients, prospective buyers and art representatives throughout the region endorse Singapore's position as an art business centre. Furthermore with English as the *lingua franca* and good exhibition venues, Singapore provides a centralised auction base where tourists and regional businesses are happy to converge.

Information connections: Singapore as a tourism ideas hub

While the preceding discussion focused on Singapore's regional connections through flows of people and capital, we turn our attention now to the flow of ideas and information. The STB envisions Singapore as a tourism hub where innovations and concepts in tourism/leisure are germinated, tested and franchised to the region. Singapore is to serve as a breeding ground for tourism ideas to take root, and also a gateway for these ideas to spread to the rest of the region. Local tourism enterprises, in particular, are encouraged to export their services and expertise (for example, in hotel management or airport construction) to regional markets after fine-tuning them on home ground.

The regional connections that tie Singapore to its hinterland are both competitive and cooperative. On the one hand, as a tourism ideas hub, Singapore will export tourism expertise to regional countries embarking on tourism development (e.g. Vietnam, Cambodia, India). These cooperative relationships are often structured as 'win–win' partnerships in which Singapore and the recipient countries benefit. At the same time, we also observe that cooperative relationships can occasionally sow the seeds of dissent, resulting in inter-country strife and neighbourly tensions. Singapore's role as a tourism information hub is therefore sustained by regional cooperation but subjected to neighbourly competition at the same time.

In terms of regional cooperation, the export of tourism expertise occurs in two ways. First, the 'Singapore Inc approach' in which the Singapore government encourages investments to be channelled to particular locales. Here the government plays an entrepreneurial role by partnering local businesses in joint ventures overseas, as well as guiding entrepreneurs to sites they would not normally consider by installing the necessary legislative and infrastructural framework to ease the setting up of business (Yeung, 1998). A good example is the Bintan Beach International Resort (BBIR), a 23,000 hectare resort complex on the Indonesian Island of Bintan developed by a consortium of Indonesian and Singaporean investors and government-linked corporations. The Economic Development Board (EDB) describes the BBIR as a "flagship project" in which "Singapore-style business climate", infrastructure, expertise and knowhow are transplanted into foreign soil (EDB, 1995:22) and where government assistance programmes like staff training are provided.

The BBIR represents one avenue through which Singapore is connected to its neighbours in a mutually cooperative partnership. Bintan will benefit from an increased inflow of tourists funnelled through Singapore as well as investments and expertise in the form of hotel developments by Singapore-owned companies like Banyan Tree, Sedona Hotels and Raffles International. Likewise Singapore also benefits because of its enlarged tourism hinterland, offering resources it cannot possibly provide at home – endless beaches, open grounds, resort hotels and water-front accommodation. The Singapore government, therefore, has a vested interest in Bintan's success. Some local companies also feel a sense of national duty by investing in Bintan while being assured of Singapore-style management. Banyan Tree Hotels and Resorts, for example, has established two hotels in Bintan because of the Singapore government's presence, according to its Vice-President (Marketing and Sales), Edwin Yeow:

At Bintan, it is not like "We went, we saw, we conquered". It's more like we went but we didn't want to [invest] but government agencies, the GLCs [government-linked companies] were all saying, "Hey, we have to do something because of this growth triangle concept." So we went in, short of national service. But of course, we succeeded. Let's be politically correct to say national service is good...At Bintan, Wah Chang went in because we saw a commercial opportunity in the project but the drive was mainly from the government. The government side like EDB was very involved...I think the government's encouragement was in opening up the doors, clearing up the land issue, the infrastructure issue. These are very huge issues which the private sector can never do on its own...Bintan is a classic case where we will never go in on our own if the government wasn't there, and the whole infrastructure wasn't resolved by the BRM and BRC [Bintan Resort Management and Bintan Resort Corporation]. They provided for and paved the road for us to go in; otherwise I don't think any private sector company would dare go in.

(Personal interview, 23 June 1999)

The second approach by which local companies 'go regional' is through the sale of expertise and tourism know-how to developing countries embarking on tourism development. Such countries include India, Vietnam, Cambodia, Myanmar and China. Regional connections of this nature are often 'win–win' partnerships as well. Recipient countries benefit with the infusion of skills in tourism development and management, while Singapore benefits because the sale of tourism knowledge helps to augment the country's export economy. Such export services include hotel management skills, staff training, consultancy, setting up and managing national air carriers and airports, implementation of tourism master plans and the development of attractions. There is much to gain by helping others: "[p]articipating in other countries' tourism development creates growth opportunities for local entrepreneurs, companies and government ministries while generating political goodwill with fellow Asians" (Chang, 1998:83). Kanai (1993) notes that tourism/leisure constitutes one of six local industries that actively contribute to the country's regionalisation and globalisation goals.

There are many examples of the export of tourism services to Asian countries. So far, the STB has helped countries like India and Vietnam develop their tourism master plans. A Singapore-based consortium is also currently building a new inter-national airport at Bangalore, while the Changi Airport Enterprises Pte Ltd helped in the conceptualisation of the same airport. Numerous tour agencies and hotel developers have also set up leisure-related businesses throughout Indo-China. Indeed, Singapore is the largest investor in Myanmar and the fourth largest investor in Vietnam with the majority of its investments in tourism properties (*Far Eastern Economic Review*, 25 April 1996). Even the Singapore Zoological Gardens has set up a consultancy department and is looking into the possibility of selling its expertise in zoo landscaping and management to cities like Madras, Hyderabad, Surabaya, Phnom Penh and Guangzhou. Bernard Harrison, Chief Executive of the Zoo, explains that "going regional" is spurred not so much by economic returns as the need to undertake "national service" and "share expertise with others" (Personal interview, 5 October, 1999).

Regional connectivities, however, are not always smooth sailing. What starts as mutual cooperation may sour into unequal relationships that undermine rather than sustain neighbourly ties. Singapore's regional forays certainly run the risk of creating tensions between Singapore and its neighbours. These tensions manifest themselves in different ways.

One tension arises with the notion of tourism as neo-colonialism. Political economy approaches often depict tourism as a way through which developed metropolitan centres impose their values on developing countries (see Britton, 1982). It is argued that the benefits derived from tourism often leak back to developed countries because of their ownership of critical services such as hotels, attractions and retail outlets. Recipient countries instead suffer from environmental, social and economic problems. While it is often assumed that the 'colonial' powers are Western, a new situation is emerging today in which newly industrialising economies such as Singapore and Thailand are taking on these positions of power. Singapore's excessive involvement in Bintan, for example, has already raised concerns over the environmental scars brought about by large-scale resort developments (*Business Traveller Asia-Pacific*, 1997b) and the socio-economic tensions engendered when locals are relegated to menial employment positions (Lim, 1999). In a study on tourism in the Growth Triangle by Lim (1999), for example, he documents that many Bintan and Johor locals perceive Singaporean tourists as arrogant and contributing to pollution and inflation. Singapore companies are also seen as elitist, employing Singaporeans in top management positions.

Another tension emerges with an increase in Singaporean tourists travelling within the region. With Singaporean expertise exported to various Asian countries, there is a strong, albeit mistaken, assumption that Singapore's characteristically high standards in tourism services will be replicated exactly in neighbouring countries. This has led many Singaporeans to complain incessantly when local standards fail to match up with what they are accustomed to back home. This 'export' of Singaporean arrogance and high expectations reflects poorly on Singapore. Kek Beng, Senior Operations Manager (OSK Mitsui Lines), explains that regional countries still lag behind in tourism services because while Singapore's 'hardware' has been successfully transplanted, 'software' has not been as easily transmitted:

Yes, everything is still not up to Singapore standards. The infrastructure and hardware is there – very good. Hardware is perfect; it's just duplication, but the software is not there. Software means the people, the workers, the environment, the character of the people you work with...Maybe we are more developed, I don't know. But I mean getting used to the Singapore five-star hotel kind of service, it's different when you go overseas. Definitely different. Software is definitely different.

(Personal interview, 20 July 1999)

The diffusion of Singaporean knowledge and expertise in the region has therefore the unfortunate effect of exporting an arrogant Singaporean mindset as well. This runs the risk of eroding regional camaraderie. Edwin Yeow of Banyan Tree Hotels and Resorts, for example, spoke of the colonial attitudes harboured by Singaporeans in Bintan, making them unpopular with locals. In his words:

I think the one feedback we always get from the locals is the mindset of Singaporeans. Some of them [Singaporeans] are delinquent in that their expectations are very high, you know. The Singaporean, as you know, pays one dollar and he wants to get more than a dollar's worth of service and value. There also seems to be an attitude, and this is not specific to Singaporeans only, of arrogance. Because their currency is stronger, the tourist has a better education and comes from a developed country, and his country is ranked number one in the world in all the competitive studies, so the mindset of the Singaporean is quite difficult. When they go on holiday, somehow they carry with them this expectation of efficiency, which a lot of Asian countries cannot deliver, even in a place like Thailand.

(Personal interview, 23 June, 1999)

The Singapore government has tried various means to combat offensive Singaporean behaviour overseas, including initiating a competition to reward the most courteous tourist. The Courtesy Campaign, a traditional local institution since 1979 when it was initiated in Singapore, is now being 'exported' to mitigate the tensions arising from regional tourism.

In conclusion, Singapore's role as a hub of tourism information and expertise ties it inextricably to the region. Cooperative links and 'win–win' partnerships connect Singapore to the rest of Asia in a mutually collusive relationship. However, these collusive ties can also give rise to regional tensions and discord that, if uncontrolled, might undermine the economic and political benefits generated through regional tourism.

Conclusion

In this chapter, we have argued that Singapore's ambition to be a tourism capital is predicated on regional connections that tie the city-state to its neighbouring countries. These connections are either competitive or collusive in nature, and are manifested in three distinct flows: business travellers visiting the country, tourism enterprises with a base in Singapore, and the export of tourism ideas and concepts from Singapore to the region. While past tourism policies focused on the development of local attractions, hotels and infrastructure, the new millennium with its emphasis on a 'borderless world' and 'shrinking earth' demands a 'transborder approach' towards tourism development. The vision of a tourism capital is Singapore's response in this globalising era. How ably Singapore fulfils this vision as a business destination, a tourism business centre and a tourism gateway ultimately depends on its ability to secure regional cooperation while negotiating the tensions and competition that inevitably arise from globalisation.

Acknowledgement

The authors acknowledge the financial support of the National University of Singapore and Singapore Tourism Board (R109-100-002-112) in the production of this chapter.

References

Baum, T. and Conlin, M.V. (1997) 'Brunei Darussalam: Sustainable tourism development within an Islamic cultural ethos', in F.M. Go and C.L. Jenkins (eds.) *Tourism and Economic Development in Asia and Australasia.* London: Cassell, 91–102.

Bianchini, F. (1991) 'Urban renaissance? The arts and the urban regeneration process', in S. MacGregor and B. Pimlott (eds.) *Tackling the Inner Cities: The 1980s Reviewed, Prospects for the 1990s.* Oxford: Clarendon, 215–50.

Bianchini, F., Fisher, M., Montgomery, J. and Walpole, K. (1988) *City Centre Culture: The Role of the Arts in the Revitalization of Towns and Cities.* Manchester: Centre for Local Economic Strategies.

Britton, S. (1982) 'The political economy of tourism in the Third World'. *Annals of Tourism Research*, 9(3), 331–58.

Business Traveller Asia-Pacific (1996), 'The best and the brightest', September, 30–49.

Business Traveller Asia-Pacific (1997a), 'The cream of the crop', October, 30–44.

Business Traveller Asia-Pacific (1997b) 'A beach for a backyard', October, 60–67.

Chang, T.C. (1998) 'Regionalism and tourism: Exploring integral links in Singapore'. *Asia Pacific Viewpoint*, 39(1), 73–94.

Economic Development Board (1995) *Singapore Unlimited: Singapore in the 21ˢᵗ Century.* Singapore: EDB.

Far Eastern Economic Review (1996) 'It's a jungle out there', April 25, 58–62.

Kanai, T. (1993) 'Singapore's new focus on regional business expansion'. *NRI Quarterly*, 2(3), 18–41.

Lim, L.H. (1999) *A Triangle Love Affair? Tourism in the Indonesia-Malaysia-Singapore Growth Triangle*, unpublished honours thesis, Department of Geography, National University of Singapore.

Low, L. and Toh, M.H. (1997) 'Singapore: development of gateway tourism', in F.M. Go and C.L. Jenkins (eds.) *Tourism and Economic Development in Asia and Australasia.* London: Cassell, 237–54.

Morris, E. (1994) 'Heritage and culture: A capital for the new Europe', in G.J. Ashworth and P.J. Larkham (eds.) *Building a New Heritage: Tourism, Culture and Identity in the New Europe.* London and New York: Routledge, 229–59.

Parnwell, M. (1998) 'Tourism, globalisation and critical security in Myanmar and Thailand'. *Singapore Journal of Tropical Geography*, 19(2), 212–31.

Poon, A. (1989) 'Competitive strategies for a "new tourism"', in C.P. Cooper (ed.) *Progress in Tourism, Recreation and Hospitality Management.* London: Belhaven Press, 91–102.

Rimmer, P. (1994) 'Regional economic integration in Pacific Asia'. *Environment and Planning A*, 24, 1599–625.

STB (1995) *Singapore: Global City for the Arts.* Singapore: STB.

STB (1996a) *Tourism 21: Vision of a Tourism Capital.* Singapore: STB.

STB (1996b) *Lifestyle and Leisure.* Singapore: STB.

STB (1999) *Singapore Annual Report on Tourism Statistics 1998.* Singapore: STB.

Smith, S. (1989) *Tourism Analysis: A Handbook.* Harlow: Longman.

Straits Times, The (1998) 'The circus comes to town', 1 June, Singapore.

Yeung, H.W.C. (1998) 'The political economy of transnational corporations: A study of the regionalization of Singaporean firms'. *Political Geography*, 17(4), 389–416.

5

Tourism in an Inter-state Borderland: The Case of the Indonesian–Singapore Cooperation

Carl Grundy-Warr and Martin Perry

Introduction

Cross-border cooperation is of obvious importance for the mutual strengthening of the tourism industries of neighbouring countries. Indeed, transnational approaches to tourism are becoming more common, as shown by the World Tourism Organisation's concept of 'inter-regional planning' and promotion of transnational tourist attractions in diverse parts of the world such as 'The Mayan World', the 'Andes Route' and 'Jewels of the Mekong' (Chang, 1998:77). As well as fitting the nature of the tourism destination, such approaches recognise that tourists will often have a regional rather than a specific destination in mind when making their travel choices. Where the political border divides geographical features, cross-border cooperation can facilitate the marketing of natural travel corridors such as a shared coastline or an archipelago. Cross-border cooperation may help to diversify the appeal of each individual destination by promoting access to complementary locations. It can rationalise investments in tourist infrastructure by encouraging the sharing of facilities such as airports. It can disperse congestion of tourists in one location and prevent the displacement of indigenous communities. Lastly, it can help to spread economic benefits accrued from tourism (Pearce, 1989; Wall, 1997).

All of these opportunities and motives for cross-border cooperation exist in the case of Singapore's tourism industry and its linkages with tourism development in the neighbouring countries of Malaysia and Indonesia. Singapore is a small city-state which has been forced to make adaptations to its own tourist image, both as a consequence of urban redevelopment and the increased accessibility of other Southeast Asian destinations. Chang (1998:82) observes that the Singapore Tourism Board (STB) has recognised the image problem related to a highly developed, sanitised and prosperous city space, replacing the slogan 'Instant Asia' with 'New Asia-Singapore'. Singapore has a continuing importance as a tourism gateway.

Its airport continues to be the region's premier international transport node through its role as a regional business and convention centre, and the city has become a relevant tour stop for big name performers. In addition, the growing affluence of its own population has increased leisure demands which are not satisfied by the limited recreation opportunities within its own built-up environment, making it a potentially important tourist generator for neighbouring countries. Singapore is also the source of considerable commercial capacity for the tourism industry in terms of its hotel and travel companies that have acquired complementary overseas assets.

The possibility of cross-border cooperation with Malaysia and Indonesia has been a large priority for Singapore since the late 1980s (Grundy-Warr and Perry, 1996; Peachey *et al.*, 1998). The principal institutional form this has taken is the Indonesia–Malaysia–Singapore (IMS) growth triangle. Singapore's international cooperation takes other forms as well, including participation in ASEAN-wide (ASEAN refers to the Association of Southeast Asian Nations) marketing projects, but the growth triangle has been the main vehicle for cooperation within its immediate hinterland. The greatest impact from this project has been on Singapore–Indonesian coopera-tion in the Riau islands of Batam and Bintan, which lie within a 30 to 45 minute fast ferry ride from Singapore. This chapter examines the impact of the IMS growth triangle on tourism development. It explains the nature of the growth triangle agree-ment and how this results in a characteristic *enclave form of investment*. By this, we mean that large joint development projects are literally built and managed in virtual isolation from the surrounding socio-cultural and economic environment. The sus-tainability of this approach to cross-border cooperation for tourism development is questioned in the light of the increasing challenges to maintaining the separation of the enclaves from the broader development of the islands. Alternative institutional and operational approaches are suggested in this chapter. Consideration is also given to the little researched socio-cultural and micro-level economic implications of the on-going joint ventures associated with industrial and tourism development schemes.

Southeast Asian growth triangles

Singapore–Indonesian cooperation in the Riau has been the most active component of the IMS growth triangle, itself the most advanced of the growth triangle projects announced subsequently. As these projects are typically presented as a new and coherent policy initiative (for example, see Toh and Low, 1993; Thant *et al.*, 1994) it is necessary to consider whether lessons from Singapore and Indonesia's coopera-tion, which form the main subject of this chapter, have wider implications. As a prelude to that judgement, this section comments on the main differences and simi-larities between the growth triangle projects. The list of localities generally included amongst such projects can be divided into three main types:

- *Indigenous* growth triangles, of which the most prominent example has been the Hong Kong and southern China (specifically the provinces of Guangdong and Fujian) region which encompass territory that has seen spontaneous integration through the action of individual traders and investors. This is a special case in the sense that pre-existing social, cultural, kinship and business linkages across the former colonial political boundary were a major motivating force underlying economic ties.

- *Resource management* growth triangles, of which the main example is the Mekong Valley (strictly not a triangle since it involves cooperation between Thailand, Laos, Vietnam, Cambodia and China) and where cooperation is primarily motivated by the need to coordinate the use of a shared resource, in this case the Mekong River that flows through multiple territories. For similar motives, the United Nations has sought to promote the Tumen River economic development area, involving cooperation between parts of North Korea, China and Russia but while cited as another growth triangle, this project has yet to see significant implementation. In a sense, all examples of cross-border cooperation have significant resource management implications. If we include the issue of human resources, then we can see that the example of the IMS growth triangle creates obvious managerial and technological functions for Singaporean employees. Natural resources are also critical in the existing agreements between Singapore and Indonesia, particularly as the former is seeking to diversify its external sources of fresh water supplies by developing watersheds in neighbouring Riau Province.

- *Economic development* growth triangles, of which the major examples are the IMS growth triangle, the Indonesia–Malaysia–Thailand (IMT) growth triangle and the East ASEAN Growth Area (EAGA) incorporating parts of Malaysia, Indonesia, the Philippines and Brunei. These triangles are recent government-led initiatives, generally encompassing territories where existing economic interaction is weak and did not develop naturally. The projects share a common development strategy based on the promotion of complementary specialisation. Thus in the case of the IMS growth triangle, the complementary nature of the ties envisaged designates Singapore as a centre for high-value manufacturing, trade and business services, Malaysia as a base for intermediary level industry and the Riau as an area of low value and labour-intensive manufacturing and recreation services. Specialisation in this way is designed to attract investment by enabling investors to retain activities in close proximity while making use of contrasting environments. The tourism sector has become one of the key exploiters of contrast between the biophysical and human-made environments within the growth triangle area.

Amongst the economic development growth triangles, three main points of contrast may be identified: (i) economic differentiation; (ii) geographical scope; and (iii) implementation. With respect to the degree of economic differentiation, the presence of Brunei in EAGA and Singapore in the IMS growth triangle, respectively Asia's second and third most wealthy territories, means that these cross-border projects encompass a large disparity in national income. This suggests greater scope for economic complementarity than in the case of the IMT growth triangle. However, while oil-rich Brunei is interested in economic diversification, it does not have the same impetus as Singapore to disperse industrial activity to neighbouring states. In terms of geographical coverage, EAGA is the most extensive project in terms of the number of participants and distance between them, while the IMS growth triangle is the most geographically compact and interconnected by existing communication and infrastructure links. A significant development with the IMS growth triangle, somewhat to the loss of this initial asset, has been the project's geographical extension, announced officially in 1997, to include West Sumatra and (in Malaysia) the states of Negri Sembilan and South Pahang.[1] Finally, with respect to implementation, only the IMS growth triangle has made headway although there has been extensive feasibility analysis in the case of the IMT growth triangle (Thant and Tang, 1996) and government agreements to investigate possible areas of cooperation in the EAGA (Mijares, 1996).

While there are therefore important differences between the growth triangle projects, they are united by the political context in which they have arisen. Most academic comments on the growth triangle projects have interpreted their initiatives as further examples of a drift towards a borderless world economy (Ohmae, 1990; 1995; Parsonage, 1992; Thant *et al.*, 1994; Friedmann, 1995). This interpretation has assumed a uniformity in borderland processes that overlooks the particular regional environment and government motives for cross-border cooperation. To explain this alternative perspective it is first helpful to distinguish between inter- and trans-state processes which, as Taylor (1995:12) emphasises, differentiate polar opposites: inter-state processes act to reproduce states, nations and territories, while trans-state processes act to undermine sovereignty based upon fixed political boundaries.

The contrast between inter- and trans-state processes identifies a spectrum of possible degrees of interdependence and integration between nation-states. The creation of an integrated borderland implies considerable merger of the economies of the adjoining nation-states facilitating the unimpeded movement of people, goods, capital and resources (Martinez, 1994:5). In this trans-state development, each national participant relinquishes its sovereignty to a significant degree for the sake of achieving mutual progress. Trans-state processes may involve a whole array of non-state mediated activities in economic, social, cultural and also political spheres of life. According to Martinez (1994), 'integrated' implies a huge dilution of national sovereignty. An interdependent borderland involves a mix of inter- and trans-state processes in which increased cross-border economic interaction and inter-state dialogue occurs alongside the continuance of two or more political sovereignties whose individual integrity remains unaffected.

There are three reasons for suggesting that the growth triangle projects in Southeast Asia, encompassing all of those identified as economic development triangles above, represent moves toward interdependent rather than integrated borderlands (Grundy-Warr and Perry, 1998):

- *Cooperation with minimal institutional innovation.* Growth triangles seek to promote greater transboundary economic activity without resolving potentially awkward institutional and legislative changes. This approach has been described as a particularly *Asian* type of government which stresses a minimum of formal, legalistic decision-making processes and fits the 'ASEAN way' and preference for dealing through networking and consensus behind closed doors (Abonyi, 1994; Thant *et al.*, 1994). Rather than transparent and accountable agencies and planning documents with clearly spelt out objectives and timeframes, the favoured mechanisms of inter-state cooperation are familiarisation tours, formal and informal contacts amongst counterparts, the constitution of *ad hoc* problem-solving committees, and visits by ministerial delegations that emphasise the establishment of inter-personal relationships (Kumar and Siddique, 1994:55). In this way, growth triangle cooperation is initiated by the decisions of senior politicians without the need for new institutional structures and without too many changes to regulatory frameworks (Abonyi, 1994). This is not to say that new institutions are not created. All joint ventures require bodies to manage and oversee developments. Rather, the implication is that there is little evidence of the kinds of new institutionalism and transnational regulations that are significant in cross-border cooperative linkages in Europe or North America.

- *National security-enhancing features.* There are certain security-enhancing consequences of transnational production for the states involved in growth triangle projects (Acharya, 1995:178). Sub-regional cooperation, to the extent that it strengthens bilateral ties between neighbours, can help to lessen political tensions without any great loss of political sovereignty. The fact that economic cooperation can progress with existing institutions, whilst regulatory changes can be restricted to particular enclave developments, helps to preserve national boundaries as protectors of state sovereignty but allows for greater economic transaction across political divides. In a sense, the Singaporean investments in the Riau islands are also one way in which the political leadership of Singapore can demonstrate its good neighbourliness and economic confidence to its huge ASEAN neighbour. This serves an important political function because Singapore's political elites are well aware of the dangers to the city-state's security if it has frictions with its militarily strong, populous and mostly Muslim neighbour to the south. Similarly, Indonesia's leaders are aware of the economic spin-offs that may arise from joint ventures with financially richer overseas partners.

- *Incremental intra-regional cooperation.* Some observers have suggested that participation in growth triangles may be viewed as a way of advancing the cause of broader intra-regional economic cooperation (for example see Kumar and Siddique, 1994:53). This interpretation tends, however, to overlook the lack of any implementation with the exception of the IMS growth triangle. The extent of cross-border integration in the Pearl River Delta (now comprising the Special Administrative Region of Hong Kong and the surrounding Guangdong province) is widely cited as an advanced growth triangle (Ohmae, 1990; Thant *et al.*, 1994) but as alluded to in the classification of growth triangles given above, this is really a special case arising from the region's political history.

As the case study of the Singapore–Indonesian border zone now goes on to show, the first two points are strongly in evidence. The consequence, we argue, is a border zone characterised by increasing problems that question its sustainability under present arrangements. However, it should also be noted that the changes in the political leadership in Indonesia and the aftermath of the late 1990s regional economic crisis could help to create an impetus for entirely new forms of cross-border cooperation.

Cross-border agreements and flagship projects

Indonesian ambition to develop the Riau islands dates back to the late 1960s, when Batam was identified as a potential logistics and operational base to support offshore oil and gas fields. A significant step in the island's development was the transfer of development responsibility to the Batam Industrial Development Authority (BIDA) in 1978 under the chairmanship of Dr B. J. Habibie, then the Minister of Research and Development. Habibie retained his control of BIDA whilst building up an influential bureaucratic and commercial industrial power base, effectively operating as a *de facto* Minister of Industry (Hill, 1996:156). More recently he became Indonesia's Vice President, and subsequently the President, before he was ousted in a democratic election in 1999 by Abdul Rahman Wahid. He retained control of BIDA up to the time of Indonesia's political upheavals in 1998 and 1999. Habibie's effective departure from high office meant that Batam had lost one of its key political figureheads and sponsors. Habibie tended to reject free market solutions in favour of attempts to engineer accelerated technological breakthroughs based on state-directed investment as well as through support of labour-intensive and resource-based industries. This belief in the ability to accelerate development processes was reflected in the revised Master Plan for Batam. This Plan envisaged a modern metropolis competing with Singapore for advanced technology and business services, and offering a high quality living and recreation environment.

The revised Master Plan, completed in 1979, took into account the island's designation in 1978 as a bonded area or duty-free zone and a population target of 700,000 to be achieved by 2004 (compared with the population of 18,640 in 1979). 10 years later, after a slump in the oil industry, total employment on Batam was just 11,000, concentrated in local services, tourism and oil-related firms using Batam as a service base (BIDA, 1991). Talks between Indonesia and Singapore to cooperate in Batam's development had been a frequent occurrence during the early 1980s without producing significant results (Regnier, 1991). One stumbling block was Singapore's preference for regulatory concessions compared with those governing foreign investments in mainland Indonesia. Such concessions were obtained following new inter-governmental discussions in the late 1980s, which resulted in an investment agreement for Singapore–Indonesian cooperation in the Riau islands.

Singapore's interest in securing cooperation with Indonesia at the time of the agreements was driven by developments in its economy (Rodan, 1993). After a recession in the mid 1980s, the manufacturing sector had been growing rapidly, exposing the city-state's limited labour and land resources. There was also concern amongst economic planners of an uncontrolled 'hollowing out' of the economy as industry moved to other parts of Asia. In response, the Economic Development Board (EDB), Singapore's premier economic promotion agency, started a programme to assist major multinationals in Singapore to relocate to an industrial estate in Bangkok, but this location presented its own congestion problems. Batam appealed to Singapore's economic planners as an alternative relocation area. The EDB promised to keep a close watch over companies shifting investments out of Singapore. Also, because Batam is so close to Singapore, it was hoped that foreign multinationals would continue to use Singapore as their main location and adopt Batam as a satellite-manufacturing base.

An industrial park was constructed on Batam as a joint Singapore–Indonesian venture and this proved to be attractive to Singapore-based multinationals. In 1999, there were around 80 firms operating in the industrial park which had been developed into a self-contained township, although around half the 60,000 workers resided outside the estate's dormitories (see section below on the migrant workers). The success of the estate resulted in a similar development on neighbouring Bintan Island, the Bintan Industrial Estate, which attracted its first tenants in 1993. The Bintan estate has yet to match the investment value attracted to Batam and has tended to attract lower value manufacturing such as clothing (Peachey *et al.*, 1998).

Although Singapore's interest in Batam and Bintan was driven originally by the opportunity to augment its industrial space, other opportunities were identified that broadened cooperation. Agreements were signed to jointly develop water resources to attend to Singapore's need to augment its existing supply. It was also clear that the available land, palm-fringed coasts, and relatively low-density populations of Bintan, and to a lesser extent, Batam, provided opportunities for joint tourism ventures. This accorded with the Indonesian ambition for the Riau islands, including high quality urban facilities and protection of marine and natural environments. From the Singapore side, tourism projects offered a way of diversifying Singapore's attractiveness to international visitors. This had been declining because of the island's rapid modernisation and international visitors. Equally important, the Riau islands offered leisure space for Singaporeans that could not be accommodated on their own crowded island and to which an increasingly affluent middle class was aspiring. Tourism investment was initially identified for Bintan and Batam but because of its larger land area and less industrial character Bintan became the site of the main tourism project, Bintan Beach International Resort.

The broadening of Singapore–Indonesian cooperation into a 'growth triangle' including southern Malaysia had investment logic but also responded to Singapore's need to be seen to share the benefits of its impressive economic growth with both regional neighbours. Singapore has gained economically, but it is also the Singapore state's desire to maintain political security with its more populous and politically volatile neighbours. Close economic integration has long been established between the southern Malaysian state of Johor and Singapore arising from their shared population and lack of an international border prior to 1965 (van Grunsven, 1995). The economic rise of the city-state benefited Johor as the industrial growth of Singapore produced linkages into Malaysia, but the disparity in economic performance, as well as racial differences, have left Malaysia ambivalent about its southern neighbour (Kamil *et al.*, 1991). From Singapore's perspective, inviting Malaysia to join the 'growth triangle' addressed any adverse reaction that they may have had regarding Singapore's assistance to Indonesia in promoting new investment locations that would potentially compete with Johor for foreign direct investments. Malaysia became party to the tripartite initiative although it was not until 1994 that a memorandum of understanding was signed by all three parties, by which time the four projects that remained the direct achievements of the growth triangle had already been put into place: Batam Industrial Park, Bintan Industrial Estate, Bintan Beach

International Resort and Karimun Marine and Industrial Complex (a project on a third Riau island that by 2000 had seen limited development).

Each of the four flagship projects follows a similar development formula, which emphasises linkages to the Singapore economy and minimal dependence on the Riau or wider Indonesian environment. They are a key test to the effectiveness of the cross-border cooperation under the 'growth triangle' concept. It should also be noted that there have been tourist developments along the east coast of Johor, including golf courses and resorts that attract Singaporean visitors and are now competing against the newer resort developments in Bintan and Batam. These alternative resort locations and the nearby Tioman Island, a popular get-away for Singaporeans, were established prior to Bintan but the Bintan Beach International Resort promised to be a much larger international tourist location with better tourist appeal.

Bintan Beach International Resort

The creation of the Bintan Beach International Resort, really a group of separate resorts and hotels, has involved the complete transformation of the landscape of the northern section of the island. Under this project, Bintan Resort Corporation, a consortium of large Singaporean and Indonesian companies including Singapore Technologies and the Salim Group, acquired the northern section of Bintan to develop the resort (Figure 5.1).

Marketing and management of the project has been given to a Singapore-based subsidiary, Bintan Resort Management. The companies involved in financing, servicing and operating the Resort include, from Singapore, Singapore Technologies Industrial, banks (Development Bank of Singapore, Overseas Chinese Banking Corporation, Overseas Union Bank), United Overseas Land Equity Investment, Keppel Land and Tropical Resorts, while the Indonesian side is dominated by KMP Bincorp Investments, a subsidiary of Salim Corporation. This is envisaged as an area for upmarket hotels, holiday chalets, condominiums, golf courses and recreational projects to be completed over 10 to 15 years by separate groups of investors. The first of these developments was opened in December 1995 and, like the others under development, involved investors linked to the partners of Bintan Resort Corporation as well as other Singapore, Indonesian and Japanese investors. Like the industrial parks, the resort area is designed to minimise reliance on other island resources in the sense that it is as self-serving as possible. Ferry connections directly link the resorts to a new ferry terminal in Singapore, avoiding the need to travel through Tanjung Pinang, the main settlement on Bintan, which is linked to the resort area by a poorly maintained road. Labour to work in the resorts is largely being recruited from other tourist centres in Indonesia.

Bintan Beach International Resort has attracted significant investments and established itself as a new tourist destination. By mid 1996, it was claimed that approximately S$1,600[2] million had been committed to projects (*The Straits Times*, 19 June 1996). Other developers with ambitious plans, such as Shangri-La International (located in Singapore), noted that it was in their interests to "open later when the infrastructure is in place and Bintan has more attractions" (*Singapore Business*,

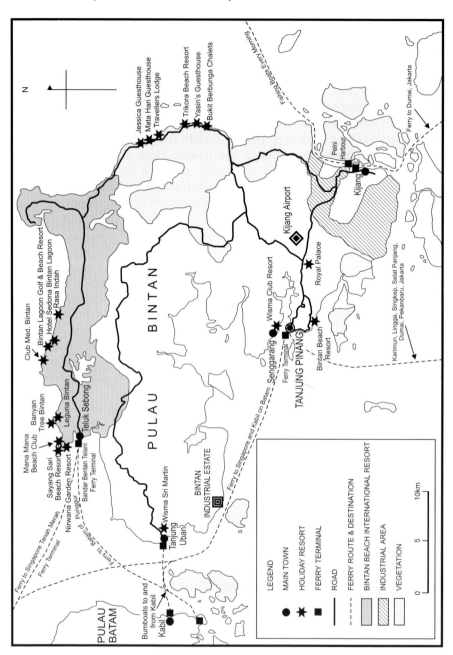

Figure 5.1 Bintan Beach International Resort

1995:25) but by mid 1997, around a quarter of the area allocated to Bintan Beach International Resort had been developed or was committed to definite projects. The total number of visitors to the Resort was projected to be around 250,000 in 1997 compared with around 100,000 in 1996 and 30,000 in 1995.[3] In 1998 and 1999, there were approximately 300,000 annual visitors (*The Straits Times*, 20 January, 2000a). The number of daily and weekly visitors varies, tending to be greater during the school and public holidays in Singapore, weekends and during the less wet periods of the year. In addition to the impressive Bintan Beach International Resort, a broader development of tourism has been encouraged in Batam and Bintan since the growth triangle project was launched.

Tourism in Batam

Batam's tourist sector attracted significant investments in the early 1990s following increased optimism about growing demand from Singaporean visitors. As well as the perceived interest amongst Singapore's increasingly affluent population in the availability of a "pleasure periphery" (Parsonage, 1992) to compensate for their congested built-up environment, tourist investment has been encouraged by Singapore's tourism promotion agencies. With its own loss of attractiveness as a tourist destination, it is keen to see the development of the region's tourist potential to retain its role as a stopover destination. Singapore government-linked and private investors have therefore been the principal investors in Batam's tourist sector, typically in joint ventures with Indonesian partners.

The tourist projects completed have mainly attempted to provide self-contained resorts, with a concentration of new developments along the northeast coastal region of Nongsa. These comprise a number of up-market hotels and recreational facilities with their own ferry service to Singapore. Batam View Beach Resort, for example, has invested around S$40 million to construct a marina, a themed pool, 250 new chalets, an amphitheatre as well as other entertainment facilities. The Nongsa Point Marina, a S$30 million marina and tourist complex was developed by Singapore's Keppel Group (a government-linked company) and Indonesian partners to provide sea-sports facilities, resort-style accommodation and entertainment facilities spread over 11 ha of waterfront. The most ambitious project, however, is being developed on the west coast as a mass-market leisure area. This is the Waterfront City which, when fully developed, is planned to cover 2,000 ha in a S$1 billion project including theme parks, country clubs, golf courses, supermarkets, accommodation, restaurants and nightclubs. A 24-hour ferry terminal has been constructed to provide direct access between the resort and Singapore.

Visitor arrivals in Batam have grown substantially since the early 1980s, encouraged by the new facilities and improved transport connections to Singapore. From around 60,000 tourist arrivals in the mid 1980s, the number of visitors exceeded a million in 1996, although since then, Batam has also had to compete for visitors to neighbouring Bintan. Average spending per visitor per day was US$180 and the average stay, two days (BIDA, 1996). The tourist image of a high-class resort based on five-star accommodation is, however, being challenged by the presence of some oil polluted beaches and the scale of industrial developments taking place elsewhere in the island. It has also to overcome the fact that seedier recreational 'attractions' have taken root in Batam, particularly forms of prostitution.

Batam's transformation during the 1990s has seen a boom in its sex industry. Male migrant workers, expatriate management and weekend visitors from Singapore fuel the industry. Batam's high-cost of living, the difficulty of securing work, expectations from family to send wages home, and the absence of community structure make prostitution a common solution to the economic woes faced by new migrants. Organised prostitution is now well observed in over 12 settlements on Batam as well as in bars, karaoke lounges, discotheques, hotels, restaurants, and massage parlours (Peachey, 1998). The number of prostitutes is increasing with every year with one estimate being that there may be as many as 40,000 sex workers in the Batam municipality (Mayor of Batam cited in Peachey *et al.*, 1998:35). The actual figures would be extremely difficult to obtain without formal surveys, but it has been suggested that some of the women working in formal jobs also engage in the recreational tourism sector in less formal occupations by night.[4]

Unemployment, underemployment and the transient nature of Batam have given rise to a high crime rate that has presented another challenge to the upgrading of Batam's tourism industry. One initiative that was attempted to upgrade the island's ambience involved incentives designed to stimulate the luxury residential property segment which, it was hoped, would have spin-offs for recreation and leisure services on the island. In early 1996, the rules governing property ownership on Batam Island were relaxed. Ownership, on a leasehold basis, which was previously set at a maximum of 30 years, was extended to up to 70 years for foreign buyers who can meet certain requirements. These requirements included: owners must belong to a golf or marina club, have a work permit for Batam, have a Smart Card for visa entry (indicating that they are frequent visitors), or have 'contributed to national development'. They must purchase houses bigger than 70 sq m, priced at a minimum of S$123,000 and meet the approval of the BIDA. As well as seeking to curb purely speculative housing provision, these changes sought to bring greater confidence to the investment market. For Singaporeans, however, residential property investment in Batam competes with China and Australia. Given the bitter experiences of shoddy construction and ambiguous legal titles from the 1990 real estate boom on Batam, this measure proved to have little investment impact. It is still possible to find large areas of vacant and never-occupied executive housing although it has been reported that some of this housing has found a market for accommodating the "second wives" of Singapore businessmen (*The Sunday Times*, 16 April 2000). Attracted by the low prices of housing, it is reported that Singapore businessmen are increasingly shunning Batam's hotels for their illicit weekends in favour of a "rented wife" permanently housed in Penuin, Tiban or Baloi Emas executive housing areas.

Top-down joint ventures, 'development enclaves' and socio-cultural tensions

The limitations of the growth triangle projects are evident when the impacts on the larger environment (ecological, social and cultural) are considered. Two local issues in particular question the sustainability of the current approaches and forms of cooperation.

Beyond enclaves: the social environment, 'ruli' housing and uncontrolled migration in Batam

The growth triangle development strategy of promoting self-contained projects with a minimal dependency on the surrounding environment has proved unrealistic. This has been most evident in the case of Batam where the island's reputation as a boom economy has overwhelmed the island with new migrants, many of them unemployed or under-employed. Almost half of the island's population, which has more than tripled since 1990, are new migrants living in illegal squatter housing called *ruli–rumah liar* (literally means 'wild houses') (Peachey, 1998; Peachey *et al.*, 1998). Extensive *ruli* or squatter areas are in open conflict with the goals of creating a high quality environment, attractive to multinational investment and international tourism. The environmental impact of unregulated housing challenges the attempt to market Batam as a clean 'Singapore-like' environment for security, public order and efficient management.

Conflicts over land clearances plus residential uncertainty and reliance on uncertain sources of poorly paid employment add to the sense of social exclusion amongst marginal groups. The proliferation of unplanned and untidy settlements also adds to the difficulty in attracting high-income residents. For instance, many managers working in Batam prefer to commute rather than live there. One impact is seen in the collapse of the executive housing market and failure to establish the island as a holiday-home location for Singaporeans. Executive housing areas, originally designed to include marinas and other recreation facilities, have become executive ghost towns deteriorating from the lack of maintenance and unwanted by Singaporean owners frightened by perceived levels of crime.

BIDA has estimated that as many as 3,000 spontaneous migrants arrive on Batam every month (Peachey, 1998:40). Recent migrants arriving in the last five years easily outnumber longer-stay residents. Many of the migrants are from West Java, West and North Sumatra and neighbouring areas in the Riau, but some migrants come from as far away as Flores in East Indonesia. Many migrants are unmarried males and females. Finding employment in the formal sectors of Batam's economy is difficult. Many men find work in the port and shipping yards, on construction sites, as security guards, as taxi drivers (both legal and illegal) or in the informal economy selling goods and services. In contrast, many young, unmarried women have managed to find employment in the factories of the Batamindo Industrial Estate, the well-managed industrial joint-venture project. But the formal sector has not managed to absorb all women migrants to the island, and Batamindo does not hire women above 24 years of age. Without sufficient housing and employment for migrants, prostitution, crime, and community disintegration tend to be the harsh realities of Batam's social landscape (Peachey, 1998; Peachey *et al.*, 1998). In fact, the darker side of tourist growth to the island partly relates to the existence of many bars, karaoke lounges, discotheques, hotels, restaurants and massage parlours frequented by casual sex workers. Another unfortunate spin-off is that Batam has become a centre for syndicates trafficking girls, drugs and other illegal goods into Malaysia (*The Straits Times*, 9 August 1994; *Riau Pos*, 14 November 1996).

Un- and under-employment combined with the transient nature of most of the housing in Batam has given rise to a high crime rate. While theft is the most reported crime, rape, weapons charges and gambling offences are on the rise (*Riau Pos*, 29 October 1996). Inter-communal tensions within the migrant communities erupted into violence in July 1999, resulting in multiple deaths and a brief period of military occupation in the island. At that time, tourist visitors were frightened off by reading lurid reports in the press, often accompanied by photos of men wielding machetes, parangs, spears, clubs, bows and arrows. The normally dry and sober press of Singapore produced stories with headlines such as "Blood must pay for blood" and "If they kill, we just have to kill" when it was reporting on a local Batam turf war between migrants from Flores and Bataks, a mostly Protestant community (*The Straits Times*, 1 August, 1999).

It is clear that joint ventures which focus exclusively on projects that are relatively protected and isolated from the surrounding social landscape may themselves be threatened by urgent social problems. Hitherto, the development authorities on Batam have taken a traditional approach to handling the squatter problem. Policies have focused on settlement clearance and relocation of residents to temporary resettlement sites. Residents are responsible for rebuilding their homes on these unserviced sites and are expected to make the transition into the formal property market, either through the purchase, lease or rental of legal accommodation within the time frame of a couple of years. In many respects, this policy has done little more than relocate the migrants from place to place, and there are few migrants who have been able to enter formal housing due to lack of availability and the expense involved. As the *relocation* settlements are poorly situated, without basic services and do not offer residents legal land title, many evictees do not choose to move to them. Instead, they secure shelter in illegal *ruli* settlements located closer to urban centres and employment opportunities. Some of the *ruli* are situated on dangerous slopes prone to mudslides. In October 1996, an early morning landslide hit such a settlement, killing at least 18 people and injuring others (*The Straits Times*, 4 October 1996). Furthermore, more and more undocumented migrants keep entering Batam everyday, which only serves to aggravate existing social problems.

The migrant and squatter problems in Batam are part of the human landscape of Batam and they are largely the consequence of the approach and type of economic development that has been implemented. It is true that the rapid establishment of Batamindo Industrial Park and several new hotels, country clubs and resorts on the island is impressive. However, these joint venture projects do begin to look incongruous if they are next door to poor squatter settlements. Attention should be given to the local social and cultural impacts of the existing joint venture projects. Indeed, we argue that the very sustainability of those projects requires serious analysis of socio-economic costs and benefits to the local population. And by 'local' this must mean all the migrants who have moved to Batam in search of employment and livelihoods. On the basis of her research of *ruli* settlements, Peachey (1998) has argued that given a degree of tenure security, squatters are eager to upgrade not only their private homes but community infrastructure as well. Together with networks of friends and family members, they persistently struggle for access to land, housing, work and fulfilment despite the often difficult and changing economic circumstances with which they are faced. Research shows that *ruli* settlements on Batam are a primary source of shelter to workers in both formal and informal employment. These workers, and the services they provide, contribute significantly to the island's growing economy. Providing opportunities for migrants to invest in their lives, their homes, their work, and their communities is a key to developing more stable, secure and sustainable industrial and tourist sectors on the island. Investments in housing, social welfare and health services will have implications for labour productivity, the local labour climate and an overall sense of security on the island. Therefore, efforts to provide services to and improve viable *ruli* settlements, provided they are located on firm ground, should be made. These measures should complement existing efforts to increase the supply of affordable legal housing (see Peachey *et al.*, 1998).

Dividing the spoils: the issues of land compensation and poor housing on Bintan

Recent protests by villagers in Bintan have threatened to close down the Bintan Industrial Park and the Bintan Beach International Resort (*The Straits Times*, 19 January 2000a). For almost one week, village protesters carrying weapons had managed to seize control of the power station supplying the industrial park. As in Batam in 1999, Bintan 'mob protests' in January 2000 made front-page news in Singapore. One of the key problems again seems to be the lack of involvement and participation of local people in the joint venture development that has completely transformed the economic and human landscape of a small island space. The angry villagers involved in the protests in Bintan were not migrants but long-term inhabitants. Thus, in two small neighbouring islands, there are completely different socio-cultural dynamics to consider. At the heart of the Bintan protests is the issue of compensation payments for land and of new land and housing promises being unfulfilled. In 1991, the Salim Group, a large Chinese corporation with close links to the former Suharto regime, bought over several small villages in northern Bintan in order to begin development on the Beach Resort and also the industrial estate (*The Straits Times*, 17 January 2000a). The developed zones are now free of local village residents. The current conflict stems from the alleged coercion used to take over land and the tiny compensation payments of between 100 and 1,000 rupiah per sq m of land sold. Many of the local villagers are now demanding 10,000 rupiah (about S$2.40) per sq m and better housing provision. One media reporter interviewed a fisherman whose former house used to be where the Bandar Bentan Telani ferry terminal servicing the Bintan Beach International Resort now stands. One day in 1991, a policeman told the fisherman and his family to leave the house, saying that they would be paid compensation later. He eventually received his 100 rupiah per sq km for a 2 ha plot of land which held his house, built in 1969, and garden plots of tapioca, vegetables and mangos. Later, developers informed him that a new housing unit would cost 1.5 million rupiah. He currently lives at Sungei Bulan, about 10 km from the main entrance of the Beach Resort, in a home without electricity, no waste disposal and poor plumbing (*The Straits Times*, 20 January, 2000a).

The protests in Bintan have sparked off various kinds of responses from officials, operators, village people and activists. These range from corporate and private sector worries about the loss of profits and concerns about the security of investments; from tour operators who are worried that the current protests will frighten away future visitors; from district officials wishing to protect investors and find a speedy resolution to the problems; from angry villagers demanding fair compensation; and from a small number of student activists who argue they are seeking social justice for ordinary people. Ironically, the Bintan protests came shortly after Singapore's Prime Minister Goh Chok Tong had announced a S$1.2 billion package of plans to help boost confidence in the Indonesian economy. The plans involve incentive schemes for small- and medium-sized companies to form partnerships with their Indonesian counterparts and to encourage further joint ventures. The PM also made clear the intention to build upon existing bilateral ventures in Batam, Bintan and Karimun islands. These plans received support from Indonesian President Wahid and his deputy Megawati Sukarnoputri. Brigadier-General George Yeo, Singapore's Minister for Trade and Industry, also made a point of stressing the fact that the Riau initiatives had stood the test of the Asian financial crisis with no workers being retrenched in Batam, Bintan or Karimun. He stressed that "The Riau projects stood out as oases of calm and sustainable development throughout the difficult period" (*The Straits Times*, 14 January, 2000). It is likely that efforts will be made to tackle at least some of the grievances of the villagers in Bintan as part of broader efforts on the part of Indonesia to improve its security image to potential investors from Singapore and elsewhere. Another aspect of the protests in Bintan is the way they have been organised with the help of student activists from other parts of Indonesia. It is these student leaders who have warned leaders in both Jakarta and Singapore to consider the socio-political context of their investments (*The Straits Times*, 26 January 2000). However, it is equally clear that the recent events in Bintan have touched raw political nerves and heightened concerns in Singapore about the stability of their investments in the Riau islands. This was indicated in the extensive reporting of the Bintan saga in the Singapore media (see for example *The Straits Times*, 16 January 2000; 17 January 2000b; 19 January 2000b; 20 January 2000b).

As in Batam, it is clear that top-down decision-making and joint venture projects like the Beach Resort and Industrial Estate have not adequately addressed local social concerns. Perhaps lessons are now being learnt about the need to involve local-level actors, be they governmental or non-governmental, much more in critical areas of the planning process that will affect local communities, be they long-term residents or migrants. There has been a tendency in some of the developments to leave big decisions to non-local decision-makers and to companies, such as the Salim Group, or agencies, such as BIDA on Batam. This has tended to leave local government officials, community agencies and leaders on the sidelines. It is necessary to address these issues for the continued viability and success of on-going projects, and to ensure investor and tourist confidence in the future of these cross-border ventures. Indeed, at the time of writing there has been an interesting suggestion coming from an economic advisor to President Wahid to make the local residents stakeholders in the investments on Bintan. Mr Sofyan Wanandi, head of the National Business

Development Council of Indonesia, pointed out that the shares in the Bintan project owned by the Salim Group now belong to the government in Jakarta through its Indonesian Bank Restructuring Agency and that it may be possible to give dividends "without voting rights" to villagers (*The Straits Times*, 26 January, 2000). Such schemes may help to lessen local tensions that arose out of modes of development that have produced enclave projects with minimal input from local communities. However, there is also a need to consider the broader aspects of transboundary cooperation that have helped to shape specific investments.

Alternative approaches to cross-border cooperation

As noted in the introduction, a key to understanding developments along the Singapore–Indonesian border zone is the wish to use the locality as a resource for strengthening national sovereignty and therefore to avoid institutional innovations that weaken national controls. These considerations are evident in the emphasis on *self-contained projects*, whether this is an industrial park, a golf course or a recreational resort. There has been very little movement towards the creation of genuine transboundary institutions or towards a harmonising of national laws in the sub-region. For instance, Indonesia's land laws are considered confusing to foreign investors and have deterred many from investing in property (Davidson, 1992). The national borders mark the limits of very different regulatory and enforcement environments for business and ordinary citizens, and the existence of pragmatic state-level economic cooperation has done little to reduce national differentiation within the sub-region itself.

The willingness of Southeast Asian states and sub-state authorities to foster transnational institutionalisation has so far been a good deal less than in parts of Europe (see Scott, 1993; Ganster *et al.*, 1997). Without the development of genuine transnational institutions and without a more complete harmonisation of regulatory systems across boundaries it is difficult to talk of the sub-regional borderlands as being in any way integrated in the sense discussed by Martinez (1994). Such developments would require political willingness to compromise over national sovereignty in a way that is currently not in prospect. It is notable in this context that one of the few innovations in border controls has been the introduction of Smart Card immigration facilities to ease the daily commuting of business executives from Singapore to Batam. This innovation symbolises the hesitant steps to border integration as one of its impacts is to reduce the need for residence in Batam amongst executives working there. A further aspect of the lack of depth in the cross-border cooperation is the over-dependence of Singaporean agencies on one joint venture partner from Indonesia, the Salim Group. This group had the political connections and privileges that initially made it the preferred joint venture partner but following Indonesia's political and economic turmoil, it has lost political patronage and privileged access to resources. Alternative investment partners may be found, but its sudden decline is a further illustration of the vulnerability of the existing cross-border cooperation. Some guidance on how to build a firmer basis for cross-border cooperation may be obtained from the experiences in Europe.

One of the critical features of transborder cooperation within western Europe, as well as and between the USA and Mexico, has been the extent to which new trans-boundary agencies have been created to handle a wide variety of border region problems, to streamline policy implementation and to manage daily transborder issues within specific border zones or sub-regions. Much of the transboundary coop-eration in Europe has arisen from informal encounters between local officials and over the course of many years has developed into more structured and institutiona-lised forms of policy-making (Scott, 1993). Entirely new cross-border institutional arrangements have evolved within Europe as a direct result of a multitude of low-key contacts between different agencies and groups, including municipal authorities, district government bodies, community organisations, academics and local business associations who have been motivated by the need to join forces across arbitrary political boundaries in order to manage common problems in a more effective man-ner. These local level initiatives have been enhanced at the supranational level by the creation of funds by the European Union set aside for transboundary regional development in different European regions, and also by the endorsement of trans-boundary planning agencies by the respective nation-states. Along the USA–Mexico borderland there are now numerous agencies, some involving federal-level officials, others being more technocratic, and still others that represent broad constituencies. As in Europe, transborder institutionalisation has been seen as necessary in order to make cooperation more effective and sustainable, notwithstanding the large cross-border economic and socio-cultural differences and big political changes over time. Officialdoms have had to adjust their national mind-sets in order to accommodate different mind-sets and to work with their new colleagues from the other side of the border.

Within Europe there has been a movement towards more integrated and harmo-nised spatial planning across borders and for new transborder agencies to tackle a wide variety of issues, including economic, social, cultural and environmental mat-ters. In contrast, sub-regional development in Southeast Asia is often limited to very specific projects and functions. The lack of established transboundary management agencies means that should there be a sudden reversal of policy by one or more national government, then the whole cooperative venture is likely to be placed in jeopardy. In contrast, transborder cooperation is less vulnerable in Europe and North America because several of the agencies responsible have developed a life of their own within their areas of competence and also because there is a stronger tradition of agencies engaging regularly in sub-national, cross-border and interna-tional para-diplomacy.

Concluding thoughts

This chapter has primarily been a case study of a *particular mode of development*. We have examined the tourism dimensions of a much larger set of projects aimed at fostering greater investments within and economic opportunities for the partners in the so-called growth triangle. As such, we view tourism projects as sharing similar benefits and costs to other kinds of investment projects. We argue that much greater attention needs to be paid to the socio-cultural and micro-level implications of projects that are effectively redesigning human geographic space to meet the needs of diverse investors and economic interests outside the specific localities of investment.

Functional transboundary cooperation has clearly produced successful ventures in the Singapore–Indonesia border zone. The sustainability of that economic success depends in part on broader market economics, the continuation of existing multinational and Singaporean investor interest, and the ability to attract mobile capital. However, we have also suggested that continued sustainability of current ventures will also require much greater linkage and more benefits being shared by the local communities, whether these are long-term residents or migrants. The joint projects have led to a huge transformation in the socio-economic and cultural landscape of the Riau islands closest to Singapore. Whilst cooperation is generating mutually beneficial economic impacts, it is clear that profits have gone to Jakarta concerns, to Singaporean investors, and mostly out of the island communities themselves. However, for Indonesians in factory and formal tourism sector employment, the incomes enjoyed are above the national average. We have also highlighted some key problems related to the extremely rapid development of Batam and Bintan, which has produced well-serviced industrial parks and beautifully finished tourist facilities, leaving social welfare and social infrastructure for residents and migrants lagging behind.

Finally, we suggest that there is still plenty of potential to strengthen and extend existing ties and to create genuine transborder institutions that could survive fluctuations of an economic and perhaps political nature. Recent high level political efforts made by the leaderships of both states point to a continued commitment to cross-border ventures. Greater attention must also be given to the socio-cultural and local political implications of top-down joint ventures on the human landscape.

Notes

[1] This extension accorded with Indonesian and Malaysian ambition to develop direct links across the Straits of Malacca, including a project to build a road bridge over the Straits, a project which was dropped under Indonesia's post-IMF budget reforms.
[2] US$1 = approximately S$1.7 at current prices.
[3] The 1997 estimate was made prior to the occurrence of smoke pollution from forest fires in mainland Indonesian that affected the region for several months from late August. The haze severely reduced tourism arrivals.
[4] Authors' correspondences with Karen Peachey, who conducted lengthy periods of fieldwork, including many interviews with local women.

References

Abonyi, G. (1994) *The Institutional Challenges of Growth Triangles in Southeast Asia*, MPP Working Paper Series, No. 3. Singapore: National University of Singapore.
Acharya, A. (1995) 'Transnational production and security: Southeast Asia's growth triangle'. *Contemporary Southeast Asia* 17(2), 173–86.
Batam Industrial Development Authority (BIDA) (1991) *Development Data*. Jakarta: BIDA.
BIDA (1996) *Development Data*. Jakarta: BIDA.

Chang, T.C. (1998) 'Regionalism and tourism: Exploring integral links in Singapore'. *Asia-Pacific Viewpoint*, 39(1), 73–94.

Davidson, P. (1992) 'An Economic Law Perspective', paper presented at the *International Symposium on Regional Cooperation and Growth Triangles in ASEAN*, Singapore, 23–24 April.

Friedmann, J. (1995) 'Where we stand: A decade of world city research', in P.Knox and P. Taylor (eds.) *World Cities in a World System*. Cambridge: Cambridge University Press, 21–47.

Ganster, P., Sweedler, A., Scott, J. and Dieter-Eberwein, W. (eds.) (1997) *Borders and Border Regions in Europe and North America*. San Diego: San Diego University Press.

Grundy-Warr, C. and Perry, M. (1996) 'Growth triangles, international economic integration and the Singapore-Indonesian border zone', in D. Rumley, T. Chiba, A. Takagi, and Y. Fukushima (eds.) *Global Geopolitical Change and the Asia-Pacific: A Regional Perspective*. Aldershot: Avebury, 185–211.

Grundy-Warr, C. and Perry, M. (1998) 'Economic integration or interdependence? The nation-state and the changing economic landscape of Southeast Asia', in L. van Grunsven (ed.) *Regional Change in Industrialising Asia: Economic Restructuring and Local Response*. Ashgate: Aldershot, 197–229.

Hill, H. (1996) The Indonesian Economy Since 1966. Cambridge: Cambridge University Press.

Kamil, Y., Pangetsu, M. and Fredericks, C. (1991) 'A Malaysia perspective', in Y. Lee Tsao. (ed.) *The Growth Triangle: The Johor-Singapore-Riau Experience*. Singapore: Institute of Southeast Asian Studies, 37–74.

Kumar, S. and Siddique, S. (1994) 'Beyond economic reality: New thoughts on the growth triangle', in Institute of Southeast Asian Studies (ed.) *Southeast Asian Affairs*, 1994. Singapore: Institute of Southeast Asian Studies, 47–56.

Martinez, O.J. (1994) 'The dynamics of border interaction: New approaches to border analysis', in C.H. Schofield (ed.) *World Boundaries, Vol. 1 Global Boundaries*. London: Routledge, 1–14.

Mijares, R. (1996) 'The BIMP-East ASEAN Growth Area'. *Pacific Business and Industries IV*, 34, 41–56.

Ohmae, K. (1990) *The Borderless World: Power and Strategy in the Global Marketplace*. London: Harper Collins.

Ohmae, K. (1995) *The End of the Nation State: The Rise of Regional Economies*. New York: The Free Press.

Parsonage, J. (1992) 'Southeast Asia's "growth triangle": A sub-regional response to a global transformation'. *International Journal of Urban and Regional Research*, 16(2), 307–17.

Peachey, K. (1998) Where there is sugar, there are ants: Planning for people in the development of Batam, Indonesia, unpublished Master of Arts Thesis, School of Community and Regional Planning, University of British Columbia.

Peachey, K., Perry, M. and Grundy-Warr, C. (1998) 'The Riau islands and economic cooperation in the Singapore-Indonesian border zone', *Boundary and Territory Briefing* 2.3. Durham: IBRU.

Pearce, D. (1989) *Tourism Development*. Harlow: Longman.

Regnier, P. (1991) *Singapore: City State in South East Asia*, (English edition). London: Hurst & Company.

Riau Pos (1996) 'Kasus pencurian dan perampokan turun', 29 October, Jakarta.

Riau Pos (1996) 'Kajati Riau: Batam rawan sindikat pengedar narkotik', 14 November, Jakarta.

Rodan, G. (1993) 'Reconstructuring divisions of labour: Singapore's new regional emphasis', in R. Higgott, J. Ravenhill and R. Leaver (eds.) *Pacific Economic Relations in the 1990s: Cooperation or Conflict*. Sydney: Allen and Unwin, 223–49.

Scott, J.W. (1993) 'The institutionalization of transboundary cooperation in Europe: Recent development on the Dutch-German border'. *Journal of Borderlands Studies VIII*, Spring, 39–66.

Singapore Business (1995) 'Can the triangle grow?', February, 14–25, Singapore.

Straits Times, The (1994) 'Batam girls sold into prostitution in Malaysia', 9 August, Singapore.

Straits Times, The (1996) 'Two new investors to give $300m boost to Bintan resorts', 19 June, Singapore.

Straits Times, The (1996) 'At least 17 killed as landslide hits Batam village', 4 October, Singapore.

Straits Times, The (1999) 'Blood must pay for blood', 1 August, Singapore.

Straits Times, The (2000) 'Projects symbolise close ties: BG Yeo', 14 January, Singapore.

Straits Times, The (2000) 'Mob protests on Bintan contained by police', 16 January, Singapore.

Straits Times, The (2000a) 'Bintan calm but tense after violence', 17 January, Singapore.

Straits Times, The (2000b) 'Tourists visiting Bintan despite riots last week', 17 January, Singapore.

Straits Times, The (2000a) 'Armed villagers stake out beach resort', 19 January, Singapore.

Straits Times, The (2000b) 'SembCorp threatens to close down Bintan park', 19 January, Singapore.
Straits Times, The (2000a) 'Its time for action, says protester', 20 January, Singapore.
Straits Times, The (2000b) 'Bintan protestors to see Gus Dur', 20 January, Singapore.
Straits Times, The (2000) 'Bintan villagers may become part-owners of island's projects', 26 January, Singapore.
Sunday Times, The (2000) 'Singapore men buy Batam houses for "girlfriends"', 16 April, Singapore.
Taylor, P.J. (1995) 'Beyond containers: Internationality, interstateness, interterritoriality'. *Progress in Human Geography*, 19(1), 1–15.
Thant, M. and Tang M. (1996) *The Indonesia-Malaysia-Thailand Growth Triangle: Theory To Practice.* Manila: Asian Development Bank.
Thant, M., Tang M. and Kakazu H. (1994) *Growth Triangles In Asia.* Hong Kong: Oxford University Press.
Toh, M.H. and Low L. (1993) *Regional Cooperation and Growth Triangles in ASEAN.* Singapore: Times Academic Press.
van Grunsven, L. (1995) 'Industrial regionalization and urban-regional transformation in Southeast Asia: The SIJORI growth triangle considered'. *The Malaysian Journal of Tropical Geography*, 26, 47–65.
Wall, G. (1997) 'Indonesia: The impact of regionalization', in F.M Go and C.L. Jenkins (eds.) *Tourism and Economic Development in Asia and Australasia.* London: Cassell, 138–49.

6

Gateways, Hubs and Transport Interconnections in Southeast Asia: Implications for Tourism Development in the Twenty-first Century

Stephen Page

Introduction

During the 1980s and 1990s, research within economic geography has focused on the concept of regional concentrations of economic activity that transcend national boundaries, in particular growth triangles (Tang and Thant, 1993) and extended metropolitan regions (EMRs) (see Douglass, 1995; Rimmer, 1995; Hall and Page, 2000). One dimension of this new spatial form of economic production has been the focus on transport hubs and gateways within these regional centres of production. The existing definitions of EMRs recognise that these urban agglomerations stretch for 20 to 100 km from the city core and are part of the wider development of global cities (Dixon and Smith, 1997). By the year 2015, of the 27 megacities predicted to exist worldwide, 17 will be located in Asia, many of which will use megaurban corridors of air, land and sea-based transport and telecommunication linkages to gain competitive production advantage (Forbes, 1999: 238). Global change and competition between transnational regions is not only assuming a greater role in the location of production in the global economy (Olds et al., 1999), but EMRs are taking on regional roles that transcend national boundaries and positioning themselves as having a primate role within the economic region or trading bloc in which they are located. According to Dick and Rimmer (1998), Southeast Asian cities have developed EMRs and what emerges is that these cities are far from 'Third World' in their characteristics. On the contrary, many of these cities have passed through a phase of decolonialisation which is accompanied by a more complex spatial structure that is unicentric and multi-nodal as wider regions and EMRs have emerged. Within the EMRs, the role of transport infrastructure is to support the growth of multi-nodal economic development. EMRs effectively collapse space and time to develop a territorial structure with linkages in the space economy where transport corridors and hubs form critical points in the spatial reconfiguration of economic activity.

Within the literature on globalisation, this "time-space compression is characterised by capitalists stretching their economic relationships to all parts of the globe to quicken the circulation of capital and to sustain profits" (Teo and Chang, 1998: 126).

Chang (1998) highlighted one of the consequences of the development of gateways in EMRs, namely that the hubs assist in the regionalisation of tourism (Tham, 1999). Hubs link locales, cities and even countries to the EMR. Low and Toh (1997) examined Singapore, where gateway tourism is reinforced by the one-stop hub role it performs for the wider Southeast Asia region. This has more recently been embodied in the Singapore Tourism Board's ambitious *Tourism 21* strategy that seeks to harness the tourism potential of Singapore's gateway and hub role in Southeast Asia. Therefore, notions of gateway tourism and hubs are now changing from an effect that was largely confined to a country or region within a country. This leads one to rethink the role and concept of hubs and gateways beyond the existing studies that have largely focused on the deregulation consequences on the airline industry in the USA (Page, 1999). As a consequence, tourism research on gateway functions and hubs as transregional entry points to developing trading blocs has only just started.

If one revisits the influential research by Britton (1982) on multinational enterprises in tourism and introduces the emerging EMRs, it is evident that the control of capital and decision-making that will affect the development and investment patterns in tourism and related infrastructure will assume a greater role within these regions. What is occurring is the growth of a pattern of primary and secondary tourism destinations functionally related to the gateway and hubs in the transnational regions and the EMRs. This is reflected in the continued spatial concentration of investments by multinational or transnational corporations in the growth triangles and EMRs. Raguraman (1997) even argues that if tourism is viewed as a form of international trade, then within the emerging role of EMRs and global cities, transport hubs and gateway entry points must be major focal points for the wider process of globalisation and regional integration of tourism in these trading blocs. What this introductory discussion highlights is that tourism is only one element of the wider economic system within Southeast Asia and that new forms of production based on EMRs are influencing the nature and spatial form of tourism production and consumption. In particular, the evolution of gateways and hubs is increasingly being recognised as a powerful spatial entity that may influence the nature of the production system that is going to shape the regionalisation of tourism patterns and activities within Southeast Asia.

It is therefore no surprise to find airline alliances (see Page, 1999) and airline cooperation such as the Star Alliance using Singapore as a strategic hub in a global network. However, since these alliances are essentially business-driven, the collaboration does not necessarily recognise the interconnectedness of tourism in the region beyond air links and markets to fill aircraft capacity. Even though the global cooperation of airline alliances has a regional manifestation in terms of regional spinoffs of air links, what should be emphasised is that local actions and activities can have implications that occur in a higher spatial order, namely, the interconnections within the region in order to harness tourism opportunities (see Hall and Page, 2000). In this respect, governments and the private sector can put up investments in the local transport infrastructure to harness the realities of global–regional–local tourism opportunities by capitalising the vital role of hubs, gateways and EMRs in the development of tourism numbers. In this respect, it is pertinent, therefore, to consider the role of air travel in association with the development of gateways and hubs.

The role of transport and tourism in EMRs in Southeast Asia

Transport is the dynamic element that links tourists from origin areas with the destination areas, and research has explored the tourist–transport interface in some detail (Hoyle and Knowles, 1992; 1998; Page, 1994; 1998; 1999). Yet within the literature on Southeast Asian tourism, most recent syntheses (e.g. Hitchcock *et al.*, 1993; Go and Jenkins, 1997) have failed to discuss the vital role of transport and infrastructure development as facilitating and potentially constraining factors in the development of tourism within the region (Leinbach and Chia, 1989; Hilling, 1996; Rigg 1997). Most tourism studies with a focus on Southeast Asia tend to assume that transport is a passive agent despite its obvious role in wider processes of economic development. Much of the published research on tourism in Southeast Asia has been devoid of any critical discussion of the role of transport in economic development in general and tourism in particular. Tourism is not any different in this context to other forms of economic development, since the rapid growth in domestic and international tourism flows and activity at different spatial scales requires transportation and associated infrastructure provision to enable the realisation of the latent potential demand. In this respect, the supply of transportation and infrastructure is a fundamental requirement for the orderly and efficient development of tourism.

   In terms of the historical development of gateways in Southeast Asia, during the 1970s, Bombay, Bangkok, Singapore, Hong Kong, Seoul, Tokyo and Sydney emerged as key hubs affecting the distribution pattern of tourism and travel within Asia. During the 1980s, competition between Bangkok, Hong Kong and Singapore for the position of major aviation hub of Asia emerged, and this continued into the 1990s. In that decade, a pattern of secondary airports linked to the hubs emerged. The recent publication of specialised studies on air transport (Findlay *et al.*, 1997), airport development (O'Connor, 1996) as well as private sector reports on aviation (Air Traffic Action Group (ATAG), 1997), together with those by Li (1998), emphasised the pivotal role gateway and hub development is assuming for the pattern of tourism development throughout Southeast Asia and the wider Asian region. One of the reasons why aviation has been the focus of much of the existing research relates to the scale and diversity of destinations within the region and the significance of airport hubs and regional air services to manage the distribution and flows of tourists into and within the region. This chapter does not consider the role of land-based transport and sea transport, of which the latter is vital for inter-island travel in the Philippines and Indonesia. Likewise, the role of tourist rail travel and tourist travel within urban areas are not considered but each is functionally linked to the emerging hubs and gateways in the region. One must, however, remember the significance of the historical antecedents set by the colonial period (Fisher, 1964) which continues to impose its legacy on the contemporary landscape. The chapter commences with a detailed discussion of air travel in the region, examining demand and supply issues. This is followed by a review of airport development and the problems facing many of the region's gateways, focusing on recent investment throughout the region to continue the expansion, concentration and dispersion of tourism through gateways and hubs.

Determinants of tourist transport in Asia

In a regional context, it is important to make an essential link in the explanation of the factors shaping the economic geography of the area, of which tourism is an integral part of the service economy (Islam and Chowdhury, 1997). Ioannides and Debbage (1998) also reinforce the argument by highlighting the need to link the regional economic context to the development of tourism in terms of consumer services such as air travel and those activities which tourists consume. As a result, there are four key forces shaping the economic landscape of the region:

- the offshore investment of Japanese, Korean and Taiwanese companies;
- the emergence of China as a market and a production location;
- rising levels of personal income in the region; and
- the rapidly expanding global role of the cities within the region.

Therefore, even without the tourism demand for travel to and within the region, it is apparent that exogenous factors are influencing economic growth and are fuelling a major demand for air travel which is resulting in an axis shift: O'Connor (1995) argues that in terms of air travel there has been a demand shift from the Europe–Asia trunk routes to a north–south axis in Asia fuelled by the growth of the above stated factors, resulting in city to city travel, of which tourism has been a part. However, in a tourism context, recreational travel has become a more significant part of the daily lives of the Asian population. In fact one could argue that the previous experience of the Japanese impact of wealth and prosperity on the global outbound tourism market and consequences for air travel is indicative of what may occur once other Asian markets begin to travel throughout the region (Hall, 1997). While transport researchers may point to the need to develop complementary modes of transport infrastructure to permit substitution in tourist travel within the region, the reality is that air transport is the only real alternative for the efficient movement of people and tourists over substantial distances. This is particularly the case in Southeast Asia because of the locations of resorts and destinations. This is supported by the research by Rimmer (1991) which investigated the potential for the development of high-speed rail corridors in the region. Rimmer concluded that the only rail links that can feasibly substitute for air travel lie within Japan, between Hong Kong, Shanghai and Beijing and between Singapore, Kuala Lumpur and Bangkok. Even then, these new networks can only cater for a small proportion of the current air travel. In fact, O'Connor (1996) observes a few linear air corridors in Southeast Asia, for example, a 300 km long corridor exists between Japan/Korea in the north through to Sumatra/Java in the south. Thus, future patterns of travel within the region for business and for other forms of tourism will be very dependent on the capacity of the existing air transport system to accommodate growth, particularly within the highly developed transport corridors.

Patterns of demand and supply in Asian air travel

Oum (1997) indicates that the Asia-Pacific region is one of the world's fastest growing regions for scheduled air travel, and Li (1998) discusses recent developments and the implications of air transport policy changes for the countries of the Association of Southeast Asian Nations (ASEAN). The main data sources for assessing the demand for tourist travel in the region have been reviewed by Hall and Page (2000) and Page (1994; 1999) and comprise the World Tourism Organisation (WTO) annual arrival statistics by country and region, and in the case of transport, data generated by the International Civil Aviation Organisation (ICAO) and the International Air Transport Association (IATA).

These data sources have recently been synthesised by the ATAG (1997) and represent one of the most detailed publicly available analyses of air travel in the region. Although many of the region's airlines have detailed market intelligence, such data remains highly sensitive due to its commercial value and is usually unavailable to researchers. In terms of growth, ATAG (1997) recorded 386 million passenger trips by scheduled aircraft in 1995 (including domestic and international passengers). Prior to the Asian crisis, the growth forecast by ICAO was 7.4 per cent growth per annum. If these growth forecasts reach their potential, then the Asia-Pacific region would by the year 2010 "record almost as many passengers as there were throughout the world in 1995" (ATAG, 1997: 5). Such growth forecasts are very dynamic and almost double the growth rates of travel in other parts of the world. Some of the key factors acting as growth drives in travel in Asia include:

- strong economic growth (prior to the Asian economic crisis);
- rising disposable income for discretionary spending on travel and tourism;
- periods of relative political stability (prior to the Asian crisis);
- progressive lifting of travel restrictions in Asian countries;
- ethnic and cultural ties between Asian countries which promote intra-regional travel;
- a continued increase in short-haul travel;
- increased travel opportunities promoted by the early stages of air transport liberalisation in the region;
- countries with a low base of travel (e.g. China) recognising and engaging in domestic and international travel; and
- the development of new airports and gateways at Kuala Lumpur, Macau and Osaka.

In terms of the Asia-Pacific region, ATAG (1997) identified five principal areas of activity:

- Central Asia comprising Kazakhstan, Tajikistan, Turkmenistan and Uzbekistan;
- South Asia comprising Afghanistan, Bangladesh, Bhutan, India, the Maldives, Nepal, Pakistan and Sri Lanka;

- Northeast Asia comprising China, Hong Kong, Japan, Macau, Mongolia, Democratic People's Republic of Korea (North Korea), Republic of Korea (South Korea), the Russian Federation (East of the Urals) and Taiwan (Chinese Taipei);
- Southeast Asia comprising Brunei Darussalam, Cambodia, Indonesia, Lao People's Democratic Republic, Malaysia, Myanmar, Philippines, Singapore, Thailand and Vietnam; and
- South Pacific comprising Australia, New Zealand, Papua New Guinea and the island nations of the Pacific including Hawaii.

Within these sub-regions, the major countries for future growth in tourism markets are likely to be:

- China, which is set to become the leading country for scheduled domestic and international travel by 2010. Its total share of Asia-Pacific air traffic is estimated to increase from 5.3 per cent in 1985 and 16 per cent in 1995 to 26 per cent in 2010. China is expected to supplant Japan as the leading market; and
- Japan, which was the largest market for air travel in 1995 with 30.8 per cent of the traffic which is expected to decrease to 20.1 per cent in 2010.

In numerical terms, the forecast growth in traffic will mean an additional 230 million passengers travelling to/from and within China in 2010 over the 1995 level. Other countries such as Vietnam are also expected by IATA to increase their volume of air traffic from 3.6 million passengers in 1995 to 28.4 million in 2010. The implications of such growth forecasts are that for 1995, 65 per cent of Asia-Pacific traffic was spatially concentrated within Northeast Asia and within the Northeast to Southeast Asia region, since average travel distances by air were under 5000 km. The most important intercontinental travel flows by air are Europe–Asia and these will remain a dominant feature of the region as:

- the principal flows are UK–Japan, with 1.2 million passenger trips in 1995 which are forecast to increase to 3.2 million by 2010;
- UK–Malaysia flows in Southeast Asia, with 755,000 passenger trips in 1995 which is expected to rise to 2.7 million in 2010.

These two dominant flows reflect the prevailing pattern of Europe–Asia travel, where the UK, Germany, France and the Netherlands accounted for 74.7 per cent of Europe–Asia-Pacific travel in 1995. This is a function of previous colonial links, business travel and a rapidly expanding medium to long-haul Europe–Asia vacation. In terms of scale, Japan–Europe passenger flows equated to 4.4 million passengers in 1995 which expanded by 13.3 per cent per annum between 1985–1995, and is forecast to rise to 10.4 million passengers by 2010, albeit at a lower growth rate of 5.9 per cent per annum.

Table 6.1 summarises the patterns of air travel and forecast growth rates for individual countries. In terms of the type of demand and likely shape of travel patterns, much of the growth will occur in terms of medium and long-haul travel to and from the region, reflected in the investment patterns of many of the airline carriers serving the region. The continued purchase of medium to long-haul fleet capacity (e.g. Boeing 767-300s with extended range capabilities, Airbus 340s and the new Boeing 777) reflect the expected pattern of growth. For example, Table 6.2

Table 6.1: Patterns of air travel and forecast growth rates in Asia Pacific, 1985–2010

| | Annual air passenger trips (in millions) | | | | | | | | | Average annual growth rate (%) | |
| | 1985 | | | 1995 | | | 2000 | | | | |
Destination	Domestic	International	Total	Domestic	International	Total	Domestic	International	Total	1985–1995	1995–2010
China	6.0	1.9	7.8	51.2	10.4	61.6	229.1	62.3	291.5	22.9	10.9
Chinese Taipei	5.9	4.8	10.7	28.7	15.8	44.6	104.1	52.8	156.9	15.4	8.8
Hong Kong	0.0	9.3	9.3	0.0	27.3	27.3	0.0	70.8	70.8	11.3	6.5
Japan	43.8	16.3	60.1	78.1	40.7	118.8	134.0	91.6	225.6	7.0	4.4
Korea	3.3	4.2	7.6	21.0	14.3	35.3	54.0	54.9	108.9	16.7	7.8
Pakistan	2.3	2.7	5.0	4.6	4.0	8.6	10.9	7.4	18.4	5.5	5.2
India	8.6	4.8	13.4	12.3	9.1	21.3	38.3	22.1	60.4	4.7	7.2
Sri Lanka	0.0	1.1	1.1	0.0	2.1	2.1	0.0	4.1	4.1	7.3	4.4
Indonesia	2.6	2.4	5.0	8.2	7.6	15.7	22.6	28.8	51.4	12.0	8.2
Malaysia	3.3	3.4	6.7	7.5	10.0	17.5	13.0	33.5	46.5	10.1	6.7
Philippines	3.3	3.1	6.4	4.7	6.7	11.4	17.4	18.3	35.7	6.0	7.9
Singapore	0.0	8.6	8.6	0.0	21.6	21.6	0.0	56.1	56.1	9.6	6.6
Thailand	1.4	5.4	6.8	6.3	15.8	22.1	22.3	49.1	71.4	12.6	8.1
Vietnam	N.A	0.1	0.1	1.5	2.1	3.6	11.3	17.1	28.4	40.9	14.8
Australia	13.1	5.5	18.7	23.5	12.8	36.3	61.4	32.5	93.9	6.9	6.5
New Zealand	2.7	2.2	5.0	4.0	4.6	8.6	8.2	10.9	19.1	5.7	5.4

Source: ATAG (1997) based on IATA data for the Asia-Pacific region and forecasts for 1980-2010.
Note: For the sake of consistency in trend analyses, traffic to and from Hong Kong has been considered separately from traffic to and from China even though Hong Kong became part of China after June 1997.

Table 6.2: Air travel by scheduled aircraft between Asia Pacific and other regions, 1985–2010

	Main world regions to and from Asia Pacific (Figures are annual passengers in millions)			
	1985	1995	2000	2010
Europe–Asia Pacific	6.9	20.7	30.1	57.8
Average annual growth (%)		11.6	7.8	6.8
Transpacific	5.1	15.5	22.8	45.3
Average annual growth (%)		11.8	8.1	7.1
Middle East–Asia Pacific	5.8	9.6	12.4	19.1
Average annual growth (%)		5.1	5.4	4.4
Africa–Asia Pacific	0.3	1.0	1.5	3.2
Average annual growth (%)		12.7	9.5	7.6

Source: ATAG (1997) based on IATA forecasts for Asia Pacific air travel, 1980–2010

shows that on the basis of IATA forecasts, average rates of growth exceeding 5 per cent per annum are likely to occur on most routes to and from Asia, although some of the higher rates of growth may need revising downwards in the short term due to the impact of the Asian crisis.

In the case of intra-regional traffic, Northeast Asia will remain a dominant high traffic area followed by Southeast Asia, with the principal flows in Northeast to Southeast Asia to South Pacific Region (including Australasia). The major flows in 1995 for inter-regional travel were generated by the China–Thailand, Hong Kong–Thailand and Japan–Singapore routes. Of the major city to city (trunk routes) flows, Hong Kong–Taipei was the dominant flow in 1995, with a volume of passengers in excess of the London–Paris route. This highlights the growing significance of gateways to the Asia-Pacific region. The consolidation and concentration of traffic in these trunk routes is reflected in the increase of city pairs with flows in excess of one million passengers. In 1993, eight international city pairs had over 1 million passengers, while in 1995 this had risen to 12 city pairs (ATAG 1997). This poses the question – how will airlines respond to the growing demand and how will they accommodate such growth?

ATAG (1997) outlines a number of strategies for airlines to meet the long-term demand for capacity growth. First, by increasing load factors (this is the technical term to describe the percentage of seats filled on each flight with fare-paying passengers), airlines are unlikely to offer more than a limited improvement to overall capacity as load factors are already high. The second option of increasing seat densities on medium to long-haul flights is also not a particularly attractive one for many airlines that are seeking to attract passengers in all classes of travel. In fact, with many airlines increasing the space allocated to business-class seating, this will continue to reduce the density of seating. Probably the most viable is the third option which is to increase the number of flights through improved utilisation of aircraft and the acquisition of additional aircraft. Yet as ATAG (1997) showed, even if the existing carriers increased flights by 200 per cent, they would still be unable to serve the 149 city pairs (sources of demand based on a daily basis) in the region. Therefore, the three main options available to airlines are:

- to open new routes;
- to increase frequencies on routes of high demand; and
- to rationalise multi-stop flights and replace them with non-stop flights.

Some improvement in capacity may also arise from the delivery of the new generation of wide-bodied aircraft to carriers serving the region. In numerical terms, ATAG (1997) expects the number of aircraft movements to increase on the Europe–Asia-Pacific routes from 79,000 in 1995 to 185,000 in 2010. Likewise, on North America–Asia-Pacific, the number of aircraft movements will increase from 64,000 in 1995 to 145,000 in 2010. These will pose major challenges for airports and the provision of airspace to accommodate rates of growth in excess of 5 per cent per annum. For this reason, it is pertinent to consider the issue of airport development and the ability of the infrastructure to cope with such demand.

Airport development in Asia: challenges and prospects

The literature on airports, airport development and the management of traffic growth is highly specialised and limited within the tourism field (see Page, 1999 for an overview). What is clear from the literature is that with the growth in tourism and recreational travel in Asia during the 1980s and 1990s, increased concern has arisen over the ability of the region's airports to accommodate the expected increase in traffic. A recent study by Rahim and Din (1999) examined a detailed range of issues now confronting governments and planners in relation to airport development within the context of one project – the Kuala Lumpur International Airport development. At a regional level, ATAG (1997) is one of a series of reports that have questioned the ability of some gateways and hubs to cope with the forecast growth. Despite the "planned spending of more than US$200 billion on airport infrastructure through to 2005, many of Asia's airports will be unable to cope with air traffic growth" (*Travel and Tourism Analyst*, 1998: 1).

Even accommodating the dampening effect of the Asian economic crisis for tourism in South Korea, Indonesia and Thailand, "economists generally expect recessionary conditions to persist for two to three years" (*Travel and Tourism Analyst*, 1998: 2). A recent IATA (1998) report argued that the Asian economic crisis should lead to a reduction of Asia-Pacific air traffic from 7.7 per cent in 1997 to 4.4 per cent in 2001, implying a reduction in passengers from 207 million to 176 million. While this may pose some fiscal problems for existing airports in Hong Kong, Seoul, Bangkok and Jakarta, ironically it may help the region's airports to cope with demand in the short term. However, a renewed period of growth is expected for 2005–2010 (*Travel and Tourism Analyst*, 1998). In fact, recent studies by APEC's Transportation Working Group recognise that most key airports in Southeast Asia would experience capacity constraints, albeit in different degrees (APEC Transportation Working Group, 1996). For this reason, it is useful to examine the recent new airport developments on greenfield sites in the region and other modernisation programmes.

New airport development projects

As Page (1999) shows, since the opening of the US$15 billion Kansai International Airport in Osaka, Japan, other developments have included the US$1.2 billion Macau International Airport, Chep Lap Kok in Hong Kong and Kuala Lumpur International Airport, Sepang, Malaysia. In addition, the government in Thailand has also approved a further airport construction project for Bangkok, with similar undertakings planned for the Philippines, Indonesia, Vietnam, Singapore, China and Taiwan. In the case of China, 10 new international airports are planned over the next decade. Further modernisation plans are also planned for China's other 140 airports. As a recent report in *Travel and Tourism Analyst* (1998:8) indicated, "Asia is the centre of an unprecedented number of expansion and modernisation projects at existing facilities, including enlargement of terminal buildings and cargo handling capacity, runway additions and updating of air traffic control (ATC) equipment".

It is clear that Singapore's Changi Airport is recognised as the region's principal hub, a position which may be challenged in the foreseeable future. For example, in 1997 it handled 25.2 million passengers, up from 24.5 million in 1996 and to accommodate future growth to retain its competitive position, the Civil Aviation Authority of Singapore is spending US$300 million on Terminal 1 to provide a further 14 aerobridges, raising the number of air bridges to 67 by the end of 1999 (*Travel and Tourism Analyst*, 1998). Work has also commenced to increase the airport's capacity to 65 million passengers a year by the year 2005, while land reclamation work has started so that a third runway can be built by the year 2015 (*Travel and Tourism Analyst*, 1998). As Table 6.3 shows, a wide range of investment projects are occurring throughout the region to accommodate new growth in air traffic. One of the notable features is the concentration of investment in the main gateways in Hong Kong, Singapore, Thailand and Malaysia to develop the main access routes to the region. From Table 6.4, it is also apparent that a wide range of airport upgrading projects is also underway to support new traffic growth at existing and new airports. Here the role of China as an emerging gateway to the region should not be underestimated.

There has also been only a limited interest in the privatisation of airports in Asia with only Australia and New Zealand following Britain's lead. However, it is evident from Tables 6.3 and 6.4 that a wide range of private sector and state funding has been used to develop the airport system in Asia. Despite the development of hubs with a growth in secondary hubs feeding the main gateways, regional concentration of traffic and tourist flows is continuing. In the case of airports, it is widely recognised that the greatest proportion of costs are capital as opposed to operating costs. Therefore the potential for efficiency gains is limited.

Some of the aspects of airport operation which private firms may perform efficiently include:

- terminal operation;
- retail outlet operation;
- building and operating runways; and
- contracted-out services.

Table 6.3: New airport projects in Asia Pacific

Country	Airport project	Cost (US$b)	Comments
Australia	Airport West, Sydney	5 (if built)	Subject to re-examination
China	Pudong International, Shanghai	2.5 (Phase 1)	Capacity of 80 million passengers a year
Hong Kong	Hong Kong International	20	2 runways; 50 aircraft movements an hour; 48 aerobridges; third runway planned to begin construction in 2005
Japan	Kansai International	15	-
Macau	Macau International	1.2	-
Malaysia	Kuala Lumpur International	3.2	Replacing Subang Airport near Kuala Lumpur; Capacity 25 million in 1999 and 60 million in 2020
South Korea	Inchon International, Seoul	8	Completion in Year 2000. Capacity for 170,000 flights a year and the first 24 hour a day airport in South Korea with two 3750m runways
Thailand	Nong Ngu Hao, Bangkok	Est. Cost 5.2	Will replace Don Muang Airport. Delayed until 2003. Will comprise one terminal and two runways and a capacity of 30 million passengers a year

However, Forsyth (1997: 62) maintains that "investment policy, and ownership of the main facilities may best be left to the public sector". In an Asia-Pacific context, privatisation has certainly opened up the opportunities for the region's airlines to become part of a global aviation industry through foreign investment, alliances and cooperation motivated by commercial motives without state protection of national/ state airlines. As Wheatcroft (1994: 24) argues, "in the long term, the privatisation of airlines seems certain to contribute to a reduction in protectionism in international aviation policies" and these changes are beginning to happen in Southeast Asia.

Conclusion

In terms of the recent Asian crisis, the impact on tourism has been a concern for intra-regional visitor arrivals although Li (1998) has pointed out a positive aspect – a rise in inbound tourism from non-ASEAN countries, an outcome of the depreciation of the Asian currencies. For airlines, the immediate consequences are the

escalation of debt service and lease costs and operating costs. Four flag carriers in ASEAN, namely, Garuda, Malaysia Airlines, Philippine Airlines and Thai Airways International, are experiencing most difficulties. Home-based air travel has drastically decreased as a result of dramatic currency depreciation.

(Li, 1998: 143).

Table 6.4: Expansion projects at existing airports in Asia Pacific

Country	Comments
Australia	Federal Airports Corporation has spent US$1 billion on capital improvements
Cambodia	Upgrading and plans for Pochentong airport at Siem Reap
China	1991-95: 8 out of 40 airports upgraded. 1996: a five-year plan launched to: • spend US$1.4 billion on infrastructure in 1997, of which US$1 billion was on airports; • aims to spend US$9 billion to rebuild and expand 32 airports including the following airports: Beijing International (cost of US$400 million and capacity of 35 million by 2005); Guangzhou (two new runways to cope with 27 million passengers a year by 2005); Shenzou; Hangzhou; Changchun; Haikou; Guiyang; Fuzhou; and Xedian.
India	Airports Authority of India is upgrading and constructing 28 airports with 75% of funds from foreign investors. Between 1995 and 1998, only US$123 million spent on airport upgrading. Only 40 of 123 airports are operational.
Indonesia	19 international airports and 6 gateways with US$1.8 billion investment underway.
Japan	Second runway by 2007 for Narita and second runway opened in 1997 for Tokyo Haneda; US$40 billion national airport expansion plan approved (including a feasibility study for a third Tokyo Airport).
Malaysia	1995-98: US$2.5 billion spent on airport redevelopments.
Philippines	New airport project for Manila at planning stage. Ninoy Aquino is receiving a terminal upgrade (US$400 million).
Singapore	Development of Terminal 1 at Changi Airport with 14 extra aerobridges (US$300 million). Terminal 3 project to be completed by 2005 to increase capacity to 65 million. Reclamation work commenced to develop a third runway by 2015.
South Korea	New airport by 2001 (Muan); Kimhae will utilise US$350 million for expansion; Yangyung will increase its capacity to 19 million passenger.
Vietnam	Plans for a doubling of airports from 16 to 32 and upgrading of airports with Japanese aid. Projects include Tan Son Nhat; Noi Bai; and Danang.

Source: Modified from *Travel and Tourism Analyst* (1998) and industry sources.

The following comments serve as a useful summary of the situation prevailing in 1998/1999 and offer both short and long-term strategic advice to both governments and policy-makers associated with transport provision for tourism:

Whilst most airport projects are unlikely to be affected by the economic crisis there is a danger that infrastructure programmes in the pipeline, or those which might have been expected to get underway soon, may be postponed or even cancelled. This would be short-sighted. It is essential that the region's airport and ATC [Air Traffic Control] infrastructure continues to be improved and expanded, not only to overcome an existing shortfall but to prepare for future growth, which will be substantial in the medium to long term.

(*Travel and Tourism Analyst*, 1998: 21).

This advice also has a more specific application to the broader context of urban tourism associated with megacities in Asia. As Shah (1996:14) argues,

Rapid urban growth, particularly in megacities, puts enormous demands on transport systems capable of moving large numbers of passengers...at affordable costs. In most megacities this demand is not met, leading to the familiar problems of air pollution and congestion, magnified in their impact in megacities because of the prevailing high densities of land use, shortage of roads, and inadequacies of public transport.

Shah's argument has a direct concern for tourism, particularly when one considers the environmental concerns of Ross and Thandanti (1995: 287) in relation to Bangkok where it "will become increasingly inhospitable and its [environmental] excesses will leak into the surrounding countryside. Foreign companies will leave and investment will dry up. Tourism will turn down". The negative impacts of rapid industrialisation and urban development and the significance for tourism in Thailand were also highlighted by Ratanakomut (1995: 92) in that "the positive impact of the growth of tourism has been the development of infrastructure in provincial towns such as Chiang Mai, Chiang Rai and Phuket. But tourism also brings problems. For example, it might create overall economic instability, increase resource leakages through import demand and environmental problems". Furthermore, in relation to Bangkok and the mounting problems of traffic congestion and a declining environmental quality, Ratanakomut (1995: 94) argues that "this would make Bangkok a less attractive place and lead tourists to shorten their stay. The growth of tourism areas such as Pattaya and Phuket is reaching its limit in terms of water supply and waste-water treatment". Therefore, whilst this chapter has predominantly emphasised the significance of air travel and tourism, there are other major infrastructure and land transportation concerns affecting megacities with a thriving tourism trade such as Bangkok. This experience is not dramatically different from the situation in other rapidly expanding urban areas in Southeast Asia. As a result, the future viability of urban tourism markets can be jeopardised although this is not just specific to urban tourism as Ross and Thandanti (1995: 273) suggest that

Tourist infrastructure such as hotels and access roads, and recreation facilities such as golf courses, contribute to the clearing of land and entail a very high per capita consumption of water. Because of the lack of planning controls, particularly in Pattaya and Phuket, untreated sewerage discharge has been allowed to pollute beaches, rivers and the corals at Phuket... This in turn has affected tourist numbers.

Yet, ironically, Rimmer (1995: 185) argues that in the case of Bangkok, "foreign trade, investment and tourism were crucial in the development of Bangkok's role as an international transport and communications hub" with the megacity status of the Bangkok metropolitan region propelling the national economy so much so that "the economic growth of Bangkok is indistinguishable from Thailand as a whole" (Rimmer, 1995: 183). Rimmer points to Bangkok's competition with other megacities in Asia-Pacific for supremacy, and tourism has become one element of the government's pursuit of this supreme status. Thus, the megacity role of many of Southeast Asia's primate cities performs a significant gateway function. This highlights their existing and future potential for urban tourism in many of the core areas of economic development of Southeast Asia. It is also a major factor in any initial explanation of the geographical distribution of international, and to a lesser degree, domestic visitors throughout the region as travel is conditioned by the availability of transport infrastructure routes and networks which are focused on the highly urbanised pattern of development. Hubs such as Singapore will certainly be influential in shaping future patterns of regional tourism as countries in the region align themselves with regional hubs and gateways that perform a range of tourism functions at different spatial scales.

In the case of transport, the relationship with environmental pollution and the significance of the tourism–transport interface in terms of declining environmental quality in cities and resort areas is becoming an issue of growing concern in Southeast Asia. In fact, Parnwell and Bryant (1996) highlight the current flaws in the economic and ecological approaches to development in Southeast Asia and the importance of political processes in relation to sustainable development. The political dimension of sustainable development is a feature subsequently analysed by Hirsch and Warren (1998) now that the environment has become an issue of public debate in the region. It is a sign of development and of the role transport plays in the facilitation of tourism development within and outside the primate cities of the region.

Some commentators have examined the contention that the arrival of the Western tourists in Southeast Asia may herald the "shock troops" of modernity (Oakes, 1997). What is clear in the 30 or more years since Fisher's (1964) seminal study of Southeast Asia is that an economic transformation has occurred in the region, with the development of an export-based economy based on primary and manufactured products. More recently, this has been complemented by the development of a service sector with a strong tourism dimension:

The distance from the major tourist supply areas of the United States and Europe may...have been a disadvantage, [but] the rapid development of the wide-bodied jet airliners has to a large degree offset this problem, while the rapid growth of incomes in the Asia Pacific region has substantially increased the potential supply of tourists.

(Walton, 1993: 214)

Thus, the transport revolution and expansion in both domestic and international tourism (both long and short-haul) has really only been possible through the facilitating role which transport has played over the last 20 years in expanding and developing Southeast Asia's tourism industry (Wood, 1979).

Acknowledgements

I would like to acknowledge the generous financial support provided by the National University of Singapore and Singapore Tourism Board in assisting with this research and for attendance at the Interconnected Worlds Conference in September 1999.

References

Air Transport Action Group (ATAG) (1997) *Asia-Pacific Air Traffic Growth and Constraints*. Geneva: ATAG.

APEC Transportation Working Group (1996) *Congestion Point Study Phase II: Final Report Volume 1 – Executive Summary; Volume 2 – Air Transport*. Singapore: APEC Secretariat & Maunsell Pte. Ltd.

Britton, S. (1982) 'The political economy of tourism in the Third World'. *Annals of Tourism Research*, 9(3), 331–58.

Chang, T.C. (1998) 'Regionalism and tourism: Exploring integral links in Singapore'. *Asia-Pacific Viewpoint,* 39(1), 73–94.

Dick, H. and Rimmer, P. (1998) 'Beyond the Third World city: The new urban geography of Southeast Asia'. *Urban Studies*, 35(12), 2303–21.

Dixon, C. and Smith, D. (eds.) (1997) *Uneven Development in Southeast Asia.* Aldershot: Ashgate.

Douglass, M. (1995) 'Global interdependence and urbanisation: Planning the Bangkok mega-urban region', in T. McGee and I. Robinson (eds.) *The Mega-Regions of Southeast Asia.* Vancouver: University of British Columbia Press, 45–77.

Findlay, C., Chia, L.S. and Singh, K. (eds.) (1997) *Asia-Pacific Air Transport: Challenges and Policy Reforms.* Singapore: Institute of Southeast Asian Studies.

Fisher, C. (1964) *Southeast Asia.* London: Methuen.

Forbes, D. (1999) 'Globalisation, postcolonialism and new representations of the Pacific Asian metropolis', in K. Olds, P. Dicken, P. Kelly, L. Kong and H. Yeung (eds.) *Globalisation and the Asia-Pacific.* London: Routledge, 238–54.

Forsyth, P. (1997) 'Privatisation in Asia-Pacific aviation', in C. Findlay, L.S. Chia and K. Singh (eds.) *Asia-Pacific Air Transport: Challenges and Policy Reforms.* Singapore: Institute of Southeast Asian Studies, 48–64.

Go, F. and Jenkins, C. (eds.) (1997) *Tourism and Economic Development in Asia and Australasia.* London: Cassell.

Hall, C.M. (1997) *Tourism in the Pacific Rim,* 2nd edition. Melbourne: Addison Wesley Longman.

Hall, C.M. and Page, S. J. (eds.) (2000) *Tourism in South and Southeast Asia: Issues and Cases.* Oxford: Butterworth-Heinemann.

Hilling, D. (1996) *Transport and Developing Countries.* London: Routledge.

Hirsch, P. and Warren, C. (eds.) (1998) *The Politics of Environment in Southeast Asia.* London: Routledge.

Hitchcock, M., King, V. and Parnwell, M. (eds.) (1993) *Tourism in Southeast Asia.* London: Routledge.

Hoyle, B. and Knowles, R. (eds.) (1992) *Modern Transport Geography.* London: Belhaven.

Hoyle, B. and Knowles, R. (eds.) (1998) *Modern Transport Geography*, 2nd edition. Chichester: John Wiley and Sons.

International Air Transport Association (IATA) (1998), *The Impact of Recent Events on the Asia-Pacific Aviation Market and Prospects for Future Growth to 2001,* March, Montreal: IATA.

Ioannides, D. and Debbage, K. (eds.) (1998) *The Economic Geography of the Tourist Industry: A Supply-Side Analysis.* London: Routledge.

Islam, I. and Chowdhury, A. (1997) *Asia-Pacific Economies: A Survey.* London: Routledge.

Leinbach, T. and Chia, L.S. (1989) *Southeast Asian Transport: Issues in Development.* Singapore: Oxford University Press.

Li, M. (1998) 'Air transport in ASEAN: Recent developments and implications'. *Journal of Air Transport Management*, 4, 135–44.

Low, L. and Toh, M.H. (1997) 'Singapore: Development of gateway tourism', in F. Go and C. Jenkins (eds.) *Tourism and Economic Development in Asia and Australasia.* London: Cassell, 237–54.

O'Connor, K. (1995) 'Airport development in Southeast Asia'. *Journal of Transport Geography*, 3(4), 269–79.

O'Connor, K. (1996) 'Airport development: A Pacific Asian perspective'. *Built Environment*, 22(3), 212–22.

Oakes, T. (1997) 'Ethnic tourism in rural Guizhou: Sense of place and the commerce of authenticity', in M. Picard and R. Wood (eds.) *Tourism, Ethnicity and the State in Asian and Pacific Societies.* Honolulu: University of Hawaii Press, 35–70.

Olds, K., Dicken, P., Kelly, P., Kong, L. and Yeung, H. (1999) (eds.) *Globalisation and the Asia-Pacific.* London: Routledge.

Oum, T. (1997) 'Challenges and opportunities for Asian airlines and governments', in C. Findlay, L.S. Chia and K. Singh (eds.) *Asia-Pacific Air Transport: Challenges and Policy Reforms.* Singapore: Institute for Southeast Asian Studies, 1–22.

Page, S.J. (1994) *Transport for Tourism.* London: Routledge.

Page, S.J. (1998) 'Transport for recreation and tourism', in B. Hoyle and R. Knowles, (eds.) *Modern Transport Geography*, 2nd edition. Chichester: John Wiley and Sons, 217–40.

Page, S.J. (1999) *Transport and Tourism.* Harlow: Addison Wesley Longman.

Parnwell, M. and Bryant, R. (eds.) (1996) *Environmental Change in Southeast Asia.* London: Routledge.

Raguraman, K. (1997) 'Airlines as instruments for nation-building and national identity: Case study of Malaysia and Singapore'. *Journal of Transport Geography*, 5(4), 239–56.

Rahim, A. and Din, K. (1999) 'Kuala Lumpur International Airport as a new tourist gateway in Southeast Asia: Assessing the potential and examining the problems', paper presented at *Interconnected Worlds: Southeast Asian Tourism in the Twenty-first Century*, Singapore, 6–7 September.

Ratanakomut, S. (1995) 'Industrializing the service sector, with special emphasis on tourism', in M. Krongakaew (ed.) *Thailand's Industrialization and its Consequences*. Basingstoke: Macmillan, 85–98.

Rigg, J. (1997) *Southeast Asia: The Human Landscape of Modernization and Development*. London: Routledge.

Rimmer, P. (1991) 'Megacities, multi-layered networks and development corridors in the Pacific Economic Zone: The Japanese ascendancy', in T. Hutton (ed.) *Conference Papers on Transportation and Regional Development*. Vancouver: Centre for Human Settlements, University of British Columbia.

Rimmer, P. (1995) 'Urbanization problems in Thailand's rapidly industrializing economy', in M. Krongakaew (ed.) *Thailand's Industrialization and its Consequences*. Basingstoke: Macmillan, 183–217.

Ross, H. and Thandanti, S. (1995) 'The environmental costs of industrialization', in M. Krongakaew (ed.) *Thailand's Industrialization and its Consequences*. Basingstoke: Macmillan, 267–88.

Shah, A. (1996) 'Urban trends and the emergence of the megacity', in J. Stubbs (ed.) *The Future of Asian Cities: Report of the 1996 Annual Meeting Seminar on Urban Management and Finance*. Manila: Asian Development Bank, 11–32.

Tang, M. and Thant, M. (1993) *Growth Triangles: Conceptual Issues and Problems, Economics*, Staff Paper Number 54. Manila: Asian Development Bank.

Teo, P. and Chang, T. C. (1998) 'Critical issues in a critical era: Tourism in Southeast Asia'. *Singapore Journal of Tropical Geography*, 19(2), 119–29.

Tham, E. (1999) 'Regionalisation as a strategy for Singapore's development', paper presented at *Interconnected Worlds: Southeast Asian Tourism in the Twenty-first Century*, Singapore, 6–7 September.

Travel and Tourism Analyst (1998) 'Asian airport development', 2, 1–21.

Walton, J. (1993) 'Tourism and economic development in ASEAN', in M. Hitchcock, V. King and M. Parnwell (eds.) *Tourism in Southeast Asia*. London: Routledge, 214–33.

Wheatcroft, S. (1994) *Aviation and Tourism Policies*. London: Routledge/World Tourism Organisation.

Wood, R. (1979) 'Tourism and underdevelopment in Southeast Asia'. *Journal of Contemporary Asia*, 9(3), 274–87.

Part Three

Reinventing Tradition in an Interconnected World

7

Globalisation, Tourism and Culture in Southeast Asia

Trevor H. B. Sofield

Introduction

One of the intriguing developments in the last 10 years has been the parallel exploration of the conceptual boundaries of globalisation and its opposite force, localisation, in the context of understanding culture. Rather than an inexorable drive
towards global homogenisation, some writers perceive a fragmentation of culture.
This seemingly paradoxical movement finds concise expression in the titles of several
works, such as Featherstone's (1995a) *Undoing Culture: Globalization,
Postmodernism and Identity;* Rojek's (1995) *Decentring Leisure*; and Bhabha's
(1994) *The Location of Culture* and his concerns with border people in interstitial
space. The thoughts expressed in this chapter are aimed at bringing tourism into this
discussion, analysing tourism as a system which is an undoubted and active agency
for globalisation yet which is simultaneously a very dynamic agency for localisation.
Interestingly, Bhabha did not focus on tourism at all although Hollinshead (1998:69)
would aver that in fact, much of his writings justify tourism being seen in the context
of globalisation as "a domain of human activity which has a hugely powerful and
dynamic role in the making and remaking of society".

The literature spawned by the topic of globalisation is far too extensive to attempt a
survey of its major scholars and the many divergent lines of research they have pursued in this chapter. It is necessary, however, to provide a brief overview of the main
themes and issues. This summary of globalisation leads into a questioning of the place
of culture in the formation of identity and image; and of place and people (society) in
the process of globalisation. Then from there, the chapter questions the role of tourism
in the development of so-called global culture; the interconnectedness of the world;
and the space that the tourism system and tourists have claimed for themselves. I term
this space 'interstitial fourth space', the space in-between, a derivative extension of
Jameson (1986), Bhabha (1994), Gupta and Ferguson (1997), and Hollinshead (1998).

Having explored the complexity of the tourism system in its global setting, I wish then to examine some of the latest theories in cultural anthropology as they relate to globalisation and the basic premise that we can no longer automatically assume that there is a bounded uniqueness about people/place/culture. There has been a paradigm shift in anthropological studies in the past two decades, with new understandings calling into question the integrity of 'culture-and-place' (Gupta and Ferguson, 1997). As anthropological studies more strongly support the notion of interconnectedness and the unpackaging of 'place + people = culture', I wish to argue that the tourism system is a very powerful force which both supports that notion and contests it. Indeed, in many instances, tourism strives to highlight difference, creates or even re-creates difference, aggressively re-imaging, re-constituting and appropriating heritage, culture and place, pursuing localisation in marked contrast to its globalising influence.

Globalisation and the tourism system

There has been an explosion in the rhetoric of globality, globalisation, internationalisation and so on. Globalisation is a process and the world-system is a structure. Two particular representations of globalisation co-exist.

The first entails the outward expansion of a particular culture to all corners of the globe; a single, homogeneous, dominating culture which integrates and incorporates all less robust cultures (Featherstone; 1995b; King, 1991; Robertson, 1991). This homogeneity is perceived in a global culture which increasingly sees the English language as the medium of communication worldwide, and the expansion to virtually all countries of Western styles of dress, food and recreation. It is also perceived in a single global economy, which is dominated by Western-style capitalism, and there is sameness in terms of the development of infrastructure, markets and business culture. The homogeneity is also perceived in a global technology based on Western computerised technology and telecommunications with faster and easier access to increasing amounts of information (mass media such as radio, terrestrial and satellite television, and communications technologies such as telephones, faxes and the Internet). Developments in the technology of transport (air, road, rail and sea) facilitate "the binding together of large expanses of time-space not only on an intra-societal level but increasingly on an inter-societal and global level" (Featherstone, 1995b:7). It is a world "of diaspora, transnational culture flows and mass movements of people" (Gupta and Ferguson, 1997:38) where a homogenising globalisation is, in the view of some, demolishing difference and moving us closer to the establishment of the so-called 'global village' (Urry, 1990).

Urry expounds in *The Tourist Gaze* (1990) that tourism contributes to the globalisation process by, *inter alia*, its dissemination of homogenous management systems; universal applications of service quality; repetition of 'touristic' architectural styles in different countries around the world; touristic marketing, promotions, and presentations; the spread of 'Western' values both through its business activities, personnel training and management; and of course through the contact travellers have with local peoples everywhere. Paradoxically, because tourism is about *difference,* at the same time it contributes to the maintenance and retention of cultural diversity. The tourism product and attractions of Southeast Asia attest to this cultural diversity.

The second image of globalisation focuses on 'interconnectedness', the way in which cultures formerly held apart are brought into contact and juxtaposition (Featherstone, 1995a, 1995b, King, 1991). Cultures pile on top of cultures in a heap that appears to have no organising principle beyond the fact that the 'culture' of communications is supported by the mass movement of people (tourists). Communication is further abetted by the ease with which contemporary information technology and telecommunications (IT&T) reaches every country and its messages are accepted and absorbed at least in part by each of the separate cultures. The movement of people is also facilitated by modern transport technologies so that over time, a certain degree of commonality evolves and echoes of different cultures will be found in every other culture.

There is much talk in the popular press of the former, and words such as 'Americanisation', 'Disneyfication' and 'McDonaldisation' are bandied about. McDonald's may be found in Singapore, Kuala Lumpur, Jakarta, Manila, Bangkok, Hong Kong, Beijing and many other cities in East Asia. Tokyo has its Disneyland and in 1999, Hong Kong reached agreement for another Disneyland near its new airport. Despite such manifestations of commonality, in reality, few observers would adhere to the belief that the endpoint of historical development would be a single, homogenous, integrated world culture bereft of linguistic, social and cultural differences. Economic differences may be lessened, political sharpness and national contestation may eventually be subdued, but certainly at the present time, in sharp contrast to the first image, the second image suggests greater clashes of cultures, with greater complexity in assertions of identity than the first image permits. There is "a spiral of relativisation of culture through increased contact" (Featherstone, 1995a:6) where not only integration but also increased conflict has occurred. Rather than the emergence of a unified global culture,

there is a strong tendency for the process of globalisation to provide a stage for global differences not only to open up a 'world showcase of cultures' in which the examples of the distant exotic are brought directly into the home, but to provide a field for a more discordant clashing of cultures.

(Featherstone, 1995b:13)

Fissiparous tendencies in the former Soviet Union (now Russia), in the Balkans (formerly united Yugoslavia) and Indonesia attest to this process.

There is now a discourse of globality although within this discourse there are many problematics. While there is some common ground on its contents, the interests that sustain the discourse vary tremendously from society to society and also within societies. The discourse itself has become an important part of globalisation and of contemporary global culture. Increasingly as the process of globalisation has gathered strength, nations and other entities have been faced "almost continuously with the problem of response to the wider, increasingly compressed, global context" in which they exist (Robertson, 1991:88). The ways in which such entities have simultaneously attempted to learn from one another and adopted elements of 'the wider world' while sustaining a sense of identity – or have attempted to isolate themselves from the pressures of contact – also constitute an important aspect of the creation of global culture. China under Mao elected to isolate itself from the world in many ways in contrast to the 'Open Door' policies pursued since 1978 when Deng delivered China's new outward approach to the world. As Robertson (1991:89) notes, "[e]ven more specifically the cultures of particular societies are, to different degrees, the result of their interactions with other societies in the global system. In other words, national-societal cultures have been differentially formed in interpenetration with significant others." In this context, the role of the tourism system as 'a significant other' interpenetrating societies and cultures across the globe, has rarely been mentioned in the sociological and political science literature of globalisation. It is this element of interpenetration, which assists a dialogic component in image-making for and between tourists and agents of the tourism system on the one hand, and host countries on the other.

The discourse on the nature of linkages between the global and the local reveals that the local can either enjoy a benign relationship with the global or be subordinated to it. While cultural integration processes are taking place on a global level, at the local level, there are increasing pluralistic or polytheistic manifestations. This situation has been variably described as

a process of cultural fragmentation and collapse of symbolic hierarchies where there are 'shifts in the value of the symbolic power and cultural capital of the west' because of the emergence of competing centres of global significance such as Japan and East Asia.

(Featherstone, 1995a:9)

This global–local interaction has also been described as "a post-colonial contra-modernity" which captures "the hybrid and syncretic perspectives...of those half-inside and half-outside of modernity, a conscious mixing of traditions and crossing of boundaries" (Bhabha, 1994:5). Postmodernism can be understood in the way it points to the decentring of culture and the introduction of cultural complexity (Featherstone, 1995a; 1995b), paradoxically away from the very universalism inherent in the concept of globalisation. Rather than contrasting autonomous local cultures (original, centred, authentic) with an opposing global cultural ecumene (which is seen as new, external, artificially imposed, inauthentic), the challenge for ethnographic theory is to seek out the ways in which connectedness between the two occurs and the ways in which dominant cultural forms may be picked up and used – and significantly transformed – by communities and nation-states in the midst of the field of power relations that links localities to the wider world (Gupta and Ferguson, 1997). Tourism provides a milieu for examining this interstitiality of local–global phenomena, in the context of what Wallerstein (1984) has called the simultaneity of particularism and universalism.

Culture and tourism

In conventional anthropological studies, 'people-place-culture' were taken as a given fact. In terms of tourism this normalised identity between people and place is presented as 'culture' for the tourist, for example in visiting Bangkok to 'experience

Thai culture', or travelling to Angkor Wat to comprehend 'the cultural achievements of vanished Asian civilisations', or staying in Singapore to appreciate 'the cultures of the East'. We live in a world where 'culture' is increasingly the province of the state as well as the community, and its definition rendered not by its peoples but by its national tourism authorities to create a signature image and differentiate the nation from its neighbours for perceived market advantage. Yet through the postmodern processes of globalisation we have "the partial erosion of spatially bounded social worlds and the growing role of the imagination of places from a distance" (Gupta and Ferguson, 1997:39). It is thus a world where Southeast Asia is positioning itself as the greatest cultural experience on the global tourist calendar, attracting very significant numbers of visitors by promoting its differences, and thus, paradoxically, participating in that globalisation which is the opposite of separateness.

The discourse on the nature of linkages between the global and the local reveals that the local can either enjoy a benign relationship with the global or be subordinated to it. In this context, the challenge for the anthropology of tourism is to explore a paradigm shift which challenges the integrity of 'culture-and-people-and-place', an anthropology "whose objects [of study] are no longer conceived as automatically and naturally anchored in space [but which] will need to pay particular attention to the way spaces and places are made, imagined, contested, and enforced" (Gupta and Ferguson, 1997:47). In its extreme form, postmodernist anthropology has moved towards 'anarchic deconstruction' in which all meaning is deferred ("the undecidability of meaning"; Derrida, 1978:2). A less extreme postmodern approach places the emphasis on a relativist position in which there are multiple realities, fragmentation, plurality, and subjectivity. It is this methodology which is utilised in this chapter to explore the imaging associated with Southeast Asia's tourism policies and the development of attractions and facilities for tourism.

A scrutiny of space implicit in theories of interstitiality points to the area of public culture and the role of the tourism system in moving beyond culture as a spatially localised phenomenon to the process of global interconnection and the interpenetration of the local by the global and vice versa. Public culture, disseminated globally by the pervasive capacity of transnational IT&T, has reached even the remotest people that anthropologists have made such a fetish of studying, and tourism has been an integral element of this process, challenging the notion of culture bounded by place and space, as if contained in a clearly defined geographical vessel. For example, Yamashita (1997:83) records the dynamic interplay of local, national and global influences accorded by the "manipulation of ethnic tradition" among the Toraja of Sulawesi, Indonesia when the funeral ceremony of a traditional aristocratic leader was filmed for television in Japan. The transformation of the funeral as more of a spectacle than a religious ceremony for consumption by a huge audience of 'outsiders' released the ritual from where it "was once unconsciously embedded in the local society" (Yamashita, 1997:101) into the world of virtual reality through the medium of television. For Yamashita, this is to be interpreted not as the 'loss' of traditional Toraja culture but as "a narrative of the emergence, or re-making of Toraja tradition in a new postmodern setting" (Yamashita, 1997:101). 'Their' space has become shared space with dimensions that reach out internationally to interconnect with societies around the world.

The fluid composition of populations in the post-Fordist era, accelerated by the immense mobility of people and the refusal of cultural products and practices to stay 'where they belong' all combine to bring about a sense of loss of territorial roots, of an erosion of the cultural distinctiveness of places (Bhabha, 1994). Deterritorialised space becomes reterritorialised space with place no longer necessarily a paramount consideration. One can find a China, an India, a Vietnam, or a Thailand in many countries in this interconnected postmodern world. The tourism system is a key agent in this reterritorialisation, often making over or manufacturing a 'Chinatown' or 'Little India' in a Singapore or a Sydney, and presenting, globally, images evocative of the original places/cultures with reconstructed ethnicity/authenticity ready for consumption by its mobile millions of tourists. According to Gupta and Ferguson (1997:48),

In this culture-play of diaspora, [aided and abetted by the tourism system], familiar lines between 'here' and 'there', centre and periphery, colony and metropole become blurred...The existence of a transnational public sphere means that the fiction that (national, regional and village) boundaries enclose homogenous cultures and regulate cultural exchange can no longer be sustained.

Rather, our premise must be that spaces have always been hierarchically interconnected, instead of naturally disconnected, and that cultural and social change becomes a matter of rethinking difference through connection.

The experience of space is always socially constructed, but important tensions arise when the relationships between place and space, and people and culture, having been 'imagined', become lived relationships in lived space. For example, we are taught that Singaporeans live in Singapore, Thais live in Thailand and Indonesians live in Indonesia. Even a casual observer, however, knows that not only Thais live in Thailand, and will question who is a 'real' Singaporean in the ethnic mix that is Singapore (Leong, 1997) or equally, a 'real' Indonesian in its multicultural society? Anthropologists and others will talk about 'Thai' culture because we assume 'a natural association' of a culture (a Thai 'way of life'), a people (Thais) and a place (Thailand) (see Cohen, in this volume). But these associations, while commonsensical at one level, are in fact contested, uncertain and in flux. Tourism has played a major role in the 'imaging' and 'recreation' of 'national cultures' and ethnicity in many Asian countries (Graburn, 1997:210). Cultural heritage may be claimed and its ownership utilised to bestow legitimacy on those with the power and authority to present it in desired form to both insiders and outsiders. Nation-states in Southeast Asia have been active in devising tourism policies to support ideologically driven definitions and symbols of national identity and ethnicity. Richter (1989:44) suggests that the Philippines under Marcos was "the classic case of using tourism development politically" in an attempt to add legitimacy to his regime. Leong's (1989; 1997) study of Singapore and the way in which the government has channelled its many different ethnicities into four official CMIO 'races' (Chinese, Malays, Indians, Others) for tourism marketing purposes is further proof of the political uses of tourism.

Touristic culture and the state

As the twentieth century comes to a close, we are confronted with the paradox of nation-states proclaiming their difference and their interconnectedness at the same time. It is a world where, as noted above, 'culture' is increasingly the province of the state rather than the community, its definition rendered not by its peoples but by its governments for political ends, with the energetic involvement of a number of agencies of the state including national tourism organisations (see Leong, 1997 on Singapore; Wood, 1997 on Asian and Pacific societies; Picard, 1997 on Bali; and Din, 1997 and Kahn, 1997 on Malaysia, for example). It is a world where Southeast Asia advocates a role for itself as the gateway between East and West, promoting itself as different yet connected, a major player in the movement of these tourists and provider of what they seek. It is thus imperative to examine tourism in the context of ethnicity, definitions of culture, and the state.

Culture, whether in its material or symbolic form, is an attribute which people(s) are said to have. A fairly standard differentiation has been culture as "the set of characteristics which distinguish one group from another" and high culture: "some set of phenomena (e.g., art, music, literature) which are different from (and 'higher') than some other set of phenomena within any one group" (Wallerstein, 1990:33). In Cultural Studies, these differences between what might be termed the older anthropological definition and the newer humanistic one are collapsed and combined so that "culture in its sense of art, literature, film, practices of representation of all kinds, both draws from and participates in the construction of culture as a way of life, as a system of values and beliefs which, in turn, affects culture as a creative, representational practice" (King, 1991:2).

In the context of postmodernism we have the ethnographer's formerly comfortable world of place/people/culture now challenged by the complexity of our growing understanding that virtually no place/people/culture had been so isolated that they had no connection with others. This understanding accepts that identity has always been based not on tightly drawn boundaries and exclusive recognition of self but on drawing differences with 'others', through external reference points (Peters, 1997). Long-held formulations about culture in the social sciences have begun to consider the question of perceptions of greater complexity. In the 1950s and 1960s, 'community studies' focused on individual towns or 'primitive' communities through territorialised limits (the ethnographer's 'dangerously delicate' local worlds where spatial confinement protected the natives' traditions, culture and primitive economies from the "power of engulfing cosmopolitan orders" (Peters, 1997:80)). However, such an approach is no longer tenable as the realisation becomes ever more apparent that even then, such entities did not exist in isolation. Connectivities did exist: 'Frontier Town America' was indeed part of mass America; the Redjang of interior Sumatra were not detached from Indonesia (Jaspen, 1964); Trobriand Islanders of Papua New Guinea were part of the socio-economic fabric of wider eastern Melanesia (Malinowski, 1922); the Ma'asai were encompassed within and across Tanzania and Kenya where colonial boundaries were largely irrelevant in a cultural context. Even for the extremely isolated Pitjantjara Aborigines of the central Australian desert, there was always an 'outside' with which links, however tenuous, were maintained. Psychologically for the inside people, there was always an 'external world' even if only dimly comprehended; and 'primitive' was a label imposed by outsiders, not part of their vision or understanding of themselves (Peters, 1997; Gupta and Ferguson, 1997).

In conventional ethnographic studies, people/place/culture was accepted as given, and the 'how' of the construction of culture was not examined. This concept of people/place/culture is graphically illustrated in any school atlas, with the boundaries of different countries clearly demarcated and the global map coloured with yellow, green, pink and blue countries. There are no fuzzy boundaries or vaguely defined unclaimed spaces. The history of national principle is reinforced and simplified for all to understand (Gellner, 1983). This national order also passes as the normal or natural order of things, for as Malkki (1996:55) writes:

...it is self-evident that 'real' nations are fixed in space and 'recognisable' on a map. One country cannot at the same time be another country. The world of nations is thus conceived as a discrete spatial partitioning of territory: it is territorialised in the segmentary fashion of the multicoloured school atlas.

The marketing and promotion activities of national tourism organisations reflect this territorialised world.

Malkki (1996) has demonstrated that it is difficult to challenge the notion of community and culture as natural and unproblematic because of what she calls 'the metaphysics of sedentarism', where the *roots* of peoples and cultures in their own territories are taken for granted. Terms such as 'the motherland' imbue this concept with 'naturalness' and reinforce the idea of nostalgia for a simple past which many societies believe may still be found to exist in isolated communities or rural settings. Yet the re-invention of rurality is characteristic of many reconstructions of image for tourism: the authentic and original exist in such an environment, everything else is contrasted as fabricated, false, substitution or modernistic replication. It has been suggested that 'nostalgia' is a Western concept out of which major tourism markets have been developed. Zeppel (1997) has captured this in her study of "meeting wild people", where Iban longhouse tourism in Sarawak is marketed for and consumed by Western tourists nostalgically searching for an assumed long-lost simplicity in the primitive and authentic Iban culture.

Gupta and Ferguson (1997:78) talk about the "waning of place as a container of experience" and this may be so for the intellectual stance currently being pursued by anthropologists as they tease out the details of the disengagement and deconstruction of people/place/culture. From the point of view of the business of tourism, however, its tourism marketing is often aimed at the opposite – of producing and projecting place as *the* container of experience. The tourist is in his/her own container, manufactured by the tourism system, and does not enter the backstage of the place of visitation except vicariously, temporarily, or on the surface, or indeed in many cases does not enter at all. They occupy interstitial space, temporarily removed from their resident space.

In anthropological studies, where identity was given as emerging naturally from community and locality (place), the ownership of culture resided in the peoples of a place. Now as stated above, nation-states have often co-opted community ownership of culture, redefined it and put it to use for national ends. There has been a 'colonisation' of culture by the new state entity, determining the particular images that shall be presented to the outside. There is in these developments an affinity between tourism and the nation-state in the sense that both have a profound interest in presenting the place as differentiated and unique, with boundaries around both geographical and socio-cultural space (Leong, 1997; Sofield and Li, 1998). This is particularly true of multiethnic states and newly independent states which in the post-colonial period may face the problem of trying to create a sense of and commitment to national unity where previously such a sentiment did not exist (Graburn, 1997). Ethnicity has become "more than a neutral social scientific term: it has become part of the way people factually and prescriptively see themselves and others ...historically constructed and re-constructed" (Wood, 1997:7).

Tourism is not a neutral agent which stands apart from power and ideology. Tourism is always involved in "the conflictual cultural economy – a participant player in the productive representation, the productive manufacture, and the productive selling of difference, and a participant player in the consumptive representation of some people and the consumptive containment of others" (Hollinshead, 1998:59). As Clifford (1988:115) argued, tourism orders the location of the objects of its gaze in ways to suit the business practices and interests of its agents: "the relentless placement of others (other people, other places, other pasts) in a present-becoming-past which can be gazed at by tourists but not with active or cultivated interest". Said's (1978) theories on cultural difference challenge Western and mainstream practices of 'othering', while Bhabha (1994) goes beyond Said's reliance on historical origins of identity to suggest a requirement to trace the dynamics of contemporary representations rather than be bound by received and authorised historical 'truth'. Richter (1999) also argues that the politics of power (particularly with reference to heritage tourism because it is bounded in issues of national identity, political communication and socialisation), will determine how history, events, people and sites will be presented. It is at this point that we may find the agents of the tourism system either actively supporting those received historical truths to promote their business of cultural heritage tourism or alternatively, dismantling prior-accepted realities. Such representations may be carried out in concert with state or government authorities which may be ideologically motivated to pursue a discontinuation of the historical reality for political ends; or the agents of the tourism system may simply be following the lead of political authorities and exploiting the 'new realities' for commercial gain.

In looking critically at the interrelationships of culture, power and place, two particular issues which cross-cut these inter-relationships are evident: place-making and identity. As Gupta and Ferguson (1997) have noted, ethnographic studies in the past few years have borrowed from writers such as Bourdieu (1977) and de Certeau (1984) the notion of active practices of social agents who never simply enact culture but interpret and reappropriate it in their own ways. Ethnographic studies have also borrowed from Foucault (1978; 1980) the idea that power relations pervade society at all levels and create fields of resistance so that culture becomes contested. It is argued in this paper that in all of these processes, tourism and its policy-makers, its marketeers and its operators, constitute together – whether consciously or otherwise

– key social agents for re-inventing, promulgating and promoting image and identity along specifically determined lines, pursuing both national separateness and inter-connectedness with the rest of the world. They carry out carefully planned, global campaigns to create awareness of national or sub-national culture, engaging in competition with neighbours, differentiating their culture-as-attraction while at the same time encouraging and promulgating connectedness through visitation and uni-versalism through such global applications as hotel chains, resorts, airlines, quality service standards, and so forth. All nations, all peoples, are welcome as tourists and the tourism system manipulates and manages all peoples as hosts also. The IT&T of the late twentieth century provide the medium by which this campaign may be waged in ways beyond the imagination – and capabilities – only three decades ago. The language of tourism, as Dann (1996) argues, has powerfully captured the imagining of peoples, cultures and destinations for presentation as commoditised objects for sale in the global capitalist economy.

Indonesia

Indonesia is a case in point where the government has attempted to use tourism to present ethnic and cultural differences in benign, non-threatening forms to prevent communalism from getting out of hand (Kipp, 1993). Taman Mini Indonesia (Beautiful Indonesia in Miniature), a theme park constructed just outside Jakarta by the Indonesian government in 1975, is a manifestation of this policy. Each of the 27 provinces has a representative architectural pavilion or similar, 'occupied' by different ethnic groups garbed in traditional dress. The park is aimed mainly at a domestic audience, and is promoted in Bahasa Indonesian tourism literature and school textbooks as the place to learn about all of Indonesia. Many more Indonesians than foreign tourists visit the park. It is ironic that Indonesia's largest ethnic minority, and one which has been the focus of much communal violence and unrest, is not represented in Taman Mini Indonesia – its Chinese nationals. The fissiparous tendencies in Aceh Province, East Timor and Irian Jaya attest to the contested nature of a unified and unifying national culture and identity in Indonesia.

   The development of Bali as a major tourist destination provides an example of the power of tourism as a force for both globalisation and localisation, and as an example of the role of governments in pre-determining the role of culture in that development. Initially seen as a place of recreation by the Dutch colonial govern-ment, the independent Indonesian state decided in 1971 to utilise the distinctive culture of the Balinese people with its temple-dominated village-scapes as the central theme for its tourism development. Concerned that tourism could degrade cultures and peoples, the Indonesian government employed a team of European anthropol-ogists to map those aspects of culture which could 'safely' be commercialised for tourism, and those sacred elements which were to be out-of-bounds to the tourist gaze. This separation of the sacred and profane is in fact alien to the Balinese, for whom the gods are always present whenever they dance, and who therefore draw little distinction between ceremonies and festivals which take place outside temple precincts and inside temple grounds and walls. The tourism development plan imposed on Bali from Jakarta also determined that major hotel development should be restricted to an enclave – Nusa Dua – again with the motive of protecting village communities from the invasive and adverse impacts of mass tourism in their midst. The concept was that major international hotel chains would be invited to construct five-star accommodation in this southern peninsula, and from its borders tourists would make daily excursions into the surrounding countryside to see approved sights, returning to their comfort zone every evening.

Globalisation is manifested firstly in the utilisation of foreign experts introducing what was at that time regarded as 'best global practice' in planning the development of tourism, and secondly through the involvement of multinational companies in the provision of the necessary superstructure, marketing and organisational framework. In terms of the cultural images of Bali which were disseminated to global markets, the local communities had little or no input. However localisation was also apparent. The marketing of Bali drew a very strong differentiation between Bali and Indonesia and promoted its culture and social environment as unique. All of the hotels in Nusa Dua were also constructed under strict guidelines in which traditional forms of Balinese architecture were to determine their external appearance. This extended to their landscaping which incorporated village elements and temples. The new airport at adjacent Den Pasar was also designed around the same principles. Everywhere, therefore, there is an emphasis on the material and spiritual culture of the Balinese in the physical appurtenances of tourism.

The way in which the Balinese have responded to the imposition of an 'outside' plan for tourism has been chronicled in the research of Picard and McKean, *inter alia,* both working independently in Bali over 25 years. Their findings demonstrate how the host communities have adapted to and in turn modified the tourism which has taken place within their social space. Picard (1993) has termed this 'touristic culture'. Through tourism, culture has been transformed into the main economic resource of Bali and by the same token, Balinese culture has become a major bargaining point with the central Indonesian government, tourism authorities and tourist operators (Picard, 1993:86). Over a period of eight years from 1971 to 1979, led by a group of Balinese academics, the Balinese held a series of seminars under the joint auspices of the Bali Directorate General of Culture and the Bali Directorate General of Tourism which resulted in the formulation of the 'doctrine of cultural tourism' for Bali and the signing of an agreement between the two Directorates General. This established the Balinese Commission of Cooperation for the Promotion and Development of Cultural Tourism *(Komisi Kerjasama Pembinaan dan Pengembangan Wisata Budaya)* whose chief objectives were to:

- increase and extend the use of culture for the development of tourism; and
- use the proceeds of tourism development for the promotion and development of culture.

(Picard, 1993:88).

Since Balinese tourism relies upon Balinese culture, if tourism were to destroy Balinese culture, it would destroy Balinese tourism (McKean, 1982). The result is one in which the Balinese, having been compelled to define their cultural heritage, in the process have put tourism to work for Bali rather than the Balinese necessarily working for tourism. They have been able to assert a significant measure of control over their tourism destiny through "on-going symbolic construction of tradition and authenticity" (Wood, 1993:60). They, rather than the central authorities in Jakarta, have determined what tourists may and may not see. And they have insisted, successfully, that rural communities should be permitted to benefit economically by constructing accommodation units outside Nusa Dua, rather than seeing, in their view, the lion's share of the tourist dollar accruing only to the multinational hotel chains located in Nusa Dua (and nearby Sanur Beach). There are now several hundred 'losman' (home-stay houses) and small to medium-sized hotels in many rural communities throughout Bali, owned and operated by local entrepreneurs.

The representation of culture for tourism has produced a number of iconic sites around Asia such as Angkor Wat in Cambodia and Borobodur in central Java. According to Kagami (1997:67), the Indonesian government decided to promote the ancient Buddhist temple site of Borobodur as "a cultural asset, especially in relation to the development and glorification of the Indonesian national culture". It was built in the ninth century, fell into disuse and was covered by the jungle for centuries until rediscovery by the English colonial officer, Sir Stamford Raffles, in 1814. In 1973, the Indonesian government took this specifically Javanese piece of heritage, one which is not linked to any surviving remnant Buddhist population in the area, and which is not of the majority national Muslim religion, restored it and reconstituted it as a national *Indonesian* historical monument. By allowing the celebration of the Buddhist *Waisak* festival there once each year, it has transformed the site from simply heritage tourism to "a newly invented cultural tradition" (Kagami, 1997:68). Visited by more than a million Indonesians each year (most of whom are not Buddhists), Borobodur has become an iconic element that constitutes a fusion of the authentic and the marker for both the Indonesians themselves and for international tourists. As Urry (citing Baudrillard) states: "what we increasingly consume are signs or representations...This world of sign and spectacle is one in which there is no originality, only what Eco terms 'travels in hyper-reality'" (Urry, 1990:85). However, Urry argues that sites which have been made into attractive spectacles are not necessarily inauthentic, but rather that there is no one simple "authentic reconstruction of history". Instead there are various kinds of interpretation and reinterpretation with their own validity (Urry, 1990:156). A visit to Borobodur, in whatever form, is an example of Nuryanti's (1996) "individual journey of self-discovery" coupled with, for the Indonesians, a re-affirmation of the Indonesian-ness of the participant observer.

Singapore

Singapore is another case in point with the invention, in 1972, of the 'Merlion' as a national symbol by the Singapore Tourism Board. The Merlion is half lion, half sea creature, and its likeness now appears in many prominent places around Singapore, most notably as the symbol for the Sentosa Island theme park. At Sentosa, the Merlion is portrayed as an ancient creature linked over many centuries to Singapore in myth and legend. In fact it did not exist until the marketing division of the Singapore government's tourism authority fabricated it because of the absence of a distinctive symbol which could be used in imaging Singapore as a tourist destination. The idea of the Merlion is drawn from a story about a local sultan who was shipwrecked on an island (not Sentosa) in the distant past and who was succoured by a wild creature, of which there are no depictions contemporary to that time. So a half lion/half fish was created. The word 'Merlion' is, like its physical manifestation, simply a figment of fertile tourism marketing: 'Mer' is French for 'sea', 'lion' is an English language word derived from the Latin word 'leo' and neither has any connection with indigenous languages or words. Yet, in the twentieth century, the Merlion has become so ubiquitous that one wonders if, in addition to most tourists, many of Singapore's younger generation now unthinkingly accept the presence and existence of the Merlion as portrayed by the tourism authority. This new myth has become a reality in modern Singapore and thousands of tourists pose before statues of the Merlion for photographs as proof of its existence and their visit to Singapore.

At Sentosa Island near to the Merlion is another example of recreated heritage, the Asian Village, which showcases ethnic foods, arts and crafts from around the region. In the Village, spatial dimensions have been collapsed and geographical boundaries as physical entities dispensed with in pursuit of differentiation. Thus one can visit Sentosa and experience Malaysian, Thai, Indonesian, Filipino, Indian and various ethnic Chinese cuisines (a case of manufactured differentiation) without having to visit Malaysia, Thailand, the Philippines, India or China. In the social and sociological sense, the preparation and consumption of food are acts of both national identification and self-identification. They are "a significant part of the differential definition of social groups and individuals" and are in one sense "an act of pure existential authenticity" (Friedman, 1995:314).

As visitors enjoy 'authentic oriental' meals they may gaze out over an artificial tropical lagoon (complete with imported white sand beach and fully-grown transplanted coconut palms). Behind the Asian food court they may perceive a formal European palace garden (along the style of the gardens in the French Palace at Versailles with fountains, statues and topiary) accompanied by a musical fountain and coloured lights, and one wonders where is Alice in Wonderland's looking glass? The global and local have become de-differentiated spatially in artful and artificial reconstruction of imagery and playful postmodernity in Sentosa, co-existing side by side with each other. To put it another way, because of the postmodern processes of globalisation we have "the partial erosion of spatially bounded social worlds and the growing role of the imagination of places from a distance" (Gupta and Ferguson, 1997:39).

Discussion

Efforts to interpret cultural and related differences are necessarily problematic because they incorporate an evaluation of 'otherness'. In so doing, in the overwhelming mass of tourism literature, there is little examination of self in determining that 'otherness', so that we have an unthinking, derived, Western, metropolitan, colonialist domination of the imagery and production of culture for tourism. In one sense, there is nothing particularly new in this; Said said much of it very clearly in his seminal work on Western representations of Orientalism in 1978 (although he was not referring to tourism in this context). Lanfant (1995) was more explicit when she commented that the construction and reconstruction of identities by and for tourism produce conflict, illusion and paradox, where the tourist objects (the primitive, exotic, and/or colourful locals) are required by the tourism industry (for which read Western, capitalist, colonialist, dominant, elitist interests) to 'preserve' an authenticity that never existed. As Hollinshead (1998) has noted, in all of this it is useful to recall the contrary words of Lanfant (1995:3–6) that tourism can be an instrument for *establishing* identities and for assisting emergent minorities (her "marginalized ethno-regional movements/groups") to gain recognition on the international stage. In short, tourism is not inherently destructive of the local even if it is totally integrated into globalisation.

Dann (1996:n.p.) on the contrary believes that tourism can inflict

all sorts of iconological violence on things through its discourse [the "sociolinguistics of tourism"], particularly through its ingrained ethnocentric styles and its form of representation. In the process it can turn other people into objects through the projection of its storylines because the very Western discourse of the industry acts as spectator, judge and jury over the topic it narrates.

This is particularly so because of the way in which the tourism system encapsulates the pre-booked package traveller, limiting contact with the people of the host communities and thereby restricting these travellers to a reliance for knowledge upon the loaded narrative provided by the travel-trade organisers of their tour. In effect, they willingly surrender themselves to the myth-making practices and culture-producing orientations of the business side of the tourism system. The independent traveller has a much better prospect of 'escaping' from this smothering embrace. Bhabha (1994:5) noted that "all representations of culture – that is, each and every projection and delineation of race/ethnicity/nationhood – are saturated with power, and that such representations of culture should increasingly be seen to be historically constituted depictions rather than being ontologically given accounts". Tunbridge and Ashworth (1996:3) similarly argue that in the context of tourism's interpretation of heritage, history is "adroitly utilised as a political tool or as a moral precedent", echoing the sentiment expressed by Richter (1989) almost a decade earlier in her analysis of the politics of tourism in Asia. As Kahn (1995:57) concluded, stereotyping via ethnocentric practice and Western discourse is "as virulent in tourism under the postmodern/post-colonial predicament as they have been found to be almost everywhere else during the so-called enlightenment of modernity".

Hollinshead has his own term for the powerful involvement of the tourism system in manufacturing, controlling and directing representations and interpretation of heritage for tourism – "fantasmatics":

This immense imaginary power to invent iconic traditions afresh or to manufacture felt authenticities amounts to the "fantasmatics" of global tourism image-making, rhetoric mongering, and discourse articulations, *viz.* the very craft [after Said, 1978:94] by which not only knowledge but life-style and life-space is created...Thus tourism...has a vast organic role in the making of peoples, in the manufacture of places, and in the manipulation of pasts.

(Hollinshead, 1998:75)

This process of global touristic managing and manufacturing may be described as "the scopic drive of the tourism system", the particular direction and force of a group's vision (in this case the marketing agents of tourism) "as orchestrated by its gaze on and over the world" (Hollinshead, 1998:74). In this context, Urry's (1990) notion of 'the tourist gaze' draws an analogy with Foucault's concept of the gaze, and argues that for tourists there are systematic ways of 'seeing', a universalisation of their gaze. Urry (1990:1) notes that "there is no single tourist gaze as such, (that) it varies by society, by social group and by historical period (and that) such gazes are constructed through difference". There is, however, a universalism brought about by the way in which these gazes are all constructed through contrast "with non-tourist social practices, particularly those based within the home and paid work" (Urry, 1990:2). Thus the touristic images of Southeast Asia are all cast in the same mould, connected by an emphasis on leisure and recreation.

The specific process by which the scopic drive of tourism has emerged is through the projection of difference. As Hollinshead (1998) has stated, tourism is essentially and fundamentally the industry of *difference*: it is at once both a leisure activity and the world's largest business. In its marketing endeavours, it is constantly striving to differentiate one destination from another, one product from another, one experience from another – to create *difference,* in other words (Dann, 1998). According to Urry (1990:3), the anticipating tourist ventures forth in pursuit of fulfilment of dreams and fantasy, achieving pleasure "on a *different* scale or involving *different* senses from those customarily encountered" (my emphasis). In Hollinshead's (1998:52) view, it is through the

projection of difference that tourism has acquired an extremely significant role in the representation of the national, cultural and ethnic character of peoples, places, and [their] pasts...These newly recognized projective architectural powers of tourism and these newly identified inventive morphological effects of international tourism [have resulted in] the invention, re-invention and de-invention of difference.

While the Southeast Asian states have a joint marketing agency and the ASEAN Tourism Council based in Kuala Lumpur combine some marketing efforts on a regional basis, for the most part, each country focuses on imaging its *differences.* Thus Sarawak advertises the authenticity of its Iban longhouses, Bali promotes the richness of its religious and cultural heritage, Thailand portrays its Buddhist temples, Singapore blends its cosmopolitan air with its fabled Merlion, and the Philippines accentuates ecotourism and its pristine beaches. Interconnection is, however, never far away, bound up in the combined image of all of these countries as part of 'the beautiful, culturally rich Orient'.

Conclusions

In the foregoing sections we examined first the process of globalisation and the multi-faceted contribution which tourism is making to that process. Second, since globalisation is concerned with both the universalisation *and* localisation of culture, we then explored the way in which the tourism system has asserted a very influential role for itself in creating representations of difference, a constructural powerhouse of design and fabrication with jurisdiction over places, spaces and peoples. We have a system which is global in its reach, both in terms of (i) all the supports it constructs – physical, social, economic, cultural – for the business of looking after the welfare and interests its client, the tourist; and (ii) its voracious appetite for utilising and consuming other global systems such as information technology and telecommunications, international transport and international financial services, amongst others. In being a major player in globalisation, tourism also strives to advance localism because destination differentiation and product distinction is essential to its capacity to be able to provide a continuing and continuous stream of different experiences globally.

As tourism is simultaneously a contributor to and part of the process of globalisation, it contributes to the interconnectedness of peoples and cultures, and in the context of the countries of Southeast Asia, has been a fundamental agent in opening these countries to visitors from neighbouring states. Both hosts and guests are defined in part by "those powerful and entwined forces of international consumer aesthetics as they observe and as they are observed by others" (Hollinshead, 1998:71).

Because of the paradigm shift in anthropological studies in the past two decades, with new understandings which question the integrity of 'culture-and-place', the notion of interconnectedness and the unpackaging of 'place + people = culture' is more strongly supported. In this chapter, I have argued that the tourism system is a very powerful force which both supports that notion and contests it. As stated previously, tourism commonly strives to highlight difference, aggressively re-imaging, reconstituting and appropriating heritage, culture and place, pursuing localisation in marked contrast to its globalising influence. To paraphrase Robertson (1991:74), we are witnesses to and participants in a massive two-fold process involving the interpenetration of the universalisation of particularisation and the particularisation of universalisation. The challenge for anthropology is not to shy away from tourism as a legitimate area of research but to explore this paradigm shift to help us better understand the complexities of the tourism system and its role in globalisation/localisation and the interconnectedness between states.

References

Bhabha, H. (1994) *The Location of Culture*. London: Routledge.
Bourdieu, P. (1977) *Outline of a Theory of Practice*, tr. R. Nice. Cambridge: Cambridge University Press.
Clifford, J. (1988) *The Predicament of Culture: Twentieth Century Ethnography, Literature and Art*. Cambridge: Harvard University Press.
Dann, G. (1996) *The Language of Tourism: A Sociolinguistic Perspective*. Wallingford: CAB International.
Dann, G. (1998) 'The pomo promo of tourism'. *Tourism, Culture and Communications*, 1(1), 1–16.
de Certeau, M. (1984) *The Practice of Everyday Life*, tr. S.Randall. Berkeley: University of California Press.
Derrida, J. (1978) *Writing and Difference*. London: Routledge.
Din, K.H. (1997) 'Tourism and cultural development in Malaysia: Issues for a new agenda', in S. Yamashita, K.H. Din and J.S. Eades (eds.) *Tourism and Cultural Development in Asia and Oceania*. Selangor: Penerbit Universiti Kebangsaan Malaysia, 104–18.

Featherstone, M. (1995a) *Undoing Culture: Globalisation, Postmodernism and Identity*. London: Sage Publications.

Featherstone, M. (ed.) (1995b) *Nationalism, Globalisation and Modernity*. London: Sage Publications.

Foucault, M. (1978) *The History of Sexuality, Volume 1, An Introduction*, tr. R. Hurley. New York: Random House.

Foucault, M. (1980) *Power/Knowledge. Selected Interviews and Other Writings, 1972–1977, Michel Foucault*, tr. C. Gordon; C. Gordon (ed.). New York: Pantheon.

Friedman, J. (1995) 'Being in the world: Globalisation and localisation', in M. Featherstone (ed.) *Nationalism, Globalisation and Modernity*. London: Sage Publications, 311–18.

Gellner, E. (1983) *Nations and Nationalism*. Ithaca: Cornell University Press.

Graburn, N.H.H. (1997) 'Tourism and cultural development in East Asia', in S. Yamashita, K. H. Din and J.S. Eades (eds.) *Tourism and Cultural Development in Asia and Oceania*. Selangor: Penerbit Universiti Kebangsaan Malaysia, 194–213.

Gupta, A. and Ferguson, J. (eds.) (1997) *Culture, Power, Place: Explorations in Critical Anthropology*. Durham and London: Duke University Press.

Hollinshead, K. (1998) 'Tourism and the restless people'. *Tourism, Culture and Communication*, 1(1), 49–78.

Jameson, F. (1986) 'Third World literature in the era of multinational capitalism'. *Social Text*, Fall, 69–79.

Jaspen, M.A. (1964) *From Patriliny to Matriliny: Structural Change among the Redjang of Southwest Sumatra*. Canberra: Australian National University.

Kagami, H. (1997) 'Tourism and national culture: Indonesian policies on cultural heritage and its utilisation in tourism', in S. Yamashita, K.H. Din and J.S. Eades (eds.) *Tourism and Cultural Development in Asia and Oceania*. Selangor: Penerbit Universiti Kebangsaan Malaysia, 61–82.

Kahn, J.S. (1995) *Culture, Multiculture, Post-culture*. London: Sage.

Kahn, J. S. (1997) 'Culturalizing Malaysia: Globalism, tourism, heritage and the city in Georgetown', in M. Picard and R.E. Wood (eds.) *Tourism, Ethnicity, and the State in Asian and Pacific Societies*. Honolulu: University of Hawaii Press, 99–127.

King, A. (ed.) (1991) *Culture, Globalisation and the World-System: Contemporary Conditions for the Representation of Identity*. London: Macmillan.

Kipp, R. (1993) *Disassociated Identities: Ethnicity, Religion and Class in an Indonesian Society*. Ann Arbor: University of Michigan Press.

Lanfant, M.F. (1995) 'Introduction', in M.F. Lanfant, J.B. Alcock and E.M. Bruner (eds.) *International Tourism: Identity and Change*. London: Sage Publications, 1–23.

Leong, W.T. (1989) 'Culture and the state: Manufacturing traditions for tourism'. *Critical Studies in Mass Communication*, 6, 355–75.

Leong, W.T. (1997) 'Commodifiying ethnicity: State and ethnic tourism in Singapore', in M. Picard and R.E. Wood (eds.) *Tourism, Ethnicity, and the State in Asian and Pacific Societies*. Honolulu: University of Hawaii Press, 71–98.

Malinowski, B. (1922) *Argonauts of the Western Pacific: An Account of Native Enterprise and Adventure in the Archipelagos of Melanesian New Guinea*. London: Routledge.

Malkki, L.H. (1996) 'National Geographic: The rooting of peoples and the territorialisation of national identity among scholars and refugees', in A. Gupta and J. Ferguson (eds.) *Culture, Power, Place: Explorations in Critical Anthropology*. Durham and London: Duke University Press, 52–74.

McKean, P. (1982) 'Tourists and Balinese'. *Cultural Survival Quarterly*, 6(3), 32–3.

Nuryanti, W. (1996) 'Heritage and postmodern tourism'. *Annals of Tourism Research*, 23(2), 249–60.

Peters, J.D. (1997) 'Seeing bifocally: Media, place, culture', in A. Gupta and J. Ferguson (eds.) *Culture, Power, Place: Explorations in Critical Anthropology*. Durham and London: Duke University Press, 75–92.

Picard, M. (1993) 'Cultural tourism in Bali: National integration and regional differentiation', in M. Hitchcock, V.T. King and M.J.G. Parnwell (eds.) *Tourism in South-East Asia*. London: Routledge, 71–98.

Picard, M. (1997) 'Cultural tourism, nation-building and regional culture: The making of a Balinese identity', in M. Picard and R. E. Wood (eds.) *Tourism, Ethnicity, and the State in Asian and Pacific Societies*. Honolulu: University of Hawaii Press, 181–214.

Richter, L.K. (1989) *The Politics of Tourism in Asia*. Honolulu: University of Hawaii Press.

Richter, L.K. (1999) 'The politics of heritage tourism development', in D. Pearce and R. Butler (eds.) *Contemporary Issues in Tourism Development*. London: Routledge, 108–26.

Robertson, R. (1991) 'Social theory, cultural relativity and the problem of globality', in A. King (ed.) *Culture, Globalisation and the World-System: Contemporary Conditions for the Representation of Identity*. London: Macmillan, 69–90.

Rojek, C. (1995) *Decentring Leisure*. London: Sage Publications.

Said, E.W. (1978) *Orientalism*. New York: Pantheon.

Sofield, T.H.B. and Li, F.M.S. (1998) 'China: Tourism development and cultural policies'. *Annals of Tourism Research*, 25(2), 362–92.

Tunbridge, J. E. and Ashworth, G.J. (1996) *Dissonant Heritage: The Management of the Past as a Resource in Conflict*. Chichester: Wiley.

Urry, J. (1990) *The Tourist Gaze: Leisure and Travel in Contemporary Societies*. London: Sage Publications.

Wallerstein, I. (1984) *The Politics of the World Economy*. Cambridge: Cambridge University Press.

Wallerstein, I. (1990) 'Culture as the ideological battleground of the modern world-system', in M. Featherstone (ed.) *Global Culture. Nationalism, Globalisation and Modernity*. London: Sage Publications, 31–56.

Wood, R.E. (1993) 'Tourism, culture and the sociology of development', in M. Hitchcock, V.T. King and M.J.G. Parnwell (eds.) *Tourism in South-East Asia*. London: Routledge, 48–70.

Wood, R.E. (1997) 'Tourism and the state: Ethnic options and constructions of otherness', in M. Picard and R. E. Wood (eds.) *Tourism, Ethnicity, and the State in Asian and Pacific Societies*. Honolulu: University of Hawaii Press, 1–34.

Yamashita, S. (1997) 'Manipulating ethnic tradition: The funerals ceremony, tourism and television among the Toraja of Sulawesi, Indonesia', in S. Yamashita, K.H. Din and J.S. Eades (eds.) *Tourism and Cultural Development in Asia and Oceania*. Selangor: Penerbit Universiti Kebangsaan Malaysia, 83–102.

Zeppel, H. (1997) 'Meeting "wild people": Iban culture and longhouse tourism in Sarawak', in S. Yamashita, K.H. Din and J.S. Eades (eds.) *Tourism and Cultural Development in Asia and Oceania*. Selangor: Penerbit Universiti Kebangsaan Malaysia, 119–40.

8

Global–Local Inter-relationships in UNESCO World Heritage Sites

Heather Black and Geoffrey Wall

Introduction

There is an ongoing struggle with the search for balance between tourism, conservation, authenticity and economic development. In the quest for balance, considerable tension in global–local relationships emerges when hosts and guests meet. Perhaps nowhere else is this tension more pronounced than when an international organisation becomes directly involved in the selection, conservation and presentation of a heritage which not only has to be defined at international and national levels, but which has a different meaning, value and expression at the local level.

This chapter is based on a study that assessed master plans developed for the management of highly significant cultural heritage sites.[1] The study set out to uncover the extent to which these plans addressed the needs and involvement of local inhabitants. Three United Nations Educational, Scientific and Cultural Organisation (UNESCO) World Cultural Heritage Sites – all religious monument sites and all historical parks[2] – were compared: Ayutthaya in Thailand and Borobudur and Prambanan in Indonesia. These international and intra-national comparisons sought to uncover the factors at work in the successful implementation of the master plans and the long-term repercussions of the planning process on the communities living adjacent to the heritage sites.

In the process of conducting the research, a theme began to emerge, which is that the values which local people attach to a heritage are different from, though no less important than, the values ascribed to it by art historians, archaeologists and government officials. These values, which have the potential to enhance the interpretation of the monuments and in fact make them more relevant to domestic and international visitors alike, are often ignored. If the meaning of a site is to be defined largely by experts who come from other places, what is lost in the process?

This chapter begins with a brief examination of planning approaches in general and how they come into play where community development, tourism and heritage conservation are concerned. The rationale for heritage conservation and the process of historical park planning, development and management are examined. Then, the case studies are introduced with descriptions of what happens to the people, neighbourhoods, monuments and landscapes when master plans are implemented on a large scale. Finally, some examples are used in the search for interconnections between community values and internationally defined classical forms of cultural expression.

Planning approaches

Planning practice has been dominated by what is known as the 'synoptic planning approach' (Hudson, 1979; Friedmann, 1987). The process relies on the idea that the technical or scientific input from experts will permit the anticipation, evaluation and informed selection from all of the possible actions and their consequences. However, upon review of past planning fiascos, there has been a growing recognition that no person or team is capable of predicting all outcomes of a particular action: "The world changes, and so will the problems planners face" (Dobbing, 1988:2). Many people involved in planning are beginning to think that planning has more to do with managing change than it does with plan crafting and implementation.

From this recognition, several counterpoint schools of planning theory have emerged since the 1960s, most of which take their point of departure from the limitations of the synoptic approach. Space does not permit a full examination of this critique here. Often a mixture of several approaches is used, the flavour of the blend depending largely on the concept of public participation, with the rationale being that through participatory planning, a more responsible, workable basis for planning and the implementation of the plans will be possible.

In the context of using tourism as a vehicle for sustainable development, for example, alternatives to the usual ways in which planning is done are called for. Those engaged in the planning and management of rural development projects are coming to realise that a participatory, stakeholder-driven process at the planning stage is a prerequisite to the success and sustainability of the project. A project's implementation is likely to be more successful, especially in terms of its socio-economic aims, if local participation is enlisted during project planning and implementation (Chambers, 1983; Kottack, 1991; Uphoff, 1991). Second, a higher degree of self-reliance is expected from the stakeholder group (Uphoff, 1991). Third, applying these experiences to tourism management, if community-centred projects encourage tourists to stay longer and/or to spend more money, the economic benefits hoped for by local communities and by governments on all levels are more likely to be forthcoming.

Historic conservation

Rationale and approaches

Before European influences began to hold sway in Asia, historical conservation focused on the maintenance of existing buildings. In 1964, the Venice Charter encouraged nations to conserve the "urban and rural settings in which was found the evidence of a particular civilisation" (International Council of Monuments and Sites (ICOMOS), 1964:n.p.). Many countries have now adopted recommendations made at international conventions and conferences, and grants and loans have been offered by international organisations. Developing countries, where conservation expertise and financial support are limited, are most dependent on international collaboration and assistance.

There is some tension involved in the rationale for and ways in which heritage is protected. The conservation of heritage might be an advantage from the perspective of tourists, tourism promoters, scholars and government administrators. However, as the values and motivations involved are largely imported, the mustering of support and involvement in such endeavours by small, local communities living in the vicinity of the sites are likely to entail more than the recognition of the site as historically significant.

Decisions concerning what is worth keeping are made at the top levels of government and dropped on the people who live near the site. Likewise, international organisations that seek to protect exceptional natural and cultural spaces take stewardship – and therefore, in some sense, ownership – of a heritage seriously because it is now shared by humankind (Peleggi, 1996). Cultural heritage site planning then is firmly rooted in the synoptic planning tradition.

The role of heritage in national ideology

While the costly conservation of these sites is motivated, in part, by an interest in preserving the artistic and architectural record of the past, governments are also anxious to preserve historical sites in order to gain economic benefits through the attraction of tourists. Furthermore, the sites selected to represent the country's heritage will also have strong implications for both collective and individual identity and hence the creation of social realities (Hall, 1994:180). In other words, some would argue that the architectural features are being reconstructed right along with the past itself.

What Blacking (1987) refers to as the "reinvention of tradition"[3] has been utilised by both Indonesian and Thai governments in promoting the symbolism of monuments as a source of political legitimacy and in the fostering of national unity. In modernising countries, the ruling class requires the creation of an often-mythological 'glorious past' which existed prior to the arrival of colonisers or other foreign influences (Evans-Pritchard, 1993:24). As Evans-Pritchard (1993:25) states, "[m]ost of the significant archaeological sites in the world that are major tourism destinations are now state-owned and operated: They are *national* monuments that present distinctive images of a country's history and culture to the outside world." In this way, she argues, archaeology has been instrumental in structuring national ideology which uses ancient symbols to create a tourism industry. National ideology has transferred the motifs of the adopted past onto everyday articles, such as banknotes. In Indonesia, a representation of the Buddhist monument of Borobudur graces the currency of a predominantly Muslim country where Buddhism as a religion barely exists. Evans-Pritchard (1993:25) goes on to suggest that by the time mass tourism arrived, the nation's psyche had already actively incorporated ancient symbols into its worldview. Preparing the local population in this way is also likely to have far-reaching effects on the promotion of the site as a domestic tourist attraction.

World Heritage

Apart from state agencies that have their own agendas, when it comes to highly significant heritage resources, international organisations impose their own mandate on local communities, all in the name of conservation. Perhaps the best known international agency that works to foster the conservation of heritage is UNESCO. At the 1972 UNESCO General Conference, the member states of UNESCO adopted the 'World Heritage Convention'. Under the terms of the Convention, a 'World Heritage List' was to be compiled which would recognise cultural and natural properties 'of outstanding universal value' from nominations submitted by the national governments of member countries. With the idea that the world's heritage transcends national boundaries and should be preserved for future generations, the Convention provides for an administrative structure, funding, inventories, technical and emergency assistance and world-wide promotion of heritage conservation. A site's acceptance to the World Heritage List signifies that it meets Convention criteria and that it is assured of adequate protection.

Historical park planning and management

The World Heritage Convention contributed significantly to the linking of what had traditionally been regarded as two different and often opposing interests: cultural environment and natural environment (ICOMOS, 1986). The notions previously used to establish natural parks would now be used to establish historical or archaeological parks.

At about the same time that the decision is made by the national government to protect significant cultural remains according to an historical park model, a master plan or management plan is usually drafted. Such a plan must be approved by the national government to ensure legislative support for the protection of the site. Once these steps have been taken, the government might then put the historical park forward as a candidate for the World Heritage List.

The process of creating an historical park generally involves the removal of existing people and houses surrounding the monumental remains; restoring the ruins; possibly erecting a fence around the site; landscaping the grounds inside the fence or designated park area; creating a parking lot and tourist facilities; building souvenir and refreshment kiosks and renting them out to vendors; and charging an admission at the gate. The historical remains are presented in their newly created, park-like setting to an admiring public and to foreign visitors.

UNESCO's recommendations for the safeguarding of sites focus on countering "the threats of modern life to landscapes and sites" (UNESCO, 1983:125) and call for "control over operations and activities liable to impair them" (UNESCO, 1983:125). Hand in hand with these concerns is the need for legislation and the power to enforce it. At the same time, UNESCO addresses the need for the 'education' of the inhabitants, presumably so that they will cooperate with the preservation mandate. References to economic pursuits, which are inevitable with restoration, promotion and subsequent tourism, have been limited to the need to control and limit such activities. Furthermore, conservation advocates must also grapple with the idea that while the intent of a World Heritage designation is to further a site's protection, the consequent and inescapable attraction of more tourists can contribute to its demise.

Heritage, tourism and economic development

Southeast Asia is rich in cultural heritage resources, the preservation and presentation of which attract much international attention. However, even in the region's rapidly industrialising countries, there is a conspicuous gap between the wealth generated by and for relatively few urbanites and the urban poor and rural population who fall well short of being able to meet basic needs for food, shelter and education. The same gap tends to exist between the few who are able to cash in on the revenue generated by tourism and the many who are unable to do so. Therefore, the serious deterioration of the built heritage must be immediately confronted but, at the same time, there is a need to attend to the integration of community development into the management of these sites.

Throughout the world, heritage and tourism have become inextricably linked (Hall, 1994:180). Tourism is used as a way to justify, economically, the preservation of heritage (Wojino, 1991; Peters, 1995). There is also the potential for financial benefit and for nation-building. The higher the profile of a monument, the more salient these possibilities become.

Once there is a realisation that historical features have the potential to bring about financial advantages, local people tend to become more enthusiastic about preserving them (Cohen, 1978; Soemarwoto, 1992). Given this argument, local involvement would serve to foster a sense of co-ownership of the historical sites by the community and there would be more of a sense of stewardship amongst residents. There are, however, also examples of cases where nearby residents have a very profound relationship with the historic features even before those features attracted wider attention. Sometimes, this relationship is due to a cultural and religious continuity with the original builders. Significantly however, as we shall see, such continuity is not a prerequisite to the affinity which community members might feel towards the historic remains.

Case studies: context

In the early part of the first millennium, the arrival of Indian merchants and missionaries in the Southeast Asian region had repercussions in what are now Java and Thailand, resulting in the creation of religious monuments, the likes of which have not been seen before or since in either place. In Thailand, Buddhism, with a bit of Hinduism mixed into it, would continue in one form or another until today. In Java, the Hindu-Buddhist ruling houses would be pushed out of the area until eventually Hinduism was practised only on the neighbouring island of Bali and, to a lesser extent, in Lombok. By the fifteenth and sixteenth centuries, Javanese rulers began to favour Islam. As a result, the existing Buddhist, Hindu and animist practices were overlaid with Islam, producing the vernacular religions which characterise much of Indonesia today. In both Thailand and Indonesia, complex pre-Hindu/Buddhist, pre-Islamic ancestor worship and animist beliefs continue unofficially, alongside mainstream religions. At the village and the household levels, for example, there is a tendency to take measures to appease potentially malevolent spirits and to ask for protection from others.

Today, Indonesia is a very culturally diverse area while Thailand is relatively homogeneous. In addition, most Thais adhere to the same religious doctrine which the builders of the monuments had revered whereas the Javanese do not. In Java, even 1,000 years ago when the monuments were constructed, neither Hinduism nor Buddhism were religions of the common people; rather, they appear to have been court religions.

The ways in which the two countries promote this cultural heritage as evidence of a 'glorious past' and as objects of shared national identity are actually quite similar. Both governments have advanced other aims such as education, international prestige and economic gain through tourism. Likewise, the reasons for needing to protect the sites were also similar. The decisions that were made to protect the monuments stemmed from the same urgent concerns: the encroachment of modern development; the tendency of people to re-use ancient building materials; and vandals.

Thailand is considered to be more 'developed' than Indonesia in terms of measures such as gross national product, per capita income, electrification, industrialisation and so on. Both countries are paying the price of entry into the global market through rapid resource exploitation and industrial development. Declining environmental quality, tremendous core-periphery problems, migration of the rural poor into urban centres, ever-widening income gaps between rich and poor, and corruption at every level of government plague (but are not limited to) the developing world. Thailand and Indonesia are no exceptions.

In both countries, about 70 per cent of the population are engaged in agriculture. Both can grow enough rice to feed their own people, with Thailand enjoying a surplus which is exported. Indonesia is a member of OPEC. Both countries have increasingly come to depend on tourism economically, with Thailand relying on it even more heavily than Indonesia. The growth of the middle class in both Indonesia and Thailand and a rise in their expendable incomes has meant more domestic tourism.

All three study sites were planned and developed and are managed and administrated at the national level. In Thailand, the Archaeology Division of the Fine Arts Department is directly responsible for all of the activities and policies concerning the historical parks. In Indonesia, a public company called P.T. Taman Wisata (Tourist Park Inc.) administers the parks and maintains the grounds, leaving only the scientific work of preserving and restoring the actual monuments to the Archaeology Department.

Indonesian sites

The Borobudur and Prambanan Districts are home to some of the most magnificent stone monuments in the world. Borobudur and Prambanan archaeological parks (Figures 8.1 and 8.2), where the most remarkable of these monuments can be visited, are situated approximately one hour apart by road. Hundreds of thousands of tourists flock to these sites each year to trudge up the ancient steps, admiring beautifully executed sculptures and the stories being told in the reliefs. Fenced, spacious, landscaped grounds encompass the colossal stone monuments. Beyond the fences, people go about their everyday lives in villages clustered around the parks. The Master Plans for these sites were drafted in 1974 and were implemented over the following decade.

Figure 8.1 Borobudur
Copyright: Victor R. Savage

Figure 8.2 Prambanan
Copyright: Victor R. Savage

Prambanan–Borobudur plan. In 1973, at Indonesia's request, the Japan International Cooperation Agency (JICA) began the surveys which would culminate in a Master Plan for the construction of Borobudur and Prambanan Archaeological Parks. The Master Plan covered the following aspects:

- legal issues (protection legislation, procedures etc.);
- administration (implementation agency, budget etc.);
- social (village reorganisation, employment etc.);
- land use; and
- primary goals (i.e. tourism, nation-building etc.).

Prambanan–Borobudur plan implementation. The Master Plan, which was drafted without the residents' knowledge, was implemented first at Borobudur and then at Prambanan. The land used to create the parks was expropriated from the people who owned it and/or lived there. The people were offered places in new settlement areas instead, outside of but near the parks. The resettlement areas were laid out with public facilities and infrastructure already installed. The local residents had previously provided goods and services to tourists, using their nearby homes as shop-fronts. When their homes were moved elsewhere, these vendors had the first option to rent a kiosk inside the park. The kiosks are identical to one another and are situated at the periphery of the parking lot.

Overall, aspects of the Master Plan which concerned the fenced areas have been successfully implemented. The monuments are well protected, conservation efforts are ongoing and visitor numbers have increased considerably. A walk through nearby neighbourhoods, however, reveals that the same cannot be said for areas outside the parks. Many factors affect the successful implementation of the Master Plan, such as: the difference in number of visitors to the respective sites (and therefore, the number of vendors who depend directly on tourism for their livelihoods[4]); lessons learnt from the first and most difficult moves and whether they have been applied to subsequent actions; and people's acceptance of the changes which the park's development would bring. The early experiences of residents, and the relationship established between the residents and the government as a result of those experiences, have also emerged as highly significant factors in the success of the implementation of the Master Plan outside the areas surrounding the parks.

In Borobudur, more so than in Prambanan, the relationship between residents and government officials was adversarial, tense and sometimes violent. This hostile relationship stems from the lack of trust between the two groups. For example, there is a great deal of tension over people's ties with the monument and with the land around it. Although one of the social objectives identified in the Master Plan is to preserve the people's ties with the land, this has not been possible. Residents who have been relocated feel that even a shift of 500 metres away from the monument weakens their connections to it. A resident further observed, "Now there is a fence around the temple. It is not our temple any more. Taman Wisata put a fence around it to keep us out." In Prambanan, when asked about their feelings towards the fence, one resident summed up the feelings of others by saying, "Taman Wisata bought it. It is normal to put a fence around something which is yours." Indeed people are losing their 'ties to the land' as their access to the monuments is now checked. This loss appears to be somewhat more poignant for the residents at Borobudur than the people in Prambanan. Apart from sentimental ties, forced relocations also weakened the people's economic links to the monuments. One reason why many opposed the shift was the reduced economic opportunities which residents would enjoy with their customers – the tourists.

Thai site

The City of Ayutthaya is a modern town of 60,000 people with a historical park. This park – the Ayutthaya Historical Park – sits on an 8.5 sq km 'island' in the middle of the city, surrounded by a ring of rivers and canals. Altogether, there are about 200 historically significant sites, some located on this city island and some outside it. The highest concentration of these historical remains is situated in the park area as are picturesque temples, monasteries and royal palaces. The green buffer zones of the park are interrupted by roads, houses, a factory and government buildings and by undeveloped tracts of land. Outside the park area, there are more densely populated neighbourhoods, temples, busy streets, shops and other businesses. There are additional ancient ruins here, a few of which are preserved and presented in their landscaped settings. However, others are more or less squashed between new buildings and roads with modern developments threatening to squeeze them out altogether. The entire island, both the historical park and the modern town within the island, has recently been added to the UNESCO World Heritage List.

Ayutthaya Master Plan. The sites within the borders of the park, established in 1982 and managed according to the 1993 Master Plan, are protected for the most part, while those outside it are protected in the legal sense but their ever-worsening condition is an ongoing concern. Many of the sites continue to deteriorate largely, but not exclusively, outside the park area due to modern development.

Similar to what was drafted for the Indonesian sites, the objectives of the Ayutthaya Historic City Master Plan are to preserve and develop the protected zone; to conserve the ruins; to develop the infrastructure; to improve the environment and atmosphere; to support education and tourism; and to support the communities in the protected area.

Ayutthaya plan feasibility. At the time of the study, the implementation of the Master Plan was underway. Therefore, it is not possible to assess whether its aims have been accomplished. Instead, some possible barriers to and opportunities for implementation are discussed.

Many of the decisions made, especially concerning overall community reorganisation and time lines, were made for political reasons. Before Ayutthaya, planners of historical parks in Thailand had taken the same approach as in Indonesia: move all of the people away from the monument, erect a fence, and find another place for the people to live. The gradual democratising forces at work in the political system in Thailand have made the government more reluctant to displace people. This is because public outcry, which frequently ensues when communities are uprooted, rarely bodes well for the government's popularity. Therefore, only people who are living on land which has been leased to them by the government and those homes situated very near to the historical sites, would be moved. In its haste to demonstrate tangible results more quickly to the public and in the hope of attracting more tourists, the Cabinet made amendments to the schedule so that the plan would move along more quickly. This very haste threatens to compromise the integrity of the archaeological research and architectural restoration (Peters, 1995).

In terms of land-use control and associated monument conservation, residents in the core protected area more or less recognise the right of the Fine Arts Department to control the government-owned land.[5] In the modern part of the town which lies outside the park area, however, the Fine Arts Department does not have the jurisdiction it has inside the park. Furthermore, a smaller proportion of the population there participates directly in the tourism economy. Businesses and residents will be expected to follow a new set of more stringent regulations. Other additional inconveniences, such as the re-routing of traffic, will inevitably make the residents wonder if living in what might come to be perceived as a 'tourist town' is really worth the trouble.

The 'blueprint' approach to historical conservation in which beautifully manicured lawns surround the ruins in a park-like setting will not augur well for the community as a whole. The interventions mandated in the Master Plan which will have a direct impact on residents are likely to be met with varying degrees of acceptance and resistance according to whether an individual has needs which are met by tourism. It appears that if the Fine Arts Department is to accomplish its goal of an overall conservation plan, in an harmonious atmosphere where old and new can co-exist, they need the support of the larger community.

Discussion: heritage from top-down

The Thai and Indonesian governments have gone about protecting the sites in somewhat different ways although the overall approach has been quite similar. The planners felt that the needs of the community were being incorporated into the plans but rather than consulting with community members, the planners tried to anticipate what those needs would be. This approach creates gaps rather than connections. There is a need to identify such gaps which, if filled, have the potential to bring groups into a more cooperative relationship. The challenges are many. They include, but are certainly not limited to, inadequate lines of communication; the failure of administrators to realise that they do not know what is best for the people affected by the plans; and the failure of those charged with coordinating the implementation of the plans to find creative and financially beneficial ways for local people to contribute to the sites. Smith (1985:142) illustrates this point by stating:

In Third World societies, the cleavages are great and the policies are devised by the educated, upper class urbanites for application on rural, uneducated, lower class, poor people. As such, many development policies are not designed by the people they are supposed to benefit, nor is there consultation; thus, policies and programmes may be very inappropriate.

In addition to decisions about land-use control and 'community improvements', both governments also consider it part of the national mandate to decide what heritage to conserve, how to define and present it, and the role that local people should play in the enhancement of this classical cultural display.

   At Borobudur, for example, the government seriously underestimated the sacred value placed on the monument by the people who lived near it. The assumption was that since the people are officially Moslem, the ancient Buddhist monument would have no spiritual value for them. This assumption was most certainly mistaken, for indeed, the people who lived near the monument valued it as a sacred place, believing that as long as they lived there, it would protect them. It is possible to discern that a very similar, expert-driven, top-down 'blueprint approach' is used in the planning of these sites with participation from local residents being practically non-existent.

Participation

The Indonesian and Thai governments gave authority to the agencies implementing the plans once they had been approved. Involving the local people in any way in the decision-making process is not officially necessary. Why then would it be in the interests of those agencies to include them? Governments stand to gain in a number of ways. First of all, projects are more successful when their planning and management rely on local control and equitable resource distribution through a wider spectrum of public participation. These principles are echoed in the prescription offered by rural development workers for project plans which are actually developed by those they are intended to benefit. To say that approaches to cultural heritage conservation are somewhat behind is an understatement.

The greatest challenge to participation lies in persuading administrators that the local people have something to offer. One of the greatest problems in implementing truly sustainable tourism is "the climate of distrust between the government and local communities" (Ioannides, 1995:590). This distrust "reflects the government's failure to accept the importance of including the communities in the decision-making process regarding their future development" (Ioannides, 1995:590). Moreover, government personnel are reluctant to consult with the public because of the information they would be required to divulge and the power struggle which might ensue. Administrative bodies tend to be interested in public participation only in so far as it is a means to foster trust and confidence, making it more likely that the people will 'buy into' the plan and work inside the system when seeking a solution to problems (Crenson, 1974:357–8). Indeed, accepting this manipulative motivation for government involvement in a more participatory process seems a far cry from the lofty, empowering goals of true participatory action. However, from these humble beginnings, a more participatory, democratic process might emerge. Besides, "even if local empowerment is not contemplated, much can still be gained from local consultation" (Wall, 1996:133).

Perhaps if the 'stakeholders' were to play a part in identifying their own needs and deciding how those needs would best be met, when those particular aims are achieved, there would be some recognition that projects and need fulfilment are connected. The project might then become more highly valued as a whole. Involvement in the process itself serves to give the people some degree of control over their lives.

Culture as a contested domain

There is a lack of will to seek out what aspects of culture are important to the local people. More than a lack of will, this study revealed that park administrators were unresponsive to local people who sought encouragement and support in the promotion of their own local expressions of cultural heritage. Local people attributed the reason for this disinterest to the high value officials place on 'classical' culture and the low value attached to local culture. Entertainment for tourists (and also for local people) at these sites generally involves dance, music and festivals. While there is much potential for local involvement, there is little effort to secure it. In Thailand, for example, the director of a branch office of the national tourism agency revealed that the failure of the local people to respond enthusiastically to suggestions made by his office to 'dress up' in traditional costumes and to participate more fully in festivals was because the people were 'inert' and not interested in culture. However, a festival held in Prambanan which consisted of a parade, a brass band, and many official speeches, had little to do with local culture, and little effort was made to tie activities, costumes, etc., to the historical context of the monuments.

In Indonesia, local cultural groups are also eager to participate but they are rarely encouraged to do so. Once in a while, a local group in Borobudur is asked to perform classical Javanese dances for special visitors but there have been no plans to expand these activities to include regular performances, dances and music which are created locally. There is potential for a link between local performing arts and tourists but the director of a performing arts school at Borobudur noted that there is no one responsible for culture in P.T. Taman Wisata. The potential of involving local performance groups is thus not realised.

In Prambanan, classical Javanese dance performances are held almost every evening with the troupes coming from Yogyakarta and other cities. However, leaders of a folk performance group have been trying for several years now to persuade P.T. Taman Wisata and tour agents in Yogyakarta to help them promote their own local folk dances and music, which they suggested could be seen by tourists during the day. The group developed a promotional pamphlet in Bahasa Indonesia and English and had spoken to people from P.T. Taman Wisata and tour agencies but to no avail. At the time of the field study, there was a growing frustration within the group. They saw their product as valuable, but no one was willing to help them make the contacts necessary to draw tourists to the performance venues.

The frustration expressed by local musicians and dancers at the Indonesian sites indicates willingness by local people to contribute but a lack of interest by the national agency to promote what they have to offer. The apparent indifference is due to a more or less single-minded interest at the national level in classical arts and a general lack of interest in more vernacular forms. In Thailand, administrators who come from outside Ayutthaya make little attempt to find out what it is that gives meaning to people's culture. In both countries, the 'classical product' is available in many other places. The local 'product' is distinctive and, at least for international visitors, especially in intimate settings such as a village venue, there is the added benefit of feeling as though one has had an 'authentic' experience.

This tension between the classical or nationally-defined cultural identity and the local or vernacular forms of culture is also evident in monuments themselves. In Borobudur, the spiritual connection felt by people with the monument might have had little in common with the ways in which Buddhists thought of the monument. It is, however, no less real. No one has bothered to find out what that relationship is and the residents continue to resent this insensitivity today. At Ayutthaya, local people have folk tales and ghost stories to tell about things that have happened at the ancient temple complexes, but again, no one has asked them to tell their stories. This chance to breathe life into the ancient remains has been ignored in order to pursue the loftier, high-status goals of classical cultural preservation. The vernacular elements of cultural expression, which tend to have so much meaning for local communities, are not generally acknowledged as being particularly valuable by national governments. The Indonesian and Thai governments appear to be more interested in culture which binds the communities together, so that the government can further its goals of political centralisation and control. The goal of cultural homogeneity is incongruent with the diverse expression of local traditions.

The UNESCO World Cultural Heritage List takes this national 'ownership' of cultural identity one step further by globalising it – by making a cultural site the shared property and responsibility of the world. The motivation of UNESCO is to preserve examples of what is unique and special, and to protect them in perpetuity. There is an element of 'freezing' the cultural remains and their contexts. While it can generally be understood why the monuments need to be separated from the destructive effects of 'progress', do the historical remains also have to be separated from the vitality of cultural expression of living peoples? Whose heritage is it, anyway? Merely because the heritage belongs to 'everyone' does not mean that it has to have the same meaning to everyone.

Concluding remarks

There appears to have been little attention by heritage protection agencies to develop, with local people, a true atmosphere of stewardship at protected sites. The need for that stewardship was articulated by residents at all three study sites. One resident at Ayutthaya summed up the issue when he said:

Somehow, people have to feel that this park and this city belong to them; they need to feel ownership. When you have to buy a ticket to see the monuments, even though that price is very small, you don't feel that those monuments belong to you and you don't belong to those monuments either. There is no sense of interdependence and that is emphasised by things like admittance fees.

(Personal interview, January 1995)

There is considerable distance between what rural and economic development project practitioners have learned and what heritage protection agencies have yet to learn. If these attitudes towards local communities pervade, those responsible for managing the sites will have to be constantly on guard against all of the elements which compromise the conservation of the site, its environment and the visitors' experience. Moreover, without the political will to democratise the planning process or to at least ensure that planning activities promote equitable distribution of social benefits, measures taken at the village level will be limited. Through the involvement of local communities in project and tourism planning, site managers might have a better idea of what community needs are. In turn, there might be a greater sense of affinity to the park by community members and, in turn, to the monuments themselves.

The international attention captured by Ayutthaya, Borobudur and Prambanan has brought into juxtaposition local and national concerns for their protection. A perusal of the Master Plans for the sites revealed that the predominant approach adopted at significant cultural heritage sites in Thailand and Indonesia to date is rooted in the synoptic planning tradition which minimises the input of local people. It is suggested that by adopting alternative approaches to monument site presentation, the potential to enhance the planning process will lead to a more equitable balance between the use and preservation of monument areas.

The builders of the monuments are dead. The ways in which they expressed their cultural identity, if not dead, are now more or less preserved or re-created and displayed for the tourist gaze. That culture, as the builders of the monuments knew it, no longer exists. The very essence of culture is that it is ever in a state of flux. The continuity lies in what humans value and, to some extent, their daily activities – the food they eat, the joys and sorrows they feel. Visitors come from great distances in order to visit these monuments as they did centuries ago. Local people look up from whatever it is they are doing – nursing their babies, tending to their gardens, working a piece of stone which will be used to repair the temple – to attend to their needs. The relationship between host and guest continues. The continuity of that relationship can be enhanced and enriched through the implementation of a constructive and creative planning process which incorporates the knowledge, skills and desires of local people, leading to more secure monument preservation, a more 'authentic' tourism experience and improved life opportunities for those living in the shadows of the monuments.

Notes

[1]This study was undertaken to fulfil the requirements of a Masters thesis in Urban and Regional Planning at the University of Waterloo. The first author engaged in a 12-week field trip at each of the study areas in 1994-1995. With the help of research assistants hired from nearby universities, this qualitative, comparative study relied on in-depth interviews with officials, academics and local residents, participant observation and land use surveys.

[2]In some countries, 'historical parks' are known as 'archaeological parks'. While there is some argument about the difference between the two terms, for the purposes of this study no distinction is made.

[3]Blacking (1987) draws on Hobsbawm and Ranger's (1983) concept in their work *The Invention of Tradition*.

[4]There are almost twice as many visitors to Borobudur than to Prambanan.

[5]A major exception is the area controlled by a modern temple and its community of monks - Wat Mongkorn Bohpit. Presently, Thai visitors who come to Ayutthaya to 'make merit' at this temple park also donate money to the temple. By far the largest tourist shopping area is located here.

References

Blacking, J. (1987) 'Development studies and the reinvention of tradition'. *World Development*, 14(4), 527–32.

Chambers, R. (1983) *Rural Development: Putting the Last First*. London: Longman.

Cohen, E. (1978) 'The impact of tourism on the physical environment'. *Annals of Tourism Research*, 5(2), 215-37.

Crenson, M. (1974) 'Organizational factors in citizen participation'. Journal of Politics, 36, 356–78.

Dobbing, N. (1988) Metastructural Planning: Toward the Self-Organization of Human Society, unpublished honours essay, Faculty of Environmental Studies, University of Waterloo, Canada.

Evans-Pritchard, D. (1993) 'Ancient art in modern context'. *Annals of Tourism Research*, 20(1), 9–31.

Friedmann, J. (1987) *Planning in the Public Domain: From Knowledge to Action*. Princeton: Princeton University Press.

Hall, C.M. (1994) *Tourism and Politics: Policy, Power and Place*. Chichester: John Wiley & Sons.

Hobsbawm, E. and Ranger, T. (eds.) (1983) *The Invention of Tradition*. Cambridge: Cambridge University Press.

Hudson, B.M. (1979) 'Comparison of current planning theories: Counterparts and contradictions'. *Journal of the American Planning Association*, 45(4), 387–98.

International Council of Monuments and Sites (ICOMOS) (1986) *ICOMOS:1964–1984*. Napoli: ICOMOS.

ICOMOS (1964) *The Venice Charter: International Charter for the Conservation and Restoration of Monuments and Sites*. Online. Available:
http://www.international.icomos.org/e_venice_htm (30 June 2000).

Ioannides, D. (1995) 'A flawed implementation of sustainable tourism: The experience of Akemas, Cyprus'. *Tourism Management*, 16(8), 583–92.

Kottack, C.P. (1991) 'When people don't come first: Some sociological lessons from completed projects', in M.M. Cernea (ed.) *Putting People First*. New York: Oxford University Press, 431–64.

Peleggi M. (1996) 'National heritage and global tourism in Thailand'. *Annals of Tourism Research*, 23(2), 432-48.

Peters, H. (1995) 'Conservation and preservation of traditional culture in the onslaught of tourism: Looking at Asia', *Workshop on Sustainable Tourism Development in World Heritage Sites – Planning for Hue, Final Report*, Bangkok: UNESCO, 47–51.

Smith, T.B. (1985) 'Evaluating development policies and programmes in the Third World'. *Public Administration and Development*, 5(2), 129–44.

Soemarwoto, O. (1992) *Cultural Tourism Development, Central Java-Yogyakarta, Activity Report No. 8, Environmental Aspects of Tourism*. Yogyakarta: Directorate General of Tourism/UNESCO/UNDP.

United Nations Educational, Scientific and Cultural Organisation (UNESCO), (1983) *Conventions and Recommendations of UNESCO Concerning the Protection of the Cultural Heritage*. Geneva: UNESCO.

Uphoff, N. (1991) 'Fitting projects to people', in M.M. Cernea (ed.) *Putting People First*. New York: Oxford University Press, 467–512.

Wall, G., (1996) 'People outside the plans', in W. Nuryanti (ed.) *Tourism and Culture: Global Civilization in Change, Proceedings of the Indonesia-Swiss Forum on Culture and International Tourism*, August 1995. Yogyakarta: Gadjah Mada University Press, 130–37.

Wojino, C.T. (1991) 'Historic preservation and economic development'. *Journal of Planning Literature*, 5(2), 296–306.

9

Negotiating Global Tourism: Localism as Difference in Southeast Asian Theme Parks

Peggy Teo and Brenda S. A. Yeoh

Introduction

Disney World is the quintessential American dream come true. It has been exalted for its enormous success and attacked by academic critics for its artificial and instant landscapes. From whichever perspective, the attention it has received bears witness to its overwhelming influence as a tourist and leisure product. It now furnishes a common iconography and is referred to as the "alpha point of hyper-reality" (Sorkin, 1992:206). Whether it is in the ability to invent or appropriate narratives, to manipulate rhetoric, to present impressive visual projections, its adroit merchandising or its creativity in marketplace synergies, Disney World has so refined the art of the theme park business that it currently provides the template on which theme parks in other parts of the world attempt to emulate (Hollinshead, 1998a). The near universality and global reach of Disney is said by Zukin (1991) and Fjellman (1992) to be so potent that it commodifies and homogenises space as it grows in tandem with the expanding tourist and leisure industry. While these are convincing trends, this chapter suggests that localism has been ignored as a contributory agent in the production of tourism landscapes. We agree with Hollinshead (1998b:121) that tourism sites, precisely because they are in the "fundamental business of 'difference' and the 'other'", become sites where negotiations on place-making occur. Rather than view tourism spaces as abstract mediums subject only to powerful global corporate forces such as Disney, this chapter argues that 'indigenisation' is as influential a countervailing force as it strives to depict meaning and subjectivity to a highly interconnected world. Where interconnections rationalise the production of tourism and strategise to build synergies across the globe (Hannigan, 1998:81; 86), local forces rein in such influences to provide the balance that is essential for establishing a raison d'être for tourism.

The chapter also argues that even though landscapes can be reduced to a few essentialist imageries for mass consumption (e.g. Goss' 1993 discussion of Hawaiian imagery), it is also true that place products are seldom static and unchanging. Place images and identities respond as much to the fluctuating needs of global tourists passing through as they do to residents who have an affective attachment to their 'own' localities (Squire, 1999). Cultural theorist Arjun Appadurai argues that hard and regular work must be undertaken to produce and maintain the materiality of locality and the local is defined as "not local *in* itself but...*for* itself" even in the face of a disjunctive mix of ideas and practices characteristic of the globalised world today (Appadurai, 1996:180–81; our emphasis). In this argument, place representation is understood not only as an active form of spatialising or of making distinct and different, it also implies that there are many components in the concept of localism. Identified by Hollinshead (1998b:139–40) as comprising many ethnic identities, state and interest groups, all localisms are said to bring to bear their imprint on place-making. In this chapter, we examine the notion of the 'local' and restore to local society its "rightful status as actor" (Lanfant, 1995:6) in a tourism undertaking. We also unpack the multiplicity of local interests that are involved in place-making using theme parks in Southeast Asia as examples. The chapter suggests that while Southeast Asian theme parks may appear to be commercially viable and internationally appealing, and akin to the universal Disney product, they also communicate and respond to the various impulses of what is often construed as 'local'.

Global connections

Landscapes can be corporate mandates (re)configured by global capitalism for touristic consumption (Urry, 1990; Boniface and Fowler, 1993; Crang, 1994). The Disney theme parks are good examples of this. They attract millions through their gates by turning the world into easily digestible capsules based on an economy of intensive representations. The parks contain many worlds which are described as "just like the real thing, only better" (Sorkin, 1992:16). The creative geographies of Disneyland and Disney World are tightly structured by a utopian discourse about society; they provide fictive narratives of a social identity that is idealised and where the idealism is maintained through spatial controls, including a boundary between its inside and the outside real world. Zukin (1995:54) describes Disney World as an ideal type of public space which is safe, clean and pleasing but with a unidimensional nature and history. The asymmetries of power so evident in real landscapes are absent in the theme park; they are absolutely displaced from any historical mooring (Hughes, 1999). What results is 'distory' (Fjellman's term), a sanitised pastiche presentation of the past which decontextualises, reduces and ultimately annihilates history (Hollinshead, 1998a). This imagery is then corporatised and spread globally through turnkey projects in Tokyo and Paris and increasingly in other parts of the world (e.g. in Hong Kong), leading Bryman (1999) to conclude that 'Disneyisation' has taken root across the globe. By this, he means that the principles of the Disney theme parks, such as a social order which is controlled by an all-powerful organisation, the "removal of any hint of production while blanketing consumption with layers of fantasy" (Warren, 1994 in Bryman, 1999:27), and the supreme capacity to consume, all come to dominate and exert salient influences on the tourism industry (Wasko, 1996).

The specific Disney traits so characteristic of this global enterprise are outlined in the next few paragraphs to show exactly how crucial they are to creating and maintaining a world-class standard theme park that will keep the cash registers ringing.

Theming

Theming is the most obvious dimension of Disneyisation (Bryman, 1999:29). The leisure industry employs theming as a drawing point, using for example, history, culture, sports or ecology to rally various aspects of the enterprise together (e.g. Hard Rock Café and Planet Hollywood). Theming is used in restaurants and eateries, shopping centres, hotels, recreation spots etc. For Disneyland and Disney World, theming creates a powerful visual and spatial reorganisation of both public and geographic space. In the former, it constructs an autonomous 'walled' city or gated community that protects its inhabitants from the menace of the real world. It provides its own transportation system, sanitation and maintenance services, security, food outlets, lighting and outdoor furniture. Visual strategy is employed to make unpleasant things such as garbage collection and maintenance work invisible. For eating, shopping, viewing of art exhibits and other similar uses, public use of space is promoted through a system of plazas, atria and lobbies. For geographic spaces, set tableaux are employed to create differentiated spaces. Stage-set landscapes depicting Main Street of USA, the old West, and children's fantasy and adventure books are utilised to provide motifs. Besides themed buildings, artefacts and costumes are introduced to complete the picture. In effect, "site is sight" (Zukin, 1995:57) in Disney World. Instead of real space, place is rubberised, compacted or stretched according to need. This is most evident in the specific geographies that the two theme parks represent within their boundaries. The frontiers of the Wild West, the Eiffel Tower and Italy's St. Mark's Square are just as easily translocated onto the park. Postcard-perfect spots offering scenic views of the world and indicated by Kodak signposts are also offered (Zukin, 1991; 1995; Marling, 1997).

Given that consumption is a key component in the survival of the park, visual strategies are also harnessed to shape consumption space. Theme-park goers are bombarded not only with the opportunity to 'see' the world – unadulterated by crime and other undesirable elements – they also have the opportunity to recall their leisure experiences by purchasing a choice of items ranging from food to souvenirs and other collectibles. In effect, in Disneyland, the distinction between theme park and shopping is obscured. There is an interlocking of consumption in different spheres – as visitors get out of one world and before they enter into another, they are bombarded by a variety of mementoes to help them remember a good experience. Even in the hotel room, the experience is reinforced through the continuation of thematic motifs. In all, shopping, eating, hotel accommodation and theme park visiting are inextricably interwoven so that visitors have the benefit of a total experience.

Service

Service in Disneyland is indeed flawless. The Disney image is one of harmony, competence and grace under pressure (Zukin, 1995:70). The Disney cast members are subject to tight controls exercised through segmented and hierarchical relations between management and labour and within labour itself. Each functional unit works at its own specific task to perfection. In fact, the relentless categorising and subdividing of work encourages workers to identify with their immediate group rather than with other workers in the park doing similar things but at different places. The reification of workspace leads to promotion from 'within' and a familiarity with one another that is sometimes regarded with envy. Most of all, Disney workers 'become' their characters and they embody the roles and magic associated with the theme park (Fish and Jameson, 1995).

A closed economy

The corporate tentacles of Disney permit it to develop a virtual seamless economy. The diversity of products and support that Disney has bought over or gained a foothold in through joint ventures with other companies ensures protection akin to trade tariffs and gives the theme park industry strong business security. For example, Disney has signed participation agreements with large corporate sponsors such as Kodak, ABC Network, General Electric, General Motors, Metropolitan Life Insurance Company and Coca-Cola. Besides corporate synergies, it has linked itself with big-name talents such as Michael Jackson, Steven Spielberg and George Lucas. Overseas, Disney franchises its products as in EuroDisney and Tokyo Disneyland (Richards and Richards, 1998).

By linking itself with others, the Disney product can be refined and communicated *en masse* to the world. For example, the Disney culture and imagery is made possible by the fact that the company is a multimedia corporation. It has film, videos, cable TV; it even owns professional sports teams. Its merchandise is sold not only within the park but franchised outside and used for promotional purposes. The theme park also has synergies with hotel and resort operations. So long as the elements relate to the leisure market, the closed economy is equivalent to an insular unit which can endure difficult times because of the multiple linkages it has established for itself. The level of competence is also greatly enhanced by a single corporate culture.

Disneyisation of the world?

When Wood (1993:50; 55) raised the issue that traditional cultures do not "dissolve and degrade" in the face of mass tourism, he was critiquing the work of sociologists who viewed culture as static, as the culmination of "things inherited from the past" and as the "opposite of modernity". Since then, his work, together with that of others such as Cohen (1988), McKean (1989) and Picard (1997) has pointed out that tourism can in fact strengthen traditional cultures and make traditional crafts and activities economically viable. Squire (1993; 1999), Lanfant *et al.* (1995) and Nicholson (1997) concur with Wood that tourism is implicated in cultural politics and postmodern viewpoints on tourism must necessarily acknowledge the dialectics that exist between itself and culture.

A contrary wave nevertheless continues to anchor the paradigm of homogenisation. Giddens (1990), Zukin (1991; 1995) and Sorkin (1992) together with geographers such as Relph (1976), Harvey (1989) and Britton (1991) maintain that the evisceration of space as a result of technology leads to time-space compression which in turn has the effect of "rolling social life away from the fixities of tradition" (Giddens, 1990:53). It results in local social practices being overwhelmed by the power of capitalist relations of production (Harvey, 1989). McLuhan's (1962 cited in Leyshon, 1995) 'global village' has the tendency to 'detraditionalise' societies and give rise to what Sorkin (1992) calls an 'ageographical' city – a city without a place attached to it. It is visible in "clumps of skyscrapers rising from well-wired fields next to the Interstate; in huge shopping malls, anchored by their national-chain departmental stores...in hermetically sealed atrium hotels cloned from coast to coast; *in uniform 'historic' gentrifications and festive markets...*" (Sorkin, 1992:xi; our emphasis). In the context of theme parks, Fjellman (quoted in Hollinshead, 1998a:105–6) accuses the Disney companies of committing global "entrepreneurial violence" which "routinely seeks to rob individuals of their thinking dignity, to obliterate 'difference' and to deny counterstories".

This outcome is facilitated by the postmodern tourist whom Rojek (1993 cited in Ritzer and Liska, 1997:102) describes as one who accepts the commodification of space because these spaces and the many products hawked along the way are manifestations of consumerism. For him, tourism is seen to be an end in itself and not a means to a loftier goal. The post-tourist relies on signs to guide him. McDonald's and Disney are key signifiers of consumption, as are icons such as the Eiffel Tower in Paris or the Taj Mahal in India (Ritzer and Liska, 1997:104). As such, Bryman (1999) propounds that Disneyisation is an inevitable outcome of postmodern tourism whereby all products, including culture, can be commodified, advertised and sold (Urry, 1990). Packaging involving a "conscious series of choices" (Ashworth, 1994) becomes a key component in the "selling of places" (Kearns and Philo, 1993). Theme parks lend themselves well to this analysis because they are consumer fetishism *par excellence*, classic examples of the power of imagineering (Archer, 1997). Tourists still seek authenticity (MacCannell, 1976) but in today's contemporary urban society, they are doomed never to find it. Instead, authenticity is substituted by simulacra (Ritzer and Liska, 1997:107) as evident in theme parks, shopping centres, hotels and food outlets. Increasingly, it has become difficult to separate the simulated from the real (Baudrillard, 1983 cited in Ritzer and Liska, 1997). Disneyland, representing the perfect model of simulation, can offer tourists seeking authenticity an 'authentic inauthenticity', and a cheaper one at that.

Although Disneyisation is prevalent, it can be argued that even in theme parks, places are "social and cultural constructions whose meanings and values are negotiated and redefined by diverse people" (Squire, 1999:82-3). For example, in Liverpool and Lancashire, Urry (1995:152-62) showed how locals were active agents in transforming declining industries into heritage sites. The reinterpretation of local culture was deemed necessary to rejuvenate the economy. In this case, history and culture were used in a strategic fashion to harness globalising forces in a way that was agreeable to the respective residents of the two areas. In a similar fashion, theme parks need not necessarily be "postmodern invaders of vernacular landscapes" (Hannigan, 1995:191) but may be viewed as active progenitors of differentiated spaces which theme-park goers engage with as a learning resource (Ley and Olds, 1988; Nuryanti, 1996). Thus, the meaning associated with the spectacle and the fantasy necessarily requires that the representations are palatable, if not acceptable, to those they signify. Wood (1993) and likewise Robins (1991) argue that tourism is in fact appropriated by locals in their symbolic constructions of culture, tradition and identity, otherwise, "cultures that do not succeed in translating some of their qualities into spectacles or commodities [will] vanish, only to become museum pieces" (Firat, 1995 cited in Picard and Wood, 1997:viii).

Disneyisation also assumes that people are passive recipients swallowed up by mega trends intent on global homogenisation. This ignores recent literature that discusses the role of agency in influencing outcomes (Lanfant, 1995; Urry, 1995; Oakes, 1997). Individuals and groups may actively respond to the constraints and opportunities provided by global tourism, yielding contrary outcomes to that suggested by Ritzer and Liska (1997). In Christchurch, New Zealand, Schöllmann, Perkins and Moore discuss the negotiations between the local council and traders to alter the "English Garden/Most English City of New Zealand" image to one that is more in keeping with its current status as a lively cosmopolitan city (Schöllmann *et al.*, 2000:62-4). Rather than globalising forces such as tourism constituting all of the meaning of place, tourism is argued to be but one of the influences in place-making. The other is, of course, the very denizens of the city itself.

Global-local dialectics is also the theme of Chang's (2000) paper on Little India in Singapore. Gazetted as a historic district in 1989, it is promoted as "the heart of Singaporean Indian heritage" (Urban Redevelopment Authority, 1988 cited in Chang, 2000:351). The transformation reflects similar efforts in other post-modern cities in which ethnic neighbourhoods are preserved conterminously with modern enterprises. It is the intermingling of the old and the new, the restoration of the "Oriental mystique" (Ministry of Trade and Industry (MTI), 1986) that will keep the tourists coming. Critiques of commodification will no doubt find enough fodder in this project to run it down. However, it would also be "presumptuous to assume that tourist-local relations are always combatory" (Chang, 2000:347). In fact, Chang concludes that local agency is more conflictive as the Indian and Chinese communities living and working in Little India assert their own sense of identity and 'insideness' within the location. Two lessons may be drawn from this fascinating example: on the one hand, global-local connections are crucial for understanding the construction of a landscape; on the other, local agencies also contribute as part of the 'connections'. Their role is under-rated and the analytical lens ought to focus more on this aspect in order for tourism research to be more complete.[1]

'Land of the Rising Fun'[2]: theme parks come to Asia

While the USA and Europe developed most of their theme parks in the 1950s to the 1970s, these are late in coming to the Asia-Pacific. For Southeast Asia, the late 1980s and especially the 1990s was the decade of theme parks. In fact, Asia is now the fastest-growing area of theme park development, with growth rates of up to 20 per cent per year (Richards and Richards, 1998:368).

With the exception of Tokyo Disneyland and the soon-to-be Hong Kong Disneyland, few of the themed developments are directly developed or franchised by the big international players such as Disney, Universal, Warner, and Six Flags. Instead, most are underwritten by local and/or regional millionaires and corporate conglomerates independently or in collaboration with state bodies. Even though North American expertise is sought after, for example, that of Landmark and Battaglia, local money has implications for the creation of identity in the parks. This will be alluded to in later sections. Suffice it to say that the demand to invest exists and that it is recent, fuelled mainly by positive feelings about the Asian travel market. In spite of recent economic woes suffered in Asia (1997-1999), including Southeast Asia, many are still very bullish about the Asian economic miracle. Overall, travel in the Asia-Pacific region has grown from 1 per cent in 1960 to 14 per cent of the 563 million international travellers in 1995 (World Tourism Organisation, 1997:5). Its share of regional tourism receipts is just as remarkable, having risen from 3 per cent in 1960 to 16 per cent in 1990 (Mak and White, 1992:14).

The Asia-Pacific region practises 'open regionalism' whereby intra-regional barriers to the economic exchange of goods and services are purposefully removed to facilitate multilateral trade (Chan, 1995 cited in Go, 1997:8). This strategy is, in fact, one of the salient factors responsible for the growth of tourism in the region. Government participation and involvement in creating conducive conditions for investment extends to national tourist boards dismantling barriers to free travel and to providing incentives to attract private entrepreneurs to invest in the tourism and leisure industries. These are in themselves aided by macro forces such as the economic boom occurring in the region (Go, 1997:14).

Under such conditions, Qu and Zhang (1997:36-42), who used data from the Pacific Asia Travel Association (PATA) to project tourism arrivals in the region (excluding the Indian subcontinent), concluded that the trend is one of growth. They calculated an average growth rate which is likely to exceed 11 per cent per annum (Table 9.1). They confirm that the relatively high rate of growth in this region is fuelled by higher disposable incomes and more leisure time. For example, the paid vacation leave entitlement in Singapore, Taipei and Hong Kong is almost comparable to cities such as London in developed countries. As per capita income increases, private consumer expenditure of individuals and families has gone up and there is more holiday travel. In fact, leisure has become a major element in the typical household budget. The World Travel and Tourism Council (WTTC, 1995:70) reported that private consumption had gone up from US$2,138.91 billion in 1987 to US$4,011.19 billion in 1995 in the Asia-Pacific region. It is further projected to increase to US$8,831 billion by 2005. From China alone, the number of people going

Table 9.1: Tourist arrivals and receipts in the major destinations, 1981–2005

Destination	Tourist Arrivals (000s)			Receipts (US$m)
	1981	1992	2005	1995
Singapore	2,829	5,990	25,493	8,378
Hongkong	2,353	6,986	23,354	9,604
Thailand	2,016	5,136	19,297	7,664
Japan	1,583	3,582	10,584	3,226
Taiwan	1,409	1,873	5,069	3,286
South Korea	1,093	3,321	12,655	5,587
Malaysia	1,006	2,346	11,071	3,910
Philippines	939	1,153	4,297	2,450
Australia	937	2,603	8,649	7,100
China	714	4,172	17,781	8,733
Indonesia	600	3,064	10,717	5,228
New Zealand	478	1,056	2,581	2,316
	1991	1995		1995
India	1,674	2,124	-	2,754
Micronesia	1,210	2,096	-	1,933
Pakistan	438	378	-	114
Melanesia	428	502	-	541
Sri Lanka	318	403	-	224
Vietnam	300	1,351	-	86
Polynesia	238	339	-	362
Cambodia	25	220	-	100
Myanmar	22	110	-	38
Laos	17	60	-	51

Source: Compiled from Qu and Zhang (1997); WTO (1997)

abroad in 1995 grew by 21 per cent over the previous year to 4.5 million (*The Economist*, 21 December 1996:33).

Agents of the 'local'

As Sofield (in this volume) argues, the relationship between the global and the local may be one of dominance-dependence or may in fact take more 'benign' forms. While theme parks, as part of the global tourism system, are important sites where local cultural heritage and place are often appropriated and reshaped by powerful global forces, we argue that locality continues to reassert itself in different ways to reclaim these sites. The task of producing locality in the business of theme parks is complex and reflects a struggle that involves many agents including the state, local people and on-site private enterprise.[3] The modern state may appropriate theme parks – particularly those containing representations of culture – as ideological space to engender allegiance and affiliation in its population as well as to represent aspects of the nation to tourists. The individual or collective agency of local people affected by theme parks may challenge the state's imagineering or resist the deterritorialisation tendencies of tourism. Local enterprises with the economic wherewithal which attempt to subscribe to profitable global trends while at the same time servicing a local population draw prodigiously from not only the global but also local resources and materials in the business of theme parks. The tensions and conflicts as well as resolutions should not be seen to be the outcome of global-local connections alone but also connections within the local arena itself. The next sections discuss each of the 'localisms' in turn as they assert themselves *vis-à-vis* the onslaught of Disneyisation.

Representing the nation: the state

With money in their pockets and time to spare, many Asians are looking for amusement within Asia. While Western analysts would argue that another Disneyland is ripe for harvest (*Asiaweek*, 12 March 1999:44-5), public investors such as the state have preferred to valorise traditional elements of local culture in cultural theme parks for two purposes: on the one hand, tourist gazing of the parks allows the nation to benefit from the tourist dollar; on the other, such parks pander to the sense of identity of the multifarious ethnic groups in the region. Oakes' (1997:41-4) short discussion of Splendid China and China Folk Culture Villages which hold miniaturised national landmarks and authentic replicas of typical dwellings and cultural displays of 21 *minzu* (minority) groups is a case in point. International tourism, with its commercialism and commodification tendencies, is not seen to collide with native culture. Instead, the state sought to "invent a landscape of nostalgia on which to build a sense of national identity...[so that the Chinese] who find themselves whirling in the maelstrom of [capitalist] Shenzhen...[can find in the park] the calming certainty of folk tradition" (Oakes, 1997:42).

Promotional images which portray a coherent national heritage become synchronic models that legitimise and affirm the existence of otherwise ignored groups. In Southeast Asia, theming around singularly 'local' elements and customs is precisely what Taman Mini Indonesia Indah ('Beautiful Indonesia') attempts to do. Conceived by the late wife of ex-President Suharto in 1971, the park reproduces, in miniature, the thousands of islands that make up the archipelago. There are exhibits, albeit static ones, of the culture and daily life of the many peoples that make up Indonesia. The nationalistic gel that Taman Mini Indonesia attempts to provide attests to the local vision of fusing a global phenomenon with a local cause. By doing so, locals are provided with a leisure outlet which provides not only an outing for the family but an appreciation/learning of the germane cultures that make up Indonesia and a historical bond that signifies a common heritage for the people.

State involvement in portraying the integrity of local cultures and showing a greater sensitivity to the indigenous people and their historical experience is also evident in Sarawak Cultural Village. This is a 'living museum' of the seven major ethnic groups dwelling in Sarawak. Ethnic associations such as the Orang Ulu Association and the Iban Association were consulted to build the correct style of houses and to ensure that the static attractions such as hunting implements and houseware as well as interactive exhibits such as dances, food preparation and mat weaving are accurately represented in the Village (Muzaini, 1997/98). The state's rhetoric with regard to the village is to "return Sarawak culture to the locals" (Jugah, 1994 cited in Muzaini, 1997/98:58) by emphasising traditional performances and crafts in the hope that through an appreciation of the rich heritage of the nation, inter-ethnic harmony can be fostered (Kedit, 1989 cited in Muzaini, 1997/98:61).[4]

Malay Village in Singapore is similarly a state initiative. In 1984, several Malay ministers and Members of Parliament appealed to the state to preserve the Malay kampong ('village') which had long since disappeared from the Singapore landscape because of rapid urban development. In order for the Malays to "retain their identity" (*The Straits Times*, 26 August 1984), a cultural theme park located in the Malay heartland and showcasing Malay architecture, arts and crafts, traditional trades and even games was mooted to help the Malays feel rooted to their heritage. Thus Malay Village was conceived and built not only as a cultural symbol as perceived by the state but also as a political symbol of Singapore's multiethnic society (the Malays being a minority in the island). Localism is defined here as a powerful political agenda which shapes not only the meaning of being local but also how the local is portrayed to the external world.

Not all theme parks in Southeast Asia harp political messages in such an obvious way. Some blend fun and enjoyment with cultural messages and it is to these that the chapter now turns.

Indigenising fun: the power of local people

A theme park which traces a meaningful history but was metamorphosed into an 'Oriental Disneyland' is Haw Par Villa in Singapore. Renamed 'Dragon World', the park was envisioned as a product of global trends that would draw visitors "the way Disneyland and Epcot Centre are doing in the U.S." (*The Straits Times*, 30 April 1986). The local consortium comprising Fraser and Neave (F&N) and Times Publishing Berhad commissioned Battaglia Associates Incorporated, an offshoot of Walt Disney Productions, to design the park (for greater discussion of this park, refer to Teo and Yeoh, 1997). The planned attractions included special effects such as lasers, animation and state-of-the-art technology to conjure hair-raising encounters with the Chinese spirit world. Visitors were to experience "earthquakes, cold winds and unseen hands reaching out unexpectedly from the dark" (*The Straits Times*, 29 April 1986) or watch "mythological battles [fought out] in a simulated sensurround undersea environment" (*Business Times*, 29 April 1986). A eight-minute boat ride through two high-speed splashdowns was touted as the way to encounter the gods of Water, Wind and Rain in the Wrath of Water Gods Flume Ride. In spite of the revamp, visitorship at the park was disappointing. Local agencies, namely Singaporeans, spurned the park because it was too commodified. To them, the park was a landscape of memories rather than a landscape of consumption. Consequently, the park reverted to what it was originally – a collection of eclectic animal tableaux embodying moral lessons. While technological wizardry is a typical Disney/global/ universalising trait, indigenous culture remains prevalent because that is what "Western visitors find fascinating and one of a kind in the world", and is something to which Asian visitors and Singaporeans are "able to relate" (MTI, 1986:n.p.). Like Sarawak Cultural Village, Dragon World initially attracted a great deal of attention.

This was, however, short-lived. Many felt that Dragon World was a one-visit attraction and the thrill-rides and hi-tech wizardry were not enough to keep them coming. Since locals spurned the attraction, huge financial losses were incurred and the company had to rethink its strategy. Ultimately, Dragon World reverted to the idiosyncratic landscape that Aw Boon Haw, the original owner, had designed it to be, and which Singaporeans had valued because of the moral lessons the park had offered to the local people. Disneyisation thus gave way to local voices and the park was restored to "the way most Singaporeans remember it" (*The Straits Times*, 26 April 1995).

The ability of local interest to assert itself is not confined to the attractions in the parks, but also extends to the way parks are run. Although it runs contrary to international safety standards, locals are permitted into the region's waterparks such as Sunway Lagoon (Selangor), A'Farmosa (Melaka) and Fantasy Island (Singapore) fully clothed in T-shirts and shorts, as these are more acceptable to the conservative dress-code required of the Islamic religion. In addition, Fantasy Island allows its clients to bring in food as picnicking is a popular pastime of families. Local agencies also influence the activities offered by the parks. For example, family days in Singapore and Malaysian theme parks are very common. On such days, the parks are closed to the public for corporate events involving staff and their families. These are part of incentive schemes to motivate the worker. Special events are planned and cater to the needs of the corporation involved.

In addition, theme parks also become the vehicle for the celebration of local festivities. During Hari Raya Puasa, Malay Village in Singapore becomes a focal point of celebration for the whole nation as Malays celebrate the breaking of the fasting month at the Village. Likewise, Chinese Garden in Singapore is the venue for the Autumn Festival, more popularly called the Lantern Festival, during which the park brings in thousands of lanterns from the Far East for the viewing pleasure of Singaporeans and tourists alike. Special events are also held to celebrate the Lunar New Year. The celebration of festivals is not incidental in the parks but forms an integral part of the park's desire to be as much a part of the local landscape as of the tourist one.

Personal visioning: private enterprise

Private enterprise, the economic powerhouse of theme parks in Asia, is keen to make profits, but often not at the expense of losing its local clientele. Private enterprise is keen to replicate the success of Disneyland or Disney World by applying some or all of the Disney traits to their theme park businesses. For example, owner entrepreneur Tan Sri Lee Kim Yew built a seamless consumption landscape akin to the Disney product in Mines Resort City, Kuala Lumpur, West Malaysia. The 1,000 acre resort city contains a world-class golf course, a shopping centre, a theme park, an exhibition hall, a business park and two hotels. Like Disney, Mines Resort City sells a lifestyle rather than a product. Its motto is "Ever searching for better living". Mines Wonderland, the theme park, is a night-time theme park and is contiguous to Mines Shopping Fair, Mines International Exhibition and Showroom (a mega convention and exhibition centre) and Mines Beach Resort and Spa (a hotel). Even in tapping international business strategies, Tan Sri Lee ensures that Mines should not alienate local people. He has done this by dotting the entire resort with local symbols. The shopping centre boasts a canal running through the belly of the building whose banks are adorned by sculptures of tropical fish spouting water from their mouths. The canal passes under 'bridges of unity' where statues adorned in local costumes keep visitors reminded of the country's cultural roots. The business park may have a conglomerate of international companies, but the facades of its buildings capture Moorish architecture in keeping with the country's strong Islamic presence. The Palace of the Golden Horses, an upmarket hotel, is like-minded in architecture and even boasts the use of local building materials such as polished granite and slate. Like the other sites, Mines Beach Resort and Spa sits on a disused open-cast tin mine whose 150 acre lake has been converted into an artificial 'tropical beach', complete with cascading waterfalls, coconut trees, palms and pavilions. The spectacle and fantasy of Mines Wonderland may not be as impressive as Disneyland's, but the astute businessman is no less able to deliver to Malaysians a similar microcosm of the world's vernacular landscapes. Tan Sri Lee built an ice-house because he felt that it would be a novelty for Malaysians accustomed to tropical heat. Within this 10,000 sq ft Snow House, ice carvings of famous landmarks such as London's Tower Bridge, Sydney Opera House and a scene of Christchurch in New Zealand have been installed. However, Malaysia's own national icons also assert a presence – Petronas and Kuala Lumpur Towers set within the Kuala Lumpur City Centre stand tall among their international counterparts. According to Tan Sri Lee:

The theme park business in Malaysia and even Southeast Asia, you have to depend on the local population. If you make your target [sic] on international tourists, you'll be making a big mistake - locals are very important.

(Personal interview, 2 April 1999)

Instead of Mickey and Donald, Mines Wonderland boasts Kamee, the local goat mascot that Tan Sri Lee wants to develop into a "household name" (Personal interview, 2 April 1999). In fact, for each of the attractions within Mines Resort City, there are plans to merchandise a symbol, e.g. a horse for the Palace of the Golden Horses, a dolphin for Mines Beach Resort and Spa and an elephant for the exhibition centre. In the figurines and soft toys, all of Mines' clients will be able to leave with gifts/mementoes to remind them of their visit and of the resort city's unique brand of Asian hospitality (Personal interview, 2 April 1999).

Theme park owners in Southeast Asia are clearly cognizant of their dependence on regional markets, namely Singapore, Indonesia, Malaysia, India, Taiwan, Japan, Korea, China and Hong Kong. Rather than surrender to the tide brought about by international tourism, indigenous culture is used as an emblem to promote its domestic and international tourism. As suggested, local private entrepreneurs play an important role in steering the vision of landscape changes in the region. According to Tan Sri Lee, "no intervention from the government is the best for entrepreneurs" (Personal interview, 2 April 1999). This sentiment is also echoed by Dato Jeffrey Cheah, the owner and developer of Bandar Sunway (Sunway City) in Petaling Jaya. Being so close to Kuala Lumpur, Malaysia's capital, Dato Cheah envisioned Bandar Sunway as "resort living within the city" (*Sunway Lagoon: Malaysia's Premier Theme Park* sales kit, n.d.:n.p.) Dato Cheah essentially ignored recommendations that the land be set aside for offices and industry. Besides these, he also invested heavily in leisure in the new township. Today, a host of synergistic activities help Sunway Lagoon, Malaysia's first international standard theme park and winner of many tourism awards, to become a resounding success. The total experience comes from the private township itself – Sunway Lagoon is flanked by Sunway Pyramid which offers 7 million sq ft of shopping, convention facilities, an internal ice-rink, a Cineplex with 10 screens, a bowling alley with 48 lanes and a look-alike Sphinx at the main entrance (see Figure 9.1). In addition, the township is home to the Moor-styled domes and spires of Sunway Lagoon Resort Hotel as well as the more modern Palmville and Lagoon View luxury resort condominiums, Sunway Lagoon Club and Menara Sungeiway, the corporate headquarters of Sungeiway Group, the company's flagship.

Sunway Lagoon has done well by attracting some 35,000 visitors a day. Divided into a waterpark and a dry park, simulacra and fantasy characteristic of Disney are liberally used in Sunway. For example, Adventure Park uses exotic themes such as Sinbad's flying carpet and the pirates' galleon as backgrounds for its rides. A 15 ft dinosaur roars to life with a "sensational display of smoke, sounds, lights and movement" (*Sunway Lagoon: Malaysia's Premier Theme Park* sales kit, n.d.:n.p.). Within its belly, 80 hi-tech simulation and virtual reality rides and video-games are

Figure 9.1 Entrance to Sunway Pyramid

housed in air-conditioned comfort. The world's longest pedestrian suspension bridge starts at a castle similar to that of Cinderella's in Magic Kingdom. Adventure also comes alive in Fort Lagoon's Wild Wild West. Here, rides are named after legendary cowboys and Indians such as Butch Cassidy, Buffalo Bill and Chief Crazy Horse or after well-known places such as the Grand Canyon and Colorado in order to bring the 'Mid-Western frontier' to Malaysia. Vultures and condors compete with heroes and villains so that "wild horses can't keep you away" from the theme park (*Sunway Lagoon: Malaysia's Premier Theme Park* sales kit, n.d.:n.p.). To add to the carnival spirit, gala fiestas abound in the park with dance performances, magic shows and music. The amphitheatre is the venue for many international performers, including All-4-One from USA and Kulcha from Australia. As with Disneyland and Disney World, accuracy in the portrayal of landscapes is not important; imagineering is the order of the day and as long as visitors' senses are stimulated, the park has achieved a measure of success. No hint of the production of the spectacle is apparent in Sunway and similarly, shopping and theme park visits are integrated so that the post-tourist is encouraged to consume.

Another Disney trait which is apparent in Sunway Lagoon is good service. The theme park is run by 'ambassadors of fun'. Service staff are sent to Disney University in Florida to participate in the Disney Approach to Service and Management Excellence course. The culture of excellence includes other in-house training programmes, goal-oriented appraisal systems and incentive schemes.

Disneyfication has not, however, completely usurped Sunway Lagoon. Although we find theming, merchandising, a culture of excellence and even a private transportation system in Sunway (the park has its own monorail system that links up the many attractions in Bandar Sunway), local culture still makes its presence felt in this theme park. Its latest attraction, 'Elephant Walk', is a themed esplanade using a local icon to enhance the tropical rainforest image of Sunway Lagoon. The Surf-wave Pool, which is 5 acres in size and capable of generating 8 foot high waves, lies adjacent to Elephant Walk and complements its tropical theme. Indeed, fully-clothed Muslims frolicking in the water provide an incongruous comparison to the bikini-clad users of Wet 'N' Wild in Brisbane or Typhoon Lagoon in Orlando.

Conclusion

We have argued in this chapter that Disneyisation as a dominant force in tourism is undoubted. However, we also suggest that in Southeast Asia as well as in other parts of the world, there is sufficient evidence to suggest that it is impossible to imagineer away local identity. In so much as there is a deterritorialisation of space as global forces operating with the tourism system erode the cultural distinctiveness of place, there is also a parallel movement in the 'reterritorialisation' of space (Sofield, in this volume) as the interplay between the 'global' and the 'local' constantly shifts, settling temporarily into different configurations.

For their part, local communities are seldom passive and often seize upon tourism as a means to establish their own legitimacy. There are a multitude of interests at play. In Southeast Asia, the state often harnesses the tourism system, including the production of cultural theme parks, to support ideologically driven definitions of natural and ethnic identities. On-site private enterprise, harkening to both the power of personalising idiosyncracies and commercial imperatives, often seeks to combine local and global icons and materials which have been scissored out from here and there, usually in uncritical and expedient ways. Local people who live with and/or consume theme parks built in their midst often express their agency in a variety of ways – by their participation or non-participation, by adapting the cultural rules underlying the parks to their own customs and purposes, and by remaining immune to the web of signification spun by the park's narratives. State, local enterprise and the people are simply generic categories that give an inkling of the gamut of localisms that can emerge. More than other tourist landscapes, theme parks, because they are contrived landscapes, are subject to forces of globalisation; however, this chapter has suggested that what is more likely to happen is a hybridisation in which both global and local elements are brought together as a result of tourism interconnections. While they are hyper-real landscapes in that they also cater to the joy of consuming, some amount of effort is made to authenticate the theme park in Southeast Asia. As with Sofield's chapter in this book, we wholeheartedly agree that tourism fosters an interpenetration of global and local connections, of universalisation and particularisation rather than the dissemination of homogeneous landscapes, management styles, service quality standards and marketing and advertising strategies.

Acknowledgements

The research projects (RP3621003 & RP3621006) leading to this chapter were undertaken under the auspices of a Memorandum of Understanding between the National University of Singapore and the Singapore Tourism Board to co-operate on tourism research. The views expressed in this chapter, however, remain solely those of the authors.

Notes

[1]Although this chapter is devoted to underscoring the local *vis-à-vis* the global, the authors would also like to bring to attention papers that call for a more balanced view in which the global and the local combine in ways that are productive to both. See, for example, McKean (1989), Roberts and Schein (1993), and Chang (1997).

[2]This term is borrowed from Hannigan (1998:175-86) in which he discussed themed entertainment in the Asia-Pacific region.

[3]There may be more than the agents suggested here but for purposes of expedient discussion, we only concentrate on these three.

[4]Although intended as an ideological landscape, Muzaini (1997/98) also found that the commodification of culture in Sarawak Cultural Village had become entrenched. The village started off as a 'living' museum, but in the end the people who lived and worked in the museum were often actors and actresses playing the part of the minority ethnic groups. The dances were not authentic but simplified and shortened versions to encourage tourist participation. Also, the selling of ethnic art and craft had become a very important motivating force for them to continue in Sarawak Cultural Village.

References

Appadurai, A. (1996) *Modernity at Large: Cultural Dimensions of Globalisation*. Minneapolis: University of Minnesota Press.

Archer, K. (1997) 'The limits of the imagineered city: Sociospatial polarization in Orlando'. *Economic Geography*, 73(3), 322–66.

Ashworth, G.J. (1994) 'From history to heritage, from heritage to history: In search of concepts and models', in G.J. Ashworth and P.J. Larkham (eds.) *Building a New Heritage: Tourism, Culture and Identity in the New Europe*. London: Routledge and Kegan Paul, 13–30.

Asiaweek (1999) 'Donald and Mickey', 12 March, 44–5.

Boniface P. and Fowler, P.J. (1993) *Heritage and Tourism in the "Global Village"*. London: Routledge.

Britton, S. (1991) 'Tourism, capital and place: Towards a critical geography'. *Environment and Planning D: Society and Space*, 9, 451–78.

Bryman, A. (1999) 'The Disneyization of society'. *The Sociological Review*, 47(1), 25–47.

Business Times (1986) 'Haw Par redevelopment project: More land and incentives needed', 29 April, Singapore.

Chang, T.C. (1997) 'Heritage as a tourism commodity: Traversing the tourist-local divide'. *Singapore Journal of Tropical Geography*, 18(1), 46–68.

Chang, T.C. (2000) 'Singapore's Little India: A tourist attraction as a contested landscape'. Urban Studies, 37(2), 343–66.

Cohen, E. (1988) 'Authenticity and commoditisation in tourism'. *Annals of Tourism Research*, 15, 371–86.

Crang, M. (1994) 'On the heritage trial: Maps and journeys to olde Englande'. *Environment and Planning D: Society and Space*, 12, 341–55.

Economist, The (1996) 'Asians at play: A good day out', 21 December, 33–6.

Fjellman, M. (1992) *Vinyl Leaves: Walt Disney World and America*. Boulder: Westview Press.

Fish, S. and Jameson, F. (1995) *Inside the Mouse: Work and Play at Disney World*. Durham and London: Duke University Press.

Giddens, A. (1990) *The Consequences of Modernity*. Cambridge: Polity Press.

Go, F.M. (1997) 'Asian and Australasian dimensions of global tourism', in F.M. Go and C.L. Jenkins (eds.) *Tourism and Economic Development in Asia and Australasia*. London: Cassell, 3–34.

Goss, J. (1993) 'Placing the market and marketing place: Tourist advertising of the Hawaiian islands, 1972–92'. *Environment and Planning D: Society and Space*, 11, 663–88.

Hannigan, J.A. (1995) 'Theme parks and urban fantasy-scapes'. *Current Sociology*, 43(1), 183–91.

Hannigan, J.A. (1998) *Fantasy City: Pleasure and Profit in the Postmodern Metropolis*. London and New York: Routledge.

Harvey, D. (1989) *The Condition of Postmodernity: An Enquiry into the Conditions of Cultural Change*. Oxford: Blackwell.

Hollinshead, K. (1998a) 'Disney and commodity aesthetics: A critique of Fjellman's analysis of "distory" and the "historicide" of the past'. *Current Issues in Tourism*, 1(1), 58–119.

Hollinshead, K. (1998b) 'Tourism, hybridity and ambiguity: The relevance of Bhabha's "third space" cultures'. *Journal of Leisure Research*, 30(1), 121–56.

Hughes, G. (1999) 'Tourism and the semiological realization of space', in G. Ringer (ed.) *Destinations: Cultural Landscapes of Tourism*. London: Routledge, 17–32.

Kearns, G. and Philo, C. (eds.) (1993) *Selling Places: The City as Cultural Capital, Past and Present*. Oxford: Pergamon Press.

Lanfant, M.F. (1995) 'Introduction', in M.F. Lanfant, J.B. Allcock and E.M. Brunder (eds.) *International Tourism: Identity and Change*. London: Sage Publications, 1–23.

Lanfant, M.F., Allcock, J.B. and Brunder E.M. (eds.) (1995) *International Tourism: Identity and Change*. London: Sage Publications.

Ley, D. and Olds, K. (1988) 'Landscape as spectacle: World's fairs and the culture of heroic consumption'. *Environment and Planning D: Society and Space*, 6, 191–212.

Leyshon, A. (1995) 'Annihilating space: The speed-up of communications', in J. Allen and C. Hamnett (eds.) *A Shrinking World: Global Unevenness and Inequality*. Milton Keynes: Open University Press and Oxford University Press, 11–54.

MacCannell, D. (1976) The Tourist: A New Theory of the Leisure Class. London: Macmillan.

Mak, J. and White, K. (1992) 'Comparative tourism development in Asia and the Pacific'. *Journal of Travel Research*, 30(20), 12–23.

Marling, K.A. (ed.) (1997) *Designing Disney's Theme Parks: The Architecture of Reassurance*. Paris and New York: Flammarion.

McKean, P. (1989) 'Towards a theoretical analysis of tourism: Economic dualism and cultural involution in Bali', in V. Smith (ed.) *Hosts and Guests*. Philadelphia: University of Pennsylvania Press, 119–38.

Ministry of Trade and Industry (MTI) (1986) *Tourism Product Development Plan*. Singapore: MTI.

Muzaini, H. (1997/98) Sarawak in a box: (Re)creating landscapes in Sarawak Cultural Village, unpublished honours thesis, Department of Geography, National University of Singapore.

Nicholson, H.N. (1997) 'Collusion, collision or challenge: Indigenous tourism and cultural experience in British Columbia, Canada', in P.E. Murphy (ed.) *Quality Management in Urban Tourism*. Chichester: John Wiley and Sons, 115–36.

Nuryanti, W. (1996) 'Heritage and postmodern tourism'. *Annals of Tourism Research*, 23, 249–60.

Oakes, T. (1997) 'Ethnic tourism in rural Guizhou: Sense of place and the commerce of authenticity', in M. Picard and R. Wood (eds.) *Tourism, Ethnicity and the State in Asian and Pacific Societies*. Honolulu: University of Hawaii Press, 35–70.

Picard, M. (1997) 'Cultural tourism, nation-building and regional culture: The making of Balinese identity', in M. Picard and R. Wood (eds.) *Tourism, Ethnicity and the State in Asian and Pacific Societies*. Honolulu: University of Hawaii Press, 181–214.

Picard, M. and Wood R. (eds.) (1997) *Tourism, Ethnicity and the State in Asian and Pacific Societies*. Honolulu: University of Hawaii Press.

Qu, H.L. and Zhang, H.Q. (1997) 'The projection of international tourist arrivals in East Asia and the Pacific', in F.M. Go and C.L. Jenkins (eds.) *Tourism and Economic Development in Asia and Australasia*. London: Cassell, 35–47.

Relph, E. (1976) *Place and Placelessness*. London: Pion.

Richards, G. and Richards, B. (1998) 'A globalised theme park market? The case of Disney in Europe', in E. Laws, B. Faulkner and G. Moscardo (eds.) *Embracing and Managing Change in Tourism: International Case Studies*. New York and London: Routledge, 365–78.

Ritzer, G. and Liska, A. (1997) '"McDisneyisation" and "post-tourism": Complementary perspectives on contemporary tourism', in C. Rojek and J. Urry (eds.) *Touring Cultures: Transformations of Travel and Theory*. New York and London: Routledge, 95–109.

Roberts, S.M. and Schein, L. (1993) 'The entrepreneurial city: Fabricating urban development in Syracuse, New York'. *Professional Geographer*, 45(1), 21–33.

Robins, K. (1991) 'Tradition and translation: National culture in its global context', in J. Corner and S. Harvey (eds.) *Enterprise and Heritage: Crosscurrents of National Culture*. London and New York: Routledge, 21–44.

Schöllman, A., Perkins, H.C. and Moore, K. (2000) 'Intersecting global and local influences in urban place promotion: The case of Christchurch, New Zealand'. *Environment and Planning A*, 32, 55–76.

Sorkin, M. (1992) 'See you in Disneyland', in M. Sorkin (ed.) *Variations on a Theme Park: The New American City and the End of Public Space*. New York: Hill and Wang, 205–32.

Squire, S. (1993) 'Valuing countryside: Reflections on Beatrix Potter tourism'. *Area*, 25(1), 5–10.

Squire, S. (1999) 'Rewriting languages of geography and tourism: Cultural discourses of destinations, gender and tourism history in the Canadian Rockies', in G. Ringer (ed.) *Destinations: Cultural Landscapes of Tourism*. London: Routledge, 80–100.

Sunway Lagoon: Malaysia's Premier Theme Park sales kit (n.d.).

Straits Times, The (1984) 'Kampung's business opportunities', 26 August, Singapore.

Straits Times, The (1986) '$30m to turn Tiger Balm Garden into a world-class theme park', 29 April, Singapore.

Straits Times, The (1986) 'Haw Par goes hi-tech', 30 April, Singapore.

Straits Times, The (1995) '$6 million revamp for Haw Par Villa', 26 April.

Teo, P. and Yeoh, B.S.A. (1997) 'Remaking heritage for tourism'. *Annals of Tourism Research*, 24(1), 192–213.

Urry, J. (1990) *The Tourist Gaze: Leisure and Tourists in Contemporary Society*. London: Sage Publications.

Urry, J. (1995) *Consuming Places*. London and New York: Routledge.

Wasko, J. (1996) 'Understanding the Disney universe', in J. Curran and M. Gurevitch (eds.) *Mass Media and Society*. London: Arnold, 348–68.

Wood, R. (1993) 'Tourism, culture and the sociology of development', in M. Hitchcock, V. King and M. Parnwell (eds.) *Tourism in Southeast Asia*. London: Routledge, 48–70.

World Tourism Organisation (WTO) (1997) *Yearbook of Statistics*. Madrid: WTO.

World Travel and Tourism Council (1995) *Travel and Tourism: A New Economic Perspective*. Oxford: Elsevier.

Zukin, S. (1991) *Landscapes of Power: From Detroit to Disney World*. Berkeley: University of California Press.

Zukin, S. (1995) *The Culture of Cities*. Cambridge, Massachusetts: Blackwell Publishers.

10

Thailand in 'Touristic Transition'

Erik Cohen

Introduction

Tourism raises complex ecological, social and cultural issues, in part because its development, particularly in third world destinations, faces a fundamental paradox. Their initial attractiveness to foreign tourists is based on an inventory of what I call (Cohen, 1995) natural attractions – pre-existing environmental, cultural and historical sites and events, which appear, or are promoted in the language of tourism (Dann, 1996) as 'authentic', 'pristine' or 'untouched', in alleged sharp contrast to the prevailing state-of-affairs in the contemporary West.[1] However, once tourism takes off and increasing numbers of mass tourists visit those destinations, a ubiquitous process takes place. As the once 'untouched' attractions come under growing pressure of sheer numbers of tourists, they become gradually transformed in order either to adapt them to tourist demand or to prevent their progressive destruction. Simultaneously new, contrived attractions are created to enhance the attractiveness of the destination and to deflect tourists from the declining natural attractions, or even to substitute for the latter. The principal thesis of this chapter is that there exists a close interconnection between the decline in the attractiveness of natural attractions and the emergence of new, contrived ones. This interconnection *en routes* countries whose tourism has initially been based on a variety of natural attractions, on a process of 'touristic transition' with far-reaching consequences for their tourist image and the composition and motivations of their tourist clientele.

The process of 'touristic transition'

While initially, the charm of many new destinations is that their natural, environmental and cultural attractions are 'unmarked' (Cohen, 1995:15) and integral to the habitat and flow of life of the local society, with the growth of tourism, a segregated tourist sphere gradually emerges. As tourism expands, these attractions become marked and gradually transformed and degraded. A growing gap (Cohen 1996:145–8) emerges between the tourist image of the destination (based on the attractiveness of its natural attractions) and reality. The newly emergent contrived attractions at first often tend to simulate, in a staged manner (MacCannell, 1973), the increasingly less attractive natural attractions: clear, blue swimming pools substitute for polluted beaches, gardens for destroyed nature, cultural shows for live ethnic customs. However, as the destination matures, such contrived attractions are increasingly implanted into the local environment, without being related to it.[2]

The boundary between the local society and the tourist sphere is, however, not fixed but permeable. Some of the initially contrived attractions become, in the course of time, 'naturalised' and incorporated into the local 'tradition' and way of life, especially if locals tend to patronise them as venues of domestic tourism or leisure activities (Cohen, 1995:26). Older contrived attractions frequently undergo a process of 'emergent authenticity' (Cohen, 1988), even as new ones are added to the tourist sphere. In the most developed destinations, the boundary between the tourist sphere and the rest of society may become blurred (Cohen, 1999).

The general process described, which I call the 'process of touristic transition', raises important issues and dilemmas in countries in which tourism plays an important role in development. I shall describe, in some detail, this process as it has evolved in Thailand. Since Thailand's transition is more advanced than in most Southeast Asian countries (excepting the city-state of Singapore) and is often held up as an example for other countries, the study of this transition may indicate incipient trends in those countries, and hence draw attention to problems and dilemmas of their future tourism development.

Recent developments in Thai tourism

The general outlines of the development of tourism in Thailand are well known and fairly well documented (see Meyer, 1988; Cohen, 1996) and need to detain us here only briefly. Thailand has enjoyed, in the West, the image of an enchanted Oriental kingdom throughout much of modern history. This image was probably the source of the prevailing favourable attitude toward the country and its people in the contemporary Western world. However, until the 1960s, Thailand was also a remote country visited by relatively few, elite tourists. The rapid development of foreign tourism to Thailand began only in the late 1960s and reached massive proportions during the 1980s and the 1990s (Table 10.1).

In the last 40 years, foreign tourism to Thailand expanded a hundred-fold and the tourists' average length of stay more than doubled. Tourist expenditure in 1997 was estimated at 120 billion baht (about US$3.24 billion at the April 2000 rate of about 37 baht to the dollar), and probably amounted to even more in 1999 when tourism picked up again after a slowdown during the 1997–1998 Asian financial crisis.

Table 10.1: Number of foreign tourist arrivals and their average length of stay 1960-1999 (selected years)

Year	Number of arrivals	Average length of stay (days)
1960	81,340	3.00
1965	225,025	4.80
1970	628,671	4.80
1975	1,180,075	5.00
1980	1,858,801	4.90
1985	2,438,270	5.58
1990	5,298,860	7.06
1993	5,760,533	6.94
1996	7,192,145	NA
1999 (target)	8,280,000	NA

Source: Tourism Authority of Thailand.

The popularity of Thailand at the outset of its tourism boom has been largely based on its 'hedonistic appeal' (Peleggi, 1996:433), particularly the easy availability of various sexual services. Partly to overcome its image as the 'brothel of Asia' and to broaden its appeal to a wider spectrum of prospective visitors, the Tourism Authority of Thailand (TAT) sought from the 1980s onward to promote the country as a destination for cultural tourism (Peleggi, 1996:433) and seaside vacationing. The TAT initiated a series of promotional campaigns such as the 'Visit Thailand Year' (1987) (*Business Review*, 1986), the 'Thailand Arts and Crafts Year' (1988–1989) (*Holiday Time in Thailand*, 1988), and the recent 'Amazing Thailand 1998–1999' (*Thaiways*, 1997). The authorities attached great importance to the latter campaign, since in a period of deep economic crisis, tourism is one of the few bright spots contributing significantly to employment and foreign exchange. The government initiated an ambitious plan to attract 17 million tourists to Thailand during the two years of the campaign. The actual effectiveness of these promotional campaigns, however, has never been reliably established.

Following the example of Thailand, other mainland Southeast Asian countries have instituted their own promotional campaigns, such as Visit Myanmar Year, 1996 (*Die Zeitung*, 1995; *Bangkok Post*, 26 November 1996) and Visit Laos Year 1999 (Tourism Authority of Lao People's Democratic Republic, circa 1998).

The sheer growth in the number of tourists is an important precondition for the process of touristic transition. Equally important are more specific trends in the composition, motivation and distribution of tourists. In the case of Thailand, several significant trends can be observed in recent years.

First, while the authorities seem to have targeted mainly affluent Western and Japanese tourists in their promotional campaigns, it is noticeable that close to half of foreign tourism to Thailand originated in Asian countries (excluding Japan), especially neighbouring Malaysia. More recently, two new major sources of tourists have opened up: mainland China (*International Herald Tribune*, 6 April 1998) and Russia (*Bangkok Post*, 21 May 1998). Though there are differences between the principal concerns of the Asian and Russian tourists, it appears that sightseeing of natural attractions is relatively low on the list of priorities of both, a fact which facilitates the process of touristic transition in Thailand.

Second, even among tourists from the West, a change of relative emphasis from sightseeing to vacationing, particularly in the seaside resorts of central and southern Thailand, appears to have taken place. This trend seems to be in tune with similar developments in other maturing tourist destinations. As once remote exotic destinations become more accessible, especially through an expanding network of cheap air links, they cease to be the preserve of elite sight-seeing visitors and become affordable to mass tourists who are more interested in vacationing than their predecessors. Moreover, first-time visitors tend to engage more in sightseeing than return visitors. Such a re-orientation also facilitates the process of touristic transition.

Third, tourism in Thailand is concentrated mainly along a north-to-south axis (Cohen, 1996:6–8) with three major nodes: Bangkok in the centre, Chiang Mai in the north and Phuket island in the south. The axis has been gradually extended further into the north and south towards the boundaries of the country and broadened to include adjoining peripheral areas. New, 'unspoilt' destinations are thus penetrated by tourism even as the natural attractions along the axis gradually decline. However, the basic geographic pattern of tourism has not changed over the period of its expansion. Outside the central axis foreign tourism is scarce, as indicated by the fact that the huge northeast of the country known as Isan, the home of 20 million inhabitants, attracted a mere 200,000 foreign tourists in 1997 (*Bangkok Post*, 10 August 1998). The recent trend to regionalisation of Southeast Asian tourism, as we shall see, encourages the further expansion of tourism into ever more peripheral areas of the country, including into Isan, while also intensifying the touristic transition of the mature tourist areas along the central axis.

Finally, during the period of rapid growth of foreign tourism, there was a parallel, though little noticed, growth in domestic tourism. Domestic tourism constitutes a significant component of tourism to some of the most popular destinations of foreign tourism, such as Phuket. It also dominates tourism in more remote, little known attractions such as in Isan which, according to one estimate, was visited by about 10 million domestic tourists in 1997. More important, domestic tourists and locals are the principal clientele of the large-scale amusement centres and other contrived attractions which have mushroomed in recent decades in the vicinity of the major cities, particularly around Bangkok.

The Thai authorities have until recently sought to attract foreign tourists to the country by emphasising its exoticism – "Exotic Thailand" was the name of a newssheet distributed by TAT, while "Thailand – the Most Exotic Country in Asia" was one of its principal promotional slogans. However, as Thailand underwent a process of rapid economic development in the decade preceding the economic crisis of 1997, with often disastrous consequences for its environment (*Bangkok Post*, 24 December 1997) and the cultural traditions of its people, the emphasis upon the exotic character of the country was attenuated. This can be seen in the substitution of the more vague and broader term 'amazing' for the former 'exotic', as in the current slogan "Amazing Thailand". In spite of the change, the emphasis remained on Thailand's natural environmental, cultural and archaeological attractions. However, with the decline of many of these attractions, the gap between the image of the more mature attractions promoted by the tourism authority and the reality encountered by the visitors has widened. As if to make up for the discrepancy, increased stress has been put on ecotourism (*Bangkok Post*, 20 December 1997), a slogan which in many instances serves as a convenient cover for the exploitation of locations such as natural parks, from which tourism was heretofore excluded (*Bangkok Post*, 1 August 1998). The contemporary promotional material reflects to a much smaller degree one of the principal current trends in Thai tourism – the emergence of a great number of often large-scale contrived attractions, besides, and often as substitutes for, the declining and transformed principal natural attractions. Thailand's touristic transition was, perhaps intentionally, largely disregarded in the promotional media and possibly also overlooked by the tourist authority itself.

The process of touristic transition in Thailand can be observed on several levels: the local, the national, and even the regional or international. I shall deal with each of these levels in some detail.

The touristic transition at the local level

The touristic transition is most advanced in the mature tourist destinations of Thailand, especially in major seaside resorts which have experienced the most intensive tourism exploitation. I shall therefore deal more extensively with one of these resorts, and then briefly describe the process in two other kinds of destination.

Seaside resorts

Though my own fieldwork took place primarily on the islands of Phuket and Koh Samui (Cohen, 1996:151–246), I chose the case study of Pattaya as the most extreme example of the touristic transition of a seaside resort. Patong on Phuket and the Chaweng and Lamai beaches on Koh Samui follow a similar trajectory, though the transition in these resorts has not yet reached the stage which has been attained by Pattaya.

Pattaya is the biggest, and in the language of its promoters, the foremost seaside resort of Southeast Asia. The resort has experienced a phenomenal growth in its relatively short history. 'Discovered' only in 1961 by American GIs stationed in Thailand (*The Nation Review*, 31 December 1978; Vielhaber, 1984), the small fishing village in the Gulf of Thailand rapidly became a centre of international vacationing due to its favourable natural endowments and convenient location in the proximity of Bangkok. Initially a popular destination of rest and recreation (R&R) trips of American GIs, Pattaya boomed in the course of the late 1970s and the 1980s into a popular destination for foreign, especially German and Arab, vacationers (Vielhaber, 1984; Montague, 1989;) who were attracted by its beaches and burgeoning nightlife. However, the rapid, uncontrolled and speculative growth which transformed the little village into an expanding city (Vielhaber, 1984; *Bangkok Post*, 25 July 1989) soon provoked environmental degradation, even as the growth of tourist-oriented prostitution, drugs and crime spoilt the initially favourable image of the resort (*Bangkok Post*, 4 July 1978; 25 July 1989; *Far Eastern Economic Review*, 28 November 1991). The pollution of the sea, which made it unfit for bathing; the destruction of marine life; the degradation of the beach environment; the rapid and mostly uncontrolled construction of hotels, shophouses, 'beer-bar' complexes and similar commercial projects, accompanied by growing tourism-related crime, engendered a deepening crisis by the mid 1990s. The authorities and the private sector sought to rehabilitate the resort and to enhance its attractiveness for wider segments of the tourist public (*Asia Magazine*, 20 March 1988; *Bangkok Post*, 26 November 1993; *The Nation*, 12 September 1993), but despite their efforts, Pattaya has not yet fully recovered from the crisis. Significantly, as efforts at environmental rehabilitation have met at best with moderate success, the private sector stepped in to enhance Pattaya's attractiveness by creating a broad spectrum of new, contrived attractions in the city and its surroundings. Often constructed on a grand scale, these attractions served to some extent to broaden the image of Pattaya as a place offering natural amenities and sexual attractions, to a multi-purpose resort with attractive offerings for all kinds of tourists. Rather than as a *beach resort*, the place is now conceived of and promoted as a *resort city*, replete with a variety of different (mainly contrived) attractions (*Bangkok Post*, 9 January 1997).

The contrived attractions of Pattaya fall into two major categories: establishments and events. The number of establishments is very large indeed, but here I shall briefly review only a few outstanding examples. The older establishments are often tenuously related in some way to the natural characteristics or the cultural or historical endowments of Pattaya or of Thailand, while the newer ones tend to be extraneous 'implants', devoid of any connection to the place or the country. The latter were brought to Pattaya or its vicinity primarily because the entrepreneurs expected that most of the visitors would come from the resort.

Probably most closely related to the local context is the Khao Khiew Open Zoo, established in 1978 in the vicinity of the main road leading from Bangkok to Pattaya and easily accessible from the resort. Covering about 1,200 acres, it houses about 200 animal species, "grouped in spacious compounds in the park which, except for the wire fences, are exact replicas of the jungles of Thailand. Perhaps...even more so than the original habitat, little of which is left due to exploitation of the forest" (*Explore Pattaya*, 1993:14).

Some of the other major older contrived attractions emphasise Thai environmental and cultural themes even though many are presented in an overtly 'staged' (MacCannell, 1973) form. Their spectacular shows are intended for the amusement of tourists and some of the items on their programmes are only tenuously, if at all, related to Thai culture. Nevertheless, they contain few, if any, purely implanted features. The Nong Nooch Orchid Wonderland, a park located on 500 acres on the road from Pattaya to Sathahip, advertises itself as "a fine example [of] Thai culture and hospitality set in a paradise of flourishing gardens" (*Nong Nooch Orchid Wonderland* brochure, *circa* 1993:n.p.). The park features a variety of differently styled gardens, a cultural spectacular as well as various hospitality and leisure services. Though the emphasis is on the Thai character of its shows, the popular elephant show includes many spectacular features which have little to do with Thai culture.

The Million Years Stone Park and Pattaya Crocodile Farm, located in the vicinity of Pattaya, is another contrived attraction, which seeks to present itself as a natural one. Thus, the somewhat garbled language of its brochure claims that its rock garden was "genuinely created in a natural way" as a "splendid combination of science and nature. Virtually [sic] for this creation proves perseverance and quest for a perfectly natural wonder" (*Million Years Stone Park and Pattaya Crocodile Farm* brochure, *circa* 1994:n.p.). The garden is said to consist of a "selection of stones [from] many places" and is thus, in a sense, similar to a zoo or botanical garden. But the park is intended more to entertain than to edify. Its logo is a crocodile fully dressed in a Western outfit. The park offers a variety of entertainment and "exciting shows featuring wild animals including tigers and bears...sword fighting, Thai games and magic shows". As in the preceding case, some of these shows have little to do with Thai culture.

Mini Siam, a theme park on the outskirts of Pattaya, is a particularly interesting case. It was initially intended, in the language of its brochure, to be "Thailand's first wonder displaying Thai heritage on a miniature scale [which] brings together more than 100 models of important art objects and historical sites throughout the Kingdom" (*Mini Siam* brochure, *circa* 1994:n.p.). Mini Siam was meant to serve "those [tourists] who cannot afford to visit and admire all the real beautiful ancient objects and ancient remains". A visit to the park will thus enable "the visitors [to] boast of a trip throughout the country" (*Hotel Information News*, 1990). At a later stage, however, new, implanted components were added to Mini Siam – Mini Europe and Mini World – probably to serve the growing number of domestic and Asian tourists who may not have a chance to travel around the world.

In contrast to the preceding examples, most of the more recently established major contrived attractions in Pattaya and its vicinity had from the outset a markedly implanted character, unrelated to the local or national environment or culture. Most prominent among such recently established attractions are the Paintball game range (*The Nation*, 7 August 1994; *Bangkok Post*, 19 May 1994), the World Dogs Centre featuring, among other things, a show which includes "dogs-boxing [sic], doing by order, protecting dogs, [dogs] jumping fire's loop, [and] jumping knife's loop [sic]" (*World of Dogs* brochure, *circa* 1998:n.p.) and a branch, established in 1995, of Ripley's Believe It or Not! museum (*Bangkok Post*, 13 January 1995).

Pattaya is also the venue of some major tourism events, especially festivals, all of which are contrived attractions. Unlike other tourism locations, no 'traditional' temple festival from the period prior to the arrival of tourism has survived to the present, if any has been celebrated at all in the little fishing village. However, while the tourist-oriented festivals created at an earlier stage resemble 'traditional' Thai festivals, the more recent ones are implanted affairs, unrelated to local or Thai culture. I shall illustrate this difference using the Pattaya Festival and the Pattaya Carnival.

The Pattaya Festival, the older of the two, replicates many of the features found in other Thai festivals. It is celebrated on, or close to, the traditional Thai New Year – the Songkran festival – and it includes a floral float parade, dragon dancers, *bong fai* (rocket) contests and a handicraft fair, all elements found in various other festivals around the country (*Bangkok Post*, 21 April 1990; 17 April 1994). The organisers of these events were able to draw upon the cultural resources of the employees of various tourist establishments in Pattaya who had migrated to the city from different regions of the country, especially from the northeast (Isan), a region rich in festival traditions.

The Pattaya Festival, however, also features some events which are extraneous to Thai culture, such as the Pattaya Midnight run, female parachute jumpers, a beach buffet and an international food festival. It is important to note that though the festival is tourist-oriented, the local Thai population takes part in it both as performers as well as spectators. Like many other newly instituted festivals in Thailand (to be discussed below), the Pattaya Festival, though initially created for foreign tourists, is becoming incorporated as an emergent local tradition.

In contrast to the Pattaya Festival, the Pattaya Carnival is primarily an implanted event unrelated to Thai culture. It is a replication of a Western, basically Christian custom for the pleasure of foreign tourists (*Thailand Traveller*, 1995). It should be noted, however, that other Christian festivals, like Christmas and Silvester, though also alien to Thai culture, are becoming popular – in a commercialised form – with the Thai public. Therefore it is possible that the carnivals may also find positive resonance among the fun-loving local public.

In the 40 years since its discovery, the fishing village of Pattaya, whose original assets were its striking natural amenities, has become a resort city whose attractions are not only increasingly contrived but also implanted, with features unrelated to the local or even the national environmental or cultural setting. Pattaya is thus suffering a loss of 'placeness' (Cohen, 1995:24) since many of its more recently established implanted attractions can be located elsewhere, and have been brought to the resort only owing to the presence of a large number of foreign tourists. In that respect Pattaya suffers a similar fate as some other large, mature resorts elsewhere in the world (cf. Butler, 1980) and like many of these, it faces an uncertain future. An analogous process of touristic transition can also be discerned in some other tourism locations in Thailand even though they may differ in their concrete manifestations from Pattaya. I shall illustrate this process in two other kinds of local situation, namely the craft villages and the hill tribes.

Craft villages

Thai handicrafts have undergone considerable transformation and a significant degree of 'heterogeneisation' (Cohen, 1993a; 2000) as they became re-oriented from their traditional clientele to an external audience (Graburn, 1976) of domestic and foreign tourists and exporters who sell to Western countries. The marketing of tourist crafts is a form of 'indirect tourism' (Aspelin, 1977) because only few consumers of such crafts come into direct contact with their producers. In Thailand, only a few craft villages have become tourist attractions in their own right, and even those are not visited by many foreign tourists. Most tourists still make their purchases in the principal craft markets, especially in the Weekend Market of Bangkok and the Night Bazaar of Chiang Mai. The process of commercialisation of their crafts has therefore not imparted major changes to the appearance of the craft villages except that in some of the more important ones, like the carvers' village of

Ban Thawai (Cohen, 1998) and the potters' village of Dan Kwien (Cohen, 1993a), big markets selling local and other craft products have emerged. An analogy to the transformation of natural attractions, and to the emergence of contrived and implanted ones in the tourist resorts, is therefore found primarily in the changes undergone by the commercialised craft objects themselves: their materials, methods of production, forms, functions and styles (Cohen, 2000).

Tourists are often enthusiastic about 'authentic' ethnic arts and crafts, but few actually purchase them in their 'unadulterated' form. In Thailand, like elsewhere in the developing world (Cohen, 1993b), the commercialisation of crafts usually necessitates their adaptation to the tastes and preferences of the external public. In its early stages, such adaptation usually remains limited to 'orthogenetic' changes. This means that although materials, forms and functions of the objects may undergo change, their style continues to resemble or constitutes merely a variation or a development of the current style during the period preceding commercialisation. This is analogous to the transformation which natural attractions undergo in resorts and other tourism locations. In some craft villages, however, especially those which produce large quantities of crafts not only for the tourist market but also for export, the link to the 'traditional' local products and styles has been gradually severed and a growing number of products presently undergo 'heterogenetic' changes (Cohen, 1993a). This means they absorb external, often foreign, influences, or are based on models or photographs of foreign craft products. Such heterogeneisation may proceed spontaneously as artisans respond to market demand, but frequently it is a result of orders placed by local businessman and foreign importers, who supply specifications, models or photos. The heterogeneisation of craft products, a trend prominent in the two above-mentioned craft villages of Ban Thawai and Dan Kwien, can be seen as analogous to the implantation of contrived attractions, unrelated to the local environment or culture, into mature tourist resorts. While the specific indicators of the process of touristic transition are different in craft villages from those in seaside resorts, the process is analytically similar in both kinds of attraction.

Hill tribes

The process of touristic transition is, in general, less advanced in hill tribe settlements, even in those most commonly frequented by tourists, than in the other kinds of tourist localities dealt with above. Few, if any, contrived attractions have been established in the tribal settlements themselves. The commercialised hill tribe crafts, though they have also been adapted to tourist tastes and preferences (Cohen, 1983; 2000) have remained on the whole within the scope of the various tribes' orthogenetic traditions. They have been transformed, but not heterogeneised like those of some of the principal Thai craft villages.

In the process of their incorporation into Thai society, the more accessible tribal villages often suffered extreme de-culturation. Consequently, a growing gap has emerged between the exotic image and the everyday reality of hill tribe people (Cohen, 1996). In many of the tribal villages visited by tourists, the inhabitants have had to stage themselves in order to preserve their attractiveness. Tribal members, especially women and children, seeking to derive some income from tourists, either by selling their crafts or other souvenirs, or by posing for photos, tend to dress in conspicuous tribal costume to attract the attention of potential clients. This is particularly the case in tribal settlements popular with tourists, such as Meo Doi Pui in the vicinity of Chiang Mai (Cohen, 1996), a village which began to attract tourists as early as the 1970s. The Hmong and the Akha tribal women hawking their crafts in the Night Bazaar of Chiang Mai also don spectacular costumes in order to attract the attention of visitors to this large and diversified market.

The case of the peculiar attire of the women of the Padaung people, a Karen sub-group in Burma (Bernard and Huteau, 1988; *Sawaddi*, 1993; Diran, 1997), illustrates how a natural, though spectacular, hill tribe attraction can be turned into a contrived one, merely by change of context. The Padaung women customarily adorn their necks and knees with brass coils, which has earned them the appellation "long-neck Karen" (*Lookeast*, 1993; Zaw, 1996) or "giraffe women" (*Bangkok Post*, 6 April 1998). Initially brought to the vicinity of the Thai border by an enterprising Padaung man in 1985 to be viewed by trekking excursions from Thailand (Mirante, 1990:36), the Padaung later fled together with Karenni rebels and refugees into Thailand, and were placed into refugee camps along the Thai–Myanmar border. Here the women became a standard attraction of tourist excursions. Their attractiveness hindered their repatriation (Mirante, 1990:37) and so they have remained in Thailand up to the present, despite periodical decisions by the authorities to send them back. In the course of the 1990s, as the Padaung women became the most popular hill tribe attraction in northern Thailand, a Thai businessman attempted to lure some of them into a compound close to a tourist location, where they could be shown to passing tourists. Here the Padaung women were virtually imprisoned in a kind of 'human zoo' until the establishment was eventually raided by the Thai police and the women returned to the refugee camps (*Bangkok Post*, 6 April 1998).

By virtue of their relocation into a 'human zoo', and exposure to the tourists' gaze, the Padaung women have become a contrived attraction or, in Mirante's phase, "hostages to tourism" (Mirante, 1990), shown to tourists against their will. But their attire did not have to be spectacularised or changed – their ordinary, natural attire was spectacular enough. The case of the tribal girls who make a living by taking photos with tourists at the northernmost point of Thailand in the vicinity of the bridge leading from the town of Mae Sai in Thailand to Kachilek in Myanmar differs significantly from that of the Padaung women. These girls willingly don a contrived tribal costume, which, while comprising some elements from various tribal attires, is altogether a free invention. Despite that, it is often featured in tourism publications as a 'traditional' tribal costume (e.g. *Saen Sanuk*, 1989). It is ironic that the author of an article in a tourist-oriented periodical chose a picture of some girls dressed in that costume for a caption stating that "Each hill tribe has its own language and culture" (*Thailand Traveller*, 1996:28–9). However, like in other cases of 'invented traditions' (Hobsbawm and Ranger, 1983), this costume may well eventually become incorporated into the evolving tribal culture of Thailand and be, for example, exhibited in a tribal museum though it did not originate in any specific tribal group.

While hill tribe people may stage themselves for tourists, and transform their crafts to catch the tourists' eye, they normally lack the financial and managerial resources to establish sustainable contrived attractions in their villages. All contrived attractions featuring Thai hill tribes have been established in non-tribal locations and initiated and owned by non-tribal entrepreneurs. The biggest and most popular of such attractions are the so-called 'tribal villages' and tribal performances staged in theme parks and similar tourism establishments in or close to urban areas in northern and even central Thailand. The process of touristic transition of the hill tribes is thus in an early stage in the tribal villages themselves, but it is in a relatively advanced stage outside those settlements, with tribal members mostly playing a passive role in the contrived attractions created and managed by others.

The touristic transition at the national level

The process of touristic transition at the national level is manifested primarily in the gradual transformation of the remaining natural attractions in the course of the expansion of tourism into previously unexploited areas, and in the proliferation of new contrived attractions primarily in more mature tourist areas. The transition has mitigated Thailand's 'exoticism', forcing a subtle reorientation of the image by which Thailand is promoted from 'exotic' to 'amazing' as the leading epithet for the country in the most recent promotional campaign.

I shall briefly illustrate the transformation of natural attractions at the national level and the creation of some major contrived attractions in four domains: the national parks, archaeological sites, festivals, and theme and amusement parks.

National parks

Although the establishment of tourist facilities in national parks is nominally prohibited, uncontrolled and often illegal, foreigner-oriented tourism development has in recent decades affected beyond repair the natural environment of Samet and Phi Phi islands (*Bangkok Post*, 26 March 1989; 17 March 1994; *The Nation*, 6 August 1991). Some other national parks have been penetrated by resort developers for domestic tourism on a smaller scale. The Thai Forestry Department and the Forest Industry Organisation recently proposed to regularise the exploitation of the national parks under the guise of ecotourism (*Bangkok Post*, 1 August 1998; 30 September 1998; *The Nation*, 14 September 1998). Their proposal also seeks to legitimise the already irreversible tourism development of Samet and Phi Phi islands (*Bangkok Post*, 24 April 1998) but it may also eventually lead to the transformation of some of the last niches of 'untouched' nature in the country.

Archaeological sites

The restoration of archaeological sites by the national authorities is officially intended to preserve the national heritage. However, this endeavour is also influenced by various political and economic considerations accompanying, and sometimes overriding, the purely historical, scientific ones. The political considerations are aimed primarily at domestic tourists and derive from the endeavour to reaffirm, in the selection of sites and the manner of their restoration, "the hegemony of the official historical narrative" that has been challenged by revisionist historians (Peleggi, 1996:433). Moreover, this endeavour is accompanied by other more practical considerations deriving from the tourism potential of restored sites. In some instances, tourism potential overrides scientific considerations in the interest of making a site more accessible or attractive to tourism. Hence, one critic of the TAT conservation policy pointed out: "[s]ince the 1980s, 'conservation' has been clearly stated in the policy of TAT... However, this is only a euphemism because it has been done for economic benefits. The conservation of tradition by TAT, for example [and by implication of archaeological and historical sites], are carried out to please tourists primarily" (Chantarotron, 1992:18). Another author points out that, according to critics, "[a]s a tourism-oriented policy prevails, archaeological sites are preserved to serve tourists rather than to help locals recognise their historical value..." (*Bangkok Post*, 7 January 1995). As a consequence, a Thai journalist complained that "our historic monuments [are turned] into tourism venues that [can] easily be mistaken for amusement parks" (*Bangkok Post*, 20 November 1996).

The desire to attract tourists led, according to one author, to the tendency for "[t]he reconstruction [of ancient sites], by adding and adapting to build up a complete structure according to ideas those in charge think are right, is thought to give a better impression to tourists than a ruined one." (*Muang Boran Journal*, 1987:11). Thus, for example, in "Sukhothai [Historical Park] Buddha images were sculpted to replace all the missing ones..." (*Muang Boran Journal*, 1987:11). The author concludes that "such renovation for commercial benefit is not based on reality and may even lead to self-indulgence" (*Muang Boran Journal*,1987:11). The invention of 'ancient traditions' to accompany the restoration of Sukhothai has led, in the blunt words of another critic, to its "Disneyfication" (*Bangkok Post*, 20 November 1996).

The context and ambience of restored archaeological sites is further transformed by their inclusion in historical parks or even by the more prosaic construction of roads, car parks, toilets, accommodation and other facilities (*Bangkok Post*, 18 March 1993) to serve the needs and convenience of tourists. Furthermore, in some extreme cases, the fanciful restoration of sites is not just a mere transformation of attractions to adapt them to tourist visits; in the case of some of the more important restored archaeological sites, such as the old capital of Sukhothai, the alterations imposed upon the site and its surroundings in fact amount to the creation of a partially contrived attraction.

Festivals

Festivals are integral to Thai folk religion and constitute the high point of communal religious activities. Temple festivals and fairs are commonly held at Buddhist temples at least once a year throughout rural Thailand, while major Buddhist, Chinese and other popular festivals are celebrated in urban centres (Gerson, 1996). Such festivals attract large numbers of visitors, and owing to their colourful rituals and accompanying events, constitute major tourist attractions. From a relatively early stage in the development of tourism in Thailand, some festivals became oriented to, and influenced by, tourism. Thus, Plion-Bernier (1973:55), after describing what he claims to have been the last traditional elephant round-up, in 1938, claims that, "[a]t the present time, round-ups are organised each year for tourists..." (Plion-Bernier, 1973:55). The elephant round-up in Surin, the principal staged representation of the traditional elephant hunt, was revived already in 1960 (Gerson 1996:53), and soon became a major tourist attraction (*Holiday Time in Thailand,* 1969). It features such events as soccer matches between elephants and the "re-enactment of an ancient battle when several 'warriors' charge on elephant back, handling long-handled weapons..." (Gerson, 1996:53). The popular Songkran festival (the Thai New Year) was already in 1980 said to have become "more colourful, more riotous and more uproarious" than it used to be 30 years earlier (*Sawasdee,* 1980); it has become even more so since then – attracting growing numbers of foreign tourists, not only as spectators but also as participants. A similar transformation has occurred in some other major established festivals, such as the Candle Festival in Ubon (*Kinnaree,* 1988) and the Chinese Vegetarian Festival in Phuket (*Phuket, Phi Phi and Krabi, circa* 1990; *The Nation,* 23 October 1998; *Bangkok Post,* 10 October 1999), at least partially under the impact of the sheer presence of growing numbers of domestic and foreign tourists, and of the desire of locals to attract and impress them. The scope of participants has increased, the principal traditional events were elaborated and spectacularised, and in some instances, various new events, unrelated to the major theme of the festival, were introduced.

Even more significant in the present context is the creation of new festivals, intended to enhance the attractiveness of an established destination, or to place a new one on the tourist map. The Flower Festival of Chiang Mai, initiated in 1977 (*Trip Info* 1997; *Kinnaree,* 1993) exemplifies the former; the Egg Banana Festival of Kamphaeng Phet (*Thailand Traveller* 1992; *Kinnaree,* 1998), the Lamyai (longan) Festival of Lamphun (*Bangkok Post,* 5 August 1993), the Straw Bird Festival of Chainat (*Kinnaree,* 1987) and the recently started Fish Festival of Singhburi, illustrate the latter. Such invented festivals, the number of which continues to grow, illustrate well the dynamics of the tourist sphere. They are initially set up as contrived attractions but are soon 'naturalised' and incorporated into the local culture, becoming an emergent 'tradition'. It appears that such incorporation is easier in the domain of festivals than in most other domains discussed here, since most festivals are not just implanted, but can be anchored in some aspects of the local environment, history or culture. They also serve to bolster local identity and pride, and are cherished by the local public even as they attract domestic and foreign tourists.

Theme parks and amusement parks

The most prominent contrived attractions are the various theme parks and amusement parks which emerged in growing numbers and at an ever bigger scale in the boom years preceding the economic crisis of 1997. Their location indicates their intended public. According to a TAT publication devoted to these types of attraction, "[m]ost of Thailand's largest and most sophisticated parks are located within easy travelling distance of Bangkok, in the city outskirts. Others are located in popular tourist spots like Pattaya or Chiang Mai" (*Exotic Thailand: Theme Parks,*

Special Events, Amusement Parks and Water Parks brochure, *circa* 1997:n.p.). Those around Bangkok are primarily oriented to the local population as centres of mass leisure activities, even though they also seek to attract domestic and foreign tourists; those around the major tourist centres are primarily oriented to foreign tourism but are also patronised by substantial numbers of domestic tourists.

All the theme and amusement parks are by definition contrived attractions. However, they differ in the extent to which they relate to, or reproduce, elements of the local or national environment, culture and history, or are completely unrelated, implanted affairs. Just as in the case of Pattaya, so at the national level, the more recently established a park, the greater the chance that it will be implanted. Some of the earliest parks, such as the Rose Garden (*Bangkok Post*, 29 July 1993), and the Ancient City (*Sawaddi*, 1972; *Saen Sanuk*, 1988), both established around 1970 in the vicinity of Bangkok, seek to reproduce some major aspects of Thai culture. The Ancient City, for example, is intended to represent Thailand in miniature and to enable visitors to "learn about many aspects of Thai culture without having to travel the length and breadth of the country" (*Bangkok Post*, 25 December 1997). The Rose Garden is said to have become "a driving force in the promotion of Thai culture and tradition throughout the four corners of the globe" (*Bangkok Post*, 29 July 1993). But some of the newer parks, like the Disney-inspired Fantasyland (*Exotic Thailand: Theme Parks, Special Events, Amusement Parks and Water Parks* brochure, *circa* 1997), King Kong Island and Siam Park City, are completely alien to local themes and, as such, purely implanted establishments. Many of the latter have been conceived on a massive scale: "the most expansive of these amusement complexes, such as Siam Park City, Dream World and Safari World in the north of Bangkok, are entire cities unto themselves, combining world-class water parks, amusement parks, and cultural attractions on sprawling premises of several hundred thousand square metres" (*Exotic Thailand: Theme Parks, Special Events, Amusement Parks and Water Parks* brochure, *circa* 1997:n.p.). Similarly, the new Phuket FantaSea park, constructed on 270 rai (67.5 ha) of land on Kamala beach (*Bangkok Post*, 27 April 1998) at a total investment of about 3.3 billion baht (about US$90 million; *The Nation*, 5 September 1998) is the largest establishment of its kind on the island. It is expected to attract 2.4 million of the 3.5 million tourists annually visiting the island (*Bangkok Post*, 27 April 1998). Joining a plethora of other contrived attractions, the size of this new project and its expected attractiveness indicates the growing significance of contrived attractions on an island whose depleting natural attractions have initially been the sole basis of its touristic attractiveness.

The touristic transition at the regional level

The late Thai Prime Minister Chatichai Choonhavan's call to transform the Southeast Asia region "from battleground to marketplace" (*Bangkok Post*, 7 December 1998) signified a re-orientation of Thailand towards its neighbours. The concrete expression of this re-orientation was the emergence of schemes of regional cooperation between Thailand and its northern and southern neighbours. In the north of Thailand, these schemes have been variously called the Economic Quadrangle (*Bangkok Post*, 6 December 1994), the Golden Quadrangle (*The Nation*, 31 March 1994; *Bangkok Post*, 28 March 1994), or the Greater Mekong Sub-region (*The Nation*, 29 July 1994; 8 August 1994) and involve up to six countries: Thailand, Laos, Burma, Vietnam, Cambodia and Southern China (*The Nation*, 29 July 1994; *Bangkok Post*, 30 January 1997). In the south of Thailand, such schemes are mostly related to a Southern Growth Triangle, involving Thailand, Malaysia and Indonesia (*Bangkok Post*, 25 March 1995). Since tourism plays a major role in the northern schemes, I shall restrict my comments to that region.

It should be noted, however, that the optimistic plans of the mid 1990s for an integrated northern regional tourism development have encountered some serious obstacles, and that therefore the extent of the regionalisation of tourism is still fairly limited (*Bangkok Post*, 4 October 1998). Hence I have to speculate on future developments because established facts are fairly scarce.

Thailand is considered as the centre or 'hub' (*The Nation*, 7 April 1995) of regional tourism development (*Bangkok Post*, 3 April 1995) and the 'gateway' to the other mainland Southeast Asian countries (TAT, n.d.; *Bangkok Post*, 30 January 1997) due to its geographical position in the region, and its relatively well developed infrastructure. Its strategic position within the region can be expected to facilitate investments by Thai entrepreneurs in the development of tourist facilities and touring services in the capital-starved countries of the region.

The Thai tourist authorities are the primary promoters of regionalisation, and consider it as one of the strategies for tourism development in the country itself. The representation of Thailand as the 'Amazing Gateways' (to other continental Southeast Asian countries) has been chosen as one of the eight principal themes of the recent 'Amazing Thailand' campaign (*Amazing Thailand 1998–1999* brochure, n.d.:19). According to one Thai tourism official, "Thailand, having reached the peak of its tourism boom in the early 1990s, risks losing its appeal unless it can be marketed as part of a more diverse region" (*Bangkok Post*, 30 January 1997). This loss of appeal of Thailand is probably a consequence of the over-exploitation of its major mature 'natural' attractions, as well as of the rapid development of the country, which affected its general attractiveness. In contrast to Thailand, according to the same official, the other "Mekong countries are considered the last frontiers of Southeast Asian tourism". These countries are said to possess great potential as tourist destinations owing to their fresh and, as yet, untouched environmental and cultural attractions.

I submit that the regional integration of tourism will have two principal consequences for the touristic transition of Thailand. On the one hand, on the national level, it will create a growing division of labour between Thailand, as the centre of regional tourism, and the rest of the mainland Southeast Asian region. Thailand will become the staging area for regional tourism, offering its developed tourism facilities and contrived attractions to foreign tourists visiting the region (cf. *Bangkok Post*, 15 December 1997). The process of touristic transition will thereby be reinforced and, in a sense, legitimised. In comparison with its neighbours, Thailand as a country will probably lose much of the exotic appeal it still possesses, and become increasingly a shopping, entertainment and vacationing destination, while the region will offer the tourists its "abundant historical and cultural heritage and unspoiled natural beauty" (*Bangkok Post*, 19 December 1994).

On the other hand, however, at the local level, regionalisation will help to expand the tourist sphere into some of the remaining remote, unexploited parts of the country. The gateway areas for overland tourism, which provide access to the neighbouring countries in the far north and deep south, will be opened up to passing foreign tourism. Hence the north-to-south tourist axis of the country will be extended right to the international boundaries. The natural attractions of these remote areas will thus be visited by growing numbers of tourists. Even more significantly, the huge northeastern region of the country (Isan), lying outside the north-to-south axis, and presently underdeveloped, can be expected to become the gateway to Indochina (cf. *The Nation*, 11 April 1997), its diverse attractions becoming part of regional itineraries which will include Isan, Laos, Cambodia and Vietnam.

Regionalisation can thus be expected to reinforce the growing importance of facilities and contrived attractions in the more mature tourist locations of Thailand and contribute to the gradual transformation of attractions in the more remote, as yet unexploited areas, thus intensifying the process of touristic transition of the country.

Conclusion

Thailand is an ambiguous example of success in tourism development. Enjoying a very positive tourist image, it succeeded in attracting rapidly growing numbers of foreign tourists. Tourism is a leading earner of foreign currency, and an important branch of the national economy. But this success was achieved at a high price: tourism contributed significantly to the often reckless destruction of natural resources, characteristic of the process of Thailand's rapid economic development as a whole, even as those resources constituted the basis of its success. Tourism has also been an important contributing factor to the process of commodification of art, culture, and sex in Thailand. It should be noted, though, that, in the domain of art and culture, tourism has contributed to the preservation of crafts and customs which would otherwise have disappeared, as well as to the emergence of new artistic styles (Cohen, 2000) and cultural performances, however their aesthetic value may be judged.

The rapid environmental and cultural changes which the country experienced in the last two decades, and the self-defeating practices in the sphere of tourism, created a growing gap between the image of the country and its reality. The impact of this gap on foreign tourism was partly mitigated by the change in the composition of the tourism flow. The expansion of mass vacationing relative to sight-seeing, and the declining interest among contemporary tourists in 'authenticity' probably ameliorated the impact which the degradation and transformation of the principal natural attractions could otherwise have had on tourist arrivals and satisfaction. The emergent development of ecotourism, and other forms of soft tourism in as yet less exploited areas (*Bangkok Post*, 20 December 1997) may also have siphoned off some of the remaining authenticity-seeking tourists from the mature tourism locations. The rapid growth in the number and scope of contrived attractions in these locations can thus be seen partly as a compensation for the depletion of natural attractions, and partly as a response to the tastes and preferences of the enjoyment-seeking vacationers who became their principal customers. The contrived attractions thus served both as a remedy as well as an incentive to vacationing tourism.

However, as we have seen, the touristic transition, the main characteristic of which is the increase in the relative number, size and significance of contrived attractions, is a nation-wide and not just a localised process. Many of the often gigantic entertainment complexes erected in the vicinity of the major cities, and especially Bangkok, were intended to serve primarily the leisure needs of the local population and of domestic, rather than foreign, tourism, although they also seek to attract foreign tourists. Such attractions are one of many expressions of the growing commercialisation and westernisation of Thai culture and, as such, provide familiar entertainment opportunities to foreign visitors.

The regionalisation of mainland Southeast Asian tourism, as was pointed out above, may well reinforce the process of Thailand's touristic transition, with Thailand as a country specialising in the provision of facilities and contrived attractions while the newly opened countries and the remote border regions of Thailand provide fresh natural environmental and cultural attractions.

The problems at the bottom of Thailand's touristic transition, and the self-defeating practices which provoked them, have not escaped the attention of the planners of the regionalisation of mainland Southeast Asian tourism. The need for 'preservation' and 'sustainability' of tourism in the areas to be newly opened up, and the emphasis upon ecotourism and other forms of soft tourism, are common themes in the planners' 'greenspeak' (Dann, 1996:238–49; *The Nation*, 2 February 1999).

It is highly questionable, however, to what extent the promoters and entrepreneurs of the regionalisation of tourism will actually be willing or able to maintain the high principles of sustainability and soft tourism, especially under the pressure of the need of governments for foreign exchange and the desire of entrepreneurs for rapid profits. It should be noted that in all the countries surrounding Thailand, transportation infrastructure and tourist facilities are hardly existent outside the major urban centres (*Bangkok Post*, 15 February 1996). However, their very establishment, accompanied by the arrival of great numbers of relatively wealthy foreigners into poor and isolated ethnic communities, may constitute a serious environmental and cultural threat, however well behaved the tourists and however 'soft' their accommodation and means of transportation (*The Nation*, 2 February 1999). Moreover, from the dire experience of other destinations, we learn that sustainability and ecotourism tend to become mere slogans used to promote the image of travel and tour companies, who in fact pay them mere lip-service. Under the circumstances, a successful regionalisation of tourism, measured in terms of numbers of tourists, length of stay and expenditures, will almost inevitably bring about the same phenomenon of transformation of natural attractions and their eventual destruction as has occurred in Thailand. It should also be noted that some of the surrounding countries are already eager to develop large-scale contrived attractions, though their natural ones have hardly been tapped. Thus both Cambodia and Vietnam have made deals with foreign companies to open casinos in various locations (*Business Day*, 17 January 1995; *Bangkok Post*, 2 May 1995) and Cambodia is planning "to organise a major Ramayana festival at Angkor in 2000" (*Bangkok Post*, 7 December 1998).

The basic question regarding regionalisation is, will international promoters and entrepreneurs become convinced that the region is sufficiently attractive to large numbers of prospective visitors to be worth the risk to initiate and construct the needed infrastructure for large-scale tourism (*The Nation*, 1 September 1998)? Or whether they will find it preferable, at least for the time being, to keep tourism in the remote areas of mainland Southeast Asia on a small scale, restricted to adventure and elite tourism, thereby saving these areas from the kind of devastation which tourism has wrought in similar areas elsewhere. Though such forms of tourism are not without detrimental environmental and cultural effects, these effects are 'softer' and considerably easier to control than the 'harder' effects of massive tourism penetration. Furthermore, they do not encourage the creation of contrived attractions, and the acceleration of the process of touristic transition, of the kind Thailand is presently undergoing.

Thailand's touristic transition represents perhaps an extreme case of a widespread type of interconnectedness between natural and contrived attractions, the latter complementing, and to an extent, substituting for, the former. Some developed urban destinations, such as Singapore, may constitute instances of a contrasting type of interconnectedness: initially based on contrived attractions, Singapore is presently opening up and promoting some complementary natural ones (Chang, 1998). How widespread this type of interconnectedness is or will become remains to be determined by further comparative research.

Notes

[1] Note, for example, the series of advertisements for Thailand in the 1980s in which the greyness of (Western) "everydayland" was contrasted with the colourful "Thailand".
[2] The dynamics of change in the character of contrived attractions resembles the process of 'heterogeneisation' of commercialised arts and crafts (Cohen, 1993a).

References

Aspelin, P.L. (1977) 'The anthropological analysis of tourism: Indirect tourism and the political economy of the Mamainde of Mato Grosso, Brazil'. *Annals of Tourism Research*, 4(3), 134–60.
Amazing Thailand 1998–1999, brochure (n.d.).
Asia Magazine (1988) 'Soft city: Just how great is Pattaya?', 20 March, 8–13.
Bangkok Post (1978) 'Pollution threat clouds Pattaya's future', 4 July, Bangkok.
Bangkok Post (1989) 'Loved to death by tourists', 26 March, Bangkok.
Bangkok Post (1989) 'Pattaya city's growth getting out of hand', 25 July, Bangkok.
Bangkok Post (1990) 'Festival attracts 30,000', 21 April, Bangkok.
Bangkok Post (1993) 'To cut or to keep', 18 March, Bangkok.
Bangkok Post (1993) 'Driving force in the promotion of Thai culture and tradition', 29 July, Bangkok.
Bangkok Post (1993) 'Lamphun Lamyai Festival', 5 August, Bangkok.
Bangkok Post (1993) '"Revive Pattaya" project aims to boost beach resort', 26 November, Bangkok.
Bangkok Post (1994) 'Jet scooters, towed floats, destroying Koh Samet', 17 March, Bangkok.
Bangkok Post (1994) 'Golden Quadrangle united by decision to make money', 28 March, Bangkok.

Bangkok Post (1994) 'A week of fun and frolics in Pattaya', 17 April, Bangkok.
Bangkok Post (1994) 'Paintball "war" games more fun than fury', 19 May, Bangkok.
Bangkok Post (1994) 'Cooperation in Quadrangle has benefits for Thai North', 6 December, Bangkok.
Bangkok Post (1994) 'TAT to host Mekong forum', 19 December, Bangkok.
Bangkok Post (1995) 'Treasures hanging in the balance', 7 January, Bangkok.
Bangkok Post (1995) 'Paradise for lovers of the weird and the wacky', 13 January, Bangkok.
Bangkok Post (1995) 'Council to review Growth Triangle projects', 25 March, Bangkok.
Bangkok Post (1995) 'TAT plans to promote tourism in "Greater Mekong"', 3 April, Bangkok.
Bangkok Post (1995) 'Controversial floating casino opens its doors', 2 May, Bangkok.
Bangkok Post (1996) 'Quadrangle tourism needs another kick-start', 15 February, Bangkok.
Bangkok Post (1996) 'Tourism versus historical accuracy', 20 November, Bangkok.
Bangkok Post (1997) '"Resort City" status a new selling point', 9 January, Bangkok.
Bangkok Post (1997) 'Thailand needs Mekong links', 30 January, Bangkok.
Bangkok Post (1997) 'Park owner aims for regional amusement centre in a decade', 15 December, Bangkok.
Bangkok Post (1997) 'A new approach to eco-tourism', 20 December, Bangkok.
Bangkok Post (1997) 'Thailand's rocky road', 24 December, Bangkok.
Bangkok Post (1997) 'Rediscovering the Ancient City', 25 December, Bangkok.
Bangkok Post (1998) 'Critics decry "human zoo" of tribeswomen', 6 April, Bangkok.
Bangkok Post (1998) '"Parks for tourism" proposed', 24 April, Bangkok.
Bangkok Post (1998) 'Phuket FantaSea on target for opening in October', 27 April, Bangkok.
Bangkok Post (1998) 'Big-spending market shows no sign of slowing', 21 May, Bangkok.
Bangkok Post (1998) 'State forestry firm eyeing eco-tourism', 1 August, Bangkok.
Bangkok Post (1998) 'Isan offers phenomenal tourism opportunities', 10 August, Bangkok.
Bangkok Post (1998) 'Tide of tourism threatens Thailand's natural beauty', 30 September, Bangkok.
Bangkok Post (1998) 'Quadrangle schemes held up', 4 October, Bangkok.
Bangkok Post (1998) 'Questions cloud bid to revive Cambodian tourism', 7 December, Bangkok.
Bangkok Post (1999) 'A piece of the action', 10 October, Bangkok.
Bernard, P. and Huteau M. (1988) *Karennis, les combattants de le Spirale d'Or.* n.l.:L'Hartman.
Business Day (1995) 'Cambodia plays its casino cards close to its chest', 17 January, Bangkok.
Business Review (1986) 'Getting ready for "Visit Thailand Year 1987"', July, 51–60.
Butler, R.W. (1980) 'The concept of a tourism area cycle of evolution: Implications for the management of resources'. *Canadian Geographer*, 24, 5–12.
Chang, T.C. (1998) 'Regionalism and tourism: Exploring integral links in Singapore'. *Asia Pacific Viewpoint*, 39(1), 73–94.
Chantarotron, M. (1992) 'Art and culture conservation in Thai society'. *Muang Boran Journal* (in Thai and English), 18(3/4), 6–19
Cohen, E. (1983) 'The dynamics of commercialized arts: The Meo and Yao of Northern Thailand'. *Journal of the National Research Council of Thailand*, 15(1), Part II, 1–34.
Cohen, E. (1988) 'Authenticity and commoditization in tourism'. *Annals of Tourism Research*, 15(3), 371(86.
Cohen, E. (1993a) 'The heterogeneization of a tourist art'. *Annals of Tourism Research*, 20(1), 138–63.
Cohen, E. (ed.) (1993b) 'Tourist arts'. *Annals of Tourism Research*, 20(1), 1–215 (special issue).
Cohen, E. (1995) 'Contemporary tourism – Trends and challenges', in R. Butler and D. Pearce (eds.) *Change in Tourism.* London and New York: Routledge, 12–29.
Cohen, E. (1996) *Thai Tourism: Hill Tribes, Islands and Open-ended Prostitution.* Bangkok: White Lotus.
Cohen, E. (1998) 'From Buddha images to Mickey Mouse figures: The transformation of Ban Thawai Carvings', in M.C. Howard, W. Wattanapun, A. Gordon (eds.) *Traditional T'ai Arts in Comparative Perspective.* Bangkok: White Lotus, 149–74.
Cohen, E. (1999) 'Ethnic Tourism in Southeast Asia', paper presented at the *International Conference on Anthropology*, Chinese Society and Tourism, 28 September–3 October, Kunming, Yunnan.
Cohen, E. (2000) *The Commercialization of the Arts and Crafts of Thailand.* London: Curzon Press.
Dann, G.M.S.(1996) 7Sociolinguistic Perspective. Wallingford, Oxon: CAB International.
Die Zeitung (1995) 'Visit Myanmar 1996, mit Sklavenarbeit und Unterdrückung (Visit Myanmar 1996 with slave-labor and suppression)', 39, 41–43, Bangkok.

Diran, R.K. (1997) *The Vanishing Tribes of Myanmar*. London: Weidenfeld and Nicolson.
Exotic Thailand: Theme Parks, Special Events, Amusement Parks and Water Parks, brochure (circa 1997).
Explore Pattaya (1993) 'Khao Khiew', 10(7), 12–14.
Far Eastern Economic Review (1991) 'Wish you were here', 28 November, 54.
Gerson, R. (1996) *Traditional Festivals in Thailand*. Kuala Lumpur: Oxford University Press.
Graburn, N.H.H. (1976) 'Introduction: Arts of the Fourth World', in N.H.H. Graburn (ed.) *Ethnic and Tourist Arts*. Berkeley: University of California Press, 1–32.
Hobsbawm, E. and Ranger T. (eds.) (1983) *The Invention of Tradition*. Cambridge: Cambridge University Press.
Holiday Time in Thailand (1969) 'Elephants at Surin', 10(3), 12-19.
Holiday Time in Thailand (1988) 'Thailand Arts and Crafts Year '88-89', 28(4), 38–41.
Hotel Information News, (1990) 'A Visit to Thailand in Brief...at Mini Siam', No. 16 B.E. 2533, 22–8.
International Herald Tribune (1998) 'Thais get an unexpected shot in the arm: Chinese tourists', 6 April, London.
Kinnaree (1987) 'The straw birds of Chainat', 4(3), 12–17.
Kinnaree (1988) 'Ubon's Buddhist Lent', 5(6), 33–5.
Kinnaree (1993) 'A fitting celebration for the flower of the north', 10(2), 74–80.
Kinnaree (1998) 'Banana Festival in Kamphaeng Phet', 15(9), 40–2.
Lookeast (1993) 'Long-neck Women – Stretching for Attention', 24(5), 36–9.
MacCannell, D. (1973) 'Staged authenticity: Arrangements of social space in tourist settings'. *American Journal of Sociology*, 79(3), 589–603.
Meyer, W. (1988) *Beyond the Mask*. Saarbrücken: Breitenbach.
Million Years Stone Park and Pattaya Crocodile Farm, brochure, (circa 1994).
Mini Siam, brochure (circa 1994).
Mirante, E.T. (1990) 'Hostages to tourism'. *Cultural Survival Quarterly*, 14(1), 35–8.
Montague, S. (1989) 'International tourism in the eastern seaboard region of Thailand'. *Crossroads*, 4(2), 9-17.
Muang Boran Journal (1987) 'Visit Thailand Year: Are we going in the right direction?', 12(2), 8–11.
Nation Review, The (1978) 'The birth of Pattaya City', 31 December, Bangkok.
Nong Nooch Orchid Wonderland, brochure (circa 1993).
Peleggi, M. (1996) 'National heritage and global tourism in Thailand'. *Annals of Tourism Research*, 23(2), 432–48.
Phuket, Phi Phi and Krabi (circa 1990) 'Phuket's amazing vegetarian festival', 1(9), 10–15.
Plion-Bernier, R. (1973) *Festivals and Ceremonies of Thailand*. n.l.: L'Hartman.
Saen Sanuk (1988) 'For time travellers only', 8(2), 33–39.
Saen Sanuk (1989) 'Mae Sai', 9(1), 44–7.
Sawaddi (1972) '"Ancient Land": Thailand's best kept secret', January/February, 15–18.
Sawaddi (1993) 'Women of Padaung', 39(2), 17–20.
Sawasdee (1980) 'Chiang Mai's Songkran Festival', July-August, 48–55.
Thailand Traveller (1992) 'Bananas, Buddhas and beauties', September, 10–16.
Thailand Traveller (1995) 'Pattaya in action', 5(39), 24–9.
Thailand Traveller (1996) 'Odyssey to the northern hill tribes', 6(59), 28–35.
Thaiways (1997) 'Amazing Thailand 1998-1999', 14(10), 41–8.
The Nation (1991) 'Another paradise lost?', 6 August, Bangkok.
The Nation (1993) 'Pattaya: Dead or alive?', 12 September, Bangkok.
The Nation (1994) 'The "Golden Quadrangle", opportunities and dangers', 31 March, Bangkok.
The Nation (1994) 'Dream of Mekong subregion nears reality', 29 July, Bangkok.
The Nation (1994) 'Thrills, spills and kills in Pattaya', 7 August, Bangkok .
The Nation (1994) 'Partners in Mekong scheme striving for an identity', 8 August, Bangkok.
The Nation (1995) 'Make Thailand Indochina tourism hub', 7 April, Bangkok.
The Nation (1997) 'Trade bustles in sleepy Mekong zone', 11 April, Bangkok.
The Nation (1998) 'ADB steps up push for tourism along Mekong', 1 September, Bangkok.
The Nation (1998) 'Safari World branches out into "fantasy"', 5 September, Bangkok.
The Nation (1998) 'National Parks for tourism', 14 September, Bangkok.
The Nation (1998) 'Holiday spirits', 23 October, Bangkok.

The Nation (1999) 'Mekong tourism brings disasters', 2 February, Bangkok.

Tourism Authority of Lao Peoples' Democratic Republic (circa 1998) Visit Laos Year 1999. Vientiane: National Tourism Authority of Lao PDR.

Tourism Authority of Thailand (TAT) (n.d.) Thailand – Gateway to the Mekong Sub-Region. Bangkok: TAT.

Trip Info (1997) 'The Flower Festival', 2(41), 8–10.

Vielhaber, C. (1984) 'Vom Fischerdorf zu einem Zentrum des Fernreisetourismus; Beispiel Pattaya, Thailand, (From fishing village to a centre of long-haul tourism: Example of Pattaya, Thailand)'. Geographischer Jahresbericht ausösterreich, 43, 31–76.

World of Dogs, brochure (circa 1998).

Zaw, M.Y. (1996) 'In search of the long-necked women'. *Geo-Australasia*, 18(1), 88–96.

11

Dialogic Heritage: Time, Space and Visions of the National Museum of Singapore

Can-Seng Ooi

Introduction

There are many ways of understanding the past. This chapter introduces a dialogic reading of the heritage preserved and the histories presented by the National Museum of Singapore (NMS). Through a dialogic perspective, I will demonstrate how time and space are structured, as well as how the past and the present animate each other in the museums. The presentations in the NMS also reflect visions of regional connections, as spelt out by the Singapore Tourism Board (STB)[1] and the Ministry of Information and the Arts (MITA). The NMS consists of three museums: the Singapore History Museum (SHM), the Singapore Art Museum (SAM) and the Asian Civilisations Museum (ACM). The National Heritage Board (NHB) manages these museums. These museums "aim to keep up with the latest museological developments to fulfil the aspirations of the visual arts community for greater professionalism and specialisation" (Singapore Tourist Promotion Board (STPB) and MITA, 1995:16).

The first part of this chapter discusses various approaches to the study of history. It offers a dialogic perspective on how history, space and time are conceptualised. The second part then examines the stories offered by the three museums in the NMS. While the SHM emphasises Singapore's past, the SAM exhibits contemporary Southeast Asian visual art and the ACM showcases Asian ancient civilisations. The final part compares the different stories. The SAM and the ACM exemplify different approaches in constructing 'regional interconnections' between Singapore and Southeast Asia, and Singapore and Asia respectively. The time–space structures tacit in these regional stories are also different. Ultimately, this chapter reconstructs the regional interconnections asserted by the SAM and the ACM.

History, space and time

Williams (1976:146–8) examined the term 'history' and noted that the term commonly refers to "a narrative account of events". However, he also observed that the study of history has evolved. He explained the three dominant approaches of historicism in the last century. The first is a relatively neutral definition of a method of study which relies on the facts of the past and traces the precedents of current events. The second is a deliberate emphasis on variable historical conditions and contexts through which all specific events must be interpreted. The third is a hostile approach, which attacks all forms of interpretations or predictors by historical necessity or the discovery of general laws of historical development. The possibility of learning from the past is severely questioned in the last approach, which suggests that history is not relevant because the past will never be repeated.

   While Williams pointed out how the past is studied, there are also issues about the nature of historical knowledge. Any study of the past can be said to be situated in the present. Since historical knowledge is interpreted today, historians are merely understanding the past from views of the present. This form of interpretation is known as 'presentism'. Presentism is the unwitting projection of a structure of interpretation that arises from a historian's own contemporary experience or context onto aspects of the past under study (Dean, 1994:28–9). To some historians, in the name of objectivity, presentism should be avoided (Dean, 1994; Pickering, 1997). An 'objective' history aims to present only what actually took place. However, any 'objective' intellectual presentation of the past is severely challenged when the very language and technology that are used have already changed from the former time (Pickering, 1997:32). This results in an inherent tension: how can history be recouped without contemporary interpretations when the past is reconstructed under present-day circumstances?

   In avoiding the dilemma of objectivism and presentism in history, Foucault's historicism offers an alternative as it privileges contemporary conditions in the articulation of the past (Dean, 1994; Ooi and Karmark, 1998). Foucault, in his book *The Archaeology of Knowledge* (1972), problematised the 'objective' manner in which history is presented. He vehemently suggested that "we...must tear away from their virtual self-evidence, and to free the problems that they pose; to recognise that they are not the tranquil locus on the basis of which other questions (concerning their structure, coherence, systematicity, transformations) may be posed, but that they themselves pose a whole cluster of questions" (Foucault, 1972:26). He also argued that a historical discourse should be treated "as and when it occurs", instead of reference to origin or their truth-value claims (Foucault, 1972:25).

   A statement is an event to Foucault (1972:25). Each statement links and fits into a narrative; he reminds us that a message is often generated via carefully selected statements. Everything that is formulated in the discourse covers and silences, it represses the not-said which can undermine what is said. Statements are strategically constructed. Dean (1994) argued that Foucault suggested a method that reveals the multiple conditions of discursive formation, which Foucault further developed through his genealogy approach. Genealogy uncovers the productive form of power underlying every movement of institutional or discursive delimitation of statements (Foucault, 1984; Dean, 1994). In other words, when Foucault looked at past and present historical statements, he interrogated these statements with the respective conditions in which they are articulated. Each statement is then examined in a contextualised present; this acknowledges the changing conditions in the on-going construction of history (Foucault, 1972; Dean, 1994; Ooi and Karmark, 1998).

Instead of treating history in an objectivist manner and trying to avoid presentist interpretations, Foucault treated history as strategic presentations. To recoup an actual past is difficult if not impossible; he considered it a futile enterprise. Instead, Foucault argued that any articulation of history has to be understood in the circumstances of presentation. The presentation and use of history is just part of strategic communication.

Comparing the objectivist and the strategist approaches accentuates fundamentally different ways of thinking about relations between the past and the present in history. A dialogic perspective offers yet another approach; like the objectivist and strategist approaches, it too addresses presentist issues.

Dialogic historicism

The dialogic perspective originates from the literary theorist Bakhtin (1981; 1984a; 1984b; 1986). His works on literary texts have been appropriated by the social sciences (e.g. van Loon, 1997; Bell and Gardiner, 1998; Ooi, 2001). The dialogic perspective stresses the importance of processes, relations, dynamics, complementarity and contradictions. It employs a dynamic rather than a static way of thinking about the world. Instead of conceptualising the world in cause-and-effect terms, a dialogic approach conceptualises a phenomenon as an ongoing interplay of ideas, structures, agents and politics. Ideas and concepts must be understood in relation to other ideas and concepts, and also within the contexts of use.

As discussed earlier, the objectivist and strategist perspectives on history consider relations between the past and the present very differently. In what I termed as dialogic historicism, neither the past nor the present dominates, but instead each animates the other. For example, a priceless Ming vase in a modern display case offers historical and aesthetic experiences to many connoisseurs whose experiences encompass the ancient object, the contemporary presentation method and the symbolism. The ancient vase and its modern presentation jointly offer a historically significant product. This example also alludes to the interplay between the world-in-the-past (the vase) and the world-of-presenting-the-past (modern presentation). This interplay between the present and the past constitutes a dialogic presentation of the past.

The interplay between the double contexts of the past and the present is encapsulated in the articulation of history; the past and present co-exist and mutually inform one another (Ooi, 2001). Communication about the past often employs languages, ideas, artefacts and contexts of both the past and present. While the objectivist tradition sees this relationship as problematic, the dialogic perspective accepts and analyses these multiple temporal contexts.

The dialogic perspective also contrasts against the Foucauldian approach. The Foucauldian way is to subsume the past under the present, privileging contemporary contexts. A dialogic reading does not discredit or discount the work of historians and museum curators in trying to rediscover the past. Remnants, documents and arte-facts from the past can tell us what happened in history, although not definitively. Besides that, historical evidences frequently offer the presence or aura that provides authority to particular interpretations of history. In other words, a narrative about the past would be better affirmed with historical artefacts.

A dialogic reading of history acknowledges that any re-presentation of the past is an act in the present and that history cannot be finalised. Dialogic historicism acknowledges objectivist and presentist concerns. However, instead of viewing the gap between the past and present as unbridgeable, it examines the gap itself. As will be elaborated next, the gap between multiple temporal contexts is discursively bridged in the presentation of history. These discursive bridges are built on chron-otopes, which are the temporal and spatial structures to story the past.

Chronotopes

The concept 'chronotope' asserts the primacy of space and time in the human experience. Chronotope literally means 'time space' (Bakhtin, 1981:84). To Bakhtin, time and space form an intricate matrix that gives body and organises narratives in the text. A chronotope is a "primary means for materialising time in space, [and it] emerges as a centre for concretising representation, as a force giving body to the entire novel" (Bakhtin, 1981:250). "In the literary artistic chronotope, spatial and temporal indicators are fused into one carefully thought-out, concrete whole" (Bakhtin, 1981:84).

Chronotopes heuristically separate time and space, and organise texts "according to the ratio and nature of the temporal and spatial categories represented" (Holquist, 1981:425–6). A chronotope points out how real historical time, space and actual historical persons are articulated, and also how time, space and char-acters are constructed in relation to one another in the story (Vice, 1997). We can theoretically frame time and space as separate and distil them from the attached emotions and values in human experiences, but Bakhtin observed that "[*l*]*iving* artistic perception...makes no such divisions and permits no such segmentation. It seizes on the chronotope in all its wholeness and fullness. Art and literature are shot through with *chronotopic values* of varying degree and scope. Each motif, each separate aspect of artistic work bears value" (Bakhtin, 1981:243, emphasis in original).

Furthermore, the multiple temporal contexts embedded in the presentation of history are assumed in chronotopes. Sandywell (1998) suggested that chronotopes encapsulate different forms of time, alterity and meaning to constitute the imaginary matrix of social experience. Van Loon (1997:93) similarly argued that the chrono-tope "articulates the dialogic structure of the utterance in 'real time/space': the world-in-the-text and the world-of-the-text". The gap between world-in-the-past and world-of-presenting-the-past discussed as presentist worries earlier is seen dia-logically not as a problem but as interplay between various temporal contexts.

This chapter examines the NMS and its spatial and temporal relationships between Singapore and its neighbours. The NMS offers products that are pregnant with historical meanings and aesthetics. The histories and aesthetics are dialogically constituted, in which objects from the past, present day circumstances and modern technologies intricately weave various stories together.

The National Museum of Singapore

The National Museum of Singapore offers both national and regional history, heritage and art. In the *National Heritage Board 1996/97 Annual Report*, Chairman Lim Chee Onn defined the goals of his organisation (NHB, 1997:5):

- as part of the National Education programme in educating young Singaporeans on post-independence history;
- supporting the state-sponsored drive to make Singapore into a gracious society; and
- transforming Singapore into a regional cultural hub and Renaissance city for the twenty-first century.

He further elaborated (1997:5):

NHB's mission is to develop in Singaporeans an awareness, understanding and appreciation of our unique heritage based on the key Asian civilisations from where our people have all come to make Singapore their home, and in the process, build a nation. The Board through its programmes seeks to provide the social glue that will help bind Singaporeans of different ethnic communities closer. It also seeks to create in us a stronger sense of belonging and identity even though more of us will eventually live and work abroad as we globalise our regionalisation efforts.

In the NHB *1997/98 Annual Report* (NHB, 1998a), he reiterated the same goals. These missions are tied to a wider national economic plan. In 1995, the Singapore Tourist Promotion Board and the Ministry of Information and the Arts published a blueprint to make Singapore a "Global City for the Arts". Among other strategies, the NMS would be reinvented (STPB and MITA, 1995; STPB, 1996a; STPB, 1996b). The STB has taken the initiative to preserve Singapore's heritage, but officers in the NHB and the various museums maintain that tourism, while important, does not dictate their work. Although only 3.3 per cent of overseas visitors to Singapore went to the museums (STB, 1998:32), tourists can contribute significantly to the museums' revenue. Mrs Tan Chee Koon, Director of Corporate Communications of the NHB, explained:

Cultural tourists are very significant in [STB's] strategies to improve tourism visitorship figures...[STB] helps us by giving us money directly to promote our events overseas. Sometimes, they help us publicise our events in their own brochures abroad. But they have very much taken it upon their shoulders to sell Singapore as the global city for the arts; basically to go after the tourist's dollar. For us, if you look at our mission, we are very much geared towards the locals but we value the tourist figures...Just take 10 per cent [of 7 million overseas visitors to Singapore a year], that will exceed our visitorship [for 1997]. So, from a very practical point of view, we want the tourists...That's where this collaboration comes in. This partnership, I think is what our chairman called 'Partnership with natural alliance'. And one of the key thrusts that we have identified for the National Heritage

Board is to identify and cultivate natural alliances with those who have interests in promoting the growth of heritage for their own benefit as well.

(Personal interview, 12 June 1998)

The NMS works within these premises, and the different heritage and histories offered by the SHM, SAM and ACM must be understood in these contexts.

The Singapore History Museum

The Singapore History Museum features a number of galleries showcasing events and artefacts relating to Singapore. The *Global City For The Arts* master plan asserts that the SHM would present "trends and developments which have characterised and shaped Singapore, highlighting those leading to the emergence of contemporary Singapore" (STPB and MITA, 1995:17).

In the SHM, Singapore's history starts in the fourteenth century with archaeological artefacts showing that Singapore was already a trading area at that time. Some permanent exhibitions in the SHM include "The Dioramas: A Visual History of Singapore" (history of Singapore from 1818 to 1965); "*Rumah Baba* – Life in a Peranakan House" (on Straits Chinese culture); "William Farquhar: His Collection of Natural History Drawings and his Public Life" (nineteenth-century flora and fauna drawings of Singapore and Malaysia); and "Colony to Nation" (mainly on Singapore's post World War II history). "Everest – Singapore at the Summit" (the adventures and triumph of the Singapore team in climbing Mount Everest in 1998, exhibited between May and October 1999); "The Forgotten Empress: The Story of the 'Empress of Asia'" (on a luxurious passenger liner which was sunk during World War II, exhibited between April and December 1999); and "The Singapore Story: Overcoming the odds" (on Singapore's social political history after World War II, exhibited from July 1998) were temporary exhibitions.

Most visitors to the SHM are pupils on school excursions. As part of the state education programme, the SHM maintains that not only must the past be preserved, the past can also offer lessons for the present and future. With reference to the racial riots in the 1950s and 1960s in Singapore, for example, the director of the SHM, Lim How Seng explained:

History repeats itself. If we don't handle the religious issues sensitively, the same riots, based on the religious issues will be revived. In that case, there is relevance of history.

(Personal interview, 4 June 1998)

The general dioramas exhibition on Singaporean history and the "Colony to Nation" permanent exhibition portray the SHM's version of Singaporean history. The story is best summarised in "The Singapore Story: Overcoming the Odds". This huge exhibition was launched as part of the National Education Programme in July 1998. The exhibition travelled around Singapore, reaching out to residents in public housing estates. There are seven themes in the story:

- Colonial period (1819–1945);
- Political awakening (1945–1955);

- Communist threat (1955–1961);
- Battle for merger (1961–1963);
- Merger years (1963–1965);
- From survival to progress (1965–present); and
- Future in our hands (future).

The political history of Singapore as presented in the SHM only began in 1945. Before then, Singapore is presented as a colonial trading post for the British. Immigrants from all over the region came to work in Singapore. The social cultural life of the island was rich and diverse. However, World War II demonstrated that the British could not defend the island. The SHM story also shows that residents lived in difficult conditions until the current ruling party came to power in 1959. Racial and communal tensions, communist threats, Malaysian and Indonesian pressures on Singapore and poverty were only some of the difficulties that the country had to face. The history from 1959 celebrates how the People's Action Party (PAP) transformed Singapore into a modern and developed city-state.

For example, in the catalogue, *Singapore: Journey into Nationhood*, for the "Singapore Story" exhibition (NHB, 1998b:115, emphasis in original), it was asserted:

Even before economic prosperity, Singapore's leaders had begun to focus on *improving the quality of life* in Singapore. When the PAP came to power in 1959, one of its first steps was to stem the spread of "yellow culture". The People's Association was formed in 1960 to bring social, cultural, educational and athletic activities to the people through the community centres. Since then, numerous *campaigns exhort Singaporeans* to do things that would improve their lives: "Girl or boy, two is enough", "Use Your Hands", "Courtesy is for you and me"... But the one campaign that has made a big physical difference to the quality of life in an urban setting is the Tree-Planting Campaign. Initiated by Lee [Prime Minister Lee Kuan Yew] in 1963, the trees, plants and small parks everywhere justify Singapore's label as *the Garden City*.

In the SHM, some aspects of the past are highlighted and made more salient than others. Before the PAP came to power in 1959, Singapore is characterised by chaos and instability. This is then contrasted with a subsequently modern and economically prosperous independent Singapore. Old documents, news clips, artefacts, photographs, reconstructed models and commentaries provide a myriad of past and present presentation tools that construct a version of Singapore's history. The story of Singapore is predominantly based on people and events that took place physically on the island. The island of Singapore is used as the linking thread among the different exhibitions.

The Singapore Art Museum

While the Singapore History Museum concentrates on the history of Singapore, the Singapore Art Museum presents twentieth-century Southeast Asian visual arts. The SAM is part of the programme to develop Singapore as a renowned arts city. It has about 4,000 pieces in its collection, which includes paintings, installations, sculptures and videos. The master plan for the SAM states that "[t]his museum is the first of its kind in the region to be primarily dedicated to the collection and display of twentieth-century Singapore and Southeast Asian visual art" (STPB and MITA, 1995:16).

Like the Singapore History Museum, the museum's facilities are of a very high standard. Besides offering twentieth-century Southeast Asian visual arts, the SAM also carries 'blockbuster' touring exhibitions. These touring exhibitions, which included "Masterpieces from the Guggenheim Museum" and "Leonard da Vinci" (NHB, 1998a; *3 Museum Guide 1999*) drew large crowds. The deputy director of the SAM, Ahmad Mashadi, explained the two main roles of the museum:

Definitely the first role is to educate Singaporeans, to expose Singaporeans to issues relating to aesthetics and beauty. And of course, to introduce them to ideas relating to art and about art. And [secondly], interrelate the appreciation for art to a sense of heritage and culture. That's why we are very much involved in the collection and study of Southeast Asian art.

(Personal interview, 27 May 1998)

In this case, the "sense of heritage and culture" extends beyond Singapore and into Southeast Asia. This assumes a relationship between Singapore and Southeast Asia, which will be elaborated next.

The thrust and agenda of the Singapore Art Museum is laid out in its inaugural exhibition, "Modernity and Beyond: Themes in Southeast Asian Art" in 1996. The Chief Curator, T.K. Sabapathy, wrote in the inaugural exhibition catalogue (1996:7, my emphasis):

Art writing by Southeast Asians is developed along turfs circumscribed by national boundaries; rarely do writers venture into neighbouring terrain, and when they do, they do so furtively, sporadically, and skirt along the surface. No doubt there are valid explanations for this situation. Be that as it may, a glaring consequence of this is the absence of a *regional outlook*. Indeed, to date, not a single perspective or framework for the study of modern artists and art of the region has been mooted by writers or scholars from countries in the region. Those from other regions are busily embarked upon the task of mapping Southeast Asian art history, most especially from Japan, Australia and the USA. Drawing attention to such occurrences is not to fuel xenophobic fever or induce withdrawal into defensive positions, on the contrary. It is undoubtedly important to know how others (from other regions) see us (in our region). Even so, it is equally important to know how we see or *regard ourselves in our region* and as *belonging in a region*.

Ahmad Mashadi also explained:

We tend to see the destinies of the various cultures in Southeast Asia as interrelated. Therefore, there is a need to promote a...multi-faceted reading, a collective reading of what Southeast Asian art is about, as a region, not just as national history.

(Personal interview, 27 May 1998)

Effectively, the symbolic scope of the SAM assumes a spatial scalar leap from country to region; it represents not only Singaporean art but also Southeast Asian art. The museum also asserts Singapore as a member of the region and it claims to offer an insider regional perspective.

'Southeast Asia' is a commonly used term. However, its definition is problematic (Acharya, 1999). Nonetheless, the Association of Southeast Asian Nations (ASEAN) has taken the initiative to define the constituent members of Southeast

Asia. ASEAN membership has increased over the years, and it is now politically defined as consisting of 10 countries, namely Burma (Myanmar), Brunei, Cambodia, Indonesia, Laos, Malaysia, the Philippines, Singapore, Thailand and Vietnam (Acharya, 1999). The Association was originally formed as an anti-Communist security alliance in 1967. The countries together have a population of over 500 million people. The various societies adhere to different religions, speak different languages and were colonised by different foreign powers in the last centuries. Despite this background, the SAM borrows this political formulation in its definition of Southeast Asia as an aesthetic region.

The SAM effectively assumes that the arts and cultures among the member countries in the region have some form of coherence and homogeneity. The SAM acknowledges that the artistic communities and their experiences amongst the member countries are diversely rich (cf. Sabapathy, 1996). The museum employs a homogeneity-in-diversity strategy to affirm Southeast Asia as a legitimate art entity. Common themes are used to bring disparate exhibits together. "Nationalism, Revolution and the Idea of the Modern", "Traditions of the Real", "Modes of Abstraction", "Mythology and Religion: Traditions in Tension", "The Self and the Other" and "Urbanism and Popular Culture" were themes used to connect the diverse exhibits in the inaugural exhibition. Such themes are still being used to establish a common Southeast Asian regional art forum in the SAM.

Organised through these linking themes, 'Southeast Asian art' is also enforced and maintained through the co-presence of various exhibits. Art works from all over the region jointly animate each other in the galleries. Although produced in different societies, the individual exhibits can, in combination, suggest and animate an impression of close cross-societal connections.

While art works from the region jointly animate each other in the SAM, alluding to an erstwhile art region, the construction of such a region remains politically sensitive. Ahmad Mashadi was cautious when I raised the issue of Singapore becoming a regional centre for Southeast Asian art:

> In terms of strategic planning, we tend to look at twentieth-century Southeast Asian art as [a space] which is vacant. No other museum is doing that. It is a niche for us. Basically, we want to spearhead research into that... There is a lot of ramifications to say that [Singapore wants to be a regional art centre]. It is basically to admit an imperialist design on our part...It is very important for us to create a kind of museum for ourselves that can stand on its own and to stand in the forefront of museology in Southeast Asia. I think it is about competition at the end of the day.... There is no one else in this region that is doing that or has the resources to do that. We have the resources to do that.

> (Personal interview, 27 May 1998)

Through the exhibition of art pieces from around the region, the SAM tries to establish a niche for itself in the museum world. ASEAN as a security arrangement, constituted by socially, culturally and politically diverse countries, has been equivocally labelled as an aesthetic region by the SAM. The various exhibits from different Southeast Asian countries not only bring the region into Singapore but also offer a sense of interconnectedness by their co-presence. However, state sovereignty and the fixity of state boundaries allude to possible intra-regional tensions. Indeed, Ahmad

Mashadi has discursively transformed these political issues into a professional and competitive one.

The SAM has effectively expanded its geographical area of representation beyond Singapore by using art pieces from all over Southeast Asia. It also offers its version of regional art history in which common themes connect various artistic communities and genres in the region. This approach suggests an interconnected Southeast Asia. This contrasts with the SHM, where the exhibitions are used to define Singaporean society within national boundaries.

The Asian Civilisations Museum

The Asian Civilisations Museum consists of two wings. At the time of this study, only the first wing was open. This first wing showcases Chinese culture and civilisation until the end of the Qing dynasty (1911 AD). In some galleries, traditional Chinese music is played to enhance the Chinese aura in the galleries. In the first wing, the permanent exhibitions introduce Chinese beliefs, symbolism, connoissseurship and the Chinese scholar tradition in various galleries. There are also galleries featuring ancient Chinese furniture, ceramics, jade and art. Each exhibit reveals a distant but revered past.

The second wing, which will only be ready in 2001, will house collections from West, South and Southeast Asia. As a whole, the ACM offers the "Story of Asia" (the title of the 'welcome' film clip in the ACM). While the SAM offers a regional perspective to modern Southeast Asian art, the ACM offers insights into ancient Asian cultures and civilisations. The reason the ACM is showcasing ancient Asian civilisations is that the Singaporean population is multi-ethnic, with a relatively recent migrant past. The ACM celebrates Singaporeans' "ancestral heritage" (STPB and MITA, 1995:17). The then Minister of Information and the Arts, George Yeo (ACM, 1997:7), asserted that "[t]he history and culture of Singapore is not intelligible without reference to the ancestral civilisations from which the different races came and with which they continue to be in contact".

Similarly, the director of the ACM, Kenson Kwok, stated (ACM, 1997:9–10):

It is sometimes forgotten that Singapore was not entirely an invention of traders, immigrant settlers and colonialists. Indigenous peoples of the region and the surrounding archipelago have always lived here, or rather, have made this island at one time or another the base for their itinerant, sea-based way of life. Our focus therefore includes Southeast Asia which, like the rest of Asia, prides itself on ancient cultures and civilisations.[...] A greater awareness of cultural history should help us gain insight into customs and societies, and endow us with greater subtlety and depth in our dealings and interactions with others, whether in Singapore or further afield.

By celebrating Singaporeans' 'ancestral heritage', the ACM effectively *lengthens* the history of Singaporean society and broadens the spatial scale in Singaporean history. Singaporeans' 'ancestral heritage' is immortalised in the ACM, but it also reclaims and animates an almost unrecognisable past for the present. The Asian region is selectively divided into areas of civilisations. When I pointed out the selectivity in the exhibits and the diversity among each Asian ancient civilisations, Kenson Kwok explained:

To a certain extent, you have to homogenise, otherwise how can you do anything? If you say that everything is different, every group and every region is different, which to a certain extent is true, you will not get anywhere. You have to make some generalisations...What is Chinese? What is Indian? These are not easy questions to answer. There has to be some overall general answers to those questions. And yet of course, it is never as simple as all that. So where do you strike a median to tell people? Chinese culture is not just Han culture, there are many influences, certainly from the other regions. We are already trying to do this to a limited extent. If you look at the gallery on Chinese history, you would see our Tang displays, the Central Asian peoples and Tang ladies wearing Central Asian costumes, and so on. So, here and there, we try to highlight but whether the message is strong enough or whether we want to make the message stronger, I don't know. It is a moot point. Because at one level, people would like a level of certainty. I don't think things can be too vague and too generalised and saying that "Well, it is very complex, even what is Chinese is a very complex question. And it is not only Han but also many other things". People need to come away with messages. If things are qualified too much, people get confused.

(Personal interview, 3 June 1998)

The above highlights the difficult task of compressing a vast amount of historical knowledge into a short story. The ACM's simplification process is synchronised with the Chinese, Malay, Indian and Others (CMIO) model (Benjamin 1997; Siddique, 1997), the way Singaporeans are ethnically classified by the state. In the ACM, various 'ancient civilisations' are contrasted against one another and must be understood within their own historical and social contexts. However, they are brought together in the ACM through Singapore's multi-ethnic population. The clusters of civilisations in the ACM are constructed in line with Singapore's multi-ethnic social engineering framework.

In sum, like the SAM, the ACM has expanded its cultural area of representation beyond the shores of Singapore into the whole continent. Furthermore, the ACM has also lengthened Singapore's history beyond its independence in 1965 by a few thousand years, by leaping back into the 'pasts' of its people. However, Asia is not imaged as a more or less coherent entity, unlike the way the SAM asserts Southeast Asia. The various Asian civilisations are woven into a Singaporean "Story of Asia". The grouping of exhibits and their co-presence, like in the SAM, assume their connectedness as they animate each other.

Dialogic links: chronotopes and visions

The NMS celebrates different histories and arts. By extending the geographical and temporal scope, the NMS offers a wide range of heritage products that go beyond the shores of Singapore. The different museums have different foci but they maintain their complementarity (see Table 11.1).

The museums of the NMS imagine Singapore differently. The SHM shows the unfolding processes of making Singaporeans into a people, especially after World War II. The ACM celebrates the origins of Singaporeans by showcasing material

Table 11.1: A comparison between the ACM, SAM and SHM exhibits

	SHM	SAM	ACM
Types of Products	Singapore recent history	Visual arts from Southeast Asia	Ancient Asian material cultures
Spatial scale	National (Singapore)	Regional (Southeast Asia)	Continental (Asia)
Temporal scale	14th century–present	From 20th century–present	"Closed" history 5000BC till 1911AD
Missions	• Presenting history for education and nation-building • Research and entertainment	• Making Singapore into a global city for the arts • Education, research and entertainment	• Making Singapore into a heritage centre for ancient Asian material cultures • Education, research and entertainment
Messages communicated	• History is still being "made": Past is source of national *pride* and *guidance* • Celebrates the leadership of the PAP	• Singapore is part of a vibrant aesthetic region • Singapore is taking leadership in promoting Southeast Asian arts	• Material cultures show glorious pasts of a multi-ethnic population • History is "closed" but is a source of *pride*
Connecting story	• Stories are based on what happened and what was found in Singapore island	• Assumes Southeast Asia as a region, with a shared destiny and aestheticism • Singapore is part of the interconnected region	• Constitutes Asia into pockets of ancient civilisations • The "Story of Asia" is woven through Singaporeans' ancestral pasts

SHM: Singapore History Museum
SAM: Singapore Art Museum
ACM: Asia Civilisations Museum

cultures of ancient Asia. The SAM envisions itself as a Southeast Asian regional visual art centre. All the museums variously appropriate history and the arts, employing different stories to connect different periods of time and spaces to modern Singapore. However, there are temporal and spatial 'gaps' in each of their stories, as will be demonstrated next.

Constructing spatial and temporal interconnections

All three museums demonstrate clearly different ways of conceptualising regional relationships and how Singapore features as a centre in the region. The SHM assumes a space marked by the boundaries of an internationally recognised nation-state. The history of Singapore is based on what happened and what was found on the island over the years. Singapore asserts its sovereignty in relation to its neighbours. The SAM, on the other hand, encompasses a space beyond Singapore's shores to include a geographical area politically defined by ASEAN. The ACM, meanwhile, divides the continent into civilisations and within each civilisation, one finds continuity and connections. Different space–time structures are embedded in the stories of the museums.

Chronotopes show how regional interconnections are constructed in these stories. Besides that, the narrated past is said to have made the present possible, but these stories of the past also betray the embedded contemporary circumstances. Leaps between the past and present (time leaps), and between Singapore, Southeast Asia and Asia (space leaps) are articulated in the assumed regional relationships in the NMS. Stories from the various museums can be mapped onto time–space matrices or chronotopes. These stories draw the past into the present and the present into the past, as well as bridging the local and the distant (see Figure 11.1).

Historical documents, artefacts and remnants are animated in these museums through contemporary technologies and interpretations. Inherent in the presentation of art and historical objects in these museums are the different periods of the past, originating from different places. From a dialogic perspective, these objects offer a presence and authority that cannot be denied; their existence asserts a past. Effectively, the *Now* and the *Then*, the *Here* and the *There* come together to form a dialogic, multi-contextual presence in the museums.

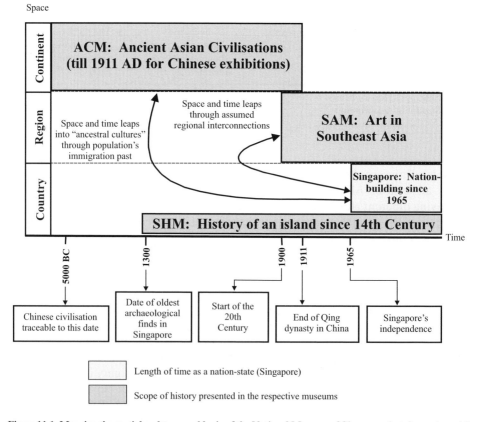

Figure 11.1 Mapping the spatial and temporal logic of the National Museum of Singapore (not drawn to scale)

Time, space and visions

The discussion so far has somewhat dichotomised the past and the present, the local and the regional. This is only a heuristic device. Dialogically, the various temporal and spatial contexts are enmeshed in the museums. Similarly, the experiences of history and space, as promoted in these museums, cannot be definitively segregated. As quoted earlier, Bakhtin (1981:84) observed that "in the literary artistic chronotope, spatial and temporal indicators are fused into one carefully thought-out, concrete whole".

By assuming wider and larger spatial and temporal representation, the NMS has expanded the heritage spaces of Singapore. The selective appropriation of cultural products from a wider region and a more distant past unleashes a set of resources for the museums. These resources are capital for economic and political management through the state involvement in the NMS. Visitors to the ACM and the SAM are also made to think that they are consuming products that have cultural significance over a wider geographical area, established over a longer period of time. Phenomenologically, if these spatial and temporal scales were cognisant to the tourists, they can feel that they have consumed a wider cultural area than the actual places they visited. Thus, not only do the new heritage spaces offer resources for economic and social engineering, the imagined horizons are also consumed by visitors to these museums.

Figure 11.2 shows a model of how time and space can map the horizons of the imagined history, culture and heritage in the museums. These horizons are the edges of the local and regional visions of the NMS. Within the visions, past cultural resources are claimed by the museums and consumed by visitors. From a dialogic historicism perspective, the concept of chronotopes is useful not only to map out the time–space logic of narrated histories; chronotopes also allow us to locate the

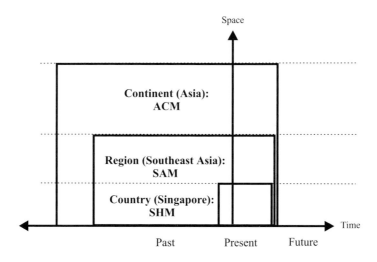

Figure 11.2 Local and regional visions: horizons of imagined heritage spaces in the NMS

assumed temporal and spatial scopes of the stories. The scopes constitute the symbolic representation of the articulated past. Effectively, the celebrated stories in the museums encapsulate the spatial and temporal visions of the narrators.

In sum, the broad spatial and temporal visions are given form and substance through specific stories. The SAM stories an interconnected Southeast Asia art region; its story is constructed and maintained through common themes and relevant exhibits. The multi-ethnic population of the Singapore story in the ACM embraces an even wider spatial and temporal vision while the SHM adopts a 'narrower' vision, showcasing only events, objects and people relating to the island-state.

Conclusion

By mapping the chronotopes, I have examined the temporal and spatial logic of the histories and stories offered by the NMS. The ways in which the chronotopes are constructed inform us of the economic, political and social contexts of present-day Singaporean society. However, the chronotopes would not be animated without the presence of the past as the exhibits not only construct the stories, they provide a focus and authority to them.

At the moment, the SAM asserts a coherent, interconnected Southeast Asia of which Singapore is a part. The ACM memorialises Singapore as a melting pot of peoples from different Asian cultures. The SHM asserts the state boundaries and sovereignty of an island-state. If the innovations taken by the SAM and the ACM are successful, the Singaporean versions of these regions would gain currency and hegemony. The SAM can thus offer the standards against which the art world must measure itself in appreciating Southeast Asian art as a genre, while at the ACM, visitors will view Asia through the eyes of the Singaporean CMIO model. The advent of these Singaporean models, however, may be hampered by political considerations. Other countries in the region would challenge these versions as they would want to protect their own cultural and historical sovereignty, just as the SHM asserts Singapore's independence and unique history.

In returning to the discussion on different approaches to history, a Foucauldian approach would concentrate only on the present circumstances surrounding the presentation of heritage products in the NMS. On the other hand, an objectivist approach questions the histories constructed by the NMS as well as challenging these stories with other 'facts' from the past. From a dialogic perspective, presentism is part of history-telling and it tries to understand the relationships between the past and the present. Even with selective modern interpretations, evidence from the past animates, focuses and offers credibility to the story.

Dialogic historicism accentuates the multiple temporal contexts in the presentation of history. The concept of chronotopes maps out the links between the past and present, Singapore and the regions. I have also drawn out the local and regional visions of the NMS through the chronotopes behind the stories. These present-day visions reclaim the past and aim to shape the future. As the present becomes the past, and the future becomes the present, the dialogic perspective respects the changing circumstances of society and culture by accepting that the past is continuously being reconstructed. Different stories will emerge as new contemporary contexts come into dialogue. Therefore, the search for heritage spaces and the imagining of Singaporean history will continue.

Acknowledgements

This study would not have been possible without the cooperation of my respondents in the National Museum of Singapore. This study is part of my PhD project. The Danish State and Copenhagen Business School financed my PhD scholarship.

Note

1 The Singapore Tourism Board (STB) is the successor to the Singapore Tourist Promotion Board (STPB). The name change came about in November 1997. This chapter uses both names to indicate the temporal context.

References

Acharya, A. (1999) 'Imagined proximities: The making and unmaking of Southeast Asia as a region'. *Southeast Asian Journal of Social Science*, 27(1), 55–76.
Asian Civilisations Museum (ACM) (1997) *The Chinese Collections*. Singapore: National Heritage Board.
Bakhtin, M. M. (1981) *The Dialogic Imagination: Four Essays*, tr. C. Emerson and M. Holquist; M. Holquist (ed.). Austin: University of Texas Press.
Bakhtin, M. M. (1984a) *Problems of Dostoevsky's Poetic*. Minnesota: University of Minnesota Press.
Bakhtin, M. M. (1984b) *Rabelais and His World*, tr. H. Iswolsky. Bloomington: Indiana University Press.
Bakhtin, M. M. (1986) *Speech Genres and Other Late Essays*, tr. V.W. MacGee; C. Emerson and M. Holquist (eds.). Austin: University of Texas Press.
Bell, M. M. and Gardiner, M. (eds.) (1998) *Bakhtin and the Human Sciences*. London: Sage Publications.
Benjamin, G. (1997) 'The cultural logic of Singapore's "multiculturalism"', in J.H. Ong, C. K. Tong and E.S. Tan (eds.) *Understanding Singapore Society*. Singapore: Times Academic Press, 67–85.
Dean, M. (1994) *Critical and Effective Histories: Foucault's Methods and Historical Sociology*. London: Routledge.
Foucault, M. (1972) *The Archaeology of Knowledge*. London: Routledge.
Foucault, M. (1984) *The Foucault Reader: An Introduction to Foucault's Thought*, P. Rabinow (ed.). London: Penguin.
Holquist, M. (1981) 'Glossary', in M.M. Bakhtin, *The Dialogic Imagination: Four Essays*, tr. C. Emerson and M. Holquist; M. Holquist (ed.). Austin: University of Texas Press, 423–34.
National Heritage Board (NHB) (1997) *Annual Report 1996/97*. Singapore: National Heritage Board.
National Heritage Board (NHB) (1998a) *Annual Report 1997/98*. Singapore: National Heritage Board.
National Heritage Board (NHB) (1998b) *Singapore: Journey into Nationhood*. Singapore: Landmark Books.
Ooi, C.S. (2001) *Mediated Cultures: Production and Consumption of Copenhagen and Singapore*, published PhD dissertation. Department of Intercultural Communication and Management, Copenhagen Business School.
Ooi, C.S. and Karmark, E. (1998) *Presentist Pasts: Articulations of History in the Danish Golden Days and LEGO*, Occasional Paper 57. Copenhagen: Department of Intercultural Communication and Management, Copenhagen Business School.
Pickering, M. (1997) *History, Experience and Cultural Studies*. London: Macmillan.
Sabapathy, T.K. (ed.) (1996) *Modernity and Beyond: Themes in Southeast Asian Art*. Singapore: National Heritage Board.

Sandywell, B. (1998) 'The shock of the old: Mikhail Bakhtin's contributions to the theory of time and alterity', in M.M. Bell and M. Gardiner (eds.), *Bakhtin and the Human Sciences*. London: Sage Publications, 196–213.

Siddique, S. (1997) 'The phenomenology of ethnicity: A Singapore case study", in J.H. Ong, C.K. Tong and S.E. Tan (eds.) *Understanding Singapore Society*. Singapore: Times Academic Press, 107–24.

Singapore Tourism Board (STB) (1998) *Survey of Overseas Visitors to Singapore 1997*. Singapore: STB.

Singapore Tourist Promotion Board (STPB) and the Ministry of Information and the Arts (MITA) (1995) *Singapore: Global City for the Arts*. Singapore: STPB and MITA.

STPB (1996a) *Destination Singapore: The Arts Experience*. Singapore: STPB.

STPB (1996b) *Destination Singapore: The Arts Tourism Directory*. Singapore: STPB

van Loon, J. (1997) 'Chronotopes: Of/in the televisualisation of the 1992 Los Angeles riots'. *Theory, Culture and Society*, 14(2), 89–104.

Vice, S. (1997) *Introducing Bakhtin*. Manchester: Manchester University Press.

Williams, R. (1976) *Keywords: A Vocabulary of Culture and Society*. London: Fontana Press.

3 Museum Guide 1999 promotional flyer (1999).

12

Imaging Melaka's Global Heritage

Carolyn Cartier

Introduction

In the late fourteenth century an Islamic trading diaspora sailed across the Indian Ocean through the archipelagos of Southeast Asia and led to the establishment of a string of sultanates and the practice of Islam (Marrison, 1951). Melaka (also known as Malacca), on the west coast of peninsular Malaysia, entered formal historical record as the first sultanate in Southeast Asia, circa 1402 (Sandhu and Wheatley, 1983a). Contemporary Melaka is a relatively small urban settlement, but it shares a global maritime history with prominent cities like London, Tokyo, New York, Amsterdam, Bombay, Buenos Aires, Hong Kong, San Francisco, Shanghai, Singapore and other places whose growth has drawn from a history of port city settlement and international trade. These world cities are also major centres of cultural transformation, economic power and political leadership whose processes shape local and global activity. They are, in contemporary transnational terms, centres of economic globalisation and cultural cosmopolitanism. Yet in all the contemporary literature about globalising and cosmopolitan processes, the origins of these cities are not well understood as products of maritime historical geographies. The idea of 'maritime' belongs to an earlier industrial era of world economic history. We have lost focus on the character of seaports, and in becoming relatively landbound and airport-oriented, increasingly lack memory of an era of travel by ship.

Historic ports marked the Asian littoral, and trade depended on a garland of coastal settlements because early mariners navigated by sight of land and regularly sought ports to re-supply. In the era before coal-fired steamships, sailing craft also depended on the seasonality of the monsoon system to sail the Asian coasts. In the heart of the Southeast Asian sea-lanes, the Strait of Malacca was the pivot of the monsoon and ports along the coasts of the Malay Peninsula and Sumatra served as sojourning stations where mariners and merchants waited out the reversal of the winds. Melaka was the most famous of these ports in the early mercantile period, and Asian regional traders dominated cultural and political life in the settlement until the colonial era transformed regional history into a series of European conquests and mercantile economies. Portuguese, Dutch, and British colonial administrations consecutively ruled over Melaka. After the British incorporated Melaka into the Straits Settlements with Singapore and Pulau Pinang (or Penang), immigrants from China and India arrived in increasing numbers and populated colonial towns. Half a millennium of colonial history inscribed in central Melaka a built environment that represents three European colonial powers and two Asian immigrant societies. But Melaka's Islamic past is missing in the cultural landscape. As a result of the colonial period, a governor, and not a sultan, sits at the head of the contemporary state, and monumental structures from the sultanate, made from wood, were destroyed and lost in the settlement's administrative transitions.

No other settlement in Malaysia shares Melaka's history, and Malaysia established Melaka town its singular designated historic city under the United Nations Educational, Scientific and Cultural Organisation (UNESCO) guidelines in 1989 (Cartier, 1997). In the early 1990s, tourism became Malaysia's number two economic growth sector and the state funded the expansion of tourism industries, including heritage tourism (*New Straits Times*, 6 February 1998). Adequately representing heritage tourism in Malaysia, though, has been a challenge for tourism planners. Melaka is an important tourist destination in Malaysia, but it is not the leading destination for domestic, regional, or international tourists. Instead, leisure activity sites from the beaches of Pulau Pinang to golf resorts and theme parks have drawn the largest numbers of visitors (Oppermann, 1992). Colonial sites are not popular tourist destinations in many postcolonial societies, especially for domestic tourists (Ashworth and Tunbridge, 1990). But the binary of colonial/postcolonial society is not a central issue in debates over contemporary formations of national culture and heritage representation in Malaysia. Instead, debates based on communal politics, or government organisation by race, have dominated debates over national culture (see Kahn and Wah, 1992; Carstens, 1999). But by contrast to these national-level debates about social organisation based on racial categories, in Melaka, a history of racial diversity and intermarriage between racial and ethnic groups has characterised the settlement (see Sandhu and Wheatley, 1983b). In Melaka, the diverse and multicultural population – borne in the historic era of the maritime settlement – has arguably worked to mediate the importance of race-based divisions, and has established a basis for a cosmopolitan outlook. These complexities, between national discourses about race, the realities of local multicultural diversity in Melaka, and the global scale history of colonialism, international trade, and migration that gave rise to Melaka, have intersected in local landscapes. Postcolonial state policies have thus produced interruptions in Melakan landscapes that symbolically uphold the ideology of the contemporary state at the expense of Melaka's global, cosmopolitan heritage. By interruptions, I mean a variety of strategies and material projects, both planned and realised, that have served to reorder the historical context and interpretations of Melakan cultural landscapes in favour of contemporary state ideologies. Ideological interruptions have displaced Melaka's remarkable global historical geography in contemporary representations of heritage, not unlike a series of state-led reclamation projects that submerged Melaka's historic harbour. All these have compromised Malaysia's attempt to gain UNESCO World Heritage Convention status for Melaka town as a cultural site of 'outstanding universal value'.

Melaka, the great historic port city, would enjoy high standing on a list of the world's most interesting places if only that history could speak for itself. Instead, people have to represent that history, retrieve it and explain it for diverse domestic and international audiences. Representing Melaka's history, by comparison to Melaka's significance in the global historical order, is an underdeveloped enterprise. Important scholarly studies of Melaka distinguish the field of Southeast Asian studies, but that field remains a discrete one and very little of it addresses the contemporary era. A stroll through Melaka town yields no bookshops vending a diverse selection of publications on local history and culture. Scant popular material is limited to colourful maps, tourist brochures, souvenir photo booklets, and just one or two more substantial publications. Residents, writers, scholars, tourism planners, heritage professionals and government officials all have had opportunity to represent Melakan history, but none of them have presented it with broad sophistication for consumption in the public sphere and for the interested traveller.

The problems and possibilities of imaging Melaka's global heritage must be understood in the context of tourism industry development in the Malaysian national economy. The state New Economic Policy (NEP), 1971–1990, emphasised capital intensive tourism development of new tourist facilities such as theme parks and golf courses, which fuelled service sector industries related to real estate development. Even in Melaka, the development of new tourist attractions received the focus of tourism planning through the 1980s and 1990s (Cartier, 1998a). The development orientation of the contemporary tourism economy, in new activity-oriented sites, arguably shifts the focus away from interest in heritage landscapes. Complicating this dilemma in Melaka is the fact that the historical origins of heritage sites are only minimally explained for the interested tourist, in small local signboards or tourist guidebooks. Alternative imaging strategies are in order for Melaka town, strategies that retrieve the richness of Melaka's globalised heritage. This chapter makes a contribution toward recapturing Melaka's global significance by critically assessing the development orientation of state tourism planning, and alternatively imaging Melaka's heritage in the contemporary terms of globalisation (see Waters, 1995; Held *et al.*, 1999). These alternative imaging strategies reorient the focus from individual tourist sites and heritage structures to the local–global contexts of Melaka's historic landscapes. Appropriately imaging Melaka's global heritage strengthens understanding of the people and places of Melaka, in the constitution of national culture and the significance of Melaka to the national tourism economy.

The maritime world economy

Maritime cities were connected to networks of seaborne diaspora and empire, and their populations represented the accumulation of people from diverse places along global trading routes. The idea of the maritime city resonates with the mercantile city, a city established during the era of mercantilism, or later industrial period through the nineteenth and early twentieth centuries (see Knox and Agnew, 1998). During these eras, oceanic trade and ship-based travel defined port cities. In the early mercantile period in Asia, according to James Scott (1997:7), "Melaka in 1500 *before* the Portuguese conquest was, with its polyglot, trading population probably more diverse, open and cosmopolitan than its contemporary trading port, Venice." On the west coast of the United States, San Francisco was the major industrial era port. The cultures and economies of both of these cities were based on long distance trade and connections to regional and world economies. Their populations were always, to use contemporary terminology, 'multicultural' and 'cosmopolitan'. What also characterises contemporary Melaka, still small enough not to be designated a 'city' in the Malaysian federal system, and San Francisco, a city whose population has barely grown beyond 750,000, is that neither of these historically great port cities functions as a major port in the contemporary era. Still, both cities have remained centres of multicultural populations and cosmopolitan cultures.

Changes in regional and world economies explain why these ports lost functional maritime status. Melaka's position declined gradually, as a result of natural, technological, and political–economic factors. Silt filled its harbour, sea-going ships increased in size, and, in 1819, the British established Singapore, which replaced Melaka's regional port function at the pivot of the monsoon. The demise of cargo shipping at the port in San Francisco was largely a spatial–technological transformation. The city of Oakland, on the eastern shore of San Francisco Bay, was the terminus of the transcontinental rail link and became the main port of the Bay after the advent of containerisation in the early 1970s. Consequently, the economies of both Melaka and San Francisco have experienced the postindustrial shift, and now depend significantly on the variety of service sector industries subsumed under the rubric 'tourism'. The tourists come to experience landscapes of cultural diversity, historic built environments, and scenes of the city along the maritime shore. As a result of the innovation of the jet aeroplane, which made mass tourism possible, travellers no longer encounter the first view of the Stadthuys, a monumental icon of the Melakan landscape built during the Dutch colonial period, or the Golden Gate Bridge, one of the leading tourist attractions in the United States (both painted in bold red), from the deck of a ship. These landscapes once existed in the traveller's geographical imagination as views from the sea. Contemporary ways of seeing these landscapes have shifted in perspective, and so too have ways of perceiving and remembering that Melaka was at the beginning of a globalising world economy and transcultural cosmopolitanism.

Tourism, heritage conservation and contested development

Colonial landscapes in Melaka town are the core of local heritage tourism resources (Figure 12.1). The outstanding colonial era structures in the town centre, including the Stadthuys, Christ Church, also built by the Dutch, and remnants of the wall that enclosed the Portuguese fort, A Famosa, have all been conserved and maintained with government support. In addition to these authentic heritage structures, beginning in the late 1980s, the state capitalised new projects to replace historic elements

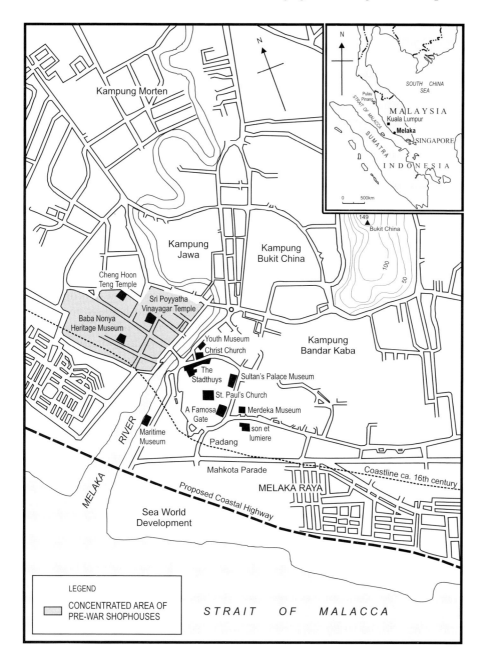

Figure 12.1 Melaka Town

lost or destroyed during the sultanate and subsequent colonial eras. A replica of the fifteenth-century Sultan's Palace and a scale model of a Portuguese carrack, which serves as the Maritime Museum, constitute two new prominent heritage tourism sites. Now, a mixed environment of both historic and new structures characterises heritage tourism resources in Melaka town. The state has also funded the construction of an international standard *son et lumière* (sound and light) attraction in the town centre. Thus state decisions to fund particular tourism development projects in Melaka reflect different rationales, including preference to conserve structures built by European colonial powers; creation of what are standard modern tourism 'products' in other world regions; and, in the case of the Sultan's Palace, projects that reflect the pro-Malay stance of the NEP, to be discussed below. The state has provided 700 million ringgit (US$269 million) over a 10-year period to develop heritage tourism in Melaka town (*Far Eastern Economic Review*, 1997).

In their analysis of heritage tourism, Ashworth and Tunbridge (1990:8) capture realities about the political economy of tourism in which "the historic city originates from architectural forms and morphological patterns...but ultimately is resolved in economic and social priorities." This realisation points to how historic conservation for tourism necessarily implies the negotiation of a range of cultural, economic and political interests which are often tied to policy goals beyond heritage conservation and tourism development. In Malaysia, by contrast to many other former colonial societies, debates over postcolonial nationalism have not focused on the impacts of the colonial period, and the built environment of colonial landscapes has generally been preserved relatively uncritically. Instead, debates about the formation of national culture have revolved around socially constructed ideas about race and ethnicity, and the accommodation of the Chinese and Indian diasporic populations in the postcolonial national order under Malay-dominated rule. For example, in the 1980s during the national culture debates, the state forbade the construction of a privately-funded Mandarin language university, discouraged practice of the traditional Chinese lion dance, and rewrote history books to replace the long-recognised Chinese founder of Kuala Lumpur with a Malay sultan (see Carstens, 1988; 1999). Through debate over these issues, the state established precedents for what constitutes nationally acceptable forms of knowledge and cultural practice. Similarly in heritage conservation, landscapes of ethnicity and diaspora, rather than colonial landscapes, are most commonly at the crux of debate – or ignored – by state interests. In the context of making choices about how to represent national heritage, the state has relatively marginalised the histories of Chinese and Indian diasporic populations. A related disjuncture emerges from the literature of diaspora studies, as the anthropologist Bruner (1996:290) has observed: "[t]he literature on diaspora and hybridity has on the whole neglected tourism...." Gaps in research at the intersections between tourism activity, heritage conservation, and the realities and representations of diasporic populations need to be explored.

The national culture debates in Malaysia found substantial support in state ideology generated under the NEP. The NEP sought to redistribute national wealth by increasing capital accumulation by Malays, and promoted the urbanisation of the Malay population (Jesudason, 1989). Its policies have had widespread influence over state patronage of various cultural, education and social institutions, and have tended to serve as a basis for legitimising the promotion of Malay cultural forms and economic opportunities. These priorities work out in the landscape. State-funded construction in the NEP era commonly featured Islamic design styles, especially for buildings in the capital (Barnard, 1984). Buildings for the new federal capital at Putrajaya, opened in 1999 south of Kuala Lumpur, bear entirely Islamic design motifs. The 'Islamicisation' of the Malaysian landscape is a partial response to the fact that, except for some prominent mosques and kampung communities, notably Kampung Baru in Kuala Lumpur, and Kampung Morten in Melaka, most historic Malay architecture lies on the fringe of towns and along the less urbanised eastern coast of the peninsula.

Focus on 'heritage tourism development' suggests ways in which the creation and promotion of heritage has reflected wider development goals, in social and economic restructuring, and representations of state ideologies about national culture. The presentation offered by the *son et lumière* attraction in the middle of Melaka town locally exemplifies intersections between capital intensive tourism development and the politics of the national culture debates. The visual spectacular offers two shows nightly, in English and in Malay, but the voice-over narrative does not focus on the global historical significance of Melaka as a settlement of diverse cultural diasporas (Islamic, Chinese, and Indian) or as a great entrepot between China, India, and Europe. Instead, the *son et lumière* presentation delivers a Malay nationalist version of Melakan history. Moreover, to control access to the nightly pageant, officials ordered the construction of a fence around the entirety of the *padang* (the former colonial parade ground), which served as a green space and a soccer field, rather than simply encircling the *son et lumière* attraction itself. The solid fence constrained both visual and pedestrian access to the major open space in the central city and projected state concern for the accumulation of revenue as a priority over access to public amenities. Thus the *son et lumière* attraction became a key element in the state's programme of heritage tourism development, in which capital intensive development combines with race-based political ideologies to support the goals of the NEP. In the process, Melaka's remarkable heritage has become obscured at best. The *son et lumière* programme could, alternatively, portray the origins and evolution of Melaka's diverse communities, and their roles in the formation of Malaysian society. But any focus on the historical geographies of Malaysia's diasporic populations challenges contemporary ideologies of national culture. Ironically, Islam is also a diasporic cultural form, but the Malaysian constitution defines the Malay race as indigenous to the peninsula and Malays as adherents of Islam.

After fencing the *padang*, Bukit China (Chinese Hill) became the only open access green space left in Melaka town. Bukit China is a 42-hectare site at the edge of the central district and the world's oldest and largest traditional Chinese cemetery. It is an important *fengshui* landscape and serves as the local jogging park. However, during a recession in the mid-1980s, the state promoted a development scheme for Bukit China that would have transformed the site into a mixed-use real estate development and a theme park. A grassroots preservation movement rose in Melaka, spread to the national level, and succeeded in halting the development project (Cartier, 1993; 1997; 1998b). The preservation movement focused attention on the historic significance of the site, and based its tactics on redefining the concepts of landscape significance and place identity, which portrayed the hill as an unparalleled landscape of Malaysian national history. Still, Bukit China does not receive any state tourism development support, even as the site holds the potential to be a significant tourist attraction for both Asian and western heritage tourism markets since *fengshui* has become popular around the world as a result of the Chinese diaspora and 'fusion culture' in many world cities.

The Bukit China preservation movement tapped two important sets of inter-scaled relations: between local values in Melaka and state nationalist ideologies, and local–global interconnections symbolised by UNESCO guidelines for historical and cultural heritage preservation. Especially through locally circulated statements and press releases, preservation activists popularised the understanding that significant historic events from each phase in Malaysian history took place at Bukit China, from the early sultanate through the colonial era to the present. One press statement, based on the locally circulated *Joint Memorandum of Melakan Graduates and Professionals* to the Chief Minister of Melaka, crystallised the substance of the community response to the movement. It focused on the symbolism of the hill as "an intimate bond between the Chinese community and Malaysia", and explained how "amidst the communalist politics that has frequently clouded inter-community relations in this country, Bukit China serves as a reminder of the bond of friendship between the Malay and Chinese communities that already existed in the early days of the Melaka Sultanate" (*The Star*, 18 October 1984). The memorandum cited several examples of material culture on the hill or historical events that took place there in which Malays played a key role. As one example, among thousands of Chinese graves on Bukit China are two especially large sacred Malay graves from the era of the sultanate, in addition to as many as 60 other Muslim graves. Such inter-ethnic community perspectives on Bukit China effectively challenged the state's implicit lack of support for ethnic group-associated monuments. Instead, it presented the state with a landscape metaphor for a multicultural version of postcolonial national culture that upheld cosmopolitan perspectives on community formation.

One landmark press statement, representing Chinese organisations from every state in Malaysia, including the Borneo states of Sabah and Sarawak, and alumni associations of Taiwan universities and Nanyang University (Singapore) drew on international heritage conservation guidelines to preserve Bukit China (*The Star*, 18 October 1984). The document invoked policy perspectives from the UNESCO World Conferences on Cultural Policies to underscore the significance of conserving local cultural sites: "historical centres and urban complexes of environmental value are being altered or impaired in the interest of what goes by the name of progress; ... such despoliation of cultural heritage is largely due to the lack of community awareness capable of appreciating and understanding with pride and of defending, preserving and extolling it" (*New Straits Times,* 19 February 1995a). This statement, by drawing support from both national and international Chinese organisations, and invoking international heritage guidelines, served to heighten ideas about local, national, and international support for the preservation of Bukit China. In the context of this inter-scaled approach, the state could no longer effectively portray

Bukit China as an 'eyesore' in small town Melaka. Bukit China had become the singular site in Malaysia to represent the history of the nation, and an internationally recognised cultural monument.

In Malaysia in the 1980s and 1990s, the state's 'megadevelopment project' ethos marginalised the conservation of both cultural and natural heritage resources (Cartier, 1998a). The largest scale real estate development projects in Melaka town have taken place on waterfront reclamations, for the construction of offices, hotels, housing, retail districts and a sea world amusement park. The reclamations destroyed the original Melaka harbour, the central site of Melaka's historic globalised economy, limiting Melaka's potential to advance an authentic tourism imaging strategy based on the historic port, and compromising Malaysia's application to the World Heritage Convention for Melaka town. Current reclamation plans for Melaka state have enlarged in scale and scope to 40 km of the coast, north and south of Melaka town, and will compromise several important cultural and natural heritage sites. The 40 km plan is so large that the state has parcelled out the pending reclamations to 19 different property developers (*New Straits Times*, 18 February 1999). By all estimates, the reclamations will destroy mangrove forests and four major nesting sanctuaries for endangered turtle species. At Ujong Pasir, 5 km south of Melaka town, the reclamation will transform the Portuguese community, one of the oldest and most rooted around Melaka town, from a seaside location into an inland site. The reclamations have already disrupted the fish and shrimp catch in the Strait, which has been the economic mainstay of the Portuguese community (*Far Eastern Economic Review*, 1995). Thus, the Portuguese community has had the basis of its livelihood undermined by reclamation, and now faces the loss of its sea front by more state-approved reclamation. The state did not initiate working with the Portuguese community to develop a sustainable community or heritage conservation plan, and government representatives met with the Portuguese community only after the reclamation project was well underway.

State promotion of rapid development in the wider Asia region in the post-Second World War period has substantially transformed pre-industrial landscapes, especially in major cities and their hinterlands. Yet by comparison to the modernisation of the built environments in Kuala Lumpur and Singapore, and the industrial growth of Pulau Pinang, Melaka has not been a major centre of industrial and high-rise redevelopment. Domestic and regional tourists find Melaka a 'sleepy backwater' by comparison to transformations in major cities (e.g., *Singapore Business*, 1993; *Malaysian Business*, 1 May 1994). The 'sleepy hollow' image is, of course, one which results from comparison with the larger national and regional experiences of Asian rapid development. But the small town image Melaka represents for domestic and Singaporean tourists arguably both further marginalises Melaka's historic significance at the origins of the global economy and fuels tourism planners to develop more contemporary activity-oriented attractions. Too frequently even Melakan tourism planners refer to how new tourism projects will transform Melaka's 'sleepy' image, rather than focusing on the strengths of Melaka's global history and its cosmopolitan culture. In these contexts, Melaka has an 'image problem'.

Representing global heritage

The perspective offered here, focused on the idea of 'global imaging', seeks to transcend these debates over the nature of tourism development, and instead focuses on the international activities of mercantile trade and migrations of cosmopolitan cultures that gave rise to the Melaka settlement and its historic built environment. Global imaging of the historic built environment also situates and enhances the significance of Melaka's diverse communities, the Malay, Chinese, Indian and Portuguese communities, in the context of international processes that gave rise to local diversity. Imaging Melaka's global heritage for the cosmopolitan global tourist, and as a local response to state discursive nationalism generated under the NEP, constructs renewed significance for Melaka town and restores the settlement's global and cosmopolitan profiles in the postcolonial national order and in regional and international tourism economies.

Representations of heritage and place imaging are different from abridged recountings of local history. Representing heritage is a challenging enterprise because careful choices must be made to distill significant elements of complex historical events for the public sphere, and in ways that grip visitors' imaginations. Strategies of heritage representation for tourism have relied on a now classic study by Freeman Tilden (1977), who set forth a set of principles for heritage interpretation. Tilden's basic formulation for the successful promotion of heritage sites was based on the idea that heritage presentation should offer much more than factual information: it should be provocative and inspirational in ways that transmit humanistic values. On this basis, Tilden's principles for heritage interpretation urged that representations of heritage should attempt to relate information to the experiences of visitors, and provide interpretations from different perspectives for different types of visitors. Most significantly, for the purposes of this discussion, Tilden advised that heritage presentations should represent large-scale perspectives and whole accounts rather than focusing only on particular phases or elements of history. In these ways, Tilden's formulation embraces a cosmopolitan worldview, perspectives which are suited to imaging Melaka as a central place in the evolving global cultural economy.

In the tourism industry, imaging strategies are "marketing images that depict the destination area as unique and distinctive" (Chang, 1997:542). T.C. Chang has discussed how tourism imaging strategies are typically the business of government tourism promotion boards, which tend to focus on national-scale or large city-scale imaging strategies. Similarly Gerry Kearns and Chris Philo (1993) have identified the many ways in which urban identities may be constructed and packaged as products to be sold. For international tourism, the Malaysian state Tourism Development Corporation concentrates on marketing the country at large and promotes the activity-oriented leisure destinations developed by the state during the 1980s and 1990s. In the national tourism profile, Melaka is the country's 'historic city' where the visitor can connect with the past and escape some of the modern intensity characteristic of other major destinations. The state's imaging strategies for Melaka are thus scaled in relation to and as subsidiary to the nation, rather than imaging Melaka independently as a destination of interest at the global scale.

Tourism imaging strategies for the industry are in many ways equivalent in meaning to socially constructed representations of place as understood in the literature of human geography. Representations of place are ways in which people produce meaning about places over time, through written records, in the media and popular culture, through activities and events, and the role of those representations in constituting identity (see Duncan and Ley, 1993). Understood as constructed representations, meanings about places are not permanently fixed but reflect prevailing norms and values, and may transform as a result of new events and the ideas they engender. From these perspectives, we can envision alternative global imaging strategies for heritage landscapes in Melaka town, strategies that situate local sites in the contexts of Melaka's interconnected worlds of maritime and mercantile history. In Melaka, this is often an exercise in recovering authenticity about local and global history from partial representations of tourist sites produced by the tourism industry and perspectives generated by postcolonial state ideologies. First, we should undertake a brief detour and visit some sites of heritage tourism information in Melaka town.

Melaka's heritage trail

During the 1990s and through the present, information boards marking the Melaka 'heritage trail' have been the most accessible source of heritage site information in Melaka town. These information boards stand in front of ten major heritage sites, including the replica of the Sultan's Palace, the Cheng Hoon Teng Temple, the oldest Chinese temple in Malaysia, and the Sri Poyyatha Vinayagar Temple, a Hindu temple (Figure 12.2).

The signs provide succinct descriptions of the heritage sites, in Malay and English, and are marked with the logo of their provider, the American Express Corporation. The American Express project was undertaken in cooperation with the Melaka state Development Corporation, and unveiled in 1992 in association with the Visit ASEAN Year programme. This transnational corporate naming mirrors private financing schemes around the world in the era of the neoliberal regime, in which corporations obtain permanent advertising in exchange for capitalising facilities and projects.

An example of text from one of the American Express information boards demonstrates both the limits and possibilities of heritage information display. The sign board in front of the Sultan's Palace tells that the structure is a replica of the original fifteenth-century sultan's palace based on a drawing in the *Sejarah Melayu* (Malay Annals), which is the earliest indigenous Malay text. The information also describes the construction of the building and some of the artefacts it houses. An alternative global imaging strategy would situate the origins of the sultanate in the context of the historic Islamic trading diaspora in Asia. Understanding the historical geography of Islamic trading migration accounts for the diffusion of Islam to Malaysia and Indonesia, as well as the pattern of sultanates and early Islamic settlements across the region, including the Moro communities in the southern Philippines and historic mosques in China. This worldly view of an Islamic population, a mobile group of explorers, traders, and clerics, speaks to visitors from diverse Asian states in a spirit

ISTANA KESULTANAN MELAKA

Bangunan ini merupakan replika istana Kesultanan Melaka pada abad ke 15 berpandukan lukisan yang dimuatkan di dalam buku Sejarah Melayu. Sungguhpun bentuk bangunannya rumit dengan tujuh serambi tertutup dan bumbungnya cerun curam, tiada sebatang paku pun digunakan dalam pembinaannya. Di dalamnya, anda akan mendapati tablo yang menggambarkan aktiviti pada zaman kegemilangan Kesultanan Melaka. Terdapat juga pamiran kraftangan dan kesenian tradisional orang-orang Melayu.

MALACCA SULTANATE PALACE

This replica of the original 15th Century palace of Malacca's extinct sultanate was based entirely on sketches found in the ancient Sejarah Melayu (Malay Annals). Despite its complex structure of seven enclosed porches and sharply sloping roofs, not a single nail was used in its construction. Inside the palace, you will find a series of tableaux recreating the many activities that took place during the heyday of the Malacca sultanate. Also well-represented are the traditional Malay arts and crafts.

Figure 12.2 Melaka heritage trail sign board in front of the Sultan's Palace

of transnational communities. Its heuristic and humanistic values remind people that regional histories were deeply intertwined long before the modern era of communal politics, and suggests a cosmopolitan sense of transnational linkages rather than differences in values tied mainly to representations of national culture. Imaging global heritage through themes of diaspora underscores common transnational and transcultural experiences.

Museums and global heritage

Melaka's Museum of History and Ethnography is housed in the Stadthuys, a formidable administrative building from the Dutch colonial era. Among several permanent exhibits, the Museum features cultural artefacts and dioramas of local ways of life. The collection is important, yet modest, and museum officials have petitioned the Portuguese government for the repatriation of material culture appropriated during the early colonial period. In Melaka as elsewhere, museum professionals are charged with providing accurate representations of history, and yet Melaka's 500 years of history raises questions about which subjects and which periods of history to highlight. On the global scale, the Museum portrays the arrival of the colonial powers in terms of the significance of the Melaka sultanate and port, a place that colonial powers fought to control. In this light, Melaka is the coveted prize, and is treated on a par with and in relation to European nation-states. The Museum gives significantly less attention to processes outside the context of state-to-state relations, especially transnational processes of diaspora during the colonial era. The British colonial administration especially encouraged labour migration from southern India and south China, and hundreds of thousands of migrants arrived at the Straits Settlements in search of work, sometimes indentured. These labourers transformed the Malay peninsula by clearing forests, planting rubber and oil palm, and settling administrative towns. Might the Museum mount an exhibition addressing the diverse origins of early settlers in Melaka? Where were the immigrants from, and why did they stay? How did new communities form and organise? Neighbourhood and community formation is an elemental characteristic of Melaka's cosmopolitan heritage, and the ways in which those diverse communities interacted over time has given rise to a multicultural population and strong local identities. Imaging Melakan identities, whose histories and geographies are simultaneously global and local, would reorient representations of Melaka toward recognition of its cosmopolitan population and its transnational origins in the mercantile period of the world economy.

Museums also house Melaka's maritime heritage. The new Maritime Museum is contained within a scale model of the Portuguese *Flor de la Mar*, which sank in the Strait in the fifteenth century. The Maritime Museum opened in 1995 and has become the most popular museum in Melaka, with nearly twice as many visitors in some years as the Museum of History. The Maritime Museum is actually a complex of three sites: the Portuguese carrack itself, containing maps and charts, models of sailing ships, and some artefacts of maritime history; a decommissioned 110-ton patrol craft of the Royal Malaysian Navy, the *KD Sri Trengganu*, built in the United Kingdom; and a godown (warehouse) displaying porcelain recovered from the *Diana*, a ship of the British Country trade that sank in the Strait in 1817. The model of the *Flor de la Mar* and the saga of the *Diana* represent the complexities of imaging Melaka's global maritime heritage. Both ships were agents for European colonial powers and their mercantile conquests: the *Flor de la Mar* is thought to have sunk after leaving Melaka with local booty, and the *Diana* was an opium trader licensed by the British East India Company. The traders operated between India and China, and when it sank, the *Diana* had just left Melaka after re-supplying en route from Canton to Madras. It was a 350-ton wooden sailing ship loaded with a mixed cargo of silk, nankeens, tea, camphor, sugar, ginseng, glass beads, and 18 tons of 'blue and white ware', a type of imperial Chinese porcelain. A private salvage company discovered the wreck of the *Diana* in 1993 after identifying scattered porcelain pieces on the sea bottom (Ball, 2000). The salvage company contracted with the Malaysian government to recover the cargo and sell it at auction, which yielded 11 tons of porcelain or over 24,000 intact pieces, and brought in 1.8 million at Christie's in Amsterdam, from buyers in 29 countries (*The Daily Telegraph*, 10 March 1995). The national museum in Kuala Lumpur, Museum Negara, kept a substantial collection of the *Diana* porcelain, but so far has not mounted an exhibition. The Melaka Maritime Museum has a small selection of the porcelain, and visitors to the Museum increased after it went on display in an old godown across the street from the *Flor de la Mar* (*New Straits Times*, 19 February 1995b). But the display of the *Diana* porcelain was not mounted as a permanent installation and its future is uncertain. The salvage company responsible for its discovery loaned the porcelain to the Maritime Museum, and installed the display as a temporary goodwill project. The Museum has not formally acquired the porcelain, and has not maintained the exhibit. Its fate lies mired in legal problems between the salvage company and the Malaysian government (Ball, 2000).

The *Diana* porcelain is a remarkable heritage tourism resource: it is authentic and internationally renowned; it demonstrates the importance of Melaka's historic port; and it represents the global maritime geographies of the mercantile era that brought Melaka into prominence along with other port cities from China to Europe. In the *Diana* porcelain, Melaka has another opportunity to image the interconnections between local and global heritage through a trading diaspora, in this case the European trade in Asian luxury goods which, according to André Gundor Frank (1998), really grafted on to Asian regional trading networks already in place. Understanding Melaka's history from this perspective provides the opportunity to foreground histories about the Asian regional trade and depend less on traditional forms of representation based on contemporary nation-states. It is important for people to know, for example, that even in the case of apparently Portuguese or British ships, such as the *Flor de la Mar* and the *Diana*, the ships' crews were almost entirely comprised of regional sailors, including Hindu merchants and members of the traditional maritime peoples of Southeast Asia such as the Mons, Funanese, the Chams, the Javanese, the Sumatrans and the Bugis (see Reid, 1993:48; SarDesai, 1997:17). Imaging global heritage in this way would require local heritage professionals to step out of the national-scale cultural and political priorities inherited from the NEP era.

Straits style shophouses

The most common element of the historic built environment in Melaka town is the Straits Chinese shophouse. The former Straits Settlements and larger towns in Malaysia are centres of Straits Chinese style architecture, which is a distinctive regional style amalgamating facade treatments of western beaux-arts, neo-classical, and art deco architecture with traditional Chinese shophouse building structure (Kohl, 1984:179–85) (Figure 12.3). The shophouse building type itself, which originated in southern China, combines both commercial and residential space in the same structure: the shop faces the street on the ground floor and the dwelling area forms the rear and upstairs of the structure. Straits style shophouses were the most common element of the urban built environment in Melaka, Penang and Singapore, and nearly everyone who opened a business in a town area set up in a shophouse, no matter their ethnic background (*The Business Times*, 16 January 1993). Their historic merits and their decorative facades were not much appreciated until they began to disappear from rapidly redeveloping urban landscapes during the 1970s and 1980s.

On a world scale, Straits Chinese style architecture exists substantially only in Malaysia and Singapore, and to a lesser degree in Xiamen, China, the home city of many migrants to the Straits Settlements, and it has increasingly come under the protection of historic conservation programmes, especially in Singapore (Kong and

Figure 12.3 Straits Chinese shophouse, Melaka

Yeoh, 1994; Teo, 1994; Teo and Huang, 1995). In Malaysia, by contrast, the state has not prioritised conservation of the Straits Chinese shophouse (Cartier, 1996). Nevertheless, appreciation for the significance of the Straits Chinese architectural style is increasing. Regional heritage planners have proposed Melaka town and the historic centre of Penang for World Heritage Site status, based on Penang's "more than 10,000 buildings of heritage value" and Melaka's "4,000 pre-war buildings" (*New Straits Times*, 1 August 1999) (see Figure 12.1). Malaysian planners and heritage professionals have been keen to rectify Malaysia's complete absence in the World Heritage Convention list of cultural and physical landscapes of global significance. Thus, ironically, in the face of losses to the heritage environment wrought by development sanctioned under the NEP, the built environment of diasporic immigrant history has become a basis for renewed application to the World Heritage Convention.

Melakans, though, have been concerned about state perspectives on shophouse conservation. In 1994, without consulting residents, the Melaka state government announced a plan to acquire 190 shophouses on Jalan Tun Tan Cheng Lock, relocate existing residents, and have the shophouses redeveloped by a Singapore company for commercial and retail use (*The Straits Times*, 7 May 1994). This street, Jalan Tun Tan Cheng Lock, is the location of the Baba Nonya Heritage Museum and is the most famous street of shophouses in Melaka, the neighbourhood of Melaka's oldest Chinese families. The plan was not carried out, but the idea was based on the Singapore model of state-led shophouse conservation. In Singapore, debates over shophouse conservation have raised questions about the nature of historic conservation schemes that focus on adaptive reuse of the buildings, in some cases transforming residential shophouse neighbourhoods into tourist shopping districts. In the process, residents have been compelled to relocate, and the ambience of the lived-in shophouse environment has been lost to new landscapes of consumption. Perhaps Melaka's greatest asset is that it is not a 'hollowed out' historic town, but a residential community where the flow of daily life infuses the urban landscape with interest and vitality.

Cosmopolitanism

Representing heritage has become increasingly complex in the contemporary era of globalising processes (see Bruner, 1996; Chang *et al.*, 1996). Different types of visitors are interested in different attractions, and heritage professionals and government officials often have different priorities about heritage conservation. Issues at stake in heritage tourism are rarely limited to processes of tourism development (see also Kahn, 1997), and tourism is often better understood as an arena in which diverse cultural, political, and economic priorities are worked out through the potential of development through tourism. In the case of Melaka, the state's focus on heritage tourism development has arguably weakened complex understandings of Melaka's role in the evolving global economy, and delinked understandings about local contemporary community formations, in the diversity of the multicultural Melakan population, from the settlement's global and diasporic heritage. In reality,

Melaka's global condition remains a vibrant force in the cosmopolitan characteristics of its contemporary populace.

'Melakan hospitality' is a phrase that circulates in tourism literature about Melaka, as well as among the town's population. Melakan hospitality may be characterised as an openness to new people and visitors, and an interest in showing them the outstanding places in the community. These gestures of hospitality include striking up conversations about various subjects, from the merits of local restaurants to international politics, and explaining details of local history otherwise missing in tourist information. For Melakans, this openness translates into a sense of community in which institutions of government and business are open to local concerns, on a walk-in basis for the local citizenry. Local quality of life is a constant topic of debate. If cosmopolitanism is about an outward-looking perspective and openness to new people and ideas, what social conditions allow cultures of openness to concentrate and flourish? The structures of society in the cosmopolitan city are regularly flexible or institutionalised in ways that embrace diversity. In historic Melaka, where diversity constituted and defined a settlement, the elite was neither large nor entrenched, and the settlement's population waxed and waned with lucrative trade opportunities or the shift of the monsoon. Maritime cities, the places of ports and sites of global mobility, were the historic places of population diversity by many categories, including race, class, ethnicity and gender. Such globalised places have regularly been the sites of highly developed civil society, which, in turn, form the basis for effective social movements, like the anti-development movement to conserve Bukit China as a cultural heritage site.

The concept of cosmopolitanism has new relevance in the contemporary era, for its ability to conceptualise shared transnational human experiences, and as a humanist counterpart to globalisation (Harvey, 2000). In the history of intellectual thought, cosmopolitanism was a central concept of eighteenth-century European philosophy and its origins antedate modern ideas about the nation-state and nationalism. Immanuel Kant, whose work is the leading source of the concept, argued that international commerce was a historical condition of the cosmopolitan community, and that cosmopolitanism lay at the basis of the formation of global civil society and the international public sphere. Thus, Kant offered early recognition of the relationship between an evolving mercantile economy and a distinctive type of community formation (Cheah, 1998:23). What are its geographies? This is Melaka in the fourteenth century when the place was likely to be more cosmopolitan than Venice. This is also San Francisco, where the leading social formation grew out of the mercantile economies generated in the wake of the Gold Rush in California. In the case of Melaka and other port cities around the Asian littoral, cosmopolitan communities evolved before the word 'international', of sixteenth-century origin, had entered the lexicon of English-speaking peoples. Thus cosmopolitanism, in signifying societal condition, may be a pre-national and post-national condition, marginalised by the hegemony of nationalism as the primary force of large-scale societal organisation during the nineteenth and twentieth centuries.

The truly contemporary cosmopolitan ethic has shed its elite edge. Substantially increased labour migration for especially low wage service sector jobs – including Indonesian women in domestic service, who work in middle and upper middle class

Malaysian homes, and Bangladeshi construction workers, who helped build Malaysia's new high-rise buildings – has changed the terms of understanding who is cosmopolitan. Contemporary cosmopolitan perspectives understand how the new global traveller lives through the challenges of differences in cultures encountered in life paths of high mobility and regardless of economic status (see Cheah and Robbins,1998). The theoretical universality of the cosmopolitan existence, in the Kantian ideal, has yielded to the idea of geographically constituted differences in internationalised consciousness, which, in the area studies mode, presupposes no western authority. Melaka has long possessed this cosmopolitan character, lived and constituted in social relations born of diversity, community, experience, tolerance, and a complex mix of local and globalised identities. Despite the vicissitudes of colonial history and postcolonial political economy, Melaka remains a vibrant settlement whose experience presents the opportunity to image and share this global cosmopolitan ideal.

Acknowledgements

This chapter is based on field work conducted in Melaka over the period 1993 to 1997. The Association of Asian Studies, the Freeman Foundation, the Luce Foundation, and the Mellon Non-Western Fund at Vassar College funded the research.

References

Ashworth, G.J. and Tunbridge, J.E. (1990) *The Tourist-Historic City*. London: Belhaven.

Ball, D. (2000) *Malaysian Historical Salvors: The Diana Adventure*. Online. Available HTTP: http://www.dianawreck.com/ (10 July 2000).

Barnard, B. (1984) *Cultural Facades: Ethnic Architecture in Malaysia*. Hanover, New Hampshire: Universities Field Staff International.

Bruner, E.M. (1996) 'Tourism in Ghana: The representation of slavery and the return of the Black diaspora'. *American Anthropologist*, 98(2), 290–340.

Business Times, The (1993) 'Early transitional facade shophouses'. 16 January.

Carstens, S. A. (1988) 'From myth to history: Yap Ah Loy and the heroic past of Chinese Malaysians'. *Journal of Southeast Asian Studies*, 19(2), 185–207.

Carstens, S. (1999) 'Dancing lions and disappearing history: The national culture debates and Chinese Malaysian culture'. *Crossroads*, 13(1), 11–64.

Cartier, C.L. (1993) 'Creating historic open space in Melaka'. *Geographical Review*, 83(4), 359–73.

Cartier, C.L. (1996) 'Conserving the built environment and generating heritage tourism in Peninsular Malaysia'. *Tourism Recreation Research*, 21(1), 45–53.

Cartier, C.L. (1997) 'The dead, place/space and social activism: Constructing the nationscape in historic Melaka'. *Environment and Planning D: Society and Space*, 15, 555–86.

Cartier, C.L. (1998a) 'Megadevelopment in Malaysia: From heritage landscapes to "leisurescapes" in Melaka's tourism sector'. *Singapore Journal of Tropical Geography*, 19(2), 151–76.

Cartier, C.L. (1998b) 'Preserving Bukit China: A cultural politics of landscape interpretation in Melaka's Chinese cemetery', in E. Sinn (ed.) *The Last Half Century of the Chinese Overseas*. Hong Kong: University of Hong Kong Press, 65–79.

Chang, T.C. (1997) 'From "Instant Asia" to "Multi-faceted jewel": Urban imaging strategies and tourism development in Singapore'. *Urban Geography*, 18(6), 542–62.

Chang, T.C., Milne, S., Fallon, D. and Pohlmann, C. (1996) 'Urban heritage tourism: The global–local nexus'. *Annals of Tourism Research*, 23(2), 192–213.

Cheah, P. (1998) 'The cosmopolitical – today', in P. Cheah and B. Robbins (eds.) *Cosmopolitics: Thinking and Feeling Beyond the Nation*. Minneapolis: University of Minnesota Press, 20–41.

Cheah, P. and Robbins, B. (eds.) (1998) *Cosmopolitics: Thinking and Feeling Beyond the Nation*. Minneapolis: University of Minnesota Press.

Daily Telegraph, The (1995) 'The week in the salesrooms: 1.8 shipwreck porcelain sale defies all expectations'. 10 March, London.

Duncan, J. and Ley, D. (eds.) (1993) *Place/Culture/Representation*. London and New York: Routledge.

Far Eastern Economic Review (1995) 'A sea change: Development on Malacca's outskirts threatens a centuries-old Portuguese enclave's links to the sea'. 158 (32), 50–1.

Far Eastern Economic Review (1997) 'The soul of cities'. 160(34), 30.

Frank, A.G. (1998) *Reorient: Global Economy in the Asian Age*. Berkeley: University of California Press.

Harvey, D. (2000) 'Cosmopolitanism and the banality of geographical evils'. *Public Culture*, 12(2), 529–64.

Held, D., McGrew, A., Goldblatt, D. and Perraton, J. (1999) *Global Transformations: Politics, Economics and Culture*. Cambridge: Polity Press.

Jesudason, J.V. (1989) *Ethnicity and the Economy: The State, Chinese Business, and Multinationals in Malaysia*. Kuala Lumpur: Oxford University Press.

Kahn, J.S. (1997) 'Culturalizing Malaysia: Globalism, tourism, heritage and the city in Georgetown', in M. Picard and R.E. Wood (eds.) *Tourism, Ethnicity, and the State in Asian and Pacific Societies*. Honolulu: University of Hawaii Press, 99–127.

Kahn, J.S. and Wah, F.L.K. (eds.) (1992) *Fragmented Vision: Culture and Politics in Contemporary Malaysia*. Honolulu: University of Hawaii Press.

Kearns, G. and Philo, C. (eds.) (1993) *Selling Places: The City as Cultural Capital, Past and Present*. Oxford: Pergamon Press.

Kohl, D.G. (1984) *Chinese Architecture in the Straits Settlements and Western Malaya: Temples, Kongsis and Houses*. Singapore: Heinemann.

Kong, L. and Yeoh, B.S.A. (1994) 'Urban conservation in Singapore: A survey of state policies and popular attitudes'. *Urban Studies*, 31(2), 247–66.

Knox, P. and Agnew, J. (1998) *The Geography of the World Economy*, 3rd edition. London: Edward Arnold.

Malaysian Business (1994) 'Sleepy hollow no more: The economy of once-slumbering Malacca is being jump-started by industrialisation and tourism'. 1 May, 50–7.

Marrison, G.E. (1951) 'The coming of Islam to the East Indies'. *Journal of the Malayan Branch of the Royal Asiatic Society*, 24(1), 28–37.

New Straits Times (1995a) 'Community must come to term with progress'. 19 February, Kuala Lumpur.

New Straits Times (1995b) 'Smooth sailing for Maritime Museum'. 19 February, Kuala Lumpur.

New Straits Times (1998) 'Boosting our tourism potential'. 6 February, Kuala Lumpur.

New Straits Times (1999) 'Future of reclamation project in DOE's hands'. 18 February, Kuala Lumpur.

New Straits Times (1999) 'Striving for World Heritage Site status'. 1 August, Kuala Lumpur.

Oppermann, M. (1992) 'International tourist flows in Malaysia'. *Annals of Tourism Research*, 19(3), 482–500.

Reid, A. (1993) *Southeast Asia in the Age of Commerce, 1450–1680, Vol.2: Expansion and Crisis*. New Haven: Yale University Press.

Sandhu, K.S., and Wheatley, P. (1983a) 'From capital to municipality', in K.S. Sandhu and P. Wheatley (eds.) *Melaka: The Transformation of a Malay Capital, ca. 1400–1980*, Vol. 1. Kuala Lumpur: Oxford University Press, 495–97.

Sandhu, K.S. and Wheatley, P. (eds.) (1983b) *Melaka: The Transformation of a Malay Capital, ca. 1400–1980*, vol. 2. Kuala Lumpur: Oxford University Press.

SarDesai, D.R. (1977) *Southeast Asia: Past and Present*, 4th edition. Boulder: Westview Press.

Scott, J. (1997) 'Futures of Asian Studies'. *Asian Studies Newsletter*, 42 (summer), 7.

Singapore Business (1993) 'Malacca sheds its small town image: The Malaysian state is determined to become an economic powerhouse and a major tourism destination'. February, 38–45.

Star, The (1984) 'Joint memorandum submitted to the Chief Minister of Melaka by the major Chinese organisations in Malaysia for the preservation of Bukit China in its entirety'. 18 October, Kuala Lumpur.

Straits Times, The (1994) 'S'pore firm set to restore old Malacca houses'. 7 May, Singapore.

Teo, P. (1994) 'Assessing socio-cultural impacts: the case of Singapore'. *Tourism Management*, 15(2), 126–36.

Teo, P. and Huang, S. (1995) 'Tourism and heritage conservation in Singapore'. *Annals of Tourism Research*, 22(3), 589–615.

Tilden, F. (1977) *Interpreting Our Heritage*, 3rd edition. Chapel Hill, University of North Carolina Press.

Waters, M. (1995) *Globalization*. London and New York: Routledge.

Part Four

Acting as One in Ecotourism

13

Southeast Asian Tourism: Traditional and New Perspectives on the Natural Environment

P. P. Wong

Introduction

The natural environment is essential and is connected to tourism in many ways. It provides myriad natural attractions. It forms the basis of tourism as witnessed in Robinson's (1976:42) quotation "were there no geographical differences between place and place, tourism would not exist". Tourism itself has multivariate impacts on the natural environment, but such impacts are less well studied than economic or socio-cultural impacts. Although dated, Mathieson and Wall (1982) provides a basic account of tourism impacts on air, water, vegetation, wildlife and various ecosystems. Research on the impact of tourism on the natural environment is on-going. For example, in Australia (Sun and Walsh, 1998), research is on vegetation and soils, an area in which basic information is still relevant. Sometimes the focus is on specific natural environments, for example, impacts on the coastal environment (Wong, 1993).

Mathieson and Wall (1982:93) made a distinction between the natural environment and the built or man-made environment, a distinction that has important research implications on the connections between tourism and the natural environment. For example, in the oft-quoted cycle of tourism development (Butler, 1980), the environment, which was undifferentiated, deteriorated as tourism progresses over time. Later, Priestley and Mundet (1998) showed that if the environment is differentiated into the natural and the built, their quality could take different paths if proper measures are instituted before tourism reaches its critical limit of development. As the natural environment takes a longer time to recover, its quality remains constant for a longer time before recovery. In contrast, the quality of the built environment shows a more immediate and continuous recovery. With the increasing availability and application of product and process innovations to the natural environment (Hjalager, 1997) it can be expected that the natural environment will recover more quickly than before. Also, research on the generation of future scenarios (e.g. Walker *et al.*, 1998) could be helpful for predicting the quality of the natural environment under different situations of tourism development. According to Allwinkle and Speed (1997), the studies on tourism impacts on the built environment still trailed behind as this is a relatively new area.

The connections between tourism and the environment (natural and built) have become progressively more complex as concerns about the environment change and in a like manner, so has tourism's response to these concerns (Hudman, 1991). In the 1950s the environment was regarded purely for enjoyment as tourism developed into a mass industry, but debates on environmental issues in the 1970s and 1980s led to new perspectives on the connections between the environment and tourism (Cater and Goodall, 1992). Starting with the 1987 Brundtland Report, environmental issues on tourism have embraced the issue of sustainability, a concept that has been further strengthened by the principles of the 1992 Earth Summit on environment and development and supported by a programme for sustainable development under Agenda 21 (Gupta and Asher, 1998). By the 1990s, environmental concerns on deforestation, climatic changes and global impacts were paralleled by ecotourism and sustainable tourism development. People and tourists have become more environmentally conscious and the tourism industry is increasingly proactive in environmental protection. Sustainable development and ecotourism have brought closer the tenuous connections between tourism and the environment.

Several *overlapping* strands of inquiry have thus emerged around tourism and the natural environment. While one group of works emphasises the impact of tourism on the natural environment and discusses basic tourism-environment interactions (e.g. Briassoulis and van der Straaten, 1992; Coccossis and Nijkamp, 1995; Mieczkowski, 1995), another provides a greater focus on creating environmentally sustainable tourism (e.g. Nelson *et al.*, 1993; Hunter and Green, 1995; Priestley *et al.*, 1996; Stabler, 1997). A sampling of recent texts shows that the discussion has moved beyond environmental impacts to strategies (Lickorish and Jenkins, 1997; Cooper *et al.*, 1998) of sustainable tourism (Gartner, 1996; Goeldner *et al.*, 1999). Even in the concept of sustainable tourism, different perspectives have come to the fore: marketing (e.g. Middleton and Hawkins, 1998), geography (e.g. Hall and Lew, 1998) and economics (e.g. Tribe, 1999) are some examples.

'Ecotourism' has perhaps become one of the best concepts to link the natural environment and tourism. It has been defined in many ways, but should cover seven basic characteristics as identified by Honey (1999:22–25) in her expanded version of the definition by The Ecotourism Society. In the tourism-environment debate, 'ecotourism' has been the biggest marketable word to emerge from the tourism industry. Ecotourism is considered as a sustainable option for natural areas (Cater and Lowman, 1994), particularly in relation to conservation, species preservation, biodiversity and protected areas (Ceballos-Lascurin, 1996; Weaver, 1998; Honey, 1999). Although the practice of sustainable tourism and ecotourism is still in question (Wheeller, 1994; Griffen and Boele, 1997), an important aspect with regard to appropriate pricing is important if any form of sustainability is to be achieved (Southgate and DeWitt, 1994; Tisdell, 1999). Irrespective of whether ecotourism can be sustainable in the long term, the fact remains that remote or untouched spots of the natural environment will continue to be affected by the onslaught of adventure tourists (Tallantire, 1993; see also *Action Asia*).

Although the Southeast Asian region has been discussed in an increasing number of tourism studies, relatively less treatment is given to the natural environment (Hitchcock *et al.*, 1993; Wong, in press). The impact studies have been restricted to coastal tourism (e.g. R.A. Smith, 1991; Wong, 1997) and ecotourism (e.g. Cochrane, 1996; Hitchcock and Jay, 1998). This lack of concern for tourism's impact on the natural environment is perhaps a reflection of the situation in Malaysia which, until recently, had been more concerned with economic and bread-and-butter issues than tourism-environment issues (Din, 1996). For example, EIA (Environmental Impact Assessment) was a late arrival and became mandatory for tourism projects only from April 1988.

This chapter attempts to analyse several issues and aspects of the connections in the natural environment of Southeast Asia which have implications for tourism. The term 'connections' is used in two perspectives: (i) the usual, familiar or traditional perspective, between the natural environment and tourism; and (ii) the new or non-traditional local-global perspective in this volume, represented by Southeast Asian tourism/natural environment on one side and regionalisation/globalisation on the other. By its nature or as a phenomenon, international tourism had a local-global feature or connection before the concept of 'globalisation' became more widely used to analyse tourism today. Thus, with reference to Southeast Asia, Pleumarom (1996:314) said, "in this new era of globalisation and Southeast Asian regionalism, authority over resources for tourism and any kind of development is to be maintained by governments *vis-à-vis* the powerful interests of the global tourism industry, and, equally important, needs to be handed down to local communities, before sustainable tourism alternatives can be delivered." In a way, this sums up the gist of prevalent issues and connections between tourism, environment (both natural and built), and globalisation. While these three components are fast becoming intertwined, it is still useful for analysis to separate tourism from the environment, and the natural environment from the built environment. Tourism itself has developed into complex forms that make classification and analysis difficult, and the globalisation process provides a further perspective in analysing tourism and the environment.

This chapter will therefore

- discuss some aspects of the natural environment which are or are becoming regional issues in Southeast Asian tourism;
- evaluate the Association of Southeast Asian Nations (ASEAN) and other regional cooperative efforts on the natural environment and tourism, including efforts with other international groups and countries and efforts within larger regional or smaller subregional groups; and
- assess the prospects on the connections between the natural environment and tourism for Southeast Asia.

Regional issues

Southeast Asia has its fair share of problems relating to the natural environment. For those that are tourism-related, tourism can be a major or contributory cause or affected by the environmental issue, or a combination of both. Traditionally, to deal with environmental problems, appropriate or mitigating measures can be implemented by the players in the tourism industry, e.g. hoteliers, resort owners, etc. Some recent regional issues of the natural environment are not caused by the tourism industry, but have serious implications and require attention outside the usual tourism trade forums. Although the issues can be regional, the response can be local, national or regional. Also, some environmental issues can easily become political issues. The following examples illustrate the nature of some regional issues relating to tourism and the natural environment, their severity and the success of mitigating measures.

Coastal degradation and coral reef destruction

A significant proportion of Southeast Asian tourism is based on coastal resorts, particularly in Indonesia, Thailand, Malaysia and the Philippines (Edwards, 1995). There are enough studies on Southeast Asian coastal tourism to show what happens to the natural environment when unplanned or spontaneous development takes place. It basically results in environmental degradation arising from a lack of, or insufficient, sewerage and refuse disposal systems leading to water pollution, environmental and ecological damage, including coastal erosion and damage to fragile ecosystems such as coral reefs. Such tourist coasts have suffered the "costa disasta" effect as experienced in Mediterranean coastal resorts (Pleumarom, 1996).

For example, within a period of 20 years, Pattaya in Thailand grew from a village to a coastal resort but suffered from coastal pollution because of the discharge of poorly treated sewerage into the sea, poor solid waste disposal, etc. By 1989, the water was declared unsafe for swimming (R.A. Smith 1992a; Charoenca, 1993). Efforts have since been made to provide sewerage treatment plants and other rehabilitative measures have also been taken. The same story is repeated in many other beach resorts in Southeast Asia, e.g. Batu Ferringhi in Penang, Malaysia (R.A. Smith 1992b; Tan, 1992), Kuta in Bali, Indonesia (Hussey, 1989), Patong Bay in Phuket, Thailand (Bunapong and Ausavajitanond, 1991) and Boracay in the Philippines (V.L. Smith, 1992). These examples should be seen as cases in which tourism is a major cause of environmental degradation. They serve as useful lessons on the fragile connections between tourism and the natural environment. They should not be repeated, but unfortunately do continue because of profit motivation, lack of enforcement, or simply a lack of knowledge (Wong, 1998).

Coral reefs in Southeast Asia are actively sought for diving, which is fast developing into an ecotourism industry. Tourism is considered as a contributory cause to the destruction of coral reefs, as their degradation is a more complex issue (Done, 1999). Coral destruction is related to blast fishing, the use of poisons in reef fishing to meet subsistence, the export of ornamental and specific restaurant fish, coral mining for construction and limemaking, and other coastal activities such as construction, dredging, etc. It is also complicated by the destruction of the reefs by the Crown-of-Thorns starfish.

The resort island of Phuket in southern Thailand provides an example of how coral reefs were saved when it was realised that reef resources were essential to tourism (Lemay and Chansang, 1989; Hinrichsen, 1997). By the mid 1980s, when unregulated coastal development threatened to ruin the reefs, it was realised that some 400 local businesses were dependent on reef-based income and that the reefs provided US$10 million annually to the local economy. In 1986, the private sector in Phuket asked the government for a coastal management system to protect the island's coral resources. The Thai government in turn called in the Coastal Resources Center of the University of Rhode Island to work out a plan that looked into the needs of the local communities. From 1989 to 1991, legislation and regulation were passed on coastal tourism. In 1992, the Thai cabinet adopted a National Coral Reef Strategy based on the Phuket model for the entire country, and provided US$2 million for its initial implementation.

Although more laymen are familiar with corals today than before, their plight is not widely appreciated as they are underwater and largely unseen. Thus, many other tourist coasts in Southeast Asia still suffer from degradation of their coral reefs (Gomez, 1988; Sato and Mimura, 1997). The major obstacle is an acute lack of public, political and media awareness about the problems confronting coral reefs. Unlike the tropical rainforest, there is no broad-based public movement to save the reefs (Hinrichsen, 1997).

Deforestation and golf courses

Tourism development in Southeast Asia has resulted in the destruction of natural vegetation and associated habitats. In particular, the construction of golf courses for Japanese tourists has led to the clearing of land, sometimes involving forest reserves. Golf courses use large amounts of water, chemicals and often non-native greenery to create an artificial ecosystem (Pleumarom, 1992).

Golf course construction is one example of an environmental issue gone political. Local concern over tourist and golf development has been increasingly expressed as political action (Pleumarom, 1992; Cameron, 1996; Din, 1996; *Travel and Tourism Analyst*, 1996). The Global Anti-Golf Movement (GAGM), which was formed in 1993, has a website and is most active in Southeast Asia and Japan. But all these have done little to halt the construction of golf courses as long as they are perceived to be profitable enterprises.

Forest fires and haze

Within Southeast Asia, the traditional slash-and-burn method is practised by farmers to clear land, especially in Indonesia. Widespread land and forest fires in Indonesia were first noted in the early 1980s and have since become a cyclical phenomenon. Their frequency means that the problem can no longer be shrugged off as a minor disturbance. Fires occurred in 1982-1983, and again in 1987, 1991, 1994, 1997 and 1998 (*New Sunday Times*, 31 January 1999).

In 1997, fires became more than just a national issue. The haze created by the fires in Sumatra and Kalimantan covered much of Southeast Asia, causing health and transport hazards. The Indonesian authorities had to admit that the fires were mainly caused by land clearance for shifting agriculture, agricultural plantations and timber estate concessions. Satellite photos showed 5 million acres of forest destroyed, an area larger than Connecticut, Delaware and Rhode Island combined. The fires were aggravated by El Nino, which brought Indonesia its worst drought in 50 years (*New Sunday Times*, 31 January 1999). By September 1997, the smoke from the fires in Kalimantan and Sumatra had enveloped Singapore and Malaysia and reached Thailand. On an air pollution scale in which 300 is dangerous to health and 500 means "stay indoors", the city of Kuching in Sarawak registered 838. The President of Indonesia issued an apology to neighbouring countries for this "natural disaster". The severity of the 1997 incident became apparent when Indonesia and Malaysia declared the haze a national disaster (Friend, 1998).

The efforts to control fires intensified and the problem drew international attention, culminating in ASEAN drawing up a regional action plan. While the monitoring of fires can be done easily, the job of tackling fires at the source is still a problem due to the lack of resources and personnel, slow response, etc.

Apart from the obvious damage to the natural environment, the fires and related haze also have an impact on the region's economy. Glover and Jessup (1999) reported that the haze-related damages from the 1997 forest fires incurred by Indonesia, Malaysia and Singapore reached US$1,396 million, affected 5 million hectares and disrupted the lives of 70 million people. The tourism sector in Indonesia, Malaysia and Singapore suffered a loss of US$70.4 million, US$127.4 million and US$58.4 million respectively. Some other specific impacts on tourism were as follows. In Singapore, the number of tourists fell dramatically in October 1997 during the height of the haze. The country's national and regional carriers, Singapore Airlines and Silk Air, had to cancel and delay flights because of poor visibility. The US State Department also issued a travel warning, urging people with respiratory conditions to consider postponing travel because of the smog.

Haze is one environmental issue that is not caused by the tourism industry and had probably never been factored into the tourism industry until it was affected. But when the haze is severe or widespread, its impact is on tourism is immense. Measures have to be taken outside the tourism sector, by appropriate state forestry, agricultural or environmental agencies, to contain the problem. As the haze crosses national boundaries, regional measures have to be taken. Haze remains an unpredictable issue for the tourism industry in Southeast Asia and only the next serious occurrence will put to the test the effectiveness of the measures undertaken.

Climate change and sea-level rise

In recent years, climate change and its associated sea-level rise have become international concerns, and these have implications for tourism. Warmer temperatures may lead to a decline in demand from tourists from cold countries (Wall, 1996). More serious is the sea-level rise, which will cause inundation and coastal erosion (Nicholls *et al.*, 1995; Wall, 1998). While countries in Southeast Asia are aware of the future sea-level rise, almost none have taken measures in relation to tourism development. Only Malaysia has looked into a suitable setback line for coastal tourism development (Teh, 1997).

The issues of climate change and sea level demonstrate that if the environmental problem does seriously affect its profits, the tourism industry is not going to take appropriate measures immediately. This is not encouraged by the fact that climate change is of a long-term nature and not clearly defined for the private sector in terms of obvious losses. As such, it is not yet accepted as a threat to tourism (but compare the Maldives, which views coastal erosion and future sea-level rise as a serious threat to its coral atolls). Much remains to be done to convince coastal resorts of the dangers of a rising sea level and the associated coastal erosion.

Regional and external cooperation

Geographically, there are many bases for considering Southeast Asia as a region. Although there have been previous experiments in regional groupings involving Southeast Asian countries, e.g. Southeast Asia Treaty Organisation (SEATO), Association of Southeast Asia (ASA), Malphilindo (acronym formed by first letters of names of its member countries), Asian and Pacific Council (ASPAC) (Palmer, 1992), the one that has served best is ASEAN. The extent of ASEAN regional and external cooperation in tackling issues in environment and tourism is illustrated in the following examples.

ASEAN regional cooperation in environment and tourism

Regional cooperation and efforts to tackle issues in environment and tourism date back to 1977 when the ASEAN Sub-Regional Environment Programme (ASEP) was adopted. Cooperation in dealing with the natural environment was carried out by six Working Groups established in 1989: ASEAN Seas and Marine Environment; Environmental Economics; Nature Conservation; Environmental Management; Transboundary Pollution and Environmental Information; and Public Awareness and Education. These groups, however, faced the daunting task of implementing measures relating to transboundary pollution which would require a demanding amount of environmental coordination between the countries concerned, technical expertise of a high standard and a source of funds yet to be found (*South China Morning Post*, 19 June 1995; *Asia Pulse*, 11 August 1997).

For a more holistic approach in tackling regional environmental problems and to encourage international communities to contribute to the regional efforts, the six working groups were restructured into three working groups focusing on transboundary haze, nature conservation and biodiversity, coastal and marine environment and multilateral environment agreements (*New Straits Times*, 5 October 1998). In the Hanoi Declaration of 1998, ASEAN stated that to ensure the sustainability of a nation's development, the protection of the environment shall be an essential part of its economic activities (*ASEAN Economic Bulletin*, 1999).

ASEAN and External Cooperation

There is also increasing ASEAN and external cooperation in environment and tourism. In an effort to save fast-dwindling wildlife species in Southeast Asia, ASEAN and the European Union (EU) established an ASEAN Regional Centre for Biodiversity Conservation (ARCBC) in Los Banos, Laguna in 1998 (*Business World*, 21 July 1997; 7 July 1998). The centre is part of an environment plan approved at the Third ASEAN Ministerial Meeting on the Environment in 1997. Under the plan, national biodiversity reference units will be set up in each ASEAN member country, while the Philippines will host the centre or network base. The biodiversity centre will promote sustainable development practices in ASEAN member countries to avoid the loss of natural resources to environmentally threatening projects. In 1999, ASEAN and the EU agreed to strengthen cooperation in such areas as market access, trade facilitation, standards, intellectual property, customs, trade in services, investment, energy, environment, transport, tourism and narcotics.

From 1986 to 1991, the ASEAN/US Coastal Resources Management Project (CRMP) was implemented for six ASEAN countries (Scura *et al.*, 1992) and its success has led to further American support for regional projects on the environment. In 1999, the US State Department approved US$4 million under the East Asia and Pacific Environmental Initiative Fund to support regional efforts to improve forestry resource management and biodiversity conservation, marine resource and coastal zone management, and to promote effective responses to the effects of climate change in the region. The new projects will specifically combat destructive fishing practices which use dynamite and cyanide to capture aquarium and food fish, study coral bleaching, protect endangered species including sea turtles, enlarge marine and forest protected areas, and introduce modern forest harvesting practices to reduce wasteful techniques currently used. A number of projects will involve the cooperation of the ASEAN countries' private sector and catalyse additional funding from international organisations.

Canada has contributed to a successful ASEAN-Canada Cooperative Programme on Marine Science. The money, through the Canadian International Development Agency (CIDA), has enabled researchers from Canada and ASEAN countries to work on joint projects on establishing environmental criteria to develop and manage marine resources and promote the protection of human health. For example, under the project, a Red Tide Network was set up in 1994 with headquarters in the Philippines to alert member countries immediately on any occurrence of algal blooms (*New Straits Times*, 27 April 1996). Australia has sponsored an ASEAN-Australian Marine Science Project to provide technical assistance in managing coastal ecology and resources in seven ASEAN countries including Vietnam, which joined in 1997. A series of symposiums on the results have been held in Southeast Asia.

In recent years, further cooperative efforts on the environment have also come from other developed countries. For example, in 1996, government agencies and non-governmental organisations from ASEAN and Germany held a meeting on Environmental Protection and Cooperation in the ASEAN Region: An International Dialogue (*New Straits Times*, 22 November 1996). In it, they emphasised the need to create a regional environmental policy. The Hanns Seidel Foundation has already initiated projects on the environment in Vietnam.

Larger regional groups and subregional groups

Regional cooperation is not restricted between ASEAN and external organisations and other countries. There is also cooperation in the larger regional groupings and subregional groups. Within the Asia-Pacific Economic Cooperation (APEC) forum, ASEAN has also participated actively in APEC's tourism and environment-related programme (APEC, 1997). APEC's efforts will complement those within ASEAN.

The Pacific Asia Travel Association (PATA) also has members from ASEAN. It supports sustainable tourism and puts out a Code for Environmentally Responsible Tourism (CERT) which awards Green Leaf logos to its members. PATA has consolidated its environmental and cultural programmes into a newly formed Office of the Environment and Culture, currently based in Monaco, to coordinate sustainable tourism services, including the PATA Green Leaf Programme.

Within Southeast Asia there are several regional 'growth triangles' for cooperative economic development, and they have implications for tourism: SIJORI (Singapore-Johore-Riau) Growth Triangle, BIMP-EAGA (Brunei, Indonesia, Malaysia, Philippines-East ASEAN Growth Area), IMT (Indonesia-Malaysia-Thailand) Growth Triangle, and the Greater Mekong Subregion (Thailand, Indochinese countries, Myanmar). The Growth Triangles in Southeast Asia are good examples of governments and private sectors working together regionally and also where tourism and the environment are viewed within a sustainable development framework.

Assessment

The various regional and regional–external ties have different roles in tackling issues related to tourism and the environment. They face various hurdles before they can be more effective. Regional initiatives involving governmental structures or institutions may not be nimble enough to tackle issues such as cross-border haze, but at least they have agreed officially on the issues for regional cooperation and that much more needs to done for the future.

Regional-external ties have the advantage of funding from external sources, thus solving a serious problem. Many of these are still linked to government agencies and their success depends on the agency selected for implementation. One of the most successful has been the ASEAN/US CRMP where 120 professionals and 200 project personnel now form a critical mass of coastal zone management (CZM) specialists in the region (*Tropical Coastal Area Management*, 1991). Apart from former colonial powers, many developed countries, e.g. Scandinavian countries, are also keen to link up bilaterally with Southeast Asian countries.

Subregional and larger regional groups in Southeast Asia play a significant role for direct private sector participation. The most successful are the regional 'growth triangles' which are at various stages of development and are enjoying varying degrees of success.

Prospects on environment–tourism connections

A common management technique for analysing organisations known as SWOT (Strengths, Weaknesses, Opportunities and Threats) is used to assess the prospects of future connections for tourism and the environment in Southeast Asia. This method lends itself well to the analysis of the strengths and weaknesses within the region, while opportunities and threats are seen as drivers from outside the region. It takes stock of the present situation, provides some useful inputs for future planning, and identifies possible ways which can be improved or utilised (Doswell, 1997).

Strengths
- Perhaps the first strength is that Southeast Asia is synonymous with ASEAN since the inclusion of Myanmar. This has important implications for future ASEAN measures on sustainable tourism and environmental protection. Such measures would have full political and administrative backing to implement strategies across the region, unlike in the past when some countries were not in ASEAN.
- A further strength comes in the form of subregional groupings in Southeast Asia. SIJORI, BIMP-EAGA, IMT and the Greater Mekong Subregion have tourist attractions based on distinctive natural environments. SIJORI and IMT offer beaches and EAGA is billed as having the largest ecotourism potential in Southeast Asia by the Asian Development Bank (ADB, 1996). The Greater Mekong Subregion offers distinctive ecotourism associated with the riverine and estuarine ecosystems. Together, these subregions offer the greatest potential for ecotourism development in Southeast Asia and could act as the main magnets for the implementation of sustainable tourism.

Weaknesses
- Despite all the cooperative measures, environmental protection is still weak and does not help tourism. The region's failure to tackle in a timely manner the problem of haze arising from forest fires during 1991-1994 and 1997-1998 has raised doubts about its methods and effectiveness.
- Another internal weakness lies in EIA in the region. While the proposal to develop a common system of conducting EIAs within the ASEAN region was made way back in 1984, the disparities in EIA systems among the ASEAN countries remain to be addressed.
- There is also inadequate manpower trained to address tourism-environment issues. Although there are cores in tourism and the environment themselves, there is still a lack of a core in appreciating the links, for example, coastal tourism and not tourism versus coastal engineering.

Opportunities
- With its potential in ecotourism, particularly in EAGA, substantial opportunities exist for external investments. Opportunities for sustainable tourism investment bring the environment and tourism closer together, for example, in the annual Mekong Tourism Forum.
- The seas in ASEAN could also form an "Aseanarean" (rhymes with Mediterranean and Caribbean) which is home to 2,500 species of marine fish

and 400 species of hard corals. It accounts for 2 per cent of the earth's water surface, twice that of the rivals it wants to best, and an array of attractions. Its potential for cruising has been utilised although it would take some time to make it as well known as the Caribbean or the Mediterranean as a cruise destination (Seward, 2000).

- A stronger connection between tourism and the environment can be made by moving beyond ecotourism attractions (Poon, 1993), for example, into environmental services and technology, ecotourism services, etc. ASEAN has a potential US$8.2 billion annual market for environmental technology and services. A consortium of Canadian environmental companies was established in 1992 to tap the urban environmental management projects in ASEAN. For coastal tourism, the provision of sewerage disposal systems and fresh water is important, particularly on small islands. There are also opportunities for the development of expertise and the provision of suitable environmental auditing frameworks.

Threats

- Perhaps the biggest threat to the region is the European Commission directive on package tourism for ASEAN member countries, hoteliers and tour operators. The demands for protection of consumers were directed particularly at developing countries which are the main tourist destinations of Europeans. European tourism operators had stressed the need for standardisation of services at hotels and restaurants, during flights and in transportation within and outside cities. For example, the Europeans demand standardisation in travel agencies' capability to give accurate descriptions of climatic conditions (Asia Pulse, 15 May 1997). This had been applied to about 30 countries in 1997. The impacts on ASEAN relate to issues on consumer protection, responsibilities and liabilities, sovereignty, laws and opportunities for legal protection, and insurance related to the directives. These have serious implications for the tourism industry, and tourism operators in ASEAN member countries would have to set up a joint insurance company to handle claims on sub-standard service from European tourists.

- Another threat from outside is the ecolabelling scheme for hotels, although this is still not widespread. Although it is not yet the industry norm in the USA, corporate agents and their clients do consider suppliers' environmental records when selecting their travel partners (West, 1995).

- The Blue Flag poses a more serious threat. This is the European ecolabel for beaches to comply with a list of standards. At present, it is applicable to European resorts where the water pollution situation is bad to begin with. In Southeast Asia, most organisations are in favour of a similar scheme imposed by a regional organisation and not from outside. The situation is still fluid and the United Nations Environment Programme-Foundation for Environmental Education in Europe-World Tourism Organisation (UNEP-FEEE-WTO) held its first meeting on the feasibility of the Asian Pacific Blue Flag in August 1999 in Bangkok. The Philippines has its own version of the Blue Flag following bad publicity on the polluted water at Boracay in 1997.

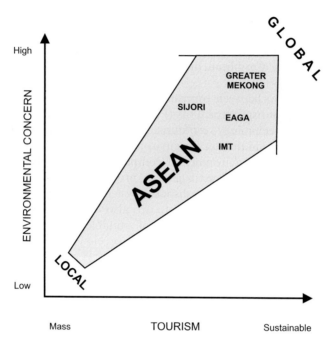

Fig. 13.1 Schematic representation of the connections between environment and tourism of Southeast Asia in a globalised world

Conclusion

Traditional and new perspectives have been used to examine the connections in the natural environment of Southeast Asian tourism under three broad areas. Such perspectives are expected to be modified, improved upon or replaced by better perspectives in future. It would be useful to reduce the discussion and analysis into guidelines that practitioners in the tourism industry can easily identify. In this respect, one could reiterate some of the points in the speech on the future of tourism delivered by the Philippines' former Secretary of Tourism at the Twelfth ASEAN Tourism Forum in Manila in 1993 (*Travel Weekly*, 1 February 1993). That speech has a strong bearing on the connections between tourism and the environment in Southeast Asia and the relevant points are re-stated as follows (my *emphasis in italics*):

(i) Measure success according to impact on the environment. The region should *not judge its tourism success purely by arrival statistics, but should use tourists' length of stay, spending and satisfaction, and the impact on the environment and local residents' quality of life as measuring sticks.*

(ii) Focus on sustainable tourism. The critical state of the environment demands that the tourism industry practise sustainable or responsible tourism. *Countries must focus on environmental protection or face the destruction of the natural resources that attract tourists.* The environment will be the single factor that will determine the volume and distribution of tourists to any destination, and which and how many wholesalers and retailers operating within the region will remain in business.

(iii) Scope for ecotourism. Tour operators with the highest standards *and those committed to the environment will survive to cater to specialised and upscale clientele seeking ecotourism programmes*; and

(iv) Tourism to protect environment. *Tourism can be used to protect the environment through revenues derived from tourism receipts* that are then funnelled back into environmental protection programmes. Also, the private sector will be encouraged to redouble its efforts toward ecologically responsible development throughout the region. Infrastructure development within the region will be affected by the 'greening of tourist facilities'. The development and operating costs of tourist facilities, such as hotels and attractions, may rise considerably as they move toward instituting environmentally sound practices, such as recycling.

In conclusion, Figure 13.1 provides a schematic summary to view the connections in the natural environment in Southeast Asian tourism from traditional and new perspectives. The trajectory of future Southeast Asian (or ASEAN) tourism is in its connections with the natural environment within a globalised world. Despite limitations and shortcomings, tourism efforts within the region and the subregions (involving national and local efforts) are working towards sustainable tourism and a high concern for the natural environment and, hopefully, to achieving the above four re-stated points. Future tourism-environment connections are based on their impact on the environment, focus on sustainable tourism and scope for ecotourism and tourism to protect the environment.

References

Action Asia, bi-monthly magazine devoted to adventure tourism and locations in Asia, published in Hong Kong since 1992.

Allwinkle, S.S. and Speed, C.E. (1997) 'Sustainability and the built environment: tourism impacts', in P.S. Brandon, P.L. Lombardi and V. Bentivegna (eds.) *Evaluation of the Built Environment for Sustainability*. London: E & FN Spon, 263–75.

ASEAN Economic Bulletin (1999) 'Hanoi Declaration of 1998: 16 December 1998', 16: 95–8.

Asia-Pacific Economic Cooperation (APEC) (1997) *Tourism and Environmental Best Practice in APEC Member Countries*. Singapore: APEC Secretariat.

Asia Pulse (1997) 'ASEAN tourism operators to set up joint insurance co.', 15 May, Sydney.

Asia Pulse (1997) 'ASEAN addresses natural resources depletion', 11 August, Sydney.

Asian Development Bank (ADB) (1996) *East ASEAN Growth Area*, Volume 3, Part 2. Manila: ADB.

Briassoulis, H. and van der Straaten, J. (1992) *Tourism and the Environment*. Dordrecht: Kluwer Academic Publishers.

Bunapong, S. and Ausavajitnond, S. (1991) 'Saving what's left of tourism development at Patong Beach, Phuket, Thailand', in O.T. Magoon, H. Converse, O. Miner, L.T. Tobin and D. Clark (eds.) *Coastal Zone '91*. New York: American Society of Civil Engineers, 1685–97.

Business World (1997) 'Los Banos to host ASEAN biodiversity', 21 July, Manila.

Business World (1998) 'ASEAN biodiversity centre in Laguna', 7 July, Manila.

Butler, R.W. (1980) 'The concept of a tourist area cycle of evolution: Implications for management of resources'. *Canadian Geographer*, 24, 5–12.

Cameron, O. (1996) 'Japan and Southeast Asia's environment', in M.J.G. Parnwell and R.L. Bryant (eds.) *Environmental Change in Southeast Asia*. London: Routledge, 67–93.

Cater, E. and Goodall, B. (1992) 'Must tourism destroy its resource base?' in A.M. Mannion and S.R. Bowlby (eds.) *Environmental Issues in the 1990s*. Chichester: John Wiley, 309–23.

Cater, E. and Lowman, G. (eds.) (1994) *Ecotourism: a Sustainable Option?* Chichester: John Wiley.

Ceballos-Lascurin, H. (1996) *Tourism, Ecotourism and Protected Areas*. Gland: IUCN.

Charoenca, N. (1993) 'Tropical coastal pollution: A case study of Pattaya', in J.E. Hay and L.M. Chou (eds.) *Contributions to Training in Coastal Zone Management in the Asia-Pacific Region and Report of the First NETTLAP Resources Development Workshop for Education and Training at Tertiary Level in Coastal Zone Management*, Publication No. 7. Bangkok: UNEP/ROAP Network for Environmental Training at Tertiary Level in Asia and the Pacific, 123–42.

Coccossis, H. and Nijkamp, P. (eds.) (1995) *Sustainable Tourism Development*. Aldershot: Avebury.

Cochrane, J. (1996) 'The sustainability of ecotourism in Indonesia: Fact and fiction', in M.J.G. Parnwell and R.L. Bryant (eds.) *Environmental Change in Southeast Asia*. London: Routledge, 237–59.

Cooper, C., Fletcher, J., Wanhill, S., Gilbert, D. and Shepherd, R. (1998) *Tourism: Principles and Practice*, 2nd edition. Harlow: Longman.

Din, A.K. (1996) 'Tourism and the environment: Some current and neglected issues', in *State of the Environment of Malaysia*. Penang: Consumers' Association of Penang, 324–29.

Done, T.J. (1999) 'Coral community adaptability to environmental change at the scales of regions, reefs and reef zones'. *American Zoologist*, 39(1), 66–79.

Doswell, R. (1997) *Tourism: How Effective Management Makes the Difference*. Oxford: Butterworth-Heinemann.

Edwards, A. (1995) *Asia-Pacific Travel Forecasts to 2050*. London: Economist Intelligence Unit.

Friend, T. (1998) 'Indonesia in flames'. *Orbis*, 42, 387–407.

Gartner, W.C. (1996) *Tourism Development*. New York: Van Nostrand.

Glover, D. and Jessup, T. (eds.) (1999) *Indonesia's Fires and Haze*. Singapore/Ottawa: Institute of Southeast Asian Studies/International Development Research Centre.

Goeldner, C.R., Ritchie, J.R.B. and McIntosh, R.W. (1999) *Tourism: Principles, Practices and Philosophies*, 8th edition. New York: John Wiley.

Gomez, E.D. (1988) 'Overview of environmental problems in the East Asian Seas Region'. *Ambio*, 17, 166–69.

Griffen, T. and Boele, N. (1997) 'Alternative paths to sustainable tourism: Problems, prospects, panaceas and pipe-dreams', in F.M. Go and C.L. Jenkins (eds.) *Tourism and Economic Development in Asia and Australasia*. London: Cassell, 321–37.

Gupta, A. and Asher, M.G. (1998) *Environment and the Developing World: Principles, Policies and Management*. Chichester: John Wiley.

Hall, C.M. and Lew, A.A. (eds.) (1998) *Sustainable Tourism: A Geographical Perspective*. Harlow: Longman.

Hinrichsen, D. (1997), 'Coral reefs in crisis'. *BioScience*, 47(9), 554–58.

Hitchcock, M. and Jay, S. (1998) 'Eco-tourism and environmental change in Indonesia, Malaysia and Thailand', in V.T. King (ed.) *Environmental Challenges in Southeast Asia*. Surrey: Curzon, 305–16.

Hitchcock, M., King, V.T. and Parnwell, M.J.G. (1993) 'Tourism in Southeast Asia', in M. Hitchcock, V.T. King and M.J.G. Parnwell (eds.) *Tourism in Southeast Asia*. London: Routledge, 1–31.

Hjalager, A.M. (1997) 'Innovation patterns in sustainable tourism: An analytical typology'. *Tourism Management*, 18, 35–41.

Honey, M. (1999) *Ecotourism and Sustainable Development: Who Owns Paradise?* Washington, D.C.: Island Press.

Hudman, L.E. (1991) 'Tourism's role and response to environmental issues and potential future effects'. *Revue de Tourism*, 4, 17–21.

Hunter, C. and Green, H. (1995) *Tourism and the Environment: A Sustainable Relationship*. London: Routledge.

Hussey, A. (1989) 'Tourism in a Balinese village', *Geographical Review*, 79, 311–25.

Lemay, M.H. and Chansang, H. (1989) *Coral Reef Protection Strategy for Phuket and Surrounding Islands*. Bangkok: Thailand Coastal Resources Management Project.

Lickorish, L.J. and Jenkins, C.L. (1997) *An Introduction to Tourism*. Oxford: Butterworth-Heinemann.

Mathieson, A. & Wall, G. (1982) *Tourism: Economic, Physical and Social Impacts*. London: Longman.

Middleton, V.T.C. and Hawkins, R. (1998) *Sustainable Tourism: A Marketing Perspective*. Oxford: Butterworth-Heinemann.

Mieczkowski, Z. (1995) *Environmental Issues of Tourism and Recreation*. Lanham: University Press of America.

Nelson, J.G., Butler, R. and Wall, G. (eds.) (1993) *Tourism and Sustainable Development: Monitoring, Planning, Managing*. Waterloo, Ontario: University of Waterloo.

New Straits Times (1996) 'Canada to fund RM5m marine studies extension', 27 April, Kuala Lumpur.

New Straits Times (1996) 'Region needs common goal for sustainable development', 22 November, Kuala Lumpur.

New Straits Times (1998) 'New approaches to tackling environmental problems', 5 October, Kuala Lumpur.

New Sunday Times (1999) 'Factors and impacts of forest fires', 31 January, Kuala Lumpur.

Nicholls, R.J., Mimura, N. and Topping, J. (1995) 'Climate change in South and Southeast Asia: Some implications for coastal areas'. *Journal of Global Environment Engineering*, 1, 137–54.

Palmer, N.D. (1992) 'SEATO, ASA, Malphilindo and ASPAC' in K.S. Sandhu, S. Siddique, C. Jeshurun, A. Rajah, J.L.H. Tan and P. Thambipillai (compilers), *The ASEAN Reader*. Singapore: Institute of Southeast Asian Studies, 27–9.

Pleumarom , A. (1992) 'Golf tourism in Thailand'. *The Ecologist*, 22, 104–10.

Pleumarom, A. (1996) 'Environmental and socio-economic implications of tourism in Southeast Asia', in *State of the Environment in Malaysia*. Penang: Consumers' Association of Penang, 314–23.

Poon, E. (1993) *Tourism, Technology and Competitive Strategies*. Wallingford: CAB International.

Priestley, G.K. and Mundet, L. (1998) 'The post-stagnation phase of the resort cycle'. *Annals of Tourism Research*, 25, 85–111.

Priestley, G.K., Edwards, J.A. and Coccossis, H. (eds.) (1996) *Sustainable Tourism?: European Experiences*. Wallingford: CAB International.

Robinson, H. (1976) *A Geography of Tourism*. London: MacDonald & Evans.

Sato, A. and Mimura, N. (1997) 'Environmental problems and current management issues in the coastal zones of South and Southeast Asian developing countries'. *Journal of Global Environment Engineering*, 3, 163–81.

Scura, L.F., Chua, T.E., Pido, M.D. and Paw, J.N. (1992) 'Lessons for integrated coastal zone management: The ASEAN experience', in T.E. Chua and L.S. Scura (eds.) *Integrative Framework and Methods for Coastal Area Management*. Manila: International Center for Living Aquatic Resources Management, 1–70.

Seward, P. (2000) *Aseanarean ahoy*! Online. Available at HTTP://www.latitude1.com/Aseanarean/index.cfm (1 February 2000).

Smith, R.A. (1991) 'Beach resorts: A model of development evolution'. *Landscape and Urban Planning*, 21, 189–210.

Smith, R.A. (1992a) 'Coastal urbanisation: Tourism development in the Asia Pacific'. *Built Environment*, 18, 27–40.

Smith, R.A. (1992b), 'Conflicting trends of beach resort development: A Malaysian case'. *Coastal Management*, 20, 189–210.

Smith, V.L. (1992) 'Boracay, Philippines: A case study in "alternative" tourism', in V.L. Smith and W.R. Eadington (eds.), *Tourism Alternatives*. Philadelphia: University Press of Pennsylvania, 135–57.

South China Morning Post (1995) 'States agree on plan to combat pollution', 19 June, Hong Kong.

Southgate, D. and DeWitt, D. (1994) *Economic Progress and the Environment: One Developing Country's Policy Crisis*. New York: Oxford University Press.

Stabler, M.J. (ed.) (1997) *Tourism and Sustainability: Principles and Practice*. New York: CAB International.

Sun, D. and Walsh, D. (1998) 'Review of studies on environmental impacts of recreation and tourism in Australia'. *Journal of Environmental Management*, 53, 323–38.

Tallantire, J. (1993) 'Adventure tourism in remote places', in S. Glyptis (ed.) *Leisure and the Environment: Essays in Honour of Professor J.A. Patmore*. London: Belhaven Press, 279–93.

Tan, P.K. (1992) 'Tourism in Penang: Its impacts and implications', in P.K. Voon and T. Shamsul Bahrin (eds.) *View from Within: Geographical Essays on Malaysia and Southeast Asia*, Kuala Lumpur: Malaysian Journal of Tropical Geography, 263–78.

Teh, T.S. (1997) 'Sea level rise implications for coastal and island resorts', in *Climate Change in Malaysia*. Serdang: Universiti Putra Malaysia, 83–102.

Tisdell, C. (1999) *Biodiversity, Conservation and Sustainable Development: Principles and Practices with Asian Examples*. Aldershot: Edward Elgar.

Travel & Tourism Analyst (1996) 'The Japanese golf holiday market', 2, 58–70.

Travel Weekly (1993) 'ASEAN nations are advised to focus on environmental issues' 1 February, Secaucus (New Jersey).

Tribe, J. (1999) *The Economics of Leisure and Tourism*, 2nd edition. Oxford: Butterworth-Heinemann.

Tropical Coastal Area Management (1991) 'The ASEAN/US Coastal Resources Management Project: Impacts and lessons learned', Editorial, *Tropical Coastal Area Management*, 6(3), 1–3.

Walker, P.A., Greiner, R., McDonald, D. and Lyne, V. (1998) 'The Tourism Futures Simulator: A systems thinking approach'. *Environmental Modelling and Software*, 14, 59–67.

Wall, G. (1996) 'The implications of climate change for tourism in small island states', in L. Briguglio, B. Archer, J. Jafari and G. Wall (eds.) *Sustainable Tourism in Islands and Small States: Issues and Policies*. London: Pinter, 205–16.

Wall, G. (1998) 'Implications of global change for tourism and recreation in wetland areas'. *Climate Change*, 40, 371–89.

Weaver, D.B. (1998) *Ecotourism in the Less Developed World*. Wallingford: CAB International.

West, K. (1995) 'Ecolabels: The industrialisation of environmental standards'. *The Ecologist*, 25, 16–20.

Wheeller, B. (1994) 'Egotourism, sustainable tourism and the environment: A symbiotic, symbolic or shambolic relationship', in A.V. Seaton, C.L. Jenkins, R.C. Wood, P.U.C. Dieke, M.M. Bennett, L.R. MacLellan and R. Smith (eds.) *Tourism: The State of the Art*. London: John Wiley, 647–54.

Wong, P.P. (ed.) (1993) *Tourism vs Environment: The Case for Coastal Areas*. Dordrecht: Kluwer Academic Publishers.

Wong, P.P. (1997) 'Coastal tourism development in Southeast Asia: Relevance and lessons for coastal zone management'. *Ocean and Coastal Management*, 38, 89–109.

Wong, P.P. (1998) 'Beach resorts: The Southeast Asian experience', in V.R. Savage, L. Kong and W. Neville (eds.) *The Naga Awakens*. Singapore: Times Academic Press, 241–60.

Wong, P.P. (in press) 'Tourism development in Southeast Asia: Patterns, issues and prospects', in L.S. Chia, (ed.) *Southeast Asia Transformed: A Geography of Change*. Singapore: Institute of Southeast Asian Studies.

14

Sinews of Interconnectivity: Tourism and Environment in the Greater Mekong Subregion

Michael J. G. Parnwell

The double-edged sword of interconnectivity

As Southeast Asia's established tourism centres have become tired and tarnished by overuse, under-management, shifting consumer preferences and changing perceptions of 'good' and 'appropriate', fresh destinations and products are constantly being sought and mobilised in order to maintain the momentum of rapid tourism growth in the region. An added urgency has come from the post-1997 regional economic crisis. Meanwhile, willing partners have been found in the five socialist states of the Greater Mekong Subregion (GMS)[1] which little more than a decade ago peered suspiciously across one of the front-lines of the Cold War but which now, courtesy of post-communist 'open doors' market reforms, lie uncomfortably on the periphery of the global capitalist system. To facilitate the process of regional integration for tourism development, alliances have readily been formed between the various agencies of tourism promotion and mobilisation – national governments, private enterprise, regional development institutions, regional travel associations, etc. – and a niche market is in the process of being carved out.[2] The advocates of tourism development point to the collective economic benefits which will accrue from cooperation across national boundaries, with the great Mekong River becoming a powerful symbol of sub-regional interconnectivity (Bakker, 1999). Furthermore, GMS tourism linkages help to give substance to the geo-political ideal of regional integration.

Meanwhile, antagonists claim that the promotion of tourism in the subregion is too strongly motivated by economic considerations and an unhealthy urgency to bring rapid 'development' to one of Pacific Asia's economic backwaters. Accordingly, tourism development is too heavily driven and controlled by commercial interests. National and supra-national bodies, blinded by prospects of joining or driving Southeast Asia's 'miracle' roller-coaster, are heavily preoccupied by regulation *for*, as opposed to the regulation *of*, tourism development (Tickell and Peck, 1992; Lipietz, 1993). They point to the considerable damage that has already occurred in Southeast Asia's established tourism heartlands and warn that the same outcome is even more likely and even more quickly in the GMS where there are inadequate safeguards and insufficient representation from non-commercial actors. The GMS periphery contains some of Pacific Asia's most vulnerable cultures and ecosystems and yet these are precisely the resources that are being singled out by and for the tourism industry (Asian Development Bank (ADB), 1998). An emerging regional coalition of antagonists cites copious evidence of damage that is already being done, issuing a clarion call for 'sustainable tourism development' and the prioritisation of protection over exploitation.

There is therefore a polarisation of positions, with a sub-regional 'protagonist alliance' pursuing an orthodox vision of development versus a regional 'antagonist alliance' pushing a more radical post-developmentalist or even anti-developmentalist ideology (Sachs, 1992; Escobar, 1995; Brohman, 1996; Rahnema and Bawtree, 1997). Arguably, however, sustainable tourism development focuses attention on the middle ground between these two positions and seeks a means of facilitating growth within limits, while transforming existing social attitudes and political power structures to allow this to happen. Conventionally, this middle ground should be patrolled by the state but in recent decades, under a neoliberal development regime, the state is claimed to have ceded economic control to the market. As a consequence of globalisation and regionalisation, political control is said to have passed to supranational agents and institutions (Peck and Tickell, 1994). In the Southeast Asian context, close connections between political, bureaucratic and economic actors have also compromised the capacity for states to regulate for sustainable development (Rodan *et al.*, 1997). This being the case, it is apt to ask what the prospects for sustainable tourism development in the 'interconnected world' of the GMS, and Southeast Asia more widely, are likely to be as we move into the twenty-first century. Will interconnectivity be a double-edged sword facilitating the rapid short-term mobilisation of tourism resources whilst doing little to conserve these resources in the longer term or to protect the interests of local communities in the subregion? Who is going to orchestrate a power balance between regional protagonist and antagonist factions? Where is regulatory strength and vision going to come from?

The aim of this chapter is to explore the process and implications of 'interconnectivity' in tourism development within the GMS. It draws initially upon recent debates on regulation, globalisation and neoliberalism to weave a loose conceptual framework for the subsequent enquiry. It then highlights some of the more important issues which are associated with regionalisation in the Mekong subregion before elucidating the protagonist and antagonist positions on tourism development. The chapter concludes that it is the principal actors in the protagonist alliance, most notably the ADB and the Thai government (which have hitherto been caricatured by the antagonists as pariahs in the subregion's recent development), that hold some of the keys to sustainable tourism development especially if they work towards strengthening the middle ground between the forces of development and conservation, guided in part by the nagging conscience of the antagonist lobby.

Sinews of interconnectivity and the regulation of development

Tourism development, as with capitalist production more generally, occurs within the framework of an established but constantly evolving 'mode of social regulation' (MSR), an ensemble of institutional forms and practices which secure the adjustment of society to the overarching principles of a regime of capitalist accumulation (Marden, 1992:753). The state is held to be the principal regulatory power (Flynn and Marsden, 1995:1184) and it is essentially charged with both regulation *for* capitalist development (e.g. delivering conditions that are conducive to the operation of business activities within a particular global regime) and the regulation *of* capitalist accumulation (e.g. protecting the welfare needs and rights of society) (Marden, 1992). The balance between these two objectives is influenced to a considerable extent by the prevailing ideology and definition of 'development', whereas the state's capacity for regulation (i.e. its 'room for manoeuvre') is conditioned by the balance of power within a given society and the prevailing political regime. The MSR is constantly evolving as a result of social and political contestation, with the regulatory state functioning as a 'mediator' between the main social actors in capitalist development (Gibbs, 1996:5).

One arena of contestation in recent years has centred around the definition of, and thus regulation for, 'development'. The orthodox vision of development around which most regulatory regimes in the South have been arrayed since at least the Second World War equated 'development' with the achievement of modernisation and growth (Brohman, 1996). Regulatory mechanisms evolved and were legitimated by the ideology of development although the regulatory process was often manipulated by social groups whose private and collective interests were best served by this "regime of over-accumulation" (Clark, 1992:622; see also Flynn and Marsden, 1995:1182). Uneven and unsustainable development was a common consequence, but in the past this mattered little because of an implicit faith in the 'trickle down effect' and the top-down directionality of development, and because of an imbalance in power which allowed élites to establish the 'rules of the game' whilst withstanding or repressing any challenge to their position and pre-eminence.

The orthodox definition of development has been seriously contested over the last few decades, sparking contestation over what constitutes an appropriate regulatory regime and leading to what Clark (1992:623) has called a plurality of competing representations and interpretations about the proper structure of society. An alternative definition of development has emerged which places a strong emphasis, *inter alia*, on the pursuit of equity, democracy and sustainability. The redefinition of development reflects the growing ascendancy and assertiveness of social actors who remained somewhat peripheral and subservient to the regulatory regime of orthodox development. An alternative, more appropriate path towards 'genuine development' is in the process of being mapped out and the foundations for an 'appropriate' regulatory environment are currently being negotiated. Sustainable development is suggested as an emerging MSR (Gibbs, 1996:6–7) which is similarly being shaped through political struggle and social conflict at the global and also the local level, leading to a challenging of the existing socio-economic order and distribution of power (Drummond and Marsden, 1995:56). However, the established order is challenging change partly by contesting the conceptual basis for change (i.e. the meaning of 'sustainable development') and in part by remodelling itself to exude an external semblance of change, for example, by calling 'dirty', 'clean' leading Gibbs (1996:7) to conclude that "certain elements of capital are already using the concept of sustainable development for the continuation of a particular set of social relations".

All said, not only is the world changing in terms of how development is defined, but there is also a quantum shift in the locus of regulatory power. The state (the traditional regulatory 'gatekeeper') is seeing its power eroded by parallel tendencies of neoliberalism and globalisation/regionalisation. However, it is not global/regionalisation *per se* that is the issue so much as the *terms of interaction* within the global system (Amin, 1997:129). As a nation becomes a player on the global stage, it inevitably cedes a degree of power, autonomy and sovereignty to supranational institutions and forces (Mittelman, 1995:291). The state by default falls into danger of becoming "outflanked" (Mittelman, 1995:291) or "hollowed out" (Peck and Tickell, 1994:317) not just by the forces of transnational capital but also by local responses to this; namely, the alliances that are forged between international capital and economic actors at the subnational level (local élites and business conglomerates).

This raises several questions and issues which will be explored below. What are the 'sinews of connectivity' that link the global with the local? What role does (or can) the state play in regulating supranational and subnational economic actors and the interaction between them? Is the state preoccupied with the regulation *of* development or regulation *for* development? Does the regulatory capacity of the state and of other bodies vary across space and time? Are there differences in regulatory styles and capacities between the free-market and former socialist states, and has the interconnection of the two given rise to unequal regulatory regimes? To what extent has the process of regional integration intensified or ameliorated the negative consequences of rapid and under-regulated development? Is regional economic integration a double-edged sword in that it allows for the more efficient mobilisation of resources in favour of economic growth whilst compromising the capacity for regulation in favour of development, however broadly defined?

Regional integration in the GMS

The Mekong River has emerged as a powerful symbol of a new era in Southeast Asia – an era of peace and integrated development (Bakker, 1999:209). What was formerly a 'front-line' of the Cold War has now become a symbol of unity and collective purpose, swept along by the currents of globalisation and a supposedly "borderless world" (Ohmae, 1990). Tourism has emerged as one of the softest and arguably least controversial means of cementing regional cooperation and integration, and it is thus apposite that culture and nature should constitute the principal resources upon which tourism development in the Mekong subregion is being built.

The end of the Cold War removed the political barriers to, and increased the incentive for, regional trade and cooperation (Rimmer, 1994:1734). Ideological differences with their capitalist neighbours have dissipated as the former socialist states of the Mekong Basin pursue the post-Cold War 'peace dividend' (Grundy-Warr, 1998:64; Bakker, 1999:214), adopting (with varying degrees of commitment and success) liberal economic reforms and 'open doors' international policies in order to breathe fresh life into moribund centrally-planned economies. As relative latecomers, they have much to gain from closer cooperation with their more advanced and experienced neighbours, principally Thailand in this instance. It is claimed that all parties stand to gain more from economic cooperation and interdependence than from interstate rivalry and unbridled competition (Rimmer, 1994:1753). However, Thailand's central involvement in GMS regional integration is in part driven by its avaricious designs on its neighbours' now-accessible natural resources at a time when its own resources and environments have become degraded as a consequence of rapid and largely unbridled economic growth (Hirsch, 1995:235). It is also argued (Mitchell, 1998:81) that the growth and increasing power of the environmental movement in Thailand has motivated its resource adventurism in neighbouring territories where fewer such constraints currently exist (see below). It is for these reasons that Thailand has attempted to style itself as a subregional development 'hub' and the 'gateway' into the Mekong subregion (Battersby, 1998:482).

One consequence of Thailand's central involvement in GMS integration, particularly within the private sector, is that it runs the risk of drawing into the frame the shadier side of Thai business practice (Battersby, 1998:484; Grundy-Warr, 1998:64). There is already plenty of evidence of the role played by Thai military, police and government officials, as well as business élites (often one and the same thing) in exploiting the timber and other natural resources of Myanmar, Laos and Cambodia, in the trafficking of women into the Thai sex industry and in the movement of drugs into and through Thailand (Hirsch, 1995; Battersby, 1998). GMS economic integration now provides a legitimate and increasingly unencumbered means by which Thai business actors can move into and control other forms of transborder business, in the process forming networks and alliances with embryonic domestic political and economic actors in neighbouring countries. These sinews of interconnectivity "rely on the Thai government to break down barriers to trade with Indochina" (Battersby, 1998:482), and as such, the Thai state can be seen essentially to be regulating *for* development.

Regional integration requires close cooperation between the public and private sectors, the former facilitating development by means of infrastructural investment and providing a conducive regulatory environment while the latter provides investment capital (Thant *et al.*, 1994:1). In the case of the GMS, however, these two sectors have been superseded by, or have coalesced with, a transnational private lending agency, the ADB. Because of its ability to mobilise quickly large amounts of investment capital (Bakker, 1999:223) for infrastructural development, the ADB has been able to encourage the subregion's states to share its grand vision for regional integration, not allowing historical antagonisms and political tensions to get in the way of good business. The ADB has thus emerged as the driving force in GMS regional development. One of the Bank's priority sectors in this regard is tourism. Crucial to the development outcomes of GMS integration in general, and for tourism development in particular, is the way that the ADB strikes a balance between regulation *for* and the regulation *of* development. Does Bakker's (1999:224) depiction of the ADB as a 'neutral broker' which is helping to bring together a once-divided region hold true?

Although civil societies of the former socialist states of the Mekong region do not have the same freedom as the ADB to influence policy and contest the definition and prioritisation of 'development' (Hirsch, 1995:251–2), there are attempts to forge grassroots regional environmental links to play an advocacy role in attempting to place environmental and local concerns higher up the policy-making agenda (Hirsch, 1995:257). As such, there is growing scope for rearranging the power context within which the contestation of development agendas takes place. The following discussion will look at how the regulatory environment in the GMS is currently being nego-tiated by what we shall call 'protagonists' and 'antagonists' in the process of tourism development.

Tourism development in the GMS: the protagonist perspective

Although there have been several attempts to mobilise the natural resources of the Mekong Basin in the past, most notably efforts to tap the hydro-power potential of the river and its tributaries in the 1950s, the ADB's current GMS scheme is the largest and most comprehensive in the subregion's history. It is also the only scheme where tourism development has formed a central pillar.[3] The GMS Programme of Economic Cooperation was initiated in 1992, and the ADB's role was to help foster economic growth to improve the livelihoods of the people in the subregion by acting as a catalyst, facilitator and 'honest broker', encouraging dialogue among the 'Mekong Six' (M6) states, and assisting in project identification, design and execu-tion (ADB, 1998:32). The ADB aims to make the GMS "the new frontier in the East Asian miracle" (ADB, 1999a) and to help raise average per capita incomes in the region three- to four-fold by the year 2020. The ADB's mandate requires it to promote regional cooperation, and this is now its highest priority (ADB, 1999b). It also aims to create an environment conducive to private sector investment in the subregion.

The ADB's GMS tourism strategy centres on the exploitation of the subregion's 'untapped' rich cultural heritage and diverse natural geography by both creating and tapping into niche ecotourism and adventure tourism markets dominated by discern-ing and relatively high-spending travellers. The attractions are already present and identified, but four principal impediments to tourism take-off remain: market aware-ness/position, availability of investment capital, accessibility and human resources. The ADB aims to facilitate tourism development by acting as a catalyst in all four fields. In relation to the first of these, the ADB, in conjunction with the National Tourism Organisations (NTOs) of the M6 states, has entered into an alliance with the private sector, most particularly by enlisting the support of the Pacific Asia Travel Association (PATA) to promote and raise market awareness of the subre-gion's tourism resources. With the exception of Thailand, which is already ahead of the game in this regard, the remaining Mekong states have experienced considerable difficulty in placing their tourism resources in the international market (ADB,

1999a). Overseen (and thus presumably regulated) by the ADB's Subregional Tourism Working Group, PATA has been promoting "this last remaining tourism frontier" under the slogan "Jewels of the Mekong" (see Figure 14.1 and Table 14.1). PATA takes overall coordinating responsibility for the joint marketing of the region's tourism 'jewels' and is particularly emphasising the themes of complementarity and interconnectivity through the promotion of multi-location holidays. However, the individual NTOs have ultimate responsibility for delivering, guaranteeing and sustaining the quality of these tourism destinations (ADB, 1999a).

In this plan, the Mekong River itself, together with some of the striking ecosystems of the Mekong Basin, are projected to become the focus of ecotourism development in the GMS. Meanwhile, the Third Meeting of the ADB Working Group on Tourism also endorsed a proposal to make village-based tourism a keystone strategy for the exploitation of the cultural resources of the GMS (ADB, 1999b). The Bank has a clear 'Policy on Indigenous Peoples' which, whilst seeking to bring to them the same development opportunities that are enjoyed by majority and mainstream groups in society, strives to ensure that they are fully consulted and ideally involved when decisions are being made which will affect their cultures, livelihoods and welfare. The ADB is in the process of rolling together its various environmental, social and governance policies into an overarching policy on sustainable development (ADB, 1999a:48) and plans to play a catalytic role in this regard in the future. With specific reference to the GMS, the ADB's "ultimate objective is to facilitate 'sustainable economic growth' and to improve the standard of living of the people in the subregion – greater awareness of the environmental impacts of infrastructure projects is being fostered at all stages of project development. The process of dialogue with non-government organisations has also been started" (ADB, 1999b:n.p.).

It is also recognised that individual states are typically concerned with environmental problems that occur within their territorial borders, whereas, in reality, environmental exploitation and its harmful effects increasingly straddle these boundaries. It is here that supranational bodies also have a role to play, especially in engendering cooperation in the confrontation and amelioration of transboundary environmental and sociocultural problems. However, as we shall see shortly, supra-

Table 14.1: GMS and the "Jewels of the Mekong"

States	Tourism resources
Yunnan, PR China	Lijiang, Dali, Kunming, Stone Forest, Xishuangbanna
Myanmar	Mingun Pagoda (Mandalay), Bagan, Inle Lake (Taunggyi), Shwedagon Pagoda (Yangon), Kyaikhtiyo (Golden Rock)
Lao PDR	Luang Prabang, Plain of Jars (Xieng Khouang), Vientiane, Sak Lao, Champassak
Vietnam	Hanoi City, Halong Bay (Haiphong), Ninh Binh Province, Thua Thien Hue, Quangnam-Danang Province
Cambodia	Angkor Wat, Phnom Penh and surroundings, Tonle Sap, Ratanakin
Thailand	Chiang Rai Province, Ubon Ratchathani, Prasat Hin Khao Phanom Rung Historical Park, The Old Royal City (Rattanakosin Island) (Bangkok)

Source: PATA (1999)

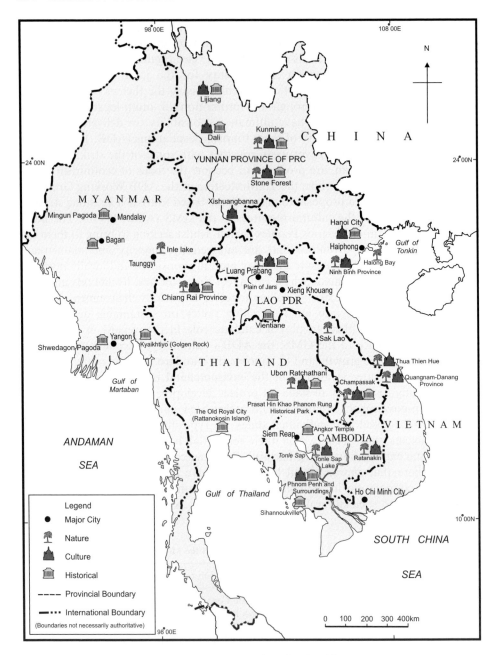

Fig. 14.1 Subregional tourism 'jewels'
Source: ADB Subregional Working Group on Tourism

national bodies such as the ADB can only influence, not control, what happens inside a sovereign territory's boundaries. At the sub-national level, other forces are in operation which may challenge and compromise their best intentions.

Tourism and environment in the GMS: the antagonist perspective

The above discussion suggests that, by and large, national and supranational institutions have been quite heavily preoccupied with regulating *for* development although there has also been a suggestion that, as awareness of and attitudes towards the harmful effects of rapid tourism growth have changed, these bodies are also beginning to turn their attention towards the regulation *of* economic growth guided, at least at the rhetorical level, by the principles of sustainable development. In general, however, supranational bodies lack effective regulatory power because, in spite of globalisation and regionalism, sovereign states still hold the ultimate right to determine what happens within their national boundaries. Meanwhile, whilst national governments too are spouting the rhetoric of sustainability, it is also often the case that their 'room for manoeuvre' is constrained by the prevailing relationship between the public and private sectors.

Given this situation, where is the power to regulate *for* sustainable development going to come from? It was suggested earlier that the environmental movement and the non-governmental sector have an important contribution to make in this regard, not as regulators *per se*, but as the 'nagging consciences' of the principal regulatory bodies. Thus, the 'antagonists' have a role to play in placing environmental conservation higher up the planning and implementation agendas and in giving regulators more 'room for manoeuvre' by challenging the established order and promoting an alternative, broader definition of 'development'.

In the GMS it is interesting to note that the strongest impulses in this regard have come from Thailand, where the orthodox development process has been in operation for longer and where the harmful effects of unbridled development have already become strongly apparent and have forced a reaction from society. The most prominent organisation in this regard has been the Project for Ecological Recovery (PER) in Thailand, which has been the driving force behind Towards Ecological Recovery and Regional Alliance (TERRA), an organisation that is committed to promoting and supporting the environmental movement in the GMS and which ultimately aims to foster genuine 'interconnectivity' within a regional environmentalist 'antagonist' movement as a counterbalance to the 'protagonist alliance'. TERRA produces a monthly *Briefing on Tourism, Development and Environment Issues in the Mekong Subregion*, appropriately entitled *New Frontiers*, which consists mainly of a critical digest of newspaper stories on tourism throughout the region. In order to give a flavour of the perspective and approach of TERRA and to highlight how the harmful effects of tourism are persisting in spite of the proliferation of words and deeds about 'sustainable tourism', the following section will present two brief case studies taken principally from recent issues of *New Frontiers* which highlight some of the problems associated with the regulation of the tourism industry in real life.

Tourism development in Yunnan, China

Yunnan Province in the People's Republic of China provides the first short case study of the mobilisation of environmental resources for tourism development in the GMS. China is in many respects quite peripheral to GMS developments but is on the verge of a veritable tourism explosion not so much from international sources but as a result of an exponential rise in domestic tourism. The way that resources and regional linkages are mobilised for the industry's expansion in Yunnan will have a significant bearing upon the impact of tourism development in a major part of the Upper Mekong region.

New Frontiers has focused on plans first to create, and then exploit for tourism, the massive Yunnan Great Rivers National Park in the vicinity of Lijiang. Covering a projected 66,870 sq. km, the Park will be some four times the size of Yellowstone National Park in the United States and will include stretches of four of Asia's greatest rivers: the Mekong, Yangtze, Salween and Irrawaddy. The area contains a massive diversity of habitats and ecosystems and within its confines can be found some 10 per cent of the world's bird species, 30 animal species which have been listed as endangered by the International Union for the Conservation of Nature (IUCN), and some 40–60 per cent of the plants that are used in traditional Chinese medicines (*The Nature Conservancy*, 1999). The principal town in the area, Lijiang, has been declared a World Heritage Site by UNESCO. On the mountain slopes and ridges that separate the major rivers can be found some of China's last remaining stands of primary forest. The proposed park is thus quite clearly an important natural resource which is in urgent need of protection from the pressures of rapid development in China, but it also constitutes an immensely attractive and hitherto untapped resource for tourism. It is the tension between these two sets of interests and the forces that lie behind them that has provided the focus of TERRA's concerns. TERRA claims that the promotion of the area for tourism will almost inevitably lead to the degradation of the natural environment and cultural erosion among the province's 26 ethnic minority groups, particularly given the recent nature of domestic tourism in China (*New Frontiers*, 1997a:7–8).

Continuing the theme of regional interconnectivity, the original driving force behind the intensified mobilisation of the region's natural resources for tourism development came from a Thai entrepreneur, Vikrom Kromadit, a Bangkok real estate developer of Chinese descent. In 1993, his original intention had been to capitalise on the growing demand in Southeast Asia for 'nearby recreational escapes' by building a ski resort on Jade Dragon Snow Mountain, one of the region's principal scenic attractions (*The Nature Conservancy*, 1999). Khun Vikrom's company, AMATA, commissioned the Colorado-based Conservation Development Corporation to undertake a feasibility study. The Corporation's conservation-minded consultant, Steve Mikol, concluded that the ski resort project was not viable, but suggested an alternative plan that would involve turning the region into a massive national park and nature reserve where ecotourism could be used as an economic means of simultaneously underpinning both conservation and development efforts. TERRA is highly sceptical about this and claims that the project will open the door to a rapid influx of tourists that neither the environment nor local cultures will be able to withstand. *New Frontiers* contains warnings of developers falling over themselves to construct golf courses, cultural theme parks and ski resorts (*New Frontiers*, 1997a:7–8). It claims that local and national officials have been easily won over to the idea of the Yunnan Great Rivers National Park because of the economic rewards that it will bring from tourism. They warn of the proliferation of karaoke bars, prostitution and 'cheesiness' (*New Frontiers*, 1998a:7). Locals who have traditionally made a living from small-scale tourism enterprises are in danger of being squeezed out as big business is attracted to the area. Tourism had started to boom even before the designation of the National Park, up from a handful in 1992 to more than 60,000 international tourists in 1997 (more than 60 per cent of whom were from Southeast Asia) following the opening of the airport in Lijiang in 1995 (*New Frontiers*, 1997a:8). In support of the tourism influx, a new road had been blasted through one of the region's main tourist attractions, the Tiger Leap Gorge (*New Frontiers*, 1997a:8).

As a counter to these developments, the US-based Nature Conservancy has become involved in the designation, design and future management of the Yunnan Great Rivers National Park. The Nature Conservancy has been behind the design and management of several national parks in the United States and in recent years has been lending its expertise to the international community (*The Nature Conservancy*, 1999). It was Steve Mikol, also a Nature Conservancy member, who first mooted this organisation's involvement in the scheme, and the Park's future prospects for sustainable tourism development would appear to rest very heavily on the partnership that has been forged between the Nature Conservancy and the Yunnan Provincial Government. By November 1997, the Nature Conservancy had helped form China's first international environmental NGO, the Institute for Human Ecology, which was responsible for presenting the consortium's plans to the national government for approval, which was duly granted in December 1997 and cemented in June 1998 during a visit by the Nature Conservancy's President, John C. Sawhill, to Yunnan. Sawhill claimed that "it was impossible to say 'No' to such an historic opportunity in such an important country" (*The Nature Conservancy, 1999*:n.p.). The Nature Conservancy believes that economic dynamism may be used as a powerful force for conservation in China:

While China reportedly has some 400 parks and nature reserves, few are actually well-protected. Environmentalists and government officials alike believe that a project combining environmental and economic strategies is the best way to demonstrate how to protect China's natural heritage while improving economic opportunities for remote rural communities.

(*The Nature Conservancy*, 1999:n.p.).

In addition to nature conservation, cultural preservation is also an important concern of the Yunnan Great Rivers National Park project.

It remains to be seen just how well the Nature Conservancy/Yunnan Provincial Government consortium will be able to achieve its conservation objectives while at the same time promoting sustainable (eco)tourism development. One vestige of China's recent past is that the provincial and state authorities have a fairly comprehensive system of regulatory and enforcement control, and thus to an extent that is not found in, for instance, Thailand, the regulatory authorities have the means to implement the best principles of the Yunnan Great Rivers National Park project. But do they have the will? The market is advancing very rapidly across China, even in peripheral areas like Yunnan,[4] and regulatory authorities are not only being swept aside by the rapid and relentless pace of business development but, in some instances, they have also become the principal actors in embryonic private sector development. As well as compromising their function as regulators *of* development, the authorities are under heavy pressure to regulate *for* development, not least in an area where average annual per capita incomes are only US$70, way below the national poverty line in China.

'Human zoos' in the GMS

The notion of 'human zoos' – contained 'villages' where indigenous peoples, together with often inauthentic or contrived manifestations of their lifestyles and material culture, can be viewed as a tourist attraction – has become something of a *cause célèbre* for the 'antagonist' movement. *New Frontiers* (1996a:7; 1996b:7; 1997b:6; 1998b:2–3; 1998c:1; 1998d:7) has featured the case of the Padaung (long-necked) people which has involved trafficking, illegal immigration, effective slavery and the erosion of personal dignity, often with the complicity of the regulatory authorities. I discuss this case here principally because of the way that it highlights the power relations which underlie the regulatory environment, but partly because it represents another form of 'ecotourism'.[5]

Females of the 7,000 strong Padaung people[6] have become renowned internationally for their practice of wearing neck rings which, over time, significantly extend the neck's length. The neck rings and elongated necks are claimed to be symbols of beauty and social ranking in Padaung society, although competing patriarchal interpretations also abound. Ever on the lookout for cultural 'differentness' as a resource for avid tourism consumption, the (Myanmese) Padaung women have become coveted for their curiosity value by tour operators. Given problems of mass tourism access to Myanmar, and a desire to gain directly from control of the 'resource', tour operators have used various devices to bring the women to the Thai market. Many of these devices have either been illegal and/or contravene the spirit of the supranational policies towards indigenous peoples that were discussed in the previous sections.

The original 'model village' (human zoo) was established in Mae Hong Song province in northern Thailand, and was quite actively promoted by both the private sector and local government officials given the relative paucity of formal tourist attractions in the province. Over time, the distinctiveness and profitability of this 'resource' attracted the attention of rival tour operators from some of the more advanced tourism destinations, particularly Chiang Mai province. These operators either sought to bring more Padaung women into the country, or lured women from the operators in Mae Hong Song province, who subsequently complained about the way that rivalry and competition from neighbours was affecting their business (*New Frontiers*, 1996a:6–7). Worse still, operators were resorting to a variety of dubious tactics to gain access to the Padaung women. Operators were apparently trafficking women illegally from Myanmar into Thailand, doubtlessly with the complicity of the regulatory 'gatekeepers' at the national borders (police, immigration officials), or were luring or even kidnapping them from refugee camps along the Thai–Myanmese border: *New Frontiers* (1996a:7) reports that a man took 46 Kayan people from a refugee camp in Mae Hong Song to a tourism centre in Chiang Mai where tourists paid US$10–12 each to view the women, whilst 30 Kayan were smuggled from Myanmar into Chiang Mai and Chiang Rai provinces to become a sight-seeing attraction for tourists who paid US$40 for the privilege (*New Frontiers*, 1996a:7).

In spite of their high profile in the tourism destinations of northern Thailand, the majority of the Padaung women are officially illegal immigrants. One can speculate that the operators who control them have also been able to control the authorities so that their illegal status does not interfere with tourism business even though it is a factor that further constrains the women's rights and lays them open to various forms of abuse. The *New Frontiers* article (1996a:7) claims:

Some years ago, business-minded people from Thailand and Myanmar made a deal with Mae Hong Song officials to allow Kayan people to live in certain villages in the province for tourism purposes, without being persecuted as illegal aliens.

Where the illegal status of the Padaung women has become an issue, their controllers have claimed that they are migrant fruit-pickers and agricultural workers, thereby forestalling any attempts to extradite them back to Myanmar (*New Frontiers*, 1997b:6).

The situation reached a head in 1997 when it transpired that a prominent Thai businessman, Thana Nakluang, had in 1996 allegedly arranged the kidnap of 34 Padaung women from Loikaw in Kayah State, Myanmar, after they had been forcibly relocated there from their home village of Panpet in the Kayah Highlands by the Myanmese military. They were apparently abducted whilst being transported to a tourist village which is under the control of the Karen Refugee Committee in the vicinity of the refugee camp at Baan Na Soi (*The Times*, 22 November 1997) and ended up instead in Mae Hong Song province in Thailand. Here they were forced to work as a tourist attraction for Thana Nakluang, with the blessing and support of the local authorities (including the Tourist Police). The 'model village' functioned quite normally and openly for 18 months until an investigative report by Andrew Drummond in the British newspaper *The Times* (22 November 1997) revealed that the Padaung were 'prisoners' being held against their will. Furthermore, while their controllers were charging tourists around £4 each to see the 'long-necked women', the Padaung themselves received only £3 per family per month for being exhibits in this human zoo (*The Times*, 22 November 1997). Their economic hardship was compounded by the vulnerability caused by their illegal status, a situation that their controllers often brutally exploited. The women were subsequently freed by the police, and Thana Nakluang was due to stand trial, although with the power of finance and connections behind him, he seemed quite confident of winning his case (*New Frontiers*, 1998c:6).

While all these shenanigans have been taking place – showing how, in reality, the market is all-powerful, particularly in instances where close alliances have been forged between exploiters and erstwhile regulators – it is the Padaung women who have suffered untold misery. In addition to receiving few of the financial rewards that their distinctive culture and appearance have yielded to the tour operators, they have also suffered the erosion of their personal dignity, functioning as curious exhibits for touristic consumption. As part of its campaign on behalf of the Padaung, TERRA representatives spoke to some of the women who had been turned into a tourist attraction. The words of one Kayan woman highlight their plight:

Sometimes when tourists take pictures of me, I am proud that they want to take my picture. But at the same time they make me feel like an animal. I have to pose in awkward positions. I have to be there, ready to do whatever they want me to do. We have no freedom here. We are just like animals in a zoo. I truly feel this is a zoo... Whether we have money or not, I can never be happy here. I have suffered a lot. I worry all the time about my children, their health and their future.

(*New Frontiers*, 1996b:7).

It is these kinds of situations that the regulators, subnational, national and supranational, have to address and ultimately eliminate if sustainable tourism development is to become a reality and not just a slogan. It is unlikely that advocacy groups such as TERRA can achieve this by themselves, particularly where their actions often consist of preaching to the already converted, but they can succeed by acting as the 'nagging conscience' of the regulatory system and by raising public awareness of the abuses that continue in the interests of tourism development.

Conclusion

This chapter has focused on the process of tourism development in what is seen by the industry's protagonists as one of Asia's 'last frontiers', the GMS. It has identified some of the principal forces and actors behind the mobilisation of natural resources for the industry's expansion, and has suggested some of the actual and latent negative consequences of inadequately controlled or managed tourism development. It has also shown where the industry's 'nagging conscience' lies, and how it might contribute towards the promotion of better practices in the longer term.

As we move into an ever more 'interconnected world' in the twenty-first century, sustainable tourism development depends crucially upon an effective means being found to strengthen and regulate the middle ground between the protagonists of orthodox development and the advocates of 'appropriate development'. It may be unpalatable to some but one conclusion that we can reach is that the ADB and the Thai government have a potentially influential role to play in this regard. The ADB, as we have seen, has gradually adopted the slogan of sustainability, and is increasingly matching actions to words. As it begins to promote and achieve genuine sustainable development, the 'antagonist alliance' will, hopefully, engage with rather than distance itself from the Bank's work, a process that, indeed, has already begun as the ADB more readily and regularly draws NGOs and other groups into its decision-making, implementation and post-project evaluation procedures (ADB, 1998:64–5; 1999a:49–52). As an important holder of the development purse strings in the GMS, particularly during a period of economic crisis, the ADB should be in a powerful position to orchestrate the power balance between the antagonist and protagonist factions, between global and local forces, and between regulation *for* and the regulation *of* the tourism industry in the subregion in a manner that is conducive to sustainable tourism development.

Meanwhile, recent changes in the other pariah of the Mekong Region, Thailand, could be employed to good effect in disseminating a potentially constructive model of 'good governance' to the Kingdom's neighbours. At a recent meeting of the ADB's Working Group on Environment, the Thai representative from the Ministry of Science, Technology and Environment, Dr Monthip Sriratana Tabucanon, claimed that civil society is increasingly being involved in environmental management in Thailand (ADB, 1999b). Such a situation is in part a consequence of the process of democratisation that has been proceeding apace in Thailand since the early 1990s and is in part reinforced by recent changes to the Thai Constitution. The latter allows for greater participation by the public and NGOs in the decision-making, implementation and evaluation components of the development process. By giving the people more power and a greater stake in both development and the environment, it is claimed that more responsible and appropriate actions will result. Although there is still a great deal of evidence to the contrary in Thailand, the empowerment of people and the creation of an alternative MSR may hold the most optimistic prospect for sustainable tourism development in the 'interconnected world' of the GMS as we move into the twenty-first century.

Acknowledgements

This chapter is related to the author's recent research on international population movements in the Mekong region which has been supported by a Senior Research Fellowship from the European Studies Programme (ESP). I gratefully acknowledge the support of the ESP, the Asia Research Center for Migration at Chulalongkorn University, Thailand, Care International in the Lao PDR, and Yunnan University in Kunming, PRC.

Notes

[1]See Table 14.1 for the constituent states.
[2]"Jewels of the Mekong" is the promotional theme for tourism development in the sub-region that is being spearheaded by the Pacific Asia Travel Association (PATA).
[3]The seven priority sectors of the GMS scheme are transport, energy, telecommunications, environment, human resource development, trade and investment, and tourism (ADB, 1998: 32).
[4]According to Eng (1997:454), there were less than a thousand foreign tourists in Yunnan in 1978. By 1990, some 23,600 foreign tourists and 1.51 million domestic tourists had visited Xishuangbanna in Yunnan.
[5]Ecotourism has been defined by Hector Ceballos-Lascurain as "travelling to relatively undisturbed or uncontaminated natural areas with the specific objective of studying, admiring, and enjoying the scenery and its wild plants and animals, as well as any existing cultural manifestations (both past and present) found in these areas" (cited in Cochrane, 1996:240-41). As such, it is not just restricted to natural environmental resources but also includes distinctive but vulnerable cultural groups such as are discussed in this brief case study.
[6]Along with the Mon, the Padaung are claimed to have been among the original inhabitants of the Irrawaddy and Salween valleys in present-day Myanmar. Calling themselves the 'ka-kaung', they have been assimilated into the much larger and ethnically diverse Karen ethnic group, although their respective languages are not mutually intelligible. Until recently the Padaung inhabited the remote hills of Kayah

State (and also the Shan State borderlands) but have subsequently been systematically forced out of the hills by the Myanmese military and many have subsequently sought protection in Karen refugee camps along the Thai-Myanmese border.

References

Asian Development Bank (ADB) (1998) *Annual Report, 1997.* Manila: ADB.

ADB (1999a) *Annual Report, 1998.* Manila: ADB.

ADB (1999b) On-Line. Available: HTTP: http://www.asiandevbank/org/ (28 June 1999).

ADB Subregional Working Group on Tourism (1999) On line. Available HTTP: http://www.asiandevbank.org/Work/GMS (28 June 1999).

Amin, A. (1997) 'Placing globalization'. *Theory, Culture and Society*, 14(2), 123–37.

Bakker, K. (1999) 'The politics of hydropower: Developing the Mekong'. *Political Geography*, 18, 209–32.

Battersby, P. (1998) 'Border politics and the broader politics of Thailand's international relations in the 1990s: From communism to capitalism'. *Pacific Affairs*, 71(4), 473–90.

Brohman, J. (1996) *Popular Development: Rethinking the Theory and Practice of Development.* Oxford: Blackwell.

Clark, G.L. (1992) 'Real regulation: The administrative state'. *Environment and Planning A*, 24, 615–27.

Cochrane, J. (1996) 'The sustainability of ecotourism in Indonesia: Fact and fiction', in M.J.G. Parnwell and R.L. Byrant (eds.) *Environmental Change in Southeast Asia: People, Politics and Sustainable Development.* London: Routledge, 237–59.

Drummond, I. and Marsden, T. (1995) 'Regulating sustainable development'. *Geoforum*, 5(1), 51–63.

Eng, I. (1997) 'Historical contingency and commercialisation in Xishuangbanna, China'. *Tijdschrift voor Economische en Sociale Geografie*, 89(4), 446–58.

Escobar, A. (1995) *Encountering Development: The Making and Unmaking of the Third World.* Princeton: Princeton University Press.

Flynn, A. and Marsden, T. (1995) 'Guest editorial: "Rural Regulation"'. *Environment and Planning A*, 27, 1180–92.

Gibbs, D. (1996) 'Integrating sustainable development and economic restructuring: A role for Regulation Theory?'. *Geoforum*, 27(1), 1–10.

Grundy-Warr, C. (1998) 'Turning the political map inside out: A view of mainland Southeast Asia', in V.R. Savage, L. Kong and W. Neville (eds.) *The Naga Awakens: Growth and Change in Southeast Asia.* Singapore: Times Academic Press, 29–86.

Hirsch, P. (1995) 'Thailand and the new geopolitics of Southeast Asia: Resource and environmental issues', in J. Rigg (ed.) *Counting the Costs: Economic Growth and Environmental Change in Thailand.* Singapore: Institute of Southeast Asian Studies, 235–59.

Lipietz, A. (1993) 'The local and the global: Regional individuality or interregionalism'. *Transactions of the Institute of British Geographers*, 18, 8–18.

Marden, P. (1992) '"Real" Regulation Reconsidered'. *Environment and Planning A*, 24, 751–67.

Mitchell, M. (1998) 'The political economy of Mekong basin development', in P. Hirsch and C. Warren (eds.) *The Politics of Environment in Southeast Asia: Resources and Resistance.* London: Routledge, 71–89.

Mittelman, J.H. (1995) 'Rethinking the international division of labour in the context of globalization'. *Third World Quarterly*, 16, 273–95.

Nature Conservancy, The (1999) Online. Available HTTP: http://www/tnc.org/magazine/main/html (28 June 1999).

New Frontiers (1996a) 'Tour operators' cut-throat competition for "long-neck" women', October, 2(10), 6–7.

New Frontiers (1996b) 'Special concern: Voices from ethnic people under "village arrest"', November, 2(11), 7.

New Frontiers (1997a) 'Lijiang trying to weather tourist influx', October, 3(10), 7–8.

New Frontiers (1997b) '"Human Zoo" report may backfire on Amazing Thailand Campaign', December, 3(12), 6.

New Frontiers (1998a) 'Yunnan Great Rivers National Park seen as a tourism gold mine', July/August, 4(4), 7.

New Frontiers (1998b) 'ADB's push for Mekong tourism', September/October, 4(5), 2–3.

New Frontiers (1998c) '"Human Zoo" operator to be charged in court', September/October, 4(5), 6.

New Frontiers (1998d) '"Human Zoos" an assault to indigenous peoples', November/December, 4(6), 7.

Ohmae, K. (1990) *The Borderless World: Power and Strategy in the Interlinked Economy*. London: Collins.

Pacific Asia Travel Association (PATA) (1999) Online. Available: HTTP: http://www.pata.org (28 June 1999).

Peck, J. and Tickell, A. (1994) 'Jungle law breaks out: Neoliberalism and global-local disorder'. *Area*, 26, 317–26.

Rahnema, M. and Bawtree, V. (eds.) (1997) *The Post-Development Reader*. London: Zed.

Rimmer, P.J. (1994) 'Regional economic integration in Pacific Asia'. *Environment and Planning A*, 26, 1731–59.

Rodan, G., Hewison, K. and Robison, R. (eds.) (1997) *The Political Economy of Southeast Asia: An Introduction*. Melbourne: Oxford University Press.

Sachs, W. (ed.) (1992) *The Development Dictionary: A Guide to Knowledge as Power*. London: Zed.

Thant, M., Tang, M. and Kakazu, H. (eds.) (1994) *Growth Triangles in Asia: A New Approach to Regional Economic Cooperation*. Oxford: Oxford University Press (for the Asian Development Bank).

Tickell, A. and Peck, J.A. (1992) 'Accumulation, regulation and the geographies of post-Fordist: Missing links in regulationist research'. *Progress in Human Geography*, 16(2), 190–218.

Times, The (1997) 'Prisoners in a "Human Zoo"', 22 November, London.

15

"Borneo, Nature's Paradise": Constructions and Representations of Nature within Nature-based Tourism

Kevin Markwell

Introduction

As a form of economic activity, nature-based tourism requires that nature be transformed into a commodity which can be readily sold to prospective tourists and a powerful way by which this commodification of nature can be achieved is through the visual and textual imagery contained in tourism media such as marketing and promotional material, postcards and published tour guides. The images contained in these media evoke Western cultural mythologies and ideas about nature and in so doing, create interconnections between the 'wild' places of the world, often but not always located in the 'East' and 'South' in the Western imagination. This chapter focuses on the visual and textual imagery employed in tourist brochures, published tour guides and postcards that serve to construct and represent Bornean nature to Western tourists.

The chapter argues the proposition put forward by Urry (1990) that tourism provides a socially constructed way of looking at and of knowing nature. Tourism practices and discourses as construed within particular social, cultural and historical frameworks can provide the boundaries within which we make sense of, and claim to understand and explain, nature. Particular ways of seeing, experiencing and knowing nature are therefore available to the tourist – as Saunders (1993:285) commented in relation to early European travellers to Borneo, "these travellers carried with them their own intellectual and cultural baggage...[including] concepts like the Noble Savage, the Romantic view of nature, Darwinian theory and the scientist's impulse to collect and classify, combined with a human fascination with the unusual and the exotic". The theoretical position adopted in this chapter is therefore similar to that articulated by Norton (1996) who argues that the cultural meanings attached to nature are fluid and that popular culture plays an important role in helping to create and sustain the ways in which we understand and attach meaning to nature. This position is echoed by Strinati (1995:123) who argues that:

Clearly all societies are confronted by a nature with which they have to deal. Therefore their cultural definitions of nature can be seen as the ways they understand nature and make it meaningful. Nature can never therefore be "innocent"; it exists as a reality which is interpreted by a society's culture.

Analysis for this chapter will be based on material described by Dann (1996:135–68) as "pre-trip written and visual/sensory media", including tourist brochures, published tour guides and postcards. These media play an important role in helping to shape the awareness, understandings and expectations of people intending to travel to selected destinations for particular experiences (see Albers and James, 1983; Thurot and Thurot, 1983; Cohen, 1993; Dann, 1993; 1996; Edwards, 1996; Bhattacharyya, 1997), although as Dilley (1986) notes, there are dangers in over-stating their importance. Indeed, tourists have some capacity, at least, to resist the messages contained within these media. For instance, individual tourists are actively involved in constructing meaning from their experiences, although this process of meaning construction largely takes place within culturally defined boundaries.

While the meaning of nature is fluid and influenced by a variety of forces, it has, at the same time, lasting qualities. The chapter also explores the perpetuation of colonial constructions of nature in contemporary Borneo. It posits that colonialism has been replaced by tourism as the global force that shapes the experience of the 'other'. The enduring qualities of Bornean nature which were constructed during colonial times, such as its exoticism, its association with the primitive and its wildness, continue to resonate in contemporary touristic constructions. In other words, ideas about Borneo's nature and the ways in which it is imagined and constructed are connected to historical meanings as well as to contemporary forces associated with globalisation. Understood this way, nature, through its intimate involvement in a variety of forms of tourism, is harnessed to serve the interests of capital. Thus, the processes of discovery and the subsequent social constructions of place and nature which occurred during colonial times are occurring again, this time within the context of the globalised tourism marketplace which connects the tropical jungles of Borneo with the other so-called 'wild' places of the world.

Constructing and representing nature

As Saunders (1993:271) has reminded us specifically in relation to Bornean tourism:

Travellers to Borneo today arrive with certain expectations...They carry with them an idea or image of Borneo, an image which tourist brochures have conveyed and tourist authorities have cultivated. What that image is [is] the culmination of a process that began when the first European traveller to Borneo's shore recorded his impressions of what he had seen.

It may well be the case that Western conceptions of the Southeast Asian region generally, and Borneo more specifically, create notions of an island that is draped in mystery, exoticism and wilderness (Savage, 1984) and that our interpretations of anything related to Borneo are filtered through this cultural lens. Many of these images were in fact constructed by colonial powers and remain prominent in promotional material today. For instance, a timeless, wild nature is often linked with "traditional war-dancing, bloodthirsty, belligerent headhunters, who live in long-houses and whose women are barebreasted" (King, 1993:111).

The constructions and representations of nature presented within tourism promotional material act as myths which help to shape the tourist imagination (Selwyn, 1993; 1996) and, in so doing, contribute to the development of expectations about particular destinations. This argument has its roots in Barthes' (1993) semiological analysis of myth-making and myth consumption within popular culture. These myths resonate within tourism promotional material, confirming existing beliefs about places and cultures, and the ways these places and cultures are positioned in relation to the Western tourist. Furthermore, the experiences portrayed to tourists by tourism promotional literature are themselves constituted within specific discourses of nature. Instead of presenting value-neutral and unmediated experiences of nature, tourism sets in place ideological frameworks within which specific ways of seeing, experiencing and knowing nature are offered to the tourist. Thus, the implicit (if not explicit) focus of tourism's engagement with nature is based largely on the consumption of nature, although admittedly much of this consumption is not material but symbolic.

Dann (1996) proposes that tourism is a form of discourse which has its own linguistic conventions and styles and which operates as a language of social control. Drawing from work carried out by Przeclawski (1994), Dann argues that tourism, although commonly associated with freedom of experience, is like leisure itself, (Rojek, 1986) constrained by a range of social, cultural, economic, spatial and temporal forces. The tourist, rather than being liberated by his/her experience, is instead regulated and controlled by an industry which is itself driven by the need to safeguard its investment and to maximise profits. Itineraries and schedules adhere to timetables, certain sites become must-see sights (see Urry, 1990) and distinct tourist routes organise the movement of tourists across space and through time. These characteristics, though clearly evident in mass tourism, are also evident in nature-based and ecotourism where certain destinations, attractions and sights have developed which serve to organise (and control) the experiences of the nature-based tourist and ecotourist. It is the images and texts of the tourism promotional material, published guide books and postcards which help create expectations which influence the subsequent actions, behaviour and experiences of tourists (see Marsh, 1985; Dilley, 1986; Dann, 1993; 1996). By advancing this position, I am not suggesting that such material determines completely the interpretations which readers make and I acknowledge the points made by Harrison (1997) in his critique of Dann's work. However, I do argue that the reading of the material occurs within particular social and cultural contexts which permit a shared understanding or meaning to be attached to the text and images. Reading a tour brochure is not, therefore, an entirely individualistic act.

The role of tourism media (postcards, brochures, published tour guides, travelogues and so on), in shaping tourists' understandings of cultural groups such as the hill tribe people of northern Thailand, the native American people of the Great Lakes, Papua New Guinean villagers and Australian aboriginal people, has been the subject of research over the last 15 or so years (see Albers and James, 1983; Cohen, 1989; 1992; 1993; Kulick and Willson, 1992; Young, 1997; Zeppel, 1997). They have discussed the ways in which cultures (and peoples) are romanticised, exoticised, idealised, and objectified for the gaze of (mostly Western) tourists. Tourism is shown to be an agent capable of stereotyping cultures and in doing so, it is implicated in the continued marginalisation and, perhaps, oppression of certain racial or cultural groups. However, little attention appears to have been paid to the role of tourism media in the construction and production of nature, although there has been some notable work from geographers, such as Dilley (1986) and Dearden and Sadler (1989) on the evaluation of landscapes. Perhaps it is because nature is culturally associated with the authentic (Phelan, 1993) that researchers have tended to neglect this area. However, I aim to show that tourism media do play a substantial role in the production and commodification of nature which can then be 'sold' to prospective tourists.

FitzSimmons (1989) was one of the first geographers to challenge the dominant ways by which nature had been conceived in the sub-discipline of human geography. She argues that while human geographers have made progress in the theorising of space and spatial relations, the same cannot be said of understandings of nature, or of its position under capitalism (see also Britton, 1991). FitzSimmons (1989:108) makes the point that "[w]e see nature through the geographical and historical experience of the urban", an assertion which can be usefully linked to Urry's (1990; 1992) "tourist gaze" – tourists experience a nature which is differentiated from their predominantly urban existences. Following Urry's argument, nature within tourism must become a spectacle, something which demands the attention of the tourist. It must be marked off and separated from the everyday experience of the tourist. Nature is defined through the discursive practices of the media, of agencies such as natural resource and protected area managers, of scientists and of popular culture. Many of these discourses operate within the tourism industry in which cultural meanings of 'place' and 'nature' are constructed, presented and represented. The industry does this "through the production of tourism marketing texts, through the facilitation and management of staged cultural attractions and 'natural' spectacles, and through material intervention in the landscape" (Norton, 1996:358). The following section now focuses specifically at the strategies used in tourism media to construct and represent Malaysian Borneo's (comprising the states of Sabah and Sarawak) nature. The material for the analysis is drawn from tourism promotional materials collected between 1991 and 1995 in Borneo and elsewhere (see Appendix). These were subject to content, semiotic and textual analyses.

Constructing and representing Bornean nature

Tourism was the third major contributor to Malaysia's GNP in 1997 and the National Economic Recovery Plan (National Economic Action Council of Malaysia, 1998) has identified this sector as playing an important role in the revitalisation of the Malaysian economy. Ecotourism and other forms of tourism such as adventure tourism which capitalise on the natural features of Malaysian Borneo will play an increasingly important role in contributing to the idea of a 'unique' experience, and thus help to give shape to a distinctive Malaysian 'brand'. The rapidly emerging eco- and adventure tourism industries highlight the imperative of making available to consumers an apparently authentic, wild, primitive and exotic nature. Promoters of tourism within Sabah and Sarawak are well aware of this need and employ a variety of images and textual strategies to appeal to the imaginations of the Western tourist. Examples of these images can be seen on the homepages of the Tourism Boards of Sabah and Sarawak where the motif of the jungle is central to the construction of nature. There is considerable emphasis on adventure and physical activity as well as a strong imagery of an untouched, natural world:

Come to Sabah and experience great moments of adventure. Be overwhelmed by the extent of her beauty and diversity; pace yourself to the myriad attractions of nature; scale the heights and witness the majestic splendour of Mount Kinabalu; dive into the depths of the azure waters off charming idyllic islands; discover wild fauna and life in nature's untouched reserves; dwell [sic] into her people's lifestyles and be fascinated

(*South East Asia Traveller* advertisement, 1992:1)

The cultural significance of mountain imagery (Schama, 1996) is also alluded to with the mention of Mount Kinabalu while the more corporeal delights of the sea are set in contrast to the grandeur of the mountain. Nature is presented in this advertisement as a medium through which multiple pleasures can be had. These pleasures are harmoniously interconnected and are both physically and culturally available to most tourists. In other words, not only are they accessible physically, but they are derived from activities (walking or trekking, canoeing, photography, visiting parks and beaches) which are culturally familiar to the tourist. Implicit within this passage is the notion that nature is, to some extent at least, able to submit to these activities, and (as will be suggested later) in order for this 'submission' to occur, nature is subjected to various forms of discipline and domestication (Norton, 1996; Macnaghten and Urry, 1998). In this way nature, however wild and exotic it may appear in the advertisements and other promotional material, has been made safe for the tourist. This tension between the 'wild' and 'tame' in the construction and representation of nature is considered to be a major theme which emerges from the analysis.

Table 15.1 presents the results of content analysis undertaken on 412 photographic images contained in 30 publications promoting Malaysian Borneo as a tourist destination. At least half the photographic images (207) contained within these publications were characterised by the author as 'nature'. Representations ranged from nature being portrayed as 'wild' and seemingly untamed, offering opportunities for adventure, through nature as an exotic 'other' waiting to be gazed upon, to nature being a suitable backdrop for rest and recreation. The task for the tourism promoter in Malaysian Borneo who, through the use of marketing tools such as brochures, published tour guides and other material mediates the "relationship between tourist and destination" (Bhattacharyya, 1997:372) is to convince the potential tourist that the 'nature' of Malaysian Borneo is sufficiently different (unique) from other competing destinations (such as Thailand, Vietnam and Indonesia) to warrant a visit, yet at the same time reassuring the tourist that the

Table 15.1: Frequencies of nature images contained in tourism brochures

Categories	n	Proportion of total photos (%)	Proportion of nature photos (%)
Total animals	64	16	30
Orang utan	23	6	11
Birds	11	3	5
Reptiles	9	2	4
Proboscis monkey	6	2	3
Invertebrates	3	1	2
Other animals	12	3	6
Total plants	36	9	17
Pitcher Plant	8	2	4
Orchids	6	1	3
Rafflesia	5	1	2
Other plants	17	4	8
Mount Kinabalu	28	7	14
Coasts/Islands	19	5	9
Rivers	14	3	7
"Adventure"	13	3	6
Mulu Caves	12	3	6
Niah Caves	9	2	4
"Jungle"	8	2	4
Waterfalls	4	1	2

Source: Collated from tourism promotional materials

experience with nature will not be so different as to lead to feelings of anxiety or discomfort (either physical or emotional). One of the strategies used to achieve this aim appears to be the selection of images of exotic yet apparently harmless and somewhat familiar aspects of nature – the use of animals and plants such as the hornbill bird, beautiful orchids, the carnivorous pitcher plant, the proboscis monkey, turtles and, of course, the orang utan.

These are considered emblematic of 'wild Borneo' and, at the same time, comparatively harmless to tourists. Dating back to colonial days, these flora and fauna have been carefully documented and aesthetically appreciated in drawings and paintings by European explorers and travellers (Savage, 1984). He shows that there has been a remarkable level of consistency across time in the aesthetic appreciation of orchids, pitcher plants, palms, tropical animals and birds, and butterflies. These colonial constructions of nature continue to evoke notions of domination and conquest over nature (Savage, 1984). The main difference is that the contemporary tourist is less of a scientific explorer than the colonisers, notwithstanding the discourse of ecotourism with its reliance on scientific (particularly ecological) language and its emphasis on observation of, and experiences with, a wild nature. Nevertheless, the contemporary tourist is, by and large, much less willing or able to spend relatively long and unstructured periods of time at particular places, and those sites which are visited have generally been transformed into 'sights' by a globalised tourism industry. I will elaborate two ways in which the 'sight' and 'site' of nature is structured: animals with human-like qualities which live in an 'authentic' environment and nature as a tamed habitat which is safe for adventure.

Animals, the comical and the cute, yet quintessentially belonging to the rainforest habitat

The apparent importance of animals in the way in which nature is constructed and promoted is evident from Table 15.1, with the total number of animal photographs almost twice that of the next largest category, plants. It should be stressed that simply because an image appears with a high frequency does not necessarily imply that it has a greater 'effect' than an image which appears less frequently. However, images which are more frequently used suggest that these are afforded greater significance (at least by the publishers of them). Many of the animals represented in tourism media, we are led to believe, perform for the entertainment and enjoyment of tourists. For instance, if we are lucky, "large predatory birds, such as the bat hawks, swoop into [caves] for a meal" (*Malaysia, Singapore and Brunei – A Lonely Planet Travel Survival Kit*, 1988:283), while the reproductive lives of marine turtles take on almost Disney-like qualities:

Visit one of the world's most important turtle breeding spots...and what excitement the islands offer...stay overnight on these islands and watch huge Green Turtles lumber ashore to lay their eggs. Then, after incubation, watch them hatch, and the hatchlings slither and scamper, helter-skelter, down to the sea.

(*Sunday Telegraph Travel Supplement*, 6 August 1995)

Proboscis monkeys are similarly "comical and clumsy...[and are] remarkably entertaining to watch as [they] leap forcefully into space" (*Sandakan Sabah, Malaysia* brochure n.d.:n.p.). The performative aspects of these animals are particularly obvious in the text as are images used to portray the orang utan, one of the most important elements in the iconography of Bornean tourism. For example, "Sabah's famous orang utan will entertain you with their antics" (*Sabah, Malaysian Borneo* brochure, n.d.:n.p.) and "watching these charming and entertaining orangs [sic] during feeding time is a sheer delight", the "orangs were friendly, with some actually hamming it up for their audience" (The *Open Road Magazine*, 1992:43). The text here is somewhat reminiscent of the chimpanzee tea parties which were once popular in zoos, where chimps were dressed in human clothes and trained to indulge in a parody of the formal high tea party (Allen *et al.*, 1994). Thus there are aspects of the contemporary portrayal of the orang utan in tourism promotion which are connected to earlier colonial discourses which emphasised European superiority and claims of cultural sophistication.

Berger (1980:2) observes that animals are both "like and unlike" humans, and are both "subjected *and* worshipped, bred *and* sacrificed" (Berger, 1980:5) and it is these fundamental ambiguities which underlie the ways in which tourism promotional materials construct and present animals and, by extension, nature. Much of what is written in tourism media about the native fauna of Borneo tends to conform to popular, anthropomorphic accounts of animals as suitable objects of the (temporary) tourist gaze. Clearly a preoccupation exists with the amusing and entertaining qualities of these animals. The orang utan, as the most 'comical', was the most commonly portrayed, with 11 per cent of all nature photographs being of this species. However, the image of the orang utan also has the potential to allow tourists to make a conceptual link with the equatorial rainforest and its associated conservation issues. One postcard examined (produced in association with the National Parks and Wildlife Office of the Sarawak Parks Department) explicitly politicised the orang utan, with its caption "Let's hang on to our forests". In this way, the orang utan acts as a "bio-logo" (Valentine, 1992:123), drawing attention to the plight of its habitat, the equatorial rainforest. However, no additional text about, for example, the relationships between rainforests and orang utans or the threats posed to tropical forests were present to reinforce what is a rather explicit conservation message. The postcard does suggest at least an attempt at connecting tourism with nature conservation goals, and of course, such connections are seen to be essential to the definition of ecotourism on a world-wide basis.

To a considerable degree, the orang utan may well signify 'wild Borneo' to Western tourists, most of whom are already familiar with this 'wild man of the jungle'. Beeckman's (1973) account of his voyage to Borneo contains a very anthropomorphic illustration of the animal he called the 'oran ootan', and his description in the text further alludes to the human qualities of the ape, noting that the "Natives do really believe that these were formerly men, but metamorphosed into beasts for their blasphemy" (Beeckman, 1973:37). Such descriptions of this 'man-like' great ape inhabiting the jungles of Borneo have excited the imagination of those in the West ever since, and so it is not surprising that its depiction in tourism promotional texts is so frequent. To some extent, the orang utan also signifies the jungle, another concept well known in the West through popular fiction, travellers' tales, film and television.

Taming the 'isolated' wild

'The jungle' is nature in its most undisciplined and seemingly most disorganised state and we are told "within these vast jungles nature has run rampant for so long that just about every type of bizarre animal or plant has survived there" (*Malaysia, Singapore, Brunei – A Lonely Planet Travel Survival Kit*, 1994:23). As Savage (1984:218–19) points out in the context of early explorers to the Southeast Asian region, "the perpetual sight of rich, dense and extensive vegetation visibly demonstrated to White travellers the fruitfulness of tropical landscapes". It was the jungle which blocked out the light in 'Darkest Africa' and it is the jungle which is inscribed with many of the West's greatest fears – becoming lost, being devoured by wild beasts or dying of some exotic 'jungle fever'. It was into the untamed jungle to which the heroic and brave (male) explorers of our childhood journeyed. And it is the jungles of Borneo, though somewhat modified and made safer, that many modern tourists are persuaded to visit. The impenetrable jungle is made penetrable for the sake of the tourist and tourism.

The jungle 'wilderness' is presented simultaneously as both wild and yet tamed, through the inclusion in photographs of physical elements such as fences at lookouts, boardwalks through the jungle – "a 45 minute walk along a plankwalk...to reach the entrance of the Great Cave without getting your feet wet...Inside the huge Great Cave the plankwalk continues so navigation is easy" (*Malaysia, Singapore, Brunei– A Lonely Planet Travel Survival Kit*, 1994:312) to end up eventually at comfortable (and European-style) lodges perched on the side of Mount Kinabalu. Dann's (1996) proposition that tourism is a language of social control is relevant here – the depiction of boardwalks, guides leading tour groups, fences, and other material interventions in the landscape may all serve to communicate to tourists the appropriate ways of experiencing such attractions and in so doing, act to control and regulate subsequent behaviour. The inclusion of tourists (as opposed to 'adventurers') in a number of the photographs also serves to locate the viewer of these images within the images themselves. Thus, nature is presented as something not completely 'raw' but rather as something which has been (at least partially) 'cooked' (Williamson, 1983; Levi Strauss, 1992). As Dann (1996:247) observes:

> One can easily observe the disadvantages of including the raw nature elements of an exotic tropical destination...since if these items were featured, it would be necessary to refer to torrential rain, hurricanes, cockroaches, poisonous snakes and so on. For these reasons such unpleasant realities are omitted...

We can 'explore' or 'trek' through the jungle, or if we wish we can board an inflatable raft for a "relaxing float through the jungle with its lush green foliage, flitting birds and nearby villages" (*Adventures Best in Borneo* brochure, n.d:n.p.). *Malaysia, Singapore and Brunei – A Lonely Planet Travel Kit* (1994:244; 283; 308; 380) refers to areas of "still unspoilt jungle", "exciting night-time jungle experiences, made easy by the plankwalk" and reassures us that "these days you won't have to hack through the jungle for several days to get to the foot" of Mount Kinabalu. We can even stay at a "jungle camp" on the floodplain of the Kinabalu River.

However, the jungle is also the site of considerable environmental, political and cultural contestation in Malaysian Borneo and the rapid rate at which forest cover is being lost was noted several decades ago by Harrisson (1970:267) who observed "[o]f the full jungle, nearly all has now vanished up to a height of about 1000 feet". While the complex issues associated with tropical forestry are often raised in the Western media, the bulk of the tourism promotional literature seeks to reassure tourists that large tracts of untouched forest still remain to be explored and enjoyed, although these are often referred to as some of the *last remaining* areas – in other words, 'see them before they disappear'. This is analogous to the commodity logic, 'buy one before they all go'. Even in those brochures promoting wildlife safari and ecotourism-type experiences, there is usually no attempt to critique the human transformation of landscapes. Instead the tourist is driven through "scenic countryside of rubber plantations" on their way to their jungle trek, although the *Malaysia, Singapore and Brunei – A Lonely Planet Travel Survival Kit* (1996:334–37) has a section on the "politics of logging". One postcard was examined which consisted of three small photographs of rainforest with the caption (on the front of the card) "Respect the Rain Forests. In their beauty, richness, age and diversity of species, they are our heritage". This postcard explicitly encourages viewers to attach heritage values to these forests and so, in this example, just as with the orang utan postcard mentioned previously, there is an explicit connection between tourism and nature conservation. The point is that such postcards are rare – I found only two in my fieldwork in Borneo in 1992 and 1993.

The 'untouched' or 'virginal' character of the forests and jungles of East Malaysia is much more problematic than the guidebooks or brochures portray. Dann (1996) discusses issues associated with the 'appropriation' of rural space by urban dwellers, and notes that such tensions are noticeably absent from what he calls 'Greenspeak', the register of ecotourism. While there is a tendency in Western discourses of nature to exclude a human dimension (apart from being the tamer or conqueror), this view ignores the strong links to nature which are embodied in many indigenous cultures. The 'untouched' forest denies the existence of many groups of indigenous peoples who have been living in it for thousands of years.

The exclusion of people from nature has been translated into practice in the establishment of protected natural areas such as national parks, which have until recently excluded or ignored the rights of indigenous groups to continue living on the land. Groups of people so affected have often resisted the acquisition of their land and their removal from it; a story which tends to be missing from tourist material promoting national parks and other reserves. Indeed, the tour brochures give a clear notion that the lands explored by tourists are largely empty, echoing the colonial myth that lands occupied by tribal peoples could be conveniently considered unoc-cupied. So, while Kinabalu Park is a paradise for nature lovers, it is not until tourists actually visit the park that they learn that the local Kadazan people have been removed from the park and now live on the flanks of the mountain.

Mount Kinabalu was another important symbol of nature in tourist brochures, accounting for 14 per cent of the total nature photographs and almost 7 per cent of the total photographs. The mountain is a highly significant and symbolic attraction in Sabah and, whilst only a minority of tourists actually climb it, most at least visit Kinabalu Park. As the *Malaysia, Singapore and Brunei – A Lonely Planet Travel Survival Kit* (1991:377) tells us, "Towering 4101 m above the lush tropical jungle of North Borneo, and the centrepiece of the vast 767 sq km Kinabalu Park, Mount Kinabalu is the major attraction in Sabah". Images of Mount Kinabalu can be construed to represent wilderness, adventure, a botanical paradise, and as a type of symbolic frontier which some tourists actually manage to penetrate by climbing to its summit:

The Park is a paradise for naturalists, botanists, bird-watchers, mountaineers and those who simply admire nature. The main attraction of the Park is Mount Kinabalu, rising majestically to a height of 4101 metres above sea level, with its granite massif dominating the surrounding landscape...As no climbing experience is required, the energetic visitor can climb Mount Kinabalu if the main route to the summit is taken.

(*Sabah, Malaysia Borneo's Paradise* brochure, 1993:n.p.).

The complex cultural significance of mountains is explored by Schama (1996), who examines the variety of ways in which mountains have been mythologised by various Western and non-Western cultures. Mountains have been invested with considerable powers – they loom large over landscapes in paintings diminishing the stature of every other element, they are regarded alternatively as benevolent and omnipotent and they have been seen to be a direct representation of the might of the Creator

(Schama, 1996:426–28). Echoes of these myths can be found in much of the tourism material examined for this present study. Mount Kinabalu "dominates" its surrounds, it sits "majestically" above the landscape, and it is "shrouded in cloud and legend". It is a "magical" place around which, to some extent, the nature-based tourism industry of Malaysian Borneo revolves. Together with the orang utan, the mountain signifies Bornean nature within the tourism media examined. The mountain has become a site of repeated conquest: initially by the English explorers, then by adventurous travellers, and today by recreational tourists.

A postcard which is an example of the conquest and subsequent taming of the mountain features the craggy granite summit upon which has been superimposed a series of white dots which mark out the summit walking trail. Each of the main peaks is also named and the height above sea level enclosed in brackets. This postcard exemplifies the taming of the mountain, and its appropriation as a key element in the landscape of tourism. This wild/tame dualistic portrayal of the mountain emerges in a number of photographs and much accompanying text in brochures and guide-books. Several photographs looking up at the summit have been taken from Park Headquarters and include sealed roadway, flagpoles, feature gardens of hibiscus and even trees pruned into 'standard' forms. We are encouraged to "savour the hill-station atmosphere" around Park Headquarters, where we can stay in a variety of accommodation including up-market chalets, and eat at cafés and restaurants. The visitor can even enjoy a "whizz-bang 15 mins. multivision slide show (using 14 projectors)" (*Malaysia, Singapore, Brunei – A Lonely Planet Travel Survival Kit* 1991:382). Not only is the mountain readily accessible, but it is also conveniently located near the more glamorous attractions of the state capital:

And today this extraordinary mountain is all so wonderfully accessible. As easy to get to as Penang, Phuket or Bali and with beach life to match those places just 2 hours down the highway at the region's main base, the port city and State capital, Kota Kinabalu
(*The Sunday Telegraph Travel Supplement*, 6 August 1995).

The passage above juxtaposes the mountain (emblematic of wild nature) with the openly synthetic and contrived pleasures of a beach-side resort in a postmodern landscape of fractured images and contradictory meanings.

Coasts and island scenes account for a further 9 per cent of the nature photographs. These photographs suggest the relaxing attributes of nature: palm trees on deserted beaches, coral reefs surrounding equally deserted islands. Adventure style photographs of people actually engaged in activities such as rafting or mountain climbing accounted for 6 per cent of the nature photographs. We can take a risk on "an adrenaline-pumping roller coaster ride crashing through thundering waves (Grade 4) in a raft, fully suited in life jacket and helmet" (*Adventure's Best in Borneo* brochure, n.d.:n.p.). Notably, it is nearly always men who are included in photographs depicting adventurous activities such as white-water rafting or mountain climbing, while images of scantily clad women are represented on postcards or in brochures depicting tropical island paradises – the sun, sea, sand and sex.

This observation conforms to the argument put forward by Swain (1995) that there is clearly a bias towards the representation of males in the overwhelming majority of 'adventure-style' tourism promotion. Men are nearly always the explorer or adventurer, while that which is to be explored or 'conquered' is frequently described, or at least alluded to, as 'feminine'. Of the 50 postcards examined, eight featured images of men (as either guides, locals or tourists) compared to three photographs of women (two shots showing local women, one shot featuring Western tourists sunbathing in bikinis). In terms of the images in brochures, 55 featured people, and of these, 34 were of men only, 12 were of women only and 9 included both women and men. However, women were overwhelmingly portrayed as either passive observers (watching nesting turtle, looking at flowers) or as an object of the male gaze (traditionally dressed young women or European women in bikinis at the beach). In a photograph showing male and female tourists together in a boat, for example, it is only the men who held cameras and binoculars (*Sandakan Sabah, Malaysia* brochure, n.d.). Men were seen climbing mountains, white-water rafting, carrying out research on turtles, or guiding groups of tourists. While not wanting to suggest that all imageries or texts examined conformed to this pattern, for this would be an over-simplification, it is proposed that in much of the material analysed, there is an observable 'feminisation' of nature and a 'masculinisation' of tourist activities associated with nature. These masculinised activities serve to control and tame nature through symbolic (if not real) conquest.

Conclusion

It is clear from this analysis of pre-trip promotional material that representations of nature play a significant role in promoting Malaysian Borneo as a tourist destination. It was found that nature was constructed and represented in a variety of ways – spectacular landscape, opportunity for adventure, and home of exotic flora and fauna – all of which reflect certain enduring myths about nature which date back to colonial days and which serve to increase the appeal of nature to a wide variety of tourists on a world-wide basis. The use of a selective number of animal species to represent nature in a specific way (e.g. the orang utan) and the relative ease with which the wild can be conquered indicate that in tourism, nature is represented as a 'wild/tame' dualism which appeals to most tourists. Just as MacCannell (1992) comments that the tourists visiting ex-cannibals in Dennis O'Rourke's 1987 film, *Cannibal Tours*, are there because of the history of head-hunting and cannibalism, the majority of tourists will only visit wilderness provided that it has been modified and mediated in order to make it palatable. Likewise, in order for ecotourism and nature tourism in Borneo to succeed, nature must be domesticated to facilitate and promote the level of tourist demand needed to earn and maintain profit. This filtering of images pervades a large number of nature attractions not only in Borneo but as far as Africa and North America. Nature as a social construction for tourism shows how influential the global reach of tourism is and serves as yet another example of how various worlds can become interconnected together.

Nature as constructed does not necessarily degrade the educational outcomes of such tourism experiences, and indeed, the very fact that more people can experience 'the wilderness' is considered by many environmental educators to be socially beneficial. However, there is a problem at one level, and that is that tourists are being sold the myth that nature exists in some form of timeless vacuum which remains unchanged in the face of industrialism and modernist paradigms of development, effectively disconnecting it from the interconnections which exist between the economy and the environment. The tourism materials promoting Malaysian Borneo as a nature destination generally pander to this myth, actively constructing nature as something in opposition to Western culture, as a place where men are actively engaged and women passively gaze, and where a multitude of pleasurable experiences can be achieved, without, it seems, any consequent damage to the environment. Thus, wild nature, created by the West through film, novels, nature documentaries and tourism is further refined and comes back to us as a sanitised and safe product, generously removed of the unequal binds of reality.

Appendix: list of tourism promotional materials subject to analysis

Adventure's Best in Borneo brochure (n.d.).
Journey through Sabah, Malaysia brochure (n.d.).
Malaysia, Singapore and Brunei – A Lonely Planet Travel Survival Kit (1988) Hawthorn: Lonely Planet Publications.
Malaysia, Singapore and Brunei – A Lonely Planet Travel Survival Kit (1991) Hawthorn: Lonely Planet Publications.
Malaysia, Singapore and Brunei – A Lonely Planet Travel Survival Kit (1994) Hawthorn: Lonely Planet Publications.
Malaysia, Singapore and Brunei – A Lonely Planet Travel Survival Kit (1996) Hawthorn: Lonely Planet Publications.
Open Road Magazine, The (1992), 'Meet the jungle man', April, 43–44.
Sabah, Malaysia Borneo's Paradise brochure (1993).
Sabah, Malaysian Borneo brochure (n.d.).
Sandakan Sabah, Malaysia brochure (n.d.).
South East Asia Traveller (1992) Borneo, Malaysia's Paradise advertisement, 7(2), 1.
Sunday Telegraph Travel Supplement (1995) 'Go ape over orang-utan', 6 August, Sydney.
Various Postcards.

References

Albers, P.C. and James, W.R. (1983) 'Tourism and the changing photographic image of the Great Lakes Indians'. *Annals of Tourism Research*, 10, 123–48.
Allen, J.S., Park, J. and Watt, S.L. (1994) 'The chimpanzee tea party: Anthropomorphism, orientalism and colonialism'. *Visual Anthropology Review*, 10(2), 45–54.
Barthes, R. (1993) *Mythologies*, 2nd Edition. London: Vintage Books.
Beeckman, D. (1973) *A Voyage To and From the Island of Borneo with a New Introduction by Chin Yoon Fong*. New York: Barnes and Noble. Reprint of the 1718 edition.
Berger, J. (1980) *About Looking*. New York: Pantheon Books.
Bhattacharyya, D.P. (1997) 'Mediating India, an analysis of a guidebook'. *Annals of Tourism Research*, 24(2), 371–89.

Britton, S. (1991) 'Tourism, capital and place: Towards a critical geography of tourism'. *Environment and Planning D: Society and Space*, 9(4), 451–78.

Cohen, E. (1989) ' "Primitive and remote": Hill tribe trekking in Thailand'. *Annals of Tourism Research*, 16, 30–61.

Cohen, E. (1992) 'The growing gap: Hill tribe image and reality'. *Pacific Viewpoint*, 33(2), 164–69.

Cohen, E. (1993) 'The study of touristic images of native people: Mitigating the stereotype of a stereotype', in D.G. Pearce and R.W. Butler (eds.) *Tourism Research: Critiques and Challenges*. London: Routledge, in association with the International Academy for the Study of Tourism, 36–69.

Dann, G.M.S (1993) 'Advertising in tourism and travel: Travel brochures', in M.A. Khan, M.D. Olsen and T. Var (eds.) *VNR's Encyclopedia of Hospitality and Tourism*. New York: Van Nostrand Reinhold, 893–901.

Dann, G.M.S. (1996) *The Language of Tourism, A Sociolinguistic Perspective*. Wallingford: CAB International.

Dearden, P. and Sadler, B. (1989) 'Themes and approaches in landscape evaluation research', in P. Dearden and B. Saddler (eds.) *Landscape Evaluation: Approaches and Applications*, Western Geographical series Volume 25. Victoria: University of Victoria, 3–18.

Dilley, R.S. (1986) 'Tourist brochures and tourist images'. *The Canadian Geographer*, 30(1), 59–65.

Edwards, E. (1996) 'Postcards: Greetings from another world', in T. Selwyn (ed.) *The Tourist Image, Myths, and Myth making in Tourism*. Chichester: Wiley, 223–31.

FitzSimmons, M. (1989) 'The matter of nature', *Antipode*, 21(2), 106–20.

Harrison, D. (1997) 'Barbados or Luton? Which way to paradise?'. *Tourism Management*, 18(6), 393–98.

Harrisson, T. (1970) *The Malays of South-West Sarawak before Malaysia: A Socio-Economic Survey*. London: Macmillan.

King, V. T. (1993) 'Tourism and culture in Malaysia', in M. Hitchcock, V. T. King and M. J. G. Parnwell, (eds.) *Tourism in Southeast Asia*. London: Routledge, 99–116.

Kulick, D. and Willson, M.E. (1992) 'Echoing images: The construction of savagery among Papua New Guinean villagers'. *Visual Anthropology*, 5(2), 143–52.

Levi Strauss, C. (1992) *The Raw and the Cooked*, translated by J. D. Weightman. Harmondsworth: Penguin.

MacCannell, D. (1992) *Empty Meeting Grounds: The Tourist Papers*. London: Routledge.

Macnaghten, P. and Urry, J. (1998) *Contested Natures*. London: Sage Publications.

Marsh, J. (1985) 'Postcard landscapes: An exploration in method'. *Canadian Geographer*, 29(3), 265–67.

National Economic Action Council (1998) *National Economic Recovery Plan*. Kuala Lumpur: Economic Planning Unit, Prime Minister's Department.

Norton, A. (1996), 'Experiencing nature: The reproduction of environmental discourse through safari tourism in east Africa'. *Geoforum*, 27(3), 355–73.

Phelan, S. (1993) 'Intimate distance: The dislocation of nature in modernity', in J. Bennett and W. Chaloupka (eds.) *In the Nature of Things, Language, Politics and the Environment*. Minneapolis: University of Minneapolis Press, 44–62.

Przeclawski, K. (1994) *Tourism and the Contemporary World*. Warsaw: Institute of Social Prevention and Readaptation, Centre for Social Problems of Education, University of Warsaw.

Rojek, C. (1986) 'Leisure and legitimation'. *Recreation Australia*, 6(4), 14–16.

Saunders, G. (1993) 'Early travellers in Borneo', in M. Hitchcock, V.T. King and M.J.G. Parnell (eds.) *Tourism in Southeast Asia*. London and New York: Routledge, 271–85.

Savage, V.R. (1984) *Western Impressions of Nature and Landscape in Southeast Asia*. Singapore: Singapore University Press.

Schama, S. (1996) *Landscape and Memory*. London: Fontana Press.

Selwyn, T. (1993) 'Peter Pan in Southeast Asia. Views from the brochures', in M. Hitchcock, M., King, V.T., and Parnell, M.J.G. (eds.) *Tourism in Southeast Asia*. London and New York: Routledge, 117–37.

Selwyn, T. (1996) 'Introduction', in T. Selwyn (ed.) *The Tourist Image, Myths, and Mythmaking in Tourism*. Chichester: Wiley, 1–33.

Strinati, D. (1995) *An Introduction to Theories of Popular Culture*. London and New York: Routledge.

Swain, M. (1995) 'Gender in Tourism'. *Annals of Tourism Research*, 22(2), 247–66.

Thurot, J. and Thurot, G. (1983) 'The ideology of class and tourism, confronting the discourse of advertising'. *Annals of Tourism Research*, 10, 173–89.

Urry, J (1990) *The Tourist Gaze, Leisure and Travel in Contemporary Societies*. London: Sage Publications.

Urry, J. (1992) 'The tourist gaze "revisited"'. *American Behavioural Scientist*, 36, 172–86.

Valentine, P.S (1992) 'Nature-based Tourism', in B. Weiler and C.M. Hall (eds.) *Special Interest Tourism*. London: Belhaven, 105–27.

Williamson, J. (1983) *Decoding Advertisements, Ideology and Meaning in Advertising*. London: Marion Boyars.

Young, T. (1997) Postcards from Australia: A Study of Touristic Images of Aboriginal Australians, unpublished B Soc Sc Honours thesis, Department of Leisure and Tourism Studies, University of Newcastle, Australia.

Zeppel, H. (1997) 'Touring the Dreamtime – Aboriginal culture in Australian tourism', in D. Rowe and P. Brown (eds.) *Proceedings of the Australian and New Zealand Leisure Studies Association Conference*. Newcastle: University of Newcastle, 218–24.

Part Five

Potentials and Problems

16

Danger-zone Tourism: Prospects and Problems for Tourism in Tumultuous Times

Kathleen M. Adams

Introduction

Over the past decade a growing number of tourism researchers have turned their attention to the effects of political instability and violence on tourism (Teye, 1986; 1988; Ryan, 1991; Gartner and Shen, 1992; Richter, 1992; Wilson, 1993; Mihalic, 1996; Pizam and Mansfield, 1996). The relationship between political turmoil and tourism is particularly salient to this volume's theme of interconnected worlds in Southeast Asia. Even very localised political violence has the potential to reverberate on tourism within national boundaries as well as regionally and internationally. In recent years, political turmoil in parts of Indonesia, Myanmar, and Cambodia appears to have slowed the flow of international tourists to other Southeast Asian nations. For this reason, even countries celebrated for their safety as tourist destinations fear declining tourism revenues when political violence erupts in neighbouring nations. While acknowledging these important concerns, this chapter explores some of the hidden dimensions and potentials of tourism in violence-tainted times.

To date, the predominant focus of research on tourism and political instability has examined political unrest in destination countries in terms of either tourist flows, economic impact, or image management (cf. Hall, 1994; Bar-On, 1996; Hall and O'Sullivan, 1996; Wall, 1996; Kelly, 1998). While these studies have been valuable, surprisingly little scholarly attention has been directed to the forms of tourism that thrive in tumultuous times. Building on the pioneering theoretical work of Richter (1989; 1992) and Picard and Wood (1997)[1] addressing the interrelations between politics and tourism in Asian nations, this chapter examines the emerging phenomenon of 'danger-zone tourism' in Indonesia and parts of mainland Southeast Asia. Drawing on ethnographic data collected in Indonesia in the 1990s, as well as interviews with returning 'danger-zone tourists' encountered in Singapore and the USA, I argue that this under-explored genre of tourism deserves our scholarly attention. Not only does danger-zone tourism appear to have commercial potential but it also may contribute to reconfiguring ethnic and national perceptions. While the numbers of 'danger-zone tourists' are currently quite small, there are indications that this unique travel pursuit is developing increasing allure in certain sectors, as suggested by websites and guidebooks devoted to tourism in dangerous places (cf. Pelton *et al.*, 1997; 1998). As I ultimately suggest in this exploratory chapter, this overlooked genre of tourism can subtly alter the ways in which groups in and adjacent to politically volatile destinations imagine themselves.

This chapter is organised into three parts. First, I begin by delineating the category of 'danger-zone tourist'. Next, I turn to outline the context for danger-zone tourism in contemporary Southeast Asia, as well as the foci of danger-zone tourists' interests in this region. Finally, I turn to an Indonesian case study to illustrate how such tourists are not merely innocuous observers of local ethnic relations, but can also play a role in the rearticulation of indigenous ethnic sensibilities.

Defining danger-zone tourism

As Crick observed, sun, sand, sea, and sex are the four 'S's often perceived as the essence of a developing nation's touristic appeal (Crick, 1989:308). And as Richter added, "a fifth 's' is even more critical: security" (Richter, 1992:36). However, these ingredients tend to be irrelevant or even antithetical to one genre of tourist generally overlooked in the tourism literature. While tumultuous Southeast Asian destinations have frightened off many package tourists, they have emerged as alluring destinations for what I term 'danger-zone tourists'. Danger-zone tourists are travellers who are drawn to areas of political turmoil. Their pilgrimages to strife-torn destinations are not for professional purposes but rather for leisure, although in some cases the professional identities of danger-zone tourists are related to their leisure pursuits.[2] The backpacker traveller in Thailand featured in Alex Garland's 1997 novel, *The Beach*,[3] captures the mindset of many danger-zone tourists when he reflects,

I wanted to witness extreme poverty. I saw it as a necessary experience for anyone who wanted to appear worldly and interesting. Of course witnessing poverty was the first to be ticked off the list. Then I had to graduate to the more obscure stuff. Being in a riot was something I pursued with a truly obsessive zeal, along with being tear-gassed and hearing gunshots fired in anger. Another list item was having a brush with my own death.

(Garland, 1997:164)

A similar mentality pervades Fielding's Black Flag Café, a website devoted to travellers returning from and planning visits to dangerous places. The site's by-line explains its unique orientation:

Looking for fun in all the wrong places? Well you've found the nets [sic] only hangout for hardcore adventurers, travel junkies, DP'ers [dangerous placers] and just about anyone who runs screaming from glossy brochures, backpacker guidebooks and Robin Leach. So let's get busy. Got a tip? Just came back from the Congo, just heading off to Albania? Let us know and don't be surprised if the staff of Fielding, the authors of DP [Dangeorous Places] or the CIA drops you a line.

(*Fielding's Black Flag Café*, 2000:n.p.)

Black Flag Café frequenters appear to have varying levels of experience with danger-zone travel, though all seem to share an intense interest in adrenaline rush travel. As one recent Black Flag Café posting reads,

A traveller in many "soft" DP [dangerous place] countries over the past ten years, I have decided it is time to go for my first war zone. Armed with my clippings, letters of intro and mas bullsh**, where should I go for my first ringside view of armed conflict? Should I dive into the thick of it "Chechnya?" or should I find a good "intro" hotspot?

(Andre, 2000:n.p.)

Among the Asian destinations suggested by repliers were sites of civil strife in Indonesia and the war zone in Afghanistan. In a different vein, another recent Black Flag Café inquiry sought a "dangerous Thai honeymoon". Declaring his fiancée was "not the swimming pool and cocktail type" but rather "a real adventurous sort who loves the unusual and unexpected", the writer requested advice on where to go for an off-the-beaten track "dangerous" honeymoon in Thailand. In this case, respondents suggested that they skip Thailand and target Laos or Cambodia "for something more adventurous" (Anon., 2000:n.p.).

The Black Flag Café website is an outgrowth of the popular travel guide, *Fielding's The World's Most Dangerous Places* (Pelton *et al.*, 1998). Hailed by *The New York Times* as "one of the oddest and most fascinating travel books to appear in a long time" (cited in Pelton *et al.,* 1998:cover page), the current edition of this volume features chapters on Cambodia, Myanmar, the Philippines, as well as shorter entries on Indonesia (Timor) and Laos. With its fourth edition in press, the book has enjoyed cult popularity among both armchair travellers and American danger-zone tourists. The brisk sales of this and other related guidebooks, as well as the touristic popularity of T-shirts with slogans such as "Danger!! Mines!! Cambodia!!"[4] not only suggest the allure of danger-zone travel but also demonstrate that some entrepreneurial individuals have begun to capitalise on this emerging genre of travel. Ironically, the political tumult that not only signals the demise of mainstream tourism but also disrupts the lives of local residents has meant prosperity for these imaginative few. The economic ramifications of a citation in *Fielding's The World's Most Dangerous Places* and the potential for revenues generated by the sale of danger-celebrating souvenirs are but some of the more concrete reasons for devoting scholarly attention to the phenomenon of danger-zone tourism. There are also more subtle dimensions of danger-zone tourism that render it of theoretical interest to tourism researchers, as I will illustrate later in this chapter.

Pitts (1996) is one of the few scholars to have made passing note of this genre of tourist, which he terms 'war tourists'. In his discussion of the impact of uprisings in Chiapas, Mexico on the tourist economy, he comments, "Just like drivers on the interstate stretching their necks trying to get a glimpse of 'what happened' at a wreck scene, these individuals [war tourists] wanted to be a part of the action" (Pitts, 1996:221). As Pitts later adds, the 'war tourists' in Chiapas were there "to experience the thrill of political violence". One magazine reported a Canadian woman explaining her reasons for visiting Chiapas as "journalism, a tan and a revolution" (*Maclean's,* 13 June 1994:28-9). Likewise, while researching the broader topic of risk creation in travel narratives, Elsrud (Personal email communication, 15 July

1999) reports that she has come across interviewees who say they are looking forward to riots in Indonesia as it is "cool to have seen/been in one". These descriptions hint at some of the activities and motivations of the genre of tourist that is the focus of this chapter.

In spite of the precedent set by Pitts (1996), I prefer to employ the term 'danger-zone tourists' instead of 'war tourists' as I believe this particular form of tourism necessitates distinction from the broader category of 'war tourism' discussed by Smith (1996). In her path-breaking exploration of war tourism, Smith focuses on the commemorative dimension of tourism to the sites of *past* wars – battlefields, cemeteries, military re-enactments, monuments and so forth.[5] My interest here, however, is not tourism pertaining to *past* wars, but rather tourism to tumultuous locations, places that are not necessarily the sites of declared wars but are nevertheless sites of *on-going* political instability, sites where there is at least an imagined potential of violent eruptions. Likewise, I have not adopted the term 'risk tourism' embraced by some writers (cf. Elsrud, under review) as this term covers a broader array of activities, including physically-challenging enterprises such as white-water rafting in Sarawak. For these reasons pertaining to precision, I prefer to adopt the term 'danger-zone tourism'.

While the numbers of danger-zone tourists appear to be rising, the allure of touristic forays into politically-risky regions has a long history, as do danger-zone travel entrepreneurs. According to Mitchell (1991:57), as early as 1830, French entrepreneurs were ferrying tourists to North Africa to witness the French bombardment of Algiers. In more contemporary times, educational tour organisers have marketed trips to Indonesia to explore the religious strife between Christians and Muslims in Indonesia. US-based Reality Tours has offered group trips to politically volatile events and destinations in Latin America and Southeast Asia. Likewise, an Italian travel agency has organised groups equipped with doctors, guards and combat gear to usher tourists to the edges of battle zones in places like Dubrovnik and the south of Lebanon (Diller + Scofidio, 1994:136). Such touristic expeditions to "the places shown on the television news" can have hefty price-tags: the aforementioned Italian tours were sold at US$25,000 per person (Phipps, 1999:83). While many danger-zone tourists are low-budget travellers, the fact that some are willing to spend extravagant amounts for their travels prompts questions concerning the compelling allure of this genre of travel.

In his exploration of the relationship between tourist discourse and tourist death, Phipps (1999) ponders the appeal of risk travel. Drawing on the work of novelist-philosopher Albert Camus, he suggests that fear gives value to travel: "[t]his threat of death and danger is something that tourism relishes so as to retain its imaginative power as a space for reconnection with the 'real' which remains so elusive...in the order of highly stratified, regulated and abstracted capitalist postmodern society" (Phipps, 1999:83). While the promise of 'authentic' encounters and experiences is intrinsic to danger-zone tourism, I believe that there are also issues of class and social differentiation at play in danger-zone tourism. Inspired by Bourdieu (1984) and Featherstone (1987), Munt (1994:102) has suggested that the consumption of unique travel experiences has increasing salience in defining social distinction. Munt argues that, in striving to establish distinction from the touristic practices of classes below them, the new middle classes have embraced a number of new forms of travel (Munt, 1994:119). According to Munt, travel to third world destinations is one of the major experiences embraced by the new middle class to establish and maintain social differentiation. Here I wish to suggest that danger-zone tourism represents one extreme practice of social differentiation, a practice which separates these 'adventurers' from the masses of package tourists, as well as from ethnic tourists. In writing on the broader topic of risk tourism, Elsrud (under review) makes a related observation. She suggests that risk narratives are a form of traveller's capital; they play into a hierarchical value system positioning travellers *vis à vis* one another and *vis à vis* their stay-at-home friends. To further illustrate the above points, I turn now to examine the imagery featured in danger-zone tourists' narratives about Southeast Asia.

The imagery of Southeast Asian danger-zone tourism

Fielding's The World's Most Dangerous Places (Pelton *et al.*, 1998), the definitive guide book for danger-zone tourists, devotes chapters to several Southeast Asian nations. In the 1998 version of this handbook, as in the corresponding website, Cambodia and Myanmar figure prominently. As tourists develop images of their vacation destinations long before they depart, through media images and guide-books, and as they draw on these glossy images in assessing their experiences in these destinations (Adams, 1984), it is apt to begin our discussion with an examination of the danger-zone imagery found in such guidebooks and travel advice websites.

In logging onto Fielding's 'danger-finder' website < *www.fieldingtravel.com/df/ intro.htm* >, one immediately knows one is in a different sort of travel zone. The background wallpaper for pages devoted to Cambodia, Myanmar and the Philippines features cartoon-like images of dynamite time bombs and rifles, shields and spears in crossbones positions. Likewise, each chapter of the book version of *Fielding's The World's Most Dangerous Places* is decorated with a comic image of a sunglass-sporting skull touting a baseball cap adorned with the DP logo. The chapters themselves are illustrated with smaller cartoons of exploding demonstrators, bazooka-carrying troops, burning dynamite sticks and fierce killer bees. These comic images seemingly 'tame' the terrors of riots and warfare, underscoring the message that dangerous travel can be something entertaining. Even the danger-themed photographs accompanying each chapter have lulling dimensions. The Myanmar chapter, for instance, opens with a shot of artificial limbs dangling decoratively from lush tropical vegetation. Other images in this chapter include two plump toddlers holding whimsically decorated guns, and troops trotting in front of a thatched-roofed pavilion. While smiling gunmen and helicopters make frequent appearances in the pages of this book, there are no images of corpses or actual warfare. This and other similar books render danger-zone travel inviting yet thrilling.

Similarly, the text of *Fielding's The World's Most Dangerous Places* tends to combine imagery of exotic settings with themes of semi-controlled risk. Dangerous destinations, for instance, are ranked on a five-star scale according to risk level. Unusually tumultous spots are awarded open palms or 'Halt' gestures. In the 1998 edition of the book, Myanmar was allotted one open palm and Cambodia was awarded four stars, indicating a spot where "danger is regional, definable, and avoidable, but the odds are that the unwary traveller will be coming home as cargo" (Pelton *et al.*, 1998:264). The narrative "Cambodia – In a Dangerous Place" underscores these themes of unpredictable danger for the unaware and excitement for the savvy traveller. As the writers recount,

> We went to Cambodia on a lark. These days, Cambodia is not necessarily the most dangerous place in the world, or even a nasty place, but it is an exotic, very inexpensive stop that every traveller to Asia should make. Is it safe? Well, if you stay inside the tourist ruts (literally), don't venture outside the ill-defined "safety" zone and watch where you step, Cambodia can be safe. Cambodia can also be brutal if you pass through the invisible safety barrier and end up in the hands of the Khmer Rouge. Just remember the advice of your first grade teacher, "Don't colour outside the lines"...One tourist can fly into Phnom Penh and Siem Reap on a modern jet, stay in a five-star hotel, and see the temple complex, complete with cold Pepsi, an air-conditioned car and a good meal, followed by an ice-cold beer at one of the many night-clubs the UN soldiers used to frequent. Another tourist can find himself kneeling at the edge of a shallow, hastily dug grave, waiting for the rifle butt that will slam into his cortex, ending his brief but adventurous life. The difference between the two scenarios might be 10 km or lingering a few too many minutes along the road.
>
> (Pelton *et al.*, 1998:364)

Similar themes of risk for the unwary or unlucky traveller to Southeast Asian danger-zones emerge in advice offered from veteran travellers on Fielding's Black Flag Café webpage. One traveller's query about the safety of bus travel from the Thai border to Siem Reap and on to Phnom Penh prompted the following advice:

> Buses don't exist in Cambodia as far as I know. They put you on the back of a pickup truck. The roads su**, but safety's not really a problem anymore. Just stay on the beaten path unless you want to get intimate with some landmines. If you're really worried, you're bound to meet some other travellers plying the same west-east route as you, so hook up with them and you'll have safety in numbers.
>
> (Raza, 2000:n.p.)

Another returnee from a trip to Siem Reap advised the poster not to go to Cambodia, as it had ceased to be a danger-zone destination – it had become a 'tourist trap'. As he declared, "It's no longer adventurous, dangerous, fun etc. to go there – every tourist in Cambodia goes there. Go to Myanmar..." (Mike, 2000:n.p.). Here we see not only the negative imagery associated with regular tourists in the danger-zone travel world, but also the impact of political shifts on the danger-zone travel circuit. As regular tourists return to once off-the-list destinations, danger-zone tourists flee to adjoining nations deemed more 'dangerous'.

Even travellers with little knowledge of political variations in Southeast Asia are advised by other posters about 'more dangerous' Southeast Asian locales. One apparently novice Black Flag Café reader recently requested advice on which Southeast Asian nation to visit, noting that he was considering Thailand, Malaysia, Singapore and Vietnam. In typical fashion, the suggestions he received outlined the varying danger levels in these very different destinations. As one poster explained,

Malaysia is VERY safe, and VERY friendly...(on the mainland)...If you want adventure in Malaysia, go to Sarawak (or however the hell you spell it). A friend of mine got his head beat in with a barstool by a Chinese gang there. [H]is crime..having a shaved head + full sleves [sic] (tattoo's) [sic]. [T]hanks to American T.V. and movies like 'romper stomper', they figure all white guys who fit this look are skinh [skinheads].

(Leon, 2000:n.p.)

While this poster highlighted bar house gang-based dangers, more typical of the Black Flag Café messages are those that highlight political danger and intrigue, such as the message below, which was posted in response to a query about the travel situation in Laos:

Also just got back from Laos (Plain of Jars, Xieng Khoang). Kept hearding [sic] these explosions in the forest. Thought it was rock blasting for road construction. Turned out to be artillery exchanges between Hmong insurgents and Lao (and perhaps Vietnamese) troops...the word on the street in [V]ientiane is that Hanoi has secretly sent in 3000 troops to Xieng Khoang to help duke it out with them (unconfirmed). Also, a couple of weeks ago, there was a grenade blast in a Vientiane backpacker cafe, injuring a couple of [G]ermans and a Brit. Could be Hmong or a simple biz [business] dispute, but things are heating up in Laos. The Lao gov [government] has put new travel restrictions in Xieng Khoang because of the fighting. Drop me a line and I'll keep ya posted.

(CAR (Wink), 2000:n.p.)

Having briefly surveyed some of the pre-travel imagery offered to budding danger-zone tourists, I now turn to examine danger-zone tourism in the Indonesian context. As the Indonesian case will illustrate, the range of danger-zone tourists is varied, as are their activities.

Close-up on danger-zone tourism in the Indonesian context: activists, adrenaline-rushers, and pursuers of the 'final frontier'

Since mid 1998, Indonesian tourism promoters have struggled against mounting negative imagery due to political, economic, ethnic, and religious unrest. As reported in a recent on-line article, "tour operators in Europe had scrapped Indonesia from their destinations lists after sparks of violent communal riots in some areas of the country" (*Asia Pulse,* 1999a:n.p.). Likewise, increasing numbers of independent travellers sharing advice on the web are painting a tableau of Indonesia as a land of travel traumas, urging fellow travellers to opt for the more predictably peaceful isles of Thailand and Malaysia. Such negative imagery has taken its toll – in 1998, the number of foreign visitors to Indonesia shrunk by 18.6 per cent (to 14.4 million), with Bali being the sole Indonesian destination to record an increase in foreign visitors (*TravelAsia,* 1999). It is precisely in this context that danger-zone tourism emerges.

Indonesian danger-zone tourism comes in various forms, reflecting the varied orientations and motivations of danger-zone tourists. At one end of the continuum are the independent budget travellers who make their way to places like Dili and

Aceh, priding themselves on slipping into off-limits destinations. At the other end of the spectrum are the 'reality tours' packaged by operations such as Global Exchange and even Indonesian travel houses. Interviews with independent travellers, examinations of danger-zone travel narratives, and perusal of advertisements for Indonesia 'reality tours' suggest a number of themes in the imagery of danger-zone travel. These include the promise of having authentic encounters with grassroots actors, the potential for enhancing one's personal identity as an activist or humanitarian, and the allure of a unique, 'exciting' travel experience that will distinguish the traveller from the growing hordes of ethnic and cultural tourists that now voyage to most corners of the globe. Let us turn to examine this imagery.

My awareness of danger-zone group tours to Indonesia was first prompted by a newspaper advertisement for a planned March 1998 'Reality Tour' to Java billed as "Democracy and Culture of Resistance in Indonesia: Suharto's Last Term?". The tour was organised by the San Francisco-based group, Global Exchange. The imagery of authentic grassroots encounters is a recurrent theme in their webpage. As explained on their webpage, Global Exchange's 'Reality Tours' are designed "to give people in US a chance to see firsthand how people facing immense challenges are finding grassroots solutions in their daily lives. [Moreover,] Reality Tours provide North Americans with a true understanding of a country's internal dynamics through socially responsible travel" (*Global Exchange*, 1999:n.p.). Here, then, we find the image of the politically-correct traveller. For US$2,150, tourists were invited to sign on to see the goings-on of the March 1998 pre-elections. The initial itinerary promised conversations with former political prisoners (including, as a possibility, the celebrated Indonesian writer, Pramoedya), factory workers, and human rights activists. The *pièce-de-résistance*, however, was to "dialogue with Indonesians and observe the election day atmosphere in the capital" (*Global Exchange*, 1999:n.p.). The repeated use of words such as 'resistance' and the emphasis on the tentative nature of the itinerary "due to circumstances beyond our control" offer a subtle background image of potential danger, as befits this particular special-interest market.

I Gede Ardika, Indonesia's Director General for Tourism, was quick to pick up on this special interest market. On March 5, 1999, he told reporters that several parties have welcomed the plan to turn the general election into a tourist attraction. For US$200 a day, three Indonesian travel agencies were selling the 'general election tourism package' which promised not only the latest update on the national election process, but a "close look" at the election process (*Asia Pulse*, 1999b). Not surprisingly, the theme of danger receded from the Indonesian packaging of the elections tours. However the theme of accessing an exciting political event to which only few foreigners are privy remained.

The commingling of politics, idealism, and the rare opportunity for authentic face-to-face dialogues with local Indonesians about potentially explosive issues does not only manifest itself in organised elections-watch tours, but also in a religion-focused tour sponsored by the Hartford Seminary. Entitled "With Muslims and Christians in Indonesia", this 1999 tour offered a first-hand experience that would "deepen participants' awareness of the state of Christian-Muslim relations and peace-making in the region by seeing the issues through the eyes of the indigenous communities" (*Hartford*

Seminary, 1999). Addressing recent upheavals in Indonesia, the webpage tour advertisement promised that "close attention will be given to the social, economic and ethnic reasons behind the recent unrest, and the role religious communities are playing, especially in relation to dialogue and understanding between Muslims and Christians" (*Hartford Seminary*, 1999:2). As in the elections watch tours, here, too, we find the imagery of 'first-hand' dialogues with local communities. In this case, however, the imagery of humanitarian and spiritual activism is even stronger.

As with the imagery found in the danger-zone group tours, the narratives of many of the independently-travelling danger-zone tourists also tend to stress the theme of the traveller's personal identity as an activist or humanitarian. As one Australian male planning a 1999 adventure in East Timor explained to me,

The reason that I'm going [to East Timor] is as much for the adrenalin as it is for the ethical side that is if I can do something, anything, to help then I'm obligated to. The crew that I'll be travelling with and myself are all environmental activists in Australia and for me that is my full-time job. Living in and touring the forests of Oz [Australia] in a kind of bourgeois, middle class, pacifist, guerrilla war gives me as much satisfaction for doing "the right thing" as it does for providing me with the rush of doing illegal stuff in the middle of the night in the forest. You see the same crew at the camps all over Australia, most are transients and all do it for the reasons that I have just mentioned.

(Personal communication, 30 August 1999)

Another theme frequently found in the narratives of many of these solo tourists that also surfaces in the danger-zone group tour imagery is that of 'first-hand' encounters. One solo American danger-zone tourist[6] told me, "I decided to go to East Timor to see what it was like. Dili was beautiful and I stayed at the Hotel Turismo where all the foreign journalists were. I got a lot of firsthand information from them on the political scene" (Personal communication, 2 September 1999).[7] And as another American, an applied social sciences researcher in his mid-thirties, explained to me,

I went to Dili for a long weekend, just to see what was happening there. That's how I spend my vacations, going to places like Kosovo and the Balkans. For a while, a few years back, I even toyed with the idea of starting a hot-spot travel agency. There are a lot of people like me, interested in experiencing these places...and understanding first-hand what is going on.

(Personal interview, 25 August 1999)

In contrast to the danger-zone group tours discussed earlier, however, the narratives of independent danger-zone tourists often draw more directly on the imagery of threat and imperilment. As the female who stayed at the Hotel Turismo in Dili went on to tell me, "I only stayed in Dili about five days because of the unsettled atmosphere, even then. Journalists were threatened and locals were intimidated" (Personal communication, 2 September 1999). The imagery of threat and imperilment also surfaces in a Canadian's web-based chronicles of his and his wife's 1991 adventures in East Timor and other parts of Indonesia:

At the first road junction we encountered, just before coming into Dili...there was a check point where we had to get out of the bus and go into a police post. The plainclothes man there took down all our particulars. We were on our way back on to the bus when we were called over to the military post on the other side of the road...where we were surrounded by soldiers in full battle dress armed with M16s, while they again took down all our particulars. It was a little tense.

(Anon., 1992:n.p.)

Peppering this writer's account of this trip are excerpts from *The Jakarta Post* and other newspapers on the violence that had transpired in Dili just weeks before their arrival. While this travel diary offers detailed descriptions of a variety of encounters as well as scenery in East Timor and nearby islands, some of the danger-zone travellers I spoke with focused almost exclusively on the imagery of extreme endangerment. As one danger-zone tourist told me,

I know another guy who goes surfing in dodgy locations around the globe. I suppose it's for the rush because when I knew him in Australia he used to surf breaks that were infamous as shark breeding and/or feedin [sic] grounds. Now he's moved on to war zones and areas of insurrection etc. This bloke has surfed places in Haiti, Vietnam and anywhere that has a conflict that attracts his attention, East Timor as recently as a month and a half ago.

(Personal email communication, 28 August 1999)

This imagery of fearless ventures to life-endangering locales was also particularly vivid in the narrative of one Australian male who had visited Dili. As he wrote in a message to me,

I've got some friends over there [East Timor] now in a non-work capacity. They had to sneak in as no tourist visas are being offered. The sh** is really going down there now and caucasion [sic] people are being targeted. The scenary [sic] is great and ordinary people are cool but unless you are like my friends who are there for an adrenalin rush then your timing sucks. Keep in mind the Indonesian people (yes I know the timorese [sic] are a hugely different ethnic group) invented the word amock [sic] ie. Run amock [sic] and in Indonesian it means to spontaneously lose control in a frenzy. I've been around when this has happened before

(Personal email communication, 2 September 1999).

For some danger-zone tourists, then, the humanitarian or spiritual motives for travels are immaterial, what matters is the adrenaline-rush factor and the allure of travelling where few dare.[8]

While the motives and specific interests of the tourists discussed above vary, two themes emerge in the imagery embedded in the narratives and advertisements for danger-zone group tours. The first involves ideas about the concept of 'authenticity'. While debates about tourists' interest in authenticity have haunted the tourism literature (cf. MacCannell, 1976; Redfoot, 1984; Cohen, 1988; 1995; Crick, 1989), Selwyn's (1996) recent distinctions between two different senses of the concept are relevant to this discussion of the imagery of authenticity in danger-zone tourism narratives. As Selwyn (1996:7) outlines, there has been some semantic confusion between two different senses of the term 'authenticity':

In the first sense, the authenticity is taken to refer to those feelings, or projections of feelings, of social solidarity pursued by tourists...In its second sense, the authenticity refers to the knowledge (about, for example, the nature, culture and society of tourist destinations) which is both sought by tourists and presented to them by [Erik] Cohen's 'intellectuals' –

museum curators, tour guides and other 'participant observers' working in, or, like anthropologists, commenting on, the tourism industry.

While recent writers have observed that some 'post-tourists' revel in the unauthentic or prefer the simulacrum (Feifer, 1985; Bruner, 1989:438; Ritzer and Liska, 1997:107), it seems clear that the individuals engaged in danger-zone tourism tend to be driven by an interest in Selwyn's second genre of 'authenticity', in their quest for privileged insider knowledge of political hot-spots. Although some, particularly the activist travellers, are also in pursuit of the first sense of authenticity (a desire for *communitas* with members of struggling foreign communities),[9] analysis of the narratives of some of the solo danger-zone tourists, especially those primarily in pursuit of adrenaline rushes, suggests a need to differentiate a third genre of authenticity pursued by some tourists. This third sense of the term authenticity, I argue, refers to a kind of visceral authenticity which includes the sense of heightened awareness (on a very physical level) experienced during endangerment.[10]

Having briefly surveyed the imagery fuelling danger-zone tourism in Indonesia, let me now turn to examine how such tourists, despite their small numbers, can also play a role in the rearticulation of indigenous ethnic sensibilities.

Danger-zone tourists as partial shapers of ethnic self-imagery

I first became aware of the role of danger-zone tourists in inadvertently moulding ethnic self-imagery when I was conducting preliminary research on the culturally heterogeneous Eastern Indonesian island of Alor, a small island 30 km off the coast of East Timor. After years of work in the heavily touristed region of Tana Toraja (Indonesia), I had selected Alor partially because it was 'off the beaten tourist track'. Alor has never figured prominently in Indonesian tourism promotion. Although a few English-language adventure tour books of the Lonely Planet genre make passing note of Alor as the "island of bronze drums and tradition", most guidebooks give it no mention whatsoever. During my first month-long visit to the island in the summer of 1989, the only other non-Indonesians I encountered were a Bali-based French ethnic arts dealer scouring the island for goods for his Kuta Beach shop and a North American consultant working on an agricultural consultancy project. Tourism figures were not available at this time and, although some tourists found their way to Alor, it is nevertheless clear that the numbers of overnight tourist stays on the island were minimal.[11]

On this first visit to Alor, I had many conversations with Alorese about their island. The Alorese with whom I spoke tended to draw on two primary images: that of their island as the homeland of bronze drums and that of their island as "the language island". As many told me, their small mountainous island was home to far more linguistic diversity than anywhere else in Indonesia, if not the world.[12] As one church leader quipped, "This is a Babylonia [sic] island" (Personal communication, 23 June 1989). Again and again, people in Alor's main town of Kalabahi heralded their island as a place of "dozens of different languages and cultures". Hand in hand with this imagery of linguistic and cultural diversity was an imagery of inter-village antipathies. As many told me, up until this century, inter-village warfare was common. As one older man animatedly recounted, "Back then, you were always watchful, as men in one village would raid other villages" (Personal communication, 22 June 1999). The self-imagery put forth by a number of Alorese on this 1989 visit, then, stressed a certain degree of ruggedness. In short, Alor was represented as a rugged place with a rugged past.

In the late 1980s, Indonesia opened East Timor to foreign tourist visitation, which had ramifications for incipient tourism on Alor, as well as for Aloreses' self-imagery. When I returned to Alor in the summers of 1993 and 1996, I found that Alor was receiving a regular trickle of overnight tourists, most arriving by ferry from Dili (East Timor) in transit to Kupang or Flores.[13] In 1994, the number of overnight tourist stays on the island had climbed to 220, admittedly still a very small number (Kantor Statistik Kabupaten Alor, 1995). Curious as to what drew these tourists to Alor, I interviewed them in 1993 and 1995. Many told me that they had not planned to visit Alor. Rather, they had targeted East Timor and their return ferry had stopped in Alor. Some were obliged to change ferries in Alor, and were faced with up to a week's wait for their desired ferry. Others jumped ship spontaneously, upon seeing the beauty of Alor's Kalabahi Bay. As one of these returning danger-zone tourists, an Australian teacher in her thirties told me,

I hadn't planned to stay here. But after the ordeal on Timor, all the tension and terror there, when the ferry cruised into Kalabahi Bay at dawn, everything here looked so beautiful and tranquil...I knew this would be a peaceful place to recover and rest up, so I grabbed my bag and got off the ship. And that's how I came to be here.

(Personal communication, 24 November 1996)

The theme of relief and the image of Alor as an idyllic place also comes through in a Canadian voyager's web-based Indonesia travel diary. Having just spent six trying days in East Timor and a sleep-deprived night on the deck of a crowded boat out of Dili, he describes his arrival on Alor as follows:

The approach to Kalabahi was up a long inlet, quite beautiful in the early morning light. We saw porpoises leaping out of the water. Immediately we got off the boat, we were approached by a man who wanted to take us to the "best hotel". It was quite a relief to find that there were three to chose from–we had been a bit concerned after the fiasco in Baucau [East Timor] that there might not be anywhere to stay...

(Anon., 1992:n.p.)

These and other returning danger-zone tourists tended to stay in one of the two small inns (*losmen*) on the shores of the Kalabahi Bay. Their stays generally lasted from three to seven days and, as there was not much to do in Kalabahi but 'rest and recover', they had ample opportunity to interact with residents of Kalabahi. Some had studied basic Indonesian in preparation for their travels and when I passed them sitting on the verandah gazing at the bay, I often overheard them gushing about the scenery to the inn's employees. While Alor is a lovely place, for these recovering danger-zone tourists, it was doubly so. The contrast between tension-filled East Timor and tranquil Alor was a repeated theme in their conversations. Many of the travellers I spoke with noted how difficult it was to fathom that peaceful Alor was just 30 km from turbulent East Timor. A number of Alorese high school students and inn employees listened to these travellers' accounts of their adventures in East Timor. Relishing the chance to practise their English, young Alorese frequently asked these foreign visitors where they had travelled in Indonesia. These conversations rapidly became terrain for additional exchanges about the contrasts between the hardships and tensions they had experienced in East Timor and the peacefulness of Alor.

By the fall of 1996, some of this danger-zone tourist-inspired imagery of "lovely", "tranquil" Alor was being embraced and repeated by the residents of Kalabahi. As several people told me, "This is a peaceful place". Stressing their lack of crime and violence, they urged me to promote Alor for its tranquil touristic charms.[14] The imagery of inter-village warfare and ruggedness appeared to be receding from their representations of their island. The conversations with these recovering danger-zone tourists seemed to be subtly shifting Alorese perceptions of themselves and their island. By late 1996, Alorese spoke of their rugged identities with much less frequency. Rather, they were shifting to a rhetoric that foregrounded the charm and loveliness of their island. While the themes of their island as a "language island" and as the homeland of *mokos* (bronze drums) endure as important elements in their self-imagery, now added to them is the new motif of beauty and tranquillity. Although it is not conclusive, the Alor case suggests one way in which danger-zone tourism can have ramifications on other groups in other, more tranquil areas. Danger-zone tourists are not merely innocuous observers of local ethnic and political relations – their comments both inside and outside these danger-zones can not only reshape place imagery, but can also play a role in the rearticulation of ethnic sensibilities.

Conclusion

Although danger-zone tourists are small in number, I believe they merit our scholarly attention. Whether inspired by humanitarian/activist interests, adrenaline rushes or the desire to voyage to the 'final frontier' of travel where few others dare to go, these tourists have been largely overlooked in the tourism literature. As the Southeast Asia examples suggest, danger-zone tourism appears to have some commercial potential, be it through small-scale T-shirt sales or special interest danger-zone tours. Perhaps more interesting for scholars of the politics of tourism, however, is the way in which danger-zone tourists become embroiled in and colour the politics of the places they are visiting. As the Alor case illustrates, even in out-of-the-way corners of the globe where tourism is embryonic at best, these returning danger-zone tourists play a role in the reshaping of indigenous ethnic sensibilities and self-imagery. Moreover, there are some indications that, in other locales, danger-zone tourists' images of the places they visit may conflict and compete with the images cherished by the residents of these destinations, or with the more idyllic (and safer) images promoted by tourism boards and hoteliers seeking mass tourism. These danger-zone tourism-related topics deserve our research attention.

Given this volume's focus on interconnected worlds, it is worth underscoring that the growing phenomenon of danger-zone tourists is very much a product of the global era (although there is certainly a precedent for danger-zone tourists in earlier eras). CNN news coverage of the world's hot spots, worldwide networks of activists, and even Internet adventure travel discussion groups have facilitated the blossoming of danger-zone tourism. Danger-zone tourists are generally fuelled by global politics, their itineraries inspired by the imagery of nightly news reports from the world's tumultuous zones. Moreover, danger-zone tourists can also contribute to non-travellers' images of these tumultuous destinations. Danger-zone tourists' web-based travelogues are read by cyber-voyagers; presumably their representations of the places they visit are digested and amplified by web surfers round the globe.

Acknowledgements

An earlier version of this paper was presented at the conference "Interconnected Worlds: Southeast Asian Tourism in the 21st Century" in Singapore (6–7 September, 1999). I would like to thank the Singapore Tourism Board and the Centre for Advanced Studies at the National University of Singapore, especially the latter for providing me with an Isaac Manasseh Meyer Fellowship to facilitate this project. My heartfelt appreciation also goes to the editors of this volume as well as to Maribeth Erb and Peter Sanchez for their thoughtful comments and encouragement. I also wish to thank Hillary Leonard and Kay Mohlman for introducing me to the work of Robert Young Pelton and Alex Garland. In addition, I have benefited from the lively discussions of 'tourism and war' in the summer of 1999 on the 'tourism anthropology' net, as well as from conversations with Joshua Caulder. Any shortcomings in these pages, however, rest solely on my shoulders.

Notes

[1] Also see Hitchcock (1999) and the essays in Picard and Wood (1997).

[2] A number of public policy planners, social science teachers and activists were also among the danger-zone tourists I interviewed.

[3] The film version of *The Beach* was released with great hoopla in early 2000. In this version, the British hero of the novel has been transformed into an American backpacker traveller. In both versions, however, the action is set in Thailand and the hero is a young man who deliberately targets dangerous off-the-beaten-track destinations believing that risk-packed experiences would make him more worldly and interesting.

[4] Torun Elsrud (Personal email communication, 15 July 1999) notes that while in Thailand conducting field research, she observed tourists sporting war-related T-shirts with slogans such as "Beware of Mines-Cambodia" or "Saigon" with an image of a gun. As Elsrud comments, "it appeared quite a few travellers and other tourists took a few weeks in Cambodia or Vietnam and at least some returned to Bangkok with these T-shirts as a symbolic expression of their trip".

[5] For related explorations of forms of war tourism, also see de Burlo (1989), Yoneyama (1995), Young (1993) and White (1997).

[6] This tourist labeled herself and others she encountered while visiting Dili as "budget travellers".

[7] In their book, Mowforth and Munt (1998) discuss some of the new forms of tourism, including what may be termed "political tourism" and/or "ego-tourism" (Munt, 1994). They note that ego-tourists "must search for a style of travel that is both reflective of an 'alternative' life-style and which is capable of maintaining and enhancing their cultural capital...ultimately it is a competition for uniqueness (Cohen, 1979; 1989) with which ego-tourists engage" (Mowforth and Munt, 1998:135). Some of these features are also embedded in danger-zone tourism.

[8] For some of these adrenaline-rush danger-zone tourists, nonchalance about the potential risks, or dismissal of concerns as 'exaggerated' by unknowing outsiders is also a dimension of the imagery. As one query on the Lonely Planet's webpage labelled "Aceh. What's the real scoop?" reads, "I'm planning a trip

to stay in Sumatra for a few months and am wondering what the real deal is with aceh [sic]. I [sic] know there is some sh** happening, but is it only confined to certain areas and does it affect travellers. I [sic] have been warned off places like south east turkey, northern [G]eorgia etc. But after visiting these places i [sic] found the warnings melodramatic. Any knowledgeable folk out there with a comment. Thankyou [sic]." (Yako, 2000:n.p.). This query prompted a number of warnings as well as a couple of lengthy narratives from danger-zone tourists who had recently returned from Aceh.

[9]For a contrasting exploration of the imagery of authenticity in ethnic tourists' narratives (both domestic Indonesian tourists and foreign tourists), see Adams (1998).

[10]This third sense of visceral authenticity also comes to the fore in some forms of extreme adventure tourism (vacations spent climbing dangerous mountain peaks, bungee jumping and so forth).

[11]It should be noted that elite cultural cruise ships began making periodic half-day stops on the island in the mid 1980s. However, according to records maintained by the Kantor Statistik Kabupaten Alor (1995), it was not until the mid 1990s that Alor began to receive more than three such cruise ship visits a year (in 1997 the island had received six half-day cruise ship visits). As the passengers are quickly sheparded to a coastal village for a dance performance and coconut milk drinks, Alorese contact with these cruise ship passengers is minimal.

[12]The island is 2,884 sq km. The linguist Stokof (1984) found 13 languages on the island, although some local sources, including the Regent, declare that there are at least 50 dialects or languages and almost as many cultural groups on Alor, which has a population of 146,000. Precise delineations of the ethnic groups on Alor are challenging, given the dearth of anthropological work on the island.

[13]There were also some group dive tourists, but most of these visitors did not stay overnight on the island and seldom interacted with Alorese, as they spent the bulk of their time underwater.

[14]A tourism consciousness campaign had been waged by the Indonesian government beginning in the early 1990s, so that even villages well off the beaten tourist track were being prompted to consider their own tourist-attracting charms.

References

Adams, K.M. (1984) '"Come to Tana Toraja, Land of the Heavenly Kings": Travel agents as brokers in ethnicity'. *Annals of Tourism Research*, 11(3), 469–85.

Adams, K. M. (1998) 'Domestic tourism and nation-building in South Sulawesi, Indonesia'. *Indonesia and the Malay World*, 26(75), 77–96.

Andre (2000) *My First War*. Online posting. Available HTTP: < www.fieldingtravel.com/blackflag/. > (10 February 2000).

Anon. (1992) *Part III- Nusa Tenggara Timor 1991-1992 Travel Diary*. Online. Available HTTP:< http://www.infomatch.com/~denysm/indon913.htm. > (29 July 1999).

Anon. (2000) *Dangerous Honeymoon*. Online posting. Available HTTP: < www.fieldingtravel.com/black-flagcafe/messages/13215.html > (29 January 2000).

Asia Pulse (1999a) 'Indonesia's tourism prospects remain glum for 1999', 17 March. Online. Available HTTP: < wysuwyg://98/http://www.skali.com/business/rtl/19990317_06.html. > (19 August 1999).

Asia Pulse (1999b) 'Indonesia travel agents to promote election tourism package', 5 March. Online. Available HTTP: < wysiwyg://98/http://www.skali.com/business/eco/199903/05/eco19990305_07.html. > (19 August 1999).

Bar-On, R.R. (1996) 'Measuring the effects on tourism of violence and of promotion following violent acts', in A. Pizam and Y. Mansfield (eds.) *Tourism, Crime, and International Security Issues*. Chichester: Wiley, 159-74.

Bourdieu, P. (1984) *Distinction: A Critique of the Judgement of Taste*. London: Routledge and Kegan Paul.

Bruner, E. (1989) 'Of cannibals, tourists, and ethnographers'. *Cultural Anthropology*, 4(4), 438–45.

CAR (Wink) (2000) *Situation in Laos*. Online posting. Available HTTP: < www.fieldingtravel.com/black-flagcafe/messages/13215.html > (21 April 2000).

Cohen, E. (1979) 'The Impact of tourism on the hill tribes of Northern Thailand'. *Internationals Asienforum*, 10(1–2), 5–38.

Cohen, E. (1988) 'Authenticity and commoditization in tourism'. *Annals of Tourism Research*, 15(3), 371–96.

Cohen, E. (1989) '"Primitive and remote" hill tribe trekking in Thailand'. *Annals of Tourism Research*, 16(1), 30–61.

Cohen, E. (1995) 'Contemporary tourism – Trends and challenges: Sustainable authenticity or contrived post-modernity', in R. Butler and D. Pearce (eds.) *Change in Tourism: People, Places, Processes*. London and New York: Routledge, 12–29.

Crick, M. (1989) 'Representations of sun, sex, sights, savings, and servility: International tourism in the social sciences'. *Annual Review of Anthropology*, 18, 307–44.

de Burlo, C. (1989) 'Islanders, soldiers, and tourists: The war and the shaping of tourism in Melanesia', in G. White and L. Lindstrom (eds.) *The Pacific Theatre: Island Representations of World War II*. Honolulu: University of Hawaii Press, 299–325.

Diller + Scofidio (1994) *Back to the Front: Tourisms of War*. Basse-Normandie (France): F.R.A.C.

Elsrud, T. (1999) *Re: Tourism + War*. Personal email communication, 15 July. Cited with permission granted on 12 September 1999.

Elsrud, T. (under review) 'Risk-creation in travelling: Backpacker adventure narration'. *Annals of Tourism Research*.

Featherstone, M. (1987) 'Lifestyle and consumer culture'. *Theory, Culture and Society*, 4(1), 55–70.

Feifer, M. (1985) *Going Places*. London: Macmillan.

Fielding's Black Flag Café (2000). Online. Available HTTP:www.fieldingtravel.com/blackflag/ (2 January 2000).

Global Exchange (1999) 'Reality tours: Travel with us to see what's really happening', Online. Available: HTTP: < http://www.globalexchange.org/tours/auto/byCountry.html > & < http://www.globalexchange.org/tours/indonesiaItin1.html > (Indonesia Itinerary) (18 August 1999).

Garland, A. (1997) *The Beach*. London: Penguin.

Gartner, W.C. and Shen, J. (1992) 'The impact of Tiananmen Square on China's tourism image'. *Journal of Travel Research*, 30(4), 47–52.

Hartford Seminary (1999) 'With Christians and Muslims in Indonesia', Online. Available HTTP: < http://www.hart.sem.edu/macd/events/Defalt.htm > (18 August 1999).

Kantor Statistik Kabupaten Alor (1995) *Kabupaten Alor Dalam Statistik*. Alor: Kalabahi.

Kelly, M. (1998) 'Tourism, not terrorism: The visual politics of presenting Jordan as an international tourist destination'. *Visual Anthropology*, 11, 191–205.

Hall, C. M. (1994) *Tourism and Politics: Policy, Power and Place*. Chichester: Wiley.

Hall, C. M. and O'Sullivan, V. (1996) 'Tourism, political stability and violence', in A. Pizam and Y. Mansfield (eds.) *Tourism, Crime, and International Security Issues*. Chichester: Wiley, 105–21.

Hitchcock, M. (1999) 'Tourism and ethnicity: Situational perspectives'. *International Journal of Tourism Research*, 1, 17–32.

Leon (2000) *Re: My 2 centz*. Online posting. Available HTTP: < www.fieldingtravel.com/blackflagcafe/messages/12787.html > (6 April 2000).

MacCannell, D. (1976) *The Tourist: A New Theory of the Leisure Class*. New York: Schocken.

Maclean's (1994) 'Down and out in Mexico: Poverty stalks a southern state', June 13, 28–29.

Mihalic, T. (1996) 'Tourism and warfare-The case of Slovenia', in A. Pizam and Y. Mansfield (eds.) *Tourism, Crime, and International Security Issues*. Chichester: Wiley, 231–46.

Mike (2000) *Cambodia*. Online posting. Available HTTP: < www.fieldingtravel.com/blackflag/ < www.zinezone.com/pubbin/login > (5 February 2000).

Mitchell, T. (1991) *Colonising Egypt*. Berkeley: University of California Press.

Mowforth, M. and Munt, I. (1998) *Tourism and Sustainability: New Tourism in the Third World*. London and New York: Routledge.

Munt, I. (1994) 'The "other" postmodern tourism: Culture, travel and the new middle classes'. *Theory, Culture and Society*, 11, 101–23.

Pelton. R.Y. (1999) *Come Back Alive: The Ultimate Guide to Surviving Disasters, Kidnapping, Animal Attacks and Other Nasty Perils of Modern Travel*. Redondo Beach (California): Fielding Worldwide, Inc.

Pelton, R.Y., Aral, C. and Dulles, W. (1997) *Fielding's Hot Spots: Travel in Harm's Way*. Redondo Beach (California): Fielding Worldwide, Inc.

Pelton, R.Y., Aral, C. and Dulles, W. (1998) *Fielding's The World's Most Dangerous Places*. Redondo Beach (California): Fielding Worldwide, Inc.

Phipps, P. (1999) 'Tourists, terrorists, death and value', in R. Kaur and J. Hutnyk (eds.) *Travel Worlds: Journeys in Contemporary Cultural Politics*. London and New York: Zed Books, 74–93.

Picard, M. and Wood, R. (eds.) (1997) *Tourism, Ethnicity and the State in Asian and Pacific Societies.* Honolulu: University of Hawaii Press.

Pitts, W. J. (1996) 'Uprising in Chiapas, Mexico: Zapata lives - Tourism falters', in A. Pizam, and Y. Mansfield (eds.) *Tourism, Crime, and International Security Issues.* Chichester: Wiley, 215–27.

Pizam, A. and Mansfield, Y. (eds.) (1996) *Tourism, Crime, and International Security Issues.* Chichester: Wiley.

Raza (2000) *Cambodia: Siam Reap to Phnom Penh.* Online posting. Available HTTP: < .www.fielding-travel.com/blackflag/ < www.zinezone.com/pubbin/login > (26 January 2000).

Redfoot, D. (1984) 'Touristic authenticity, touristic angst, and modern reality'. *Qualitative Sociology,* 7(4), 291–309.

Richter, L. (1989) *The Politics of Tourism in Asia.* Honolulu: University of Hawaii Press.

Richter, L. (1992) 'Political instability and tourism in the third world', in D. Harrison (ed.) *Tourism and the Less Developed Countries.* London: Belhaven, 35–46.

Ritzer, G. and Liska, A. (1997) '"McDisneyization"' and "Post-Tourism": Complementary perspectives on contemporary voyeurism', in C. Rojek and J. Urry (eds.) *Touring Cultures: Transformations of Travel and Theory.* London and New York: Routledge, 96–109.

Ryan, C. (1991) *Tourism, Terrorism and Violence: The Risks of Wider World Travel.* London: Research Institute for the Study of Conflict and Terrorism.

Selwyn, T. (ed.) (1996) *The Tourist Image: Myths and Myth-Making in Tourism.* Chichester: Wiley.

Smith, V. (1996) 'War and its tourist attractions', in A. Pizam and Y. Mansfield (eds.) *Tourism, Crime, and International Security Issues.* Chichester: Wiley, 247–64.

Stokof, W.A.L. (1984) 'Annotations to a text in the Abui Language (Alor)'. *Bijdragen tot de Taal land en Volkenkunde,* 140(1), 106–62.

Teye, V. (1986) 'Liberation wars and tourism development in Africa: The case of Zambia'. *Annals of Tourism Research,* 13(4), 589–608.

Teye, V. (1988) 'Coup d'etat and African tourism: A study of Ghana'. *Annals of Tourism Research,* 15(3), 329–56.

TravelAsia (1999) 'Election packages, anyone?'. Online. Available HTTP: < http://www.incentives-asia.-com/travel-asia/03_19_99/stories/election.html> (19 August 1999).

Wall, G. (1996) 'Terrorism and tourism: An overview and an Irish example', in A. Pizam and Y. Mansfield (eds.) *Tourism, Crime, and International Security Issues.* Chichester: Wiley, 143–58.

White, G. (1997) 'Museum/memorial/shrine: National narrative in national spaces'. *Museum Anthropology,* 21(1), 8–26.

Wilson, D. (1993) 'Tourism, public policy and the image of Northern Ireland since the troubles', in B. O'Connor and M. Cronin, M (eds.) *Tourism in Ireland: A Critical Analysis.* Cork: Cork University Press, 138–61.

Wood, R. (1984) 'Ethnic tourism, the state and cultural change in Southeast Asia'. *Annals of Tourism Research,* 11(3), 353–74.

Wood, R. (1997) 'Tourism and the state: Ethnic options and constructions of otherness', in M. Picard and R. Wood (eds.) *Tourism, Ethnicity and the State in Asian and Pacific Societies.* Honolulu: University of Hawaii Press, 1–34.

Yako (2000) *Aceh: What's the Real Scoop?* Online. Available HTTP: < http://www.lonelyplanet.com/thorntree/seaisl/fett.htm. > (22 August 2000).

Yoneyama, L. (1995) 'Memory matters: Hiroshima's Korean atom bomb memorial and the politics of ethnicity'. *Public Culture,* 7(3), 499–527.

Young, J. E. (1993) *The Texture of Memory: Holocaust Memorials and Meaning.* New Haven: Yale University Press.

17

Interconnections, Planning and the Local–Global Nexus: A Case from Vietnam

Peter Burns

Introduction

Local culture is viewed as a prime resource for global tourism. It is therefore hardly surprising that interconnections at the local–global nexus should be considered important. With regard to planning for tourism, there has been only a slight shift towards seeing participation by the local people as being a necessary part of developing destinations and attractions for global tourism. Almost two decades ago, Murphy (1985) wrote what was probably the first cohesive work on what he termed a community approach to tourism planning. The book was well received and had important points to make about participation in planning at a local level. Some of these points crossed political philosophies and boundaries, such as acknowledging the need for social, economic, aesthetic and environmental trade-offs, the importance of cross-sector linkages, and the building up of a complete tourist product and image. However, the devil (as always) is in the detail. The ideas on planning participation illustrated in Murphy's work are rooted in the politics of capitalism and multi-party democracy as constructed by the West, and possess a distinctly North American flavour. It might be suggested that this approach does not necessarily work within all political and social situations. Other authors such as Doswell (1997) in his distinctly muddled text on destination management, fail to acknowledge community participation. Doswell refers instead to the co-ordinating role of the national tourism authority and "major companies...entertainment complexes, trade unions and consumer groups" (1997:187) as being the most pre-eminent players. Laws (1995) makes several references to community action within tourism development but his examples, such as Hawaii, come from a range similar to that of Murphy (1985). This is not to say that approaches to community participation in planning have not been discussed. The UK-based pressure group Tourism Concern often reports on community issues (cf. *In Focus*) but the articles circulate mainly among its members and within a few academic libraries. Its voice, while rooted in direct experience, action and passion, is somewhat marginal to the scientific debates taking place in journals and volumes such as the present one.

While the main purpose of this chapter is to examine the various interconnections that frame the relationship between the local, the national and the global, I will also suggest that community participation does not necessarily have to be constructed in, or bounded by, Western European/North American multi-party democratic processes. I will reflect on tourism planning at a town level, using the case of Cua Lo in Nghe An province on the north-central coast of Vietnam to explore some of the local–national–global interconnections and barriers.

The chapter comprises four parts: first, a national context in which the present political economy of Vietnam is lightly touched upon; second, a brief profile of tourism in Vietnam; third, the case study and findings; and finally, a concluding section which considers some of the relational issues that may be inferred from the interconnections between the local and the global.

The national context

Vietnam is in an interesting position, being one of very few surviving communist states. Central planning has been and is still very evident in all areas of life: from education through industrial policy to tourism. Global politics, on the other hand, has changed dramatically from the former East–West bipolarity to the existing tripolarity in which the world is effectively divided into three super-regions framed by three super-economic agreements: the US-dominated North American Free Trade Agreement (NAFTA) (Todaro, 1997); the Japan-dominated Asia-Pacific Economic Cooperation forum (APEC) (Stubbs and Underhill, 1994); and the Franco-German-dominated European Union (EU) (Isaak, 1995). It has been forcefully argued that all three regions are dominated, in the face of the virtual economic and political collapse of the former Soviet Union, by the US-inspired World Trade Organisation (Kiely and Marfleet, 1998) and relationships between political allies and former economic partners have undergone dramatic changes. These changes are taking place within a very unstable global-political climate. There is ethnic and political confrontation in Eastern Europe and a paradoxical and strained relationship between the US and China where commercial interests seem to be winning over the US' natural distaste for socialism/communism. Within the Asian region, Vietnam, China and Mongolia's transition to the market system (especially agricultural production) is taking place under the leadership of their respective communist parties in a sort of mix between 'stabilisation-cum-privatisation' and 'family responsibility' where large decision-making power extends to the family within a collective framework (Lavigne, 1995:111).

Coming out of the post-Cold War chaos has been the changing relationship between central and local governments. While the communist system in Vietnam has always operated through local cadres and local Peoples' Committees of one form or another, fieldwork for this paper undertaken in 1998 revealed the sense that the former 'heavy hand' of centralised government is becoming lighter. In the particular case of Vietnam, this higher profile for political and economic engagement at a global level has been a policy shift rather than policy drift. The perception of democracy held by the rulers can be summarised as "the party leads, the state administers and the people exercise collective mastery" (Vietnamese political adage cited by Thayer, 1994:1). The economic and agricultural crises during the decades following the Vietnam war forced the ruling Communist Party to develop and introduce plans for the wholesale renovation/renewal of the country (the *doi moi*) based on three fundamentals:

- *shifting* from a highly centralised planned economy based chiefly on public ownership of the means of production to a multi-sector economy operating under a market mechanism with state management and a socialist orientation;
- *democratising* social life with the aim of developing the rule of law in a state of the people, by the people and for the people (whereby the law stands above other considerations such as party membership or patronage); and
- *implementing* an open door policy and promoting cooperation and relations between Vietnam and all other countries in the world community in the spirit of developing amiable relations for peace, independence and development (United Nations Development Programme (UNDP), 1998:3).

These three aims can be contextualised by the following from a speech made in 1990 by the Chairman of the National Council of Ministers:

It stands to reason that the continuation of the process of *doi moi* constitutes an imperative need and a vital issue for our country. Ours is a principled implementation of renewal. That is a creative application of Marxism-Leninism to the specific conditions of our country. Renewal in order to build up socialism more effectively, not to renounce socialism.

(Thayer, 1994:7)

In ideological terms, national stabilisation and development and international relations have been framed by the following basic concept:

The strategy is to place human beings at the centre of development and to promote the potential of individuals and communities as well as of the whole nation. The strategy also seeks to harmoniously combine economic development with socio-cultural development so that the people's cultural and spiritual lives will improve together with their material well-being. Under this strategy, economic development is considered the basis as well as a tool and prerequisite for the realisation of social policies.

(UNDP, 1995:2)

In more concrete terms, the general objectives were to:

- *overcome* the economic crisis and to stabilise the country's socio-economic situation;
- *move* beyond the status of a poverty-stricken and under-developed country; and
- *improve* the living standards of the population and create favourable conditions for more rapid development in the early twenty-first century.

In many ways, Vietnam has successfully translated the benefits of economic growth into improvement in the lives of its people. Evidence for this is that

Vietnam has improved its ranking in the annual UNDP Human Development listings. It is now 122nd out of 174 countries, and has caught up with many other countries of the Association of Southeast Asian Nations (ASEAN) in terms of life expectancy (66.4 years) and functional adult literacy (93.7 per cent) (UNDP, 1999).

Some population and employment issues

Any number of issues may be chosen to contextualise Cua Lo's problems in relation to national challenges and tourism development. Given that Vietnam's underlying purpose in developing tourism is one of economic development, and moreover, the personal experience of economic development as felt by ordinary people is through enhanced employment opportunities, it is worth providing a brief profile of population and employment characteristics. In particular (as will be seen later in this chapter), tourism has the capacity to provide some employment and entrepreneurial opportunity with minimal start-up capital, as has happened in Cua Lo. Without doubt, if the fieldwork was more extensive or opportunities arose for further studies, the next priorities for detailed investigation would be issues relating to how women and ethnic minorities fare in the new range of economic activities, for it is here that "material relations...[are] analysed within the larger framework of social reproduction...and the way in which the concrete historical reality is embodied in agents through personal and collective identities" (Narotzky, 1997:158).

In 1998, the population of Vietnam was estimated at 76.2 million. Almost 60 million live in rural areas. The country has 54 ethnic groups with a total of 9.6 million (13 per cent of the population), each with distinctive characteristics of language, modes of dress and lifestyle patterns. Many of these minority people live in mountainous areas that tend to have more harsh climatic conditions and poor infrastructure. A number of policy measures have been undertaken by the government to preserve the social integrity and traditions of such ethnic groups while ensuring equal rights in political, economic, cultural and social domains (UNDP, 1995:22). Creating meaningful and legitimate employment that will enable the population to support itself is probably Vietnam's biggest challenge.

Finding productive employment for the youthful population represents a particularly important challenge for Vietnam. Working towards this end, the government has created, as the UNDP states, fundamental changes in the thinking and awareness by both the state and workers regarding employment and job creation:

The unemployed no longer wait for the government to provide jobs as they did in the past, but actively look for and generate employment instead while the state's role is to create a favourable socio-economic and legal environment.

(UNDP, 1995:6)

Unemployment and underemployment remain, as the UNDP reports, "a thorny problem" with the UNDP indicating that:

In big cities such as Hanoi and Ho Chi Minh City the unemployment situation puts pressure on both the economy and society. In rural areas 30–35 per cent of workforce are still underemployed due to limited agricultural economic activities.

(UNDP, 1995:6)

Urban drift, which is placing enormous environmental and social strain on Hanoi and Ho Chi Minh City, also remains a problem, adding to the pressure on the government to produce (through the creation of favourable conditions) more jobs in both urban and rural areas.

Tourism in Vietnam

Vietnam's tourism has shown erratic trends during the past decade and in a sense shadows Vietnam's global interconnections. Whereas overall numbers have increased (rising from a total of 250,000 in 1990 to 1.7 million in 1997, and down to 1.5 million in 1998), arrival figures from individual countries have shown declines. These have been counterbalanced by phenomenal growth in arrivals from China, which we may speculate to be a result of the reunification of China and Hong Kong. Table 17.1 shows some arrival statistics.

In a fundamental sense, these figures are meaningless until contextualised and the reasons behind the trends are identified. So, for example, it is important to know that 1994 saw the end of the US embargo and 1995 the entry of Vietnam into the ASEAN group. Similarly, the drop in US arrivals and sudden increase in Vietnamese arrivals can be explained by the Vietnamese immigration authority's decision to make an explicit category for *Viet Kieu* (Vietnamese nationals permanently residing abroad).

Table 17.1: International visitor arrivals

	1993	1994	1995	1996	1997
Total	600,438	1,018,214	1,351,296	1,607,155	1,715,637
Country of Origin					
Taiwan	96,257	185,067	224,127	175,486	154,566
Japan	31,320	67,596	119,540	118,310	122,083
France	61,883	111,657	118,044	73,599	67,022
USA	102,892	152,176	57,515	43,171	40,409
UK	20,231	39,237	52,820	40,692	44,719
Hong Kong	16,845	24,223	21,133	14,918	10,696
Thailand	16,695	24,233	23,117	19,626	18,337
China	17,509	14,381	62,640	337,555	405,369
Overseas Vietnamese	152,672	194,055	261,300	196,907	272,157
Others	84,134	206,014	411,060	546,891	580,369
Purpose of visit					
Vacation	242,867	475,825	610,647	661,716	691,402
Business	141,004	263,420	308,015	364,896	403,175
Visiting friends/ relatives	141,368	210,064	202,694	273,784	371,849
Other	75,199	68,935	229,940	306,759	249,211
Domestic tourism	5,100,000	6,214,000	6,908,000	7,254,000	8,500,000

Source: VNAT (1998a)

The 1995 increase in arrivals for Vietnamese is probably due to the centenary celebrations for the birth of Ho Chi Minh, a revered figure in Vietnam.

Organisational structures of tourism

Burns and Holden (1995) have argued that if a useful understanding of tourism at a particular location or destination is to be developed, then tourism as a social and economic phenomenon must be analysed through a systems approach, whereby its inter-related parts are drawn together and made sense of. In the case of a centrally planned economy such as Vietnam, the central role of a national organisation for tourism cannot be ignored. The question of organisational and institutional arrangements is, in the case of Vietnam, a very delicate one. The official picture is that the Vietnam National Administration of Tourism (VNAT) represents the central government while at a provincial and local level, People's Committees are the administrative authority. People's Committees are involved in tourism through the ownership, management and operation of various tourism enterprises ranging from hotels to inbound tour operations. However, the local–national situation is more than this: relationships between VNAT and the provinces are thus complex and political. To put it bluntly, VNAT wants to 'own' tourism, and sees the local level as inefficient, ineffective and slowing down VNAT's ambitious goals (Personal communication, October, 1998).

The organisation and activities of each committee differ depending on the strength of tourism in the region. People's Committees in the larger tourist areas have established tourism departments that are responsible to the local People's Committee but liaise with VNAT on professional and national policy matters. In effect, the local People's Committee tourism departments are considered to be VNAT's provincial offices. VNAT must obtain local approval when designating tourism zones while local tourism departments will refer to VNAT for national tourism policy issues. However, given that VNAT has control over the senior tourism appointments at the local level, the decisions are almost certain to be skewed towards VNAT's priorities.

At the national level, the organisation for tourism is illustrated in Figure 17.1. It can be seen that state involvement is still a fundamentally important feature of hotel ownership patterns. This involvement is not only by VNAT but also the military, trade unions, and other government departments (for example, the largest hotel in Cua Lo is owned and run by the military). Privatisation is being discussed at both national and local levels but the government has been somewhat coy about reporting details and progress.

Nghe An Province

Nghe An province is located within one of the poorest areas of Vietnam: the north central coast, which is the third most impoverished region where 26.4 per cent of households are officially designated as "very poor" (defined as having an annual per capita income of less than US$60). Furthermore, 5.1 per cent of households are designated "extremely poor" (i.e. with less than US$36 per capita per year)

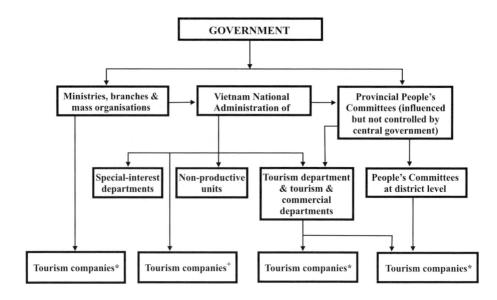

Notes:

* A total of 650 government owned companies, private companies, limited liability companies and joint ventures with foreign investment (including a large number of hotels)

+ 20 companies owned by the Vietnam National Administration of Tourism

Fig. 17.1 Vietnam tourism organization chart (1998)
Source: VNAT, 1998b

(UNDP, 1997:9). As the *doi moi* reforms (economic restructuring started in 1986) take effect, this level of poverty is being ameliorated as part of the macro reforms, which include rural roads/communications, focused assistance to ethnic groups, and development of rational micro-finance systems with particular emphasis on the role of women in development.

Table 17.2 contextualises the workforce showing that a large proportion of men and women (43 per cent) make their living directly from the land or sea, emphasising the rural nature of Cua Lo. The Nghe An Province People's Committee has identified four labour force priorities which will frame their future development actions:

- *continuing* social development;
- *reintegrating* complementary labour (including demobilising military conscripts);
- *helping* secondary and high school graduates who do not qualify for university; and
- *assisting* in the resettlement of returning overseas contract workers.

Table 17.2: Labour structure for Nghe An Province, 1998

Productive sectors	Men (18-60 years)	Women (18-55 years)	Total No.	%
Agricultural/forestry	4,303	4,148	8,451	20.00
Fisheries	5,120	4,880	10,000	23.00
Industry/construction	1,398	2,684	18,550	6.99
Services	5,378	8,052	19,948	31.08
Other	1,312	1,708	25,326	6.99
Unemployed	2,830	1,400	26,638	9.79
Total	20,341	22,872	29,468	97.85[a]

[a]percentages do not add due to rounding
Source: Nghe An Labour Department (1999)

It can be seen that these objectives are as much social as they are economic and this is a reflection of the priority given to social development by local and national authorities.

The provincial tourism department bears responsibility for initiating and co-ordinating labour force training and other issues within the context of the province's economic development. However, the structure of the provincial tourism department (shown in Figure 17.2) shows that it has little capacity to do this given that there is no dedicated official looking after human resource development. The Director is appointed by the Nghe An People's Committee Chairman in consultation with the VNAT. The Vice-Directors are appointed by the Nghe An People's Committee Chairman in consultation with the tourism department's Director. Thus it can be

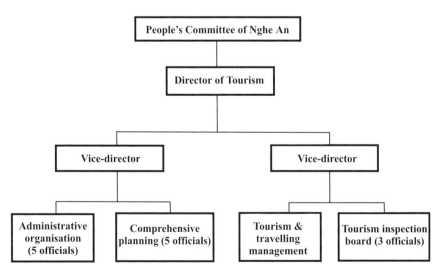

Fig. 17.2 Institutional arrangements for tourism in Nghe An Province
Source: Nghe An Labour Department, 1999

seen that the top three officials will almost certainly be under the direct influence of, or owe distinct allegiance to VNAT.

Cua Lo Town

The town of Cua Lo has three officials in its tourism department responsible for inspections and planning. The tourism product itself is geared towards the domestic market, including day-trippers. The major employers in the tourism sector are hotels, guesthouses and other accommodation. Other tourism related employment is in non-hotel restaurants, bars and other services (provision of deck chairs, hire of swimsuits etc.) in seasonal units on the beach, with small numbers in sea and ground transport, and retail property partly providing tourism services. Other tourism activities are very limited so that employment in travel agencies, local tour operations, recreational services, and tourist oriented shops that might be found in more economically advanced areas barely exists. Table 17.3 shows official data on tourism employment in Cua Lo.

The estimated number of employees in tourism, excluding seasonal employees, was 350 in 1995, rising to 450 and 500 in 1996 and 1997 respectively. These figures appear to be rounded approximations. Table 17.3 gives more precise data for 1998 with permanent staff reported as 696 and contract (seasonal) workers as 104 (Cua Lo Department of Employment, n.d.). Seasonal staff are drawn from both within the locality and outside. Even so, the data for seasonal staff appear to be low, not entirely in line with evidence gathered from the field research interviews and observations. There may be under-reporting of seasonal employment but the precise reason for this is difficult to ascertain. The seasonality of employment is a key issue for the local economy, but may, in a sense, be something of a Western construct in that local people develop a seasonal portfolio of employment that matches the ebb, flow and seasons of the rural economy (see later comment).

Officials perceive the lack of jobs during the rest of the year for local people as a problem. Populations stuck in a portfolio of seasonal work are unlikely to make significant economic progress and are almost certain to make no contribution to a tax base. The potential to draw in migrants seeking temporary employment is also a concern.

Table 17.3: Tourism employment in Cua Lo

Activity	Estimated jobs
Hotels and guesthouses:	
permanent workers	696
seasonal (contract) workers	104
Cua Lo public sector	100
Micro-enterprises/food stalls etc.	1,895
Total	2,795

Source: Cua Lo Department of Employment (n.d.)

The official data on contract employment shown in Table 17.3 indicate a seasonal increase of about 15 per cent to hotel employment. This was both for skilled and unskilled workers. However, interviews with hotel managers suggested that seasonal employment adds anything from 60 per cent to 100 per cent.

Within the accommodation sector, the 1998 staff:room ratio for Cua Lo was 0.7 while the staff:bed ratio was 0.3. These ratios are low compared to other parts of Southeast Asia and even within Vietnam. For example, the Friendship Hotel in Vinh City has a ratio of 1.2 (90 staff/75 rooms); the Daewoo Hotel in Hanoi has a 1.5 ratio (640 staff/411 rooms in 1998). The large proportion of simple government and guesthouse accommodation and the generally low occupancy rates explains the low staffing situation in Cua Lo. This latter point is a statistical paradox that reflects the short season of tourism activity (not much longer than three months). The implications from these data are that while low-investment entrepreneurship creates opportunities for families (especially in rural areas where paid employment is scarce), it is large and complex projects such as five-star resorts or city hotels that provide significant employment. Furthermore, this employment will add value to the general labour pool because of the highly skilled and technical nature of operations in large hotels (including engineering, accountancy, marketing as well as the range of food and beverage jobs). Efforts towards local participation in planning should reflect these realities and both sides of the argument need to be understood. Put simply, small-scale development will enable local people to retain control over parts of the destination tourism system but will not provide high levels of employment and will not add value to the national labour force through an enlarged and enhanced skills pool. On the other hand, while big projects will provide large numbers of jobs, local control will almost certainly be in the hands of outsiders (Burns and Holden, 1995).

Micro-enterprises and female-headed households in Cua Lo

As with many countries struggling for economic independence whilst the economy is still structured around subsistence farming, the role of women as entrepreneurs is extremely important. During the short tourist season, within the town of Cua Lo, local agricultural and fishing families set up micro-enterprises in the form of temporary sidewalk cafés and stalls. In 1998, there were 203 sidewalk operations and 176 pitches on the beach employing almost 1,900 people (Cua Lo Department of Employment, n.d.). No particular skills are required for this activity beyond average household skills such as cleaning, serving and cooking. These are typical of many food-based micro-enterprises in South and Southeast Asia in that they require minimal investment and are distinctly family affairs.

At one level, the micro-enterprises might be termed low productivity enterprises. However, they provide an important safety net for those without formal education or with social reasons (such as family obligations) that exclude them from employment in the formal sector. Observations during the fieldwork indicated that most of these businesses were run by women, accompanied by children (men were not much in evidence). A research survey was not possible during the time-constrained visit, but informal conversations through a translator indicated that many of the women were the supporting figure in what are termed female-headed households. In a way, it might be concluded that these entrepreneurial women are side-stepping the problem of allocating resources and loans to the very poor. However, it might also be said that they are unlikely to step beyond their marginal economic activity given the relatively low gross income of micro-enterprises. These businesses and these women remain largely unconnected with the 'world out there'. That being said, there is little evidence that on a national or local level, women are being excluded from technical training. However, the age-old problem of traditional gender obligations does impact on the women's ability to be integrated into the economic mainstream.

The local authorities including the Cua Lo tourism office seem to take a benign attitude towards the micro-enterprises. They are unlicensed and not strictly legal, yet seem to remain free from harassment. Having discussed issues of employment and business at the localised level within the context of the broader national situation, I now turn to examining some of the issues arising.

Discussion

This chapter started with a mention of Murphy's (1985) approach to community participation. It was suggested that this model was rooted in a Western paradigm but has been portrayed as being a sort of 'normal' approach. This brief peep behind the disintegrating bamboo curtain has revealed that definitions and perceptions of community have no 'normal' bedrock, but are social constructions bounded by the politics of place, space and time. For example, community participation in Vietnam is often in the context of development that is supposed to prevent at least some of the probable causes of continued poverty in various parts of the country including:

- *isolation*: geographic, linguistic, social and intellectual;
- *inability to manage risks*: such as typhoons, flooding, pests, illness, unplanned births, price fluctuations;
- *lack of access*: to resources such as land, credit, technology, useful information;
- *inadequate participation*: in the planning and implementation of government programmes; and
- lack of sustainability: both financial and environmental.

Although the above are regional and national factors, evidence from the fieldwork suggests that each of these issues impacts upon life and participation in democratic processes in Cua Lo Town in one way or another. For example, insofar as isolation is concerned, the rail link with Hanoi is both slow and unreliable, the road is slow, and the local airport has safety problems that mitigate against its opening. Poverty and subsistence living means that local people cannot plan against events (such as price rises or changing weather patterns) taking place at a global level. Enterprise is stifled due to a generalised lack of access to micro-financing, especially for small-scale tourism projects that lie outside VNAT's grand plans.

The following model (Figure 17.3) tentatively suggests one interpretation of the relationship between the global and the local in Vietnam. It shows how tourism planning is affected by at least two of the five factors listed above (lack of access to useful information and inadequate participation in planning and implementation of government programmes).

Item 1 (Global Inputs), takes account of a number of ways in which VNAT is connected with the 'world out there'. Officials attend all the major tourism trade fairs (for example, London, Berlin, Madrid) and have a steady stream of contact with foreign consultants, business opportunists and educators ensuring a steady and fairly consistent exchange of information. Items 2 and 3 (VNAT) illustrate the pivotal role of VNAT in gathering and distributing knowledge. VNAT is the technical gate-keeper of knowledge, controlling the flow of knowledge to the provinces. Item 4 (Cua Lo) shows that those involved in tourism in Cua Lo are effectively excluded

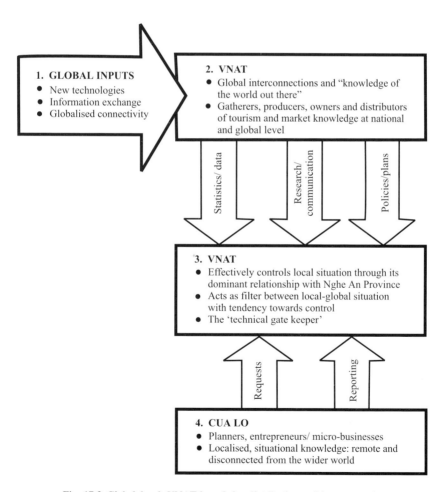

Fig. 17.3 Global–local, VNAT knowledge distribution and interconnections

from global–local interconnections through the powerful hand of VNAT. As such, the town remains disconnected.

While it is quite clear that the ideas collected together as Figure 17.3 could be considerably enhanced through further fieldwork, certain preliminary deductions may be intuited. For example, there is very little 'new knowledge' being generated or entering the tourism system. The flow of information is one way and it is filtered so as to reinforce the dominant position of VNAT (i.e. knowledge of 'the world out there' is generated and owned by VNAT which gathers intelligence through its international and pan-national activities). These data are then passed through information channels 'owned' by VNAT and through 'its' (VNAT's) people to the various provinces. This may impact negatively on product development by stifling locally-based innovation. This structure thus reinforces the current system and, it might even be argued, dilutes whatever quality that exists. This closed loop of knowledge will have unintentional negative impacts on product development (as mentioned above) and from a development perspective, it reinforces the current tourism system which has not demonstrated a capacity to tackle poverty.

The original question raised in this chapter concerned participation and democracy in planning. If we take the original meaning of 'democratic' to mean 'rule by the people', it might be argued that planning under Vietnam's communist system is no less democratic than planning in some other countries. In India, for example, the most senior tourism technocrats in some states are members of the elite Indian Civil Service (ICS) and appointed by the Government of India (GOI). In the United Kingdom, planning permission for out of town mega-developments or roads refused in the light of popular resistance is regularly reversed in long, expensive legal battles where the power of the large corporation or government has both the finance and stamina to push through their ideas. For example, development of a huge multi-screen cinema in Crystal Palace in the south London suburb of Sydenham has been rejected time and time again by local people (including protest sit-ins and violent disorder), but the local borough council has given in to the wishes of the developer.

Even though local communities are isolated in many ways, what the system of People's Committees in Vietnam appears to do is to try to understand the central concerns of such local communities and where the knowledge gaps are. Party members are expected to take part in local discussions, though further evidence of the effectiveness of their participation and whether or not they can actually stop something VNAT wants to push ahead is lacking. Based on lengthy interviews with local and regional tourism officials, several generalised themes emerge as reflecting VNAT's attitude towards the provinces and People's Committees. First, concerns have been raised about mutual respect between 'host' and 'guest'. Is this possible, or is the relationship flawed by inequality? VNAT does not appear to be particularly interested in pursuing this line of enquiry for while 'global' knowledge exists about social impacts of tourism at a local level, this type of specialised data is not sent down to local People's Committees.

Second, a gap appears to exist because the VNAT is not particularly interested in the culture/nature of the local industry. For example, it is not interested in knowing when and how the local tourism industry began, nor its stages of development. VNAT's knowledge does not extend beyond promoting particular programmes or developments (such as large-scale hotels). Third, with regard to structure and organisation of the industry, it is again difficult to see the sustained effort of VNAT in shaping the future industry to ensure its ownership patterns remain local and that tourism is making sufficient contribution towards poverty alleviation. It is, however, quite clear that VNAT understands very well tourism and the national economy. Officials know about investment levels (especially direct foreign investment) and indeed, are actively promoting investment opportunities through their presence at various international forums and travel trade shows.

Conclusions

There are certain contradictions in this chapter, but in a very real sense these reflect the current state of flux in Vietnam. VNAT is still working out its relationships/ interconnections with the variety of localised agencies in the country. Table 17.4 is an attempt to codify some of the issues raised by local people (entrepreneurs, citizens, officials) made during the fieldwork, a categorisation of matters and themes that have been raised on a number of occasions.

Referring back to the *doi moi* (political and economic renovation/renewal) mentioned earlier in this chapter, tourism is making a contribution to the *doi moi* fundamentals:

- *decentralisation*: attempting to shift tourism planning to a local level through the local People's Committees will help the shift towards easing central control (though beware replacing a national gerontocracy (rule by the elderly) with a local oligarchy!);
- *multi-sector economy*: tourism has attracted private investment and entrepreneurship which will contribute towards the deinstitutionalisation of the economy (though this is particularly difficult in a communist country where economics is embedded into social institutions to an extent where its separate analysis is difficult);

Table 17.4: Characteristics of local concerns

Cui Bono (who benefits)	• What is the level of investment and what are the benefits and costs? • How can the interconnections between local–global bring equitable distribution of benefits?
Economic development	• How can this be differentiated from economic enlargement (i.e., development without progress)? • What are the most effective approaches to people-centred development? (i.e., global ideas working at a local level)
Impacts on the cultural environment	• How can better communication and interconnections bring about positive benefits to local culture? • Are there specific changes to culture and society bought about by tourism that need special monitoring and public awareness?
Impacts on the natural and built environment	• How can tourism be used as a tool for environmental awareness and conservation? • How can touristic consumption of the natural environment benefit local people?

- *democracy*: while not specific to Vietnam, there is little doubt that international tourism, as a global social phenomenon, assists the passage towards more openness through exposure of oligarchic regimes to external view and criticism (though a shift towards democracy as defined by the West is somewhat ironic given the inequalities inherent in global capitalism); and
- *foreign relations:* the notion of "amiable relations for peace, independence and development" can be strengthened through international tourism (although it might be argued that industrial-scale tourism in developing countries tends to be dominated by foreign enterprises which may, in effect, distort development and create dependency) (Burns, 1999a).

From the above list, it may be seen that tourism is making a contribution to Vietnam's development even though the positive aspects are balanced by some important caveats.

In summary, tourism planning involving local–global connections is framed by something of a 'chicken and egg' or 'Catch 22' situation. For the most part, the Cua Lo People's Committee does not have the technical capacity or educational infrastructure to deliver specific tourism plans or recommendations while at the same time, it feels obliged to plan at the local level so as to fulfil Vietnam's political ideal of popular power. VNAT, in an unusually participative manner, acknowledged that something needs to happen to break the deadlock at the local level. In practical terms, this means an injection of 'know-how' from outside. However, this brings along the danger that interconnections will be characterised by an external agenda: usually a focus on markets, supply-side development and development as an accidental spin-off from tourism (Burns, 1999b). There have been certain unresolved paradoxes and contradictions in this chapter for which I make no apology: such is the nature of writing about the complexities of Vietnam.

In order to further investigate the notion of interconnections, the next stage of research should be to examine the interaction of the global (hyper-mobile capital; producer-driven commodity chains controlled by the core; inequalities whereby economic globalisation does not mean economic homogenisation; the increasing irrelevance of the state) and the *local* (class; consumers; social institutions; power relationships) with the purpose of developing some new assumptions about power, tourism, and its socio-economic potential.

This chapter started with the premise that local culture is considered a prime resource for global tourism. While the particular issue of culture was not pursued (the opening sentence was making a point about why tourists are interested in the 'local'), the point about interconnections was explored through an examination of the power relationship between VNAT and the People's Committee at a very localised situation: the town of Cua Lo. It was argued that democracy remains a social construct with more than one interpretation. Finally, it was suggested that while tourism is making a definite contribution towards the national goals of *doi moi* (which are, in a very real sense, also international goals!), strengthening localised interconnections (local–national) and developing interconnections at an international level (national–global) are hampered by the centralising characteristics of the existing political culture.

References

Burns, P. (1999a) *An Introduction to Tourism and Anthropology*. London: Routledge.

Burns, P. (1999b) 'Paradoxes in planning: Tourism elitism or brutalism?'. *Annals of Tourism Research,* 26(2), 329–40.

Burns, P. and Holden, A. (1995) *Tourism: A New Perspective*. Englewood Cliffs: Prentice Hall.

Cua Lo Department of Employment (n.d.) *Annual Labour Report*. Vinh City: Cua Lo People's Committee.

Doswell, R. (1997) *Tourism. How Effective Management Makes a Difference*. Oxford: Butterworth-Heinemann.

In Focus (passim) Quarterly journal of Tourism Concerns, published in London since 1991.

Isaak, R. (1995) *Managing World Economic Change: International Political Economy*. Englewood Cliffs: Prentice Hall.

Kiely, R. and Marfleet, P. (eds.) (1998) *Globalisation and the Third World*. London: Routledge.

Lavigne, M. (1995) *The Economics of Transition: From Socialist Economy to Market Economy*. Basingstoke: Macmillan.

Laws, E. (1995) *Tourism Destination Management: Issues, Analysis and Policies*. London and New York: Routledge.

Murphy, P. (1985) *Tourism: A Community Approach*. New York and London: Routledge.

Narotzky, S. (1997) *New Directions in Economic Anthropology*. London: Pluto Press.

Nghe An Labour Department (1999) *Annual Statistical Report*. Vinh City: Nghe An People's Committee.

Stubbs, R. and Underhill, G. (eds.) (1994) *Political Economy and the Changing Global Order*. Basingstoke: Macmillan.

Thayer, C. (1994) 'Renovation and Vietnamese society: The changing roles of government and administration', *Proceedings of Vietnam's Economic Renovation: Policy and Performance*, 19–21 September 1990. Canberra: Australian National University. Online. Available ftp://coombs.anu.edu.au/coombspapers/othes/politics/vietnam-doi-moi-renovation.txt (2 April 2000).

Todaro, M. (1997) *Economic Development*, 6th edition. Harlow: Addison Wesley Longman.

United Nations Development Programme (UNDP) (1995) *Poverty Elimination in Vietnam*. Hanoi: UNDP.

UNDP (1997) *Some Lessons Learned in Supporting the Transition from Poverty to Prosperity*, UNDP Staff Paper. Hanoi: UNDP.

UNDP (1998) *East Asia: From Miracle to Crisis, Lessons for Vietnam*, UNDP Staff Paper. Hanoi: UNDP.

UNDP (1999) *Annual Human Development Report for 1998*. New York: UNDP.

Vietnam National Administration of Tourism (VNAT) (1998a) *Annual Statistical Report*. Hanoi: VNAT.

VNAT (1998b) *The Vietnam Tourist Book*. Hanoi: VNAT.

18

Bali and Beyond: Locational Effects on the Economic Impact of Tourism

Wiendu Nuryanti

The role of Bali in Indonesia's regional framework

This chapter explores the role of Bali as a tourism gateway into other tourist regions within Indonesia. It does so as part of a larger research to understand the role of a given tourism destination location and the characteristics of accessibility within the context of regional development.

Unquestionably, Bali is Indonesia's most important tourist destination. In fact, for much of the potential visitor market from Asia, Europe or North America, Bali has a stronger image as a destination than Indonesia itself. In state planning, Bali is positioned as an important connector to other regions of Indonesia, besides its own importance as a destination attracting 1.2 million visitors in 1997 (Directorate General of Tourism (DGT), 1997).

In terms of performance, tourism has fared well for the country as a whole. From tenth place among the top ten destinations in Asia Pacific in 1990, it went up to sixth place by 1997 with some 5 million international arrivals prior to the economic and social crisis that swept Southeast Asia ((World Tourism Organisation) WTO, 1996). By the end of 1997, however, Indonesia was surpassed as a destination by China (23.7 million arrivals), Hong Kong (10.4 million), Thailand (7.2 million) and Singapore (6.5 million). It should be noted that travel by air is the only effective access by international visitors to Indonesia, an archipelago with some 17,000 islands, unlike those other destinations where access by land is a vital factor for tourism's success.

The connector role that Bali is perceived to have is predicated on the infrastructure networks built by the former colonial regime of Indonesia. These networks enabled many economic linkages and allowed for the exploitation of resources in different parts of Java, Bali included. This historical background is also responsible for the modern importance of Bali as a tourism destination in Indonesia.

Therefore, from a very early time, infrastructure in terms of accessibility has been a central concept in understanding the spectrum of levels in tourism development within Indonesia.

When the first national plan for development began in an independent Indonesia in the late 1960s, it was argued that Bali would be Indonesia's best tourism 'asset' given its long exposure to the outside world and its image in Western culture as a mystical, exotic destination. Government policy dictated that Bali would become Indonesia's 'show window' to the world (Picard, 1996:39). In addition, the lessons learnt from the growth of tourism in Bali would enable it to be used as a model for future tourism development throughout the archipelago. This concept of Bali's dual role – as a primary destination and also as a development model – was to become the foundation for a national tourism policy that would prevail in subsequent decades of government planning in Indonesia.

For a variety of reasons which space prevents elaboration on in this chapter, Bali has remained the anchor of Indonesian tourism over the last three decades. Its unique combination of resources and attractions has given it the title of the Arts & Entertainment (A&E) television network's No. 1 tropical destination in the world (the programme was aired on cable television on 25 March 2000). The Indonesian government has tried to develop other regions for tourism by using Bali as a core attraction as well as a gateway, attempting to persuade visitors to explore places close by. Slogans such as 'Bali and Beyond' and 'Bali Plus' became the centre-pieces of marketing efforts in the 1980s and 1990s that would turn Bali into a platform from which tourism would reach other regions in Indonesia. This chapter will review the creditability of this notion, given the implications of distance and access within the Indonesian archipelago.

From an economic point of view, where tourism acts in a demand–supply relationship, there are three important aspects involved: tourism as a flow of income, trade and foreign exchange. The tourism supply–demand relationship requires resource allocations and by accepted definition, involves physical movement outside habitual living spaces. From a tourism product viewpoint, the image of tourism destinations in Indonesia may be described as being dominated by Bali, followed in second place by Java for its cultural monuments and striking landscapes. So-called 'special interest types' of tourism such as marine tourism or ecotourism products dominate the remainder of destinations in the country. The types of fragile resources involved in these special interest tourism products are found in the less developed regions of Indonesia. These include regions containing tropical forests, wildlife and marine resources in the eastern parts of Indonesia, as well as cultural-ethnic tourism potentials in many rural villages throughout the country.

The main problem associated with these types of tourism products is that they are in low volume and that they tend to be associated with subsistence levels of development, fragile environments and remoteness. The areas in Indonesia that reflect this profile include East, Central, South and West Kalimantan, Irian Jaya, Maluku, North and Southeast Sulawesi. These are regions characterised not only by low GRDP (Gross Regional Development Product) per capita (averaging 0.08 compared to the national mean of 0.97) but also low hotel value added per capita and low accessibility.

The vulnerability of these regions to external pressures such as tourism can be explained as follows (Nuryanti, 1998):

- their lower GRDP indicates that their natural and cultural assets are not easily available and they need better accessibility to gain wider appeal;
- the low populations found in these regions tend to be associated with low availability of human resources both in terms of quantity and skills. It should be noted that the total combined population of these regions represents only 5 per cent of the population of Indonesia as a whole; and
- these regions also generate the lowest *domestic* tourism activities, a pre-condition for international tourism. Without economies of scale and sectoral linkages, they can scarcely graduate to become an international attraction.

The importance of tourism as an external linkage contributing to changes in the sociocultural and economic structures of countries is therefore apparent. The scale of this phenomenon is shown in the amount of space that the literature devotes to the impacts of tourism in national development for a country as a whole (Bull, 1991). However, relatively little research to date has focused on the impacts of tourism in *regional* development.

In the past few decades of intensive development work around the world, the principle of regional development has emerged as an important strategy for countries to attempt to balance the social as well as economic inequalities typically found in almost every country. The broadening of the concept of development (both as a process and a state) away from only narrow considerations of economic growth to encompass wider economic, environmental and social concerns has contributed to enrich the range of definitions of the term (Pearce, 1989). Regional development has traditionally been considered to be a process that operates with two complementary characteristics. First, there is linkage with the exterior (or external linkages), including flows of goods, services, capital, information and foreign exchange earnings. Second, there is the internal differentiation or internal structural change reflecting a country's capacity to process the external linkages through such aspects as skills improvement in the workforce and organisational development in the public and private sectors (Young, 1966; Capener *et al.*, 1969). Regional development, therefore, may be considered to be a function of the interplay between these external and internal linkages.

Location, accessibility and interconnections

Tourism is a unique phenomenon compared to other consumer exports because of the all-important fact that tourists (consumers) must travel to the location of the destination in order to consume its product. It therefore places itself as a possible tool for regional development, a notion that is not lost to the Indonesian government.

Although the effect of distance on movement is recognised intuitively in a variety of fields, Losch's (1954) work was the first introduction of a spatial dimension into an economic framework. Losch saw fundamental parallels between biological and economic forms and his theory suggests that natural events reach their goal by the shortest possible route. In the field of physics, it appears for the first time in the eighteenth century with the principle of least action. In the twentieth century, it shows up in systems analysis as the concept of minimum potential energy, and it is also discussed in the social sciences as the principle of least efforts (Isard, 1979).

It is within this framework that the concept of mobility in tourism has been approached, using Bali as a study area within the context of the regional systems of Indonesia. The role of a given location of a tourism destination and the characteristics of accessibility within the context of regional development are essential elements of this research.

There are three basic determinants involved – the structure of consumer preferences, the economic potential of a given location (destination), and the characteristics of accessibility (Vickerman, 1975). The characteristics of accessibility, the thrust of analysis in this chapter, are represented by the *opportunity* cost of time and money involved in the travel distance. In a tourism context, this may be termed the 'economic distance'.

Economic distance in this chapter is represented by an index of accessibility within the various regional economic structures. The level of accessibility between regions is calculated based on the following formula:

$$\text{Access(ij)} = \frac{\{(Tm_{ij} + Tc_{ij}) \times F_{ij}\} \times \{(Tm_{ji} + Tc_{ji}) \times F_{ji}\}}{(F_{ij} + F_{ji})}$$

where:

Access (ij)	is the accessibility level between region ij and ji
Tm(ij)-ji	the sum of travel times of each mode in the network (e.g. total flight times) from region ij and ji
Tc(ij)-ji	is the sum of times of the connection between network ij and ji
F(ij)-ji	frequency between region ij and ji.

The price distance is calculated in each region by multiplying the total number of tourists who visited the region by the average air ticket price to the region from each of the five main international air gateways (Jakarta, Bali, Medan, Surabaya, and Manado). The result is then divided by the total number of tourists who entered the five gateways.

In order to be able to put this into a scale, a price index was calculated from the price distances obtained in order to reflect the level of accessibility for each region. The price index was then calculated in an inverse relationship by dividing the results of each price distance into one and multiplying by 1,000 to obtain a manageable number. The calculations work within practical difficulties such as measurement problems of regional accessibility and economic potential at the regional level, the difficulties coming from the absence of complete data.

Vickerman (1995) states that the economics of location depend on two inter-related features: the existence of increasing returns and the differentiation of travel time and costs within regions. The research reported in this chapter investigated whether variations in location or accessibility between regions (using Bali as an example) can be a cause of the variations in tourism performance, as shown by multiplier effects. Accessibility has generally been defined as some measure of spatial separation of human activities. Essentially it denotes the ease or difficulty with which activities may be reached from a given location using a particular transportation system (Morris, Dumble and Wigan, 1979).

Several broad applications of accessibility indicators may be identified, including evaluation of the travel choice as well as measures of the trip distribution system. When analysing tourism, measures such as *time* and *cost*, which determine network quality and performances, seem more appropriate than measures of network distance only in terms of simple geographical or physical distance.

Clearly, the operational effect of distance is not therefore directly proportional to the unit distance (e.g. airline miles) because it is not only mileage that affects the concept of distance. There is a tendency to underestimate the impact of distance because distance decay can occur. Distance decay or the friction of distance effect – meaning the accumulated effect of distance on attractiveness of a given destination – will vary depending on the particular flows being examined (Morris, Dumble and Wigan, 1979; Haynes and Fotheringham, 1984; Bull, 1991).

Accessibility, within a tourism context, therefore, becomes an even more important indicator because it provides a useful analytical tool in explaining consumer demand in relation to the time and price of the trip distribution pattern. For example, the cost per mile of travelling may decrease with distance. A plane ticket from Jakarta to Bali may be only two-thirds the cost of a ticket from Jakarta to Irian Jaya, although the actual distance between the two points is three times greater.

However, there are other important factors that affect trip decision-making besides distance – these include vital elements such as cost, amount of travel time, convenience, comfort, safety, status and so forth. For some market segments, travel in itself may have a high attractiveness as it offers enjoyment of the point-to-point journey which can be a form of pleasurable experience rather than simply transport. This may be significant especially for special interest tourists who tend to search for more meaningful experiences during their journeys. Therefore, there is no reason why accessibility should not also vary between trip purposes and motivation.

Inter-regional tourism system

In the tourism context where consumers have to come to the production site in order to consume the product, the location factor regarding any destination is vital. The location reflects a complex relationship involving consumer production, consumer markets and inter-regional differentiation. Location is also affected by interconnection factors in terms of access, economies of scale of operation, and concentration.

In tourism studies in developing countries, the concept of an inter-regional system which emphasises the concept of 'core and periphery' has been used extensively regarding both studies of international tourism (Friedmann, 1966; Frank, 1969; Ibbery, 1984; Ecumenical Coalition on Third World Tourism (ECTWT), 1988; Lea, 1988) as well as domestic tourism scales (Weaver, 1998). Typically within this concept, tourism is interpreted as the post-colonial or post-industrial equivalent of exploitation by some form of 'international force' of another country's resources and spaces.

In the inter-regional tourism system, we can see that the economic objective for the destination country is to increase its share of income, employment and so forth, while for the tourism industry it is principally to increase profits. The political objective for the destination country is that it should have better control over the use of local resources. Hence, given these varied stakeholders and motivations, the role of the state or government as a mediating structure becomes very important. Also, the complexities of the inter-regional relationship among different regions often result in significant inter-regional disparities in terms of position, population and power. Such inter-regional imbalances have not received enough attention within tourism studies or at a policy level by governments in developing countries (exceptions include Conlin and Baum, 1995; Briguglio *et al.*, 1996).

According to Weaver (1998), the involvement of inter-regional tourism regions is not clear-cut or obvious when it comes to issues such as facilitation or restrictions in the fields of foreign investment, tourist entries and effective control over tourism policy. Often, these external influences act as a 'broker' or as external foci dealing with cores within the destination country. This also affects operational issues such as quality standards within the destination's core as well as periphery. It has to be acknowledged that this relationship between external foci, internal core, and periphery is a tangled one where it is often difficult to separate clearly fields of control and influence.

To illustrate this disparity, small island states and dependencies which are located mainly within developing countries (and are defined as having less than 3 million residents and a land mass of less than 28,000 sq km) account for only about 0.3 per cent of the global population, but receive approximately 4.6 per cent of all international visitors (WTO, 1996). In the case of Indonesia, more than 60 per cent of international tourists visit less than 0.3 per cent of the total landmass of Indonesia – only some 6,000 sq km. In contrast, regarding tourist expenditures, this tiny percentage of the land generates more than 61 per cent of the total. For instance, in 1997, Bali alone received some 25 per cent of the total number of overseas visitors to Indonesia – 1.2 million out of a total of 5.2 million.

Furthermore, that 0.3 per cent of land is accessible within two hours average travel time from Bali makes the island very appealing as a gateway. This illustration clearly shows the instances of regional subordinate-dominant systems, where tourism has functioned as a centrifugal force reflecting the core-periphery relationship of Bali with other regions.

Economic multipliers and interconnections

As is well known, the principal concept underlying tourism multipliers is based on the recognition that the various sectors that make up any economy are interdependent. Multiplier analysis and values are important indicators of the overall economic impact within pre-defined regions brought about by a change in the level of external demand. Therefore, any change in the level of tourist expenditure by visitors from outside the local economy will not only affect the industry which produces the final goods but also the industry's suppliers and so forth, right through the economic chain within and between regional systems.

Multiplier values will vary from region to region depending on different factors such as the level of regional development, the level of diversification in the regional economy and various socio-cultural aspects related to regional development. The complexities of multiplier analysis depend on the intricate transactions taking place between economic sectors in each region.

Tourism, in contrast to most other large-scale and export industries, is not recognised as a separate industry by widely used international data analysis tools such as *Industry Classification Standards.* This is due to the fact that tourism by its very nature has a highly inter-sectoral dimension in its economic transactions. Therefore the sectoral transaction data which are used in the multiplier calculation for tourism are normally categorised into three different groups of transactions: accommodation/hotels and restaurants; transportation; and goods and services including souvenirs.

Any change in regional tourist expenditure brings about a change in the regional economy's level of output, income, employment, government revenue and foreign exchange flows which may be greater than, equal to or less than the value of the initial change. The ratio of the change in one of the above variables to the change in the final demand (tourist expenditure) which brought it about is known as the *multiplier.*

Therefore, there will be a value given for an output multiplier, income multiplier, employment multiplier, government revenue multiplier and foreign exchange multiplier. The technique employed in this research is *input–output analysis,* which is a method by which the flow of production can be traced among the various sectors of the economy through the changes in final demand or exports.

Input–output analysis involves the construction of a table, analogous to a table of national/regional accounts, which shows the economy of the country or region in matrix form. Each industrial, commercial and service sector of the economy is shown first in column form as a purchaser of goods and services from other sectors and second as a row where its sales to each of the other sectors are listed (Table 18.1). The basic structure of input–output transaction tables can be subdivided into four quadrants (Archer, 1977; Fletcher, 1989; Archer and Fletcher, 1990):

Quadrant A	Quadrant B
Quadrant C	Quadrant D

Quadrant A is a matrix of inter-industry transaction flows. The economy is disaggregated into homogeneous productive sectors and the rows of Quadrant A represent the sales of intermediate goods and services from each sector to each other sector of the economy. Therefore the columns of Quadrant A show the purchases that each sector makes from each of the other sectors. Quadrant B is a matrix of primary inputs for each of the productive sectors listed in Quadrant A. For instance, the rows of Quadrant B will represent factors such as salaries, profits, taxation and imports. Therefore, the columns demonstrate the purchases of each of these factors by the productive sectors listed in Quadrant A. Quadrant C is a matrix of final demand. The columns of this quadrant will represent the purchases of the government, households, capital and exports from each of the productive sectors. By definition, the rows of Quadrant C show the sales of each of the productive sectors to

Table 18.1 A basic input–output transaction table

		Intermediate Demand						Final Demand of Good & Service				
	Sales To	Productive Sectors						Final Demand Sectors				
	Purchases From	Industry										
		1	2	.	. . . .	m		H	I	G	E	
Productive Sectors	Industry 1	X_{11}	X_{12}	.	. . . .	X_{1m}		C_1	I_1	G_1	E_1	X_1
	Industry 2	X_{21}	X_{22}	.	. . . .	X_{2m}		C_2	I_2	G_2	E_2	X_2
	Industry 3	X_{31}	X_{32}	.	. . . .	X_{3m}		C_3	I_3	G_3	E_3	X_3
	.	.	.	.	. . . . .			.	.	.	.	.
	.	.	.	.	. . . . .			.	.	.	.	.
	.	.	.	.	. . . . .			.	.	.	.	.
	.	.	.	.	. . . . .			.	.	.	.	.
	Industry m	X_{m1}	X_{m2}	.	. . . .	X_{mm}		C_m	I_m	G_m	E_m	X_m
Primary Inputs	Wages & Salaries	W_1	W_2	.	. . . .	W_m		W_C	W_I	W_G	W_E	W
	Profits & Dividends	P_1	P_2	.	. . . .	P_m		P_C	P_I	P_G	P_E	P
	Taxes	T_1	T_2	.	. . . .	T_m		T_C	T_I	T_G	T_E	T
	Imports	M_1	M_2	.	. . . .	M_m		M_C	M_I	M_G	M_E	M
	Total Input (Purchases)	X_1	X_2	.	. . . .	X_m		C	I	G	E	X

where: X = Output
        C = Consumption (household)
        I = Investment (private)
        G = Government expenditure
        E = Exports
        M = Imports
        W = Wages & Salaries
        P = Profits & Dividends
        T = Taxes

FINAL DEMAND SECTORS
H = Household consumption sector
I = Investment expenditure sector
G = Government expenditure sector
E = Exports sector

each category of final demand. Quadrant D is a matrix which shows the purchase of primary inputs by each of the categories of final demand. Therefore, goods and services which are imported for re-exportation would be entered in the import row of the export column in Quadrant D. The table has three main sections:

- The primary input quadrant which shows how each productive sector purchases its labour, imports goods and services, and the taxes it pays to the government on profits generated from its business activity;
- the productive sector quadrant which demonstrates how each industrial sector buys from/sells to each other industrial sector; and
- the final demand quadrant which shows how each of the various elements of final demand purchases from each of the productive sectors.

The transaction table may be then described algebraically as:

$$X_i = \sum_{j=1}^{n} x_{ij} + Y_i$$

where: X_i = the total output of the *i*th industry;
            x_{ij} = sales of industry I to industry j;
            Y_i = final demand for industry i.

The essence of this simplification model is that the basic economy is shown within the A matrix and that all other sectors are treated as an exogenous power of the basic economy. By the use of simple matrix algebra, it is possible to trace the flow of additional tourist expenditure through the economy. Tourism's impact on each sector, as well as the amount of income, public sector revenue and imports are monitored. The main concept of the input–output method is based on the recognition that the various sectors that make up the economy are interdependent. The focus upon the sectoral interdependencies represents the comprehensive nature of actual inter-sectoral transactions that exist within the real economy. The input–output model also has the ability to analyse the *total* economic impact of tourism throughout the economy – that is, its direct, indirect and induced effects.

The input–output analysis in this chapter used Indonesia's national input–output tables accompanied by 27 input–output tables established at the regional level, of which three are main cities and the remainder, provinces (Biro Pusat Statistik (BPS), 1986–1994; 1990; 1995a; 1995b; 1995c; 1995d; 1995e). Though the regional tables are less sophisticated in technical detail and accuracy compared to the national one, they can still be used in constructing regional models. Using this method, it is possible to determine the impact of change in international tourist expenditures by tracing the flow of additional tourist expenditure through the economy. The method also enables us to study the impact tourism expenditures have on each sector, as well as the amount of income, government revenue and imports created at each round of transactions. The result of the calculation is shown in the total income multiplier values (Figure 18.1).

Using data collected from 27 provinces in Indonesia, a regression analysis of income multipliers on price distance was carried out (Nuryanti, 1998). An important finding from this analysis is that when the price index increases (which means the price distance decreases), the total income multiplier values increase (Figure 18.2). In other words, the further the regions move economically from the centre, the lower the total income values generated by tourists in the regions.

The contribution of tourism to regional development involves a number of factors. One of the most important indicators is the pattern of tourism multipliers – its direct, indirect and induced impacts on income, employment, and output. In this context, the concept of regional interconnections is revealed through the effects of tourism on regional development using the link between income multiplier values and spatial interaction.

Besides the input–output model, the *gravity model* was also used to help determine the effect of location on tourism multipliers on the regional economies of Indonesia. The gravity model, one of the most productive borrowings from physical science, has

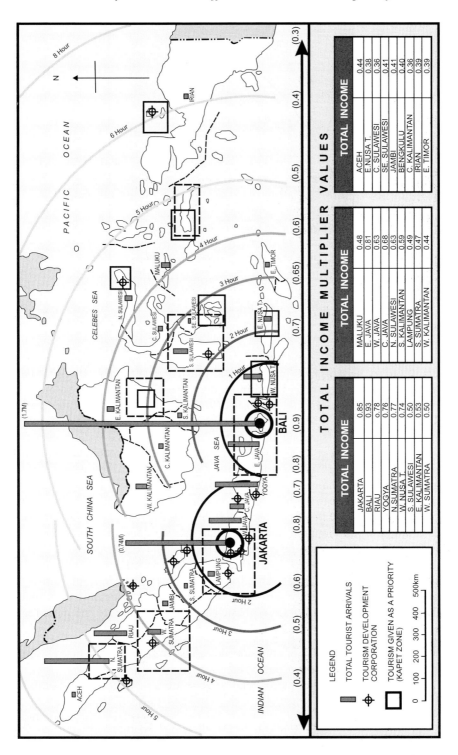

Fig. 18.1 Gradation multiplier values by location

TOTAL INCOME MULTIPLIER VALUES

TOTAL INCOME			TOTAL INCOME			TOTAL INCOME	
JAKARTA	0.85		MALUKU	0.48		ACEH	0.44
BALI	0.93		E. JAVA	0.81		E. NUSA T.	0.38
RIAU	0.78		W. JAVA	0.63		C. SULAWESI	0.36
YOGYA	0.76		C. JAVA	0.68		SE. SULAWESI	0.41
N.SUMATRA	0.77		N. SULAWESI	0.63		JAMBI	0.41
W. NUSA T.	0.74		S. KALIMANTAN	0.59		BENGKULU	0.40
S. SULAWESI	0.50		LAMPUNG	0.49		C. KALIMANTAN	0.36
E. KALIMANTAN	0.53		S. SUMATRA	0.47		IRIAN	0.39
W. SUMATRA	0.50		W. KALIMANTAN	0.44		E. TIMOR	0.39

LEGEND

■ TOTAL TOURIST ARRIVALS

✛ TOURISM DEVELOPMENT CORPORATION

□ TOURISM GIVEN AS A PRIORITY (KAPET ZONE)

0 100 200 300 400 500km

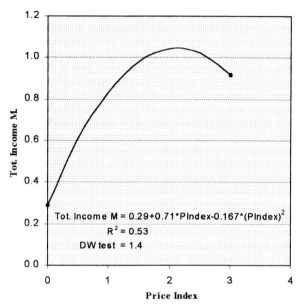

Fig. 18.2 Regression analysis

been employed by geographers in the field of gravitational theory (Haggett, 1965). Gravity based models are widely used in modern scientific geography because they make explicit and operational the idea of relative (as opposed to absolute) distance as well as location. Gravity-based models have the ability to measure such relative location concepts by integrating measures of relative distance with measures of relative size. They enable a review of the structure of a spatial economy as a structural schema involving ordered arrangements of groups, sub-groups, aggregated and disaggregated sectors. The importance of the relative concepts of location, distance, and spatial interaction can be seen in the continued use of wider applications of gravity based models in different fields. The disciplines that use gravity-based models include city and urban planning, transport analysis, retail and location firms, shopping centre investments, land developments (Haynes and Fotheringham, 1984), as well as archaeology (Adams, 1977; Clark and Stankey, 1979).

In practical terms, these gravity-based approaches can provide important inputs for both public and private decision-makers, especially when dealing with macro-level development issues. In brief, two basic elements that capture the most fundamental principles of the gravity model are:

- scale effects: that larger or more developed masses tend to generate more activities than smaller or less developed ones; and
- distance effects: that further places tend to generate less interaction or output of activities than closer ones.

In sum, the gravity model offers a robust analytical technique to present more effectively the space-economy as a hierarchy of focal points and access. Combined with the results of the input–output analysis shown in Figure 18.1, a visual representation of the effects of distance on regional economies becomes apparent.

Conclusion

Figure 18.1 clearly indicates that Bali (0.93) and Jakarta (0.85) are the two main centres for Indonesian tourism. These two destinations have the highest income multiplier values. More important, the multiplier values drop steeply the further regions are from these two centres. This evidence suggests that tourism in Indonesia is related strongly not only to development disparities but also to locational constraints (Nuryanti, 1998). These are significant indicators that government policy in the form of national inter-sectoral development planning for tourism should address. For instance, it implies that the marketing rationale behind the 'Bali and Beyond' campaign may not be realistic from a locational point of view.

The flow of tourism in the regions presupposes a certain level of development such as the existence of necessary infrastructure, services and facilities. In many cases, these can be employed for many public uses within the regions besides tourism. Facilities such as roads, airports, water systems, telephone networks and other public facilities that are constructed to support tourism can also provide greater access to wider markets for many locally produced goods, thus benefiting other economic sectors as well. The relationship between location effect on economic impacts of tourism can be explained by Figure 18.2 that as price distance decreases, the total income values increase. The further the regions are from economic centres, the more likely it is that they lack close sectoral interlinkages to support tourism demand, and thus are less able to absorb the benefits from tourism. In other words, in order to supply tourism demand, the 'remote' category of regions must import goods and services from outside the region (or even outside the country). Therefore, these regions are necessarily associated with higher import values. When these forms of 'import dependency' tourism grow without developing the ability to offer import substitution, it can lead to dependency and create regional imbalances.

This research supports the key insight that it is not the geographical or physical size of a region (sq km per capita) that determines total numbers of tourists and multiplier effect values. Rather, it is the size of the regional economy that is a significant factor in determining the multiplier effect values (Fletcher and Archer, 1990; Archer and Fletcher, 1996). Research carried out on scale and locational effects on tourism multipliers in Indonesia found that the size of the community in terms of both population and geographical size do not act as significant factors in explaining the generation of tourism multiplier values (Nuryanti, 1998). Rather, it is the size of the economic structures and the infrastructure within the region that should be the concern. The size of the local or regional economy has been found to be significant in influencing the degree to which economic benefits leak out of the region.

Furthermore, the research suggests that the gravity model combined with interlinkage principles can play a useful role in helping formulate tourism policy in the context of regional development. More appropriate national and regional development policies will encourage greater numbers of visitors and produce a higher quality of development, generate higher income multiplier values and reduce leakages. This policy role is fundamental in developing the tourism sector which is characterised by resource immobility, capacity constraints, seasonality and, most of all, the consumer's inability to experience the product before purchase.

The research presented here suggests that market proximity to the centres and easy accessibility are the main factors in explaining the hypothesis that accessibility factors strongly influence not only the total number of visitor arrivals but also the value of multiplier effects from visitor spending. These findings confirm the importance of spatial interconnections as well as intersectoral linkages that occur within regions with a higher level of development and easier access. It underscores the importance of these linkages in supporting the development of tourism that is associated with higher income multiplier values as seen in Figure 18.1. It is suggested that these findings, with the importance and understanding of the concept of *location*, may be a key concept for planners in addressing national and regional tourism development with the aim of minimising regional imbalances.

As borders and barriers to travel dissolve daily, especially among the ASEAN countries of Southeast Asia, regional cooperation in the form of tourism development has become a central pillar among governments to promote stronger regional growth. In many areas – human resource training, marketing and promotion, infrastructure, transportation – the links are being put in place that already enable visitors to visit easily different destinations in different countries.

At the same time, competitor countries in Southeast Asia such as Thailand, Malaysia and the Philippines project a similar image in the major tourism markets of Europe, North America, and Asia Pacific. That is, they all market themselves as having a tropical climate, good beaches, warm hospitality, varied marine and land environments, exotic local cultures and inexpensive services and accommodation. Therefore, while cooperation will continue to be an important feature of the relationship between these sister countries, there will simultaneously be an effort to distinguish one from the other by emphasising regional characteristics to increase market share.

Within this context of cooperation and competition, it is evident that well-founded policies of tourism planning in a regional framework will encourage development and offer more social and economic benefits to the populations in the regions concerned.

References

Adams, J.G.L. (1977) 'Tourism as a means of development in remote areas', in B.S. Duffield (ed.) *Tourism: A Tool for Regional Development*. Edinburgh: Tourism and Recreation Research Unit, University of Edinburgh, 8.1–8.9.

Archer, B.H. (1977) 'The economic costs and benefits of tourism', in B.S. Duffield (ed.) *Tourism: A Tool For Regional Development*. Edinburgh: Tourism and Recreation Research Unit, University of Edinburgh, 5.1–5.11.

Archer, B.H. and Fletcher, J.E. (1990) 'Multiplier analysis in tourism'. *Cahiers du Tourisme*, 3, 28–47.

Archer, B.H. and Fletcher, J.E. (1996) 'The economic impact of tourism in the Seychelles'. *Annals of Tourism Research*, 23(1), 32–47.

Biro Pusat Statistik (BPS) (1986–1994) *Foreign Tourist Opinion Survey*. Jakarta: BPS

BPS (1990) *Input–Output Table (Indonesia) Volumes I, II, III*. Jakarta: BPS.

BPS (1995a) *Studi Dampak Ekonomi Pariwisata di Indonesia, Indikator Sosekpar, Laporan Akhir*. Jakarta: BPS.

BPS (1995b) *Studi Dampak Ekonomi Pariwisata di Indonesia, Hasil Analisis*. Jakarta: BPS.

BPS (1995c) *Survey Opini Wisatawan Asing di Indonesia 1988–1995*. Jakarta: BPS.

BPS (1995d) *Data Pariwisata Indonesia*. Jakarta: BPS.

BPS (1995e) *Data Statistik Pariwisata Indonesia*. Jakarta: BPS.

Briguglio, L., Butler, R., Harrison, D. and Filho, D. (1996) *Sustainable Tourism in Islands and Small States*. London: Pinter.

Bull, A. (1991) *The Economics of Travel and Tourism*. London: Pitman.

Capener, H., Jones, B. and Clavel, P. (1969) *Alternative Organisational Models for District Development*. Ithaca, New York: Cornell University.

Clark, R.N. and Stankey, G.H. (1979) *The Recreation Opportunity Spectrum: A Framework for Planning, Management, and Research*. Washington D.C.: US Department of Agriculture Forest Service.

Conlin, M. and Baum, T. (ed.) (1995) *Island Tourism: Management Principles and Practice*. New York: Wiley.

Directorate General of Tourism (DGT) (1997) *Pariwisata Indonesia*. Jakarta: DGT.

Ecumenical Coalition on Third World Tourism (ECTWT) (1988) *Tourism: An Ecumenical Concern*. Bangkok: ECTWT.

Fletcher, J.E. (1989) 'Input–output analysis and tourism impact studies'. *Annals of Tourism Research*, 16(4), 514–29.

Frank, A. (1969) *Capitalism and Underdevelopment in Latin America*. New York: Monthly Review Press.

Friedmann, J. (1966) *Regional Development Policy: A Case Study of Venezuela*. London: MIT Press.

Haggett, P. (1965) *Locational Analysis in Human Geography*. London: Edward Arnold.

Haynes, K.E. and Fotheringham, A.S. (1984) *Gravity and Spatial Interaction Models*. London: Sage.

Ibbery, B. (1984) 'Core-periphery contrast in European social well-being'. *Geography*, 69, 289–302.

Isard, W. (1979) 'General theory: Social, political, economic and regional', in W. Isard (ed.) *Location and Space-Economy*. Massachusetts: MIT Press, 172–206.

Lea, J. (1988) *Tourism and Development in the Third World*. New York: Routledge.

Losch, A. (1954) *The Economics of Locations*. New Haven: Yale University.

Morris, J.M., Dumble, P.L., and Wigan, M.R. (1979) 'Accessibility indicators for transport planning'. *Transportation Research*, 13A, 91–109.

Nuryanti, W. (1998) 'Scale and Locational Effects on Tourism Multipliers – Tourism and Regional Development in Indonesia', Unpublished Ph.D. thesis, Department of Service Industries, Bournemouth University, UK.

Pearce, D. (1989) *Tourism Development*. New York: Longman Scientific.

Picard, M. (1996) *Bali: Cultural Tourism and Touristic Culture*, tr. D. Darling. Singapore: Archipelago Press.

Vickerman, R.W. (1975) *The Economics of Leisure and Recreation*. London: Macmillan Press.

Vickerman, R.W. (1995) 'Accessibility and regional development', paper presented at the *European Science Foundation Conference on European Transport and Communications, Espinho, Portugal*.

Weaver, D. (1998) 'The evolution of 'plantation' tourism landscape on the Caribbean Islands of Antigua'. *Tijdschrift voor Economische en Social Geografie*, 79, 319–31.

World Tourism Organization (WTO) (1996) *Yearbook of Tourism Statistics*. Madrid: WTO.

Young , F. (1966) 'A proposal for co-operative cross-cultural research on intervillage systems'. *Human Organization*, 25(1), 46–50.

19

Conclusion: Southeast Asian Tourism Connections – Status, Challenges and Opportunities

Geoffrey Wall

Introduction

Thoughts on the millennium

This chapter, indeed this book, was begun in the twentieth century and completed in the twenty-first century. In the middle of 1999, while checking out of a small hotel in Indonesia, the author was surprised to be offered birthday greetings by the cashier. Date of birth had been an item on the registration form completed on checking into the hotel and the perceptive cashier had noticed this. The greeting was all the more surprising in that the author was not aware that it was his birthday until it was pointed out to him. On the other hand, when visiting a Chinese restaurant in Canada in February 2000, the author surprised the staff with New Year greetings and best wishes for the 'Year of the Dragon'. The Chinese staff wondered how a Caucasian Canadian from the United Kingdom would know about such things. As one who is prone to overlook his own birthday as well as the special anniversaries of others, it should not be surprising that the approaching millennium was viewed with some scepticism.

It is impossible to deny the importance of the passage of time as each new day brings us one day closer to our eventual demise. Most individuals and societies have important rites associated with the passage of time – and sometimes these celebrations become tourist attractions. The passing of the old millennium and the onset of the new, being rarer than a new year, was seen by many as a particularly special time for celebration as well as assessment. This was so even though there was uncertainty concerning the date from which the millennium should be counted as well as the precise year in which the new millennium would begin. Although the celebration of specific rites are largely culture-bound and one might be cynical concerning the reasons why one day might be accorded special significance as compared to the next, the millennium achieved global recognition. Locations competed with claims to be the first place in which to experience the millennium and special events to celebrate it were arranged in many parts of the world and shared in rapid succession by the global media. It was a spectacle of global significance, albeit one of questionable authenticity.

Although in many ways an idea, the notion of the millennium had tangible significance. The disruptions to computer systems may not have occurred on the scale which was predicted, nevertheless, the consequences were very real in the vast amounts of money which were spent to prepare for, avoid or respond to possible catastrophe. The millennium was also a tourism phenomenon, spawning numerous events around the world (Olsen and Timothy, 1999). However, uncertainty concerning computer systems caused many to avoid flying and, at least in my home area, the inflated rates charged by organisers of special events caused many to celebrate at home with the result that advance ticket sales were slow and some commercial events were cancelled.

The conference that led to the publication of this book as, indeed, the publication of the book itself, are both events linked to the millennium. The conference was also a tourism event in that it brought together people from a variety of locations for a mix of business and pleasure. Although Southeast Asia has had its share of millennial spectacles, when viewed in retrospect, it is very likely that the passage of the millennium *per se* will prove not to have been a watershed in the evolution of tourism in Southeast Asia. However, it did provide a good excuse to celebrate, take stock and chart new directions and thereby contribute to tourism research and education in the twenty-first century.

The Asian economic crisis

The latter years of the twentieth century had been a time of turbulence in Southeast Asia. More than a decade of growth in tourism was suddenly terminated by a period of sharp declines associated with the so-called Asian economic crisis, leading to a period of retrenchment and re-evaluation. The Asian economic crisis which, fortunately, appears to be subsiding, demonstrates both the global ties and local nuances of Southeast Asian economies and destinations, with the consequences being inconsistent across the region (Wall, 1998a). In a world in which economies are intertwined, the crisis was not restricted to Southeast Asia but it became a phenomenon with global implications. Furthermore, it was not one crisis but many with varied causes and consequences in different locations. For example, elsewhere I have argued that Indonesia has been experiencing at least five crises: economic, political, racial and two related environmental crises in the form of drought and forest fires (Wall, 1998b). Each of these crises has its implications for tourism but their individual roles are difficult to determine since they are occurring at the same time with inter-related repercussions.

If we consider each of these crises in turn, some of the differences in their implications for tourism can be teased out. The economic crisis reduced the discretionary spending of those market segments which had previously been expanding most rapidly, i.e. the middle classes of the expanding and economically vibrant Asian cities. Thus there was a reduction in the regional demand. Those living in peripheral locations and relying on subsistence economies, living hand-to-mouth existences and lacking discretionary incomes, were essentially not consumers of tourism products. Paradoxically, although their incomes were often low, they were partially insulated from the failings of the monetary economy because of their minimal linkages to it. On the other hand, their well-being was adversely affected by recurring droughts, which curtailed agricultural productivity, thereby encouraging the clearing of more land both by small subsistence farmers and large operators of commercial plantations. Slash-and-burn land clearing techniques were more difficult to control in the dry conditions with the result that forest fires were rampant. Not only did these fires and slash-and-burn techniques destroy large areas of great biological diversity with considerable tourism potential, the smoke haze drifted across nearby countries such as Singapore and Malaysia. Indonesia literally smoked out some of its most important markets! One suspects that the onset of rain will have increased erosion on the denuded slopes, leading to increased sedimentation in coastal locations, possibly threatening coral reefs.

Meanwhile, the economic crisis in Indonesia was accompanied by political dislocation as Suharto, the long-time President, was forced to step down amidst riots and loss of life. Fearing for their safety, potential tourists shunned Indonesia but they did so to differing degrees, for varied lengths of time and selectively with respect to location. For example, following an immediate decline, Bali was viewed as a safe haven and, initially aided by bargain basement prices, rebounded fairly rapidly, particularly in the Australian market. On the other hand, riots in neighbouring Lombok subsequently resulted in the evacuation of tourists and undermined tourism there (*Sunday Morning Post Magazine*, 9 April 2000). The racial and religious aspects of the violence in Indonesia particularly threatened Chinese Indonesians. Thus, the racial violence was especially unsettling to the regional market, a large proportion of which was expatriate Chinese. While some Indonesian Chinese fled, at least temporarily, the low value of the rupiah, the reduction in the number of flights and the imposition of large departure taxes on Indonesian residents reduced the participation of Indonesians in international travel.

The above description of recent events in one country indicates the complexity of forces influencing Southeast Asian tourism, their far-reaching consequences and the poverty of single-factor explanations. While it would be nice to be able to distinguish the relative importance of each event and to separate out their individual consequences, it is virtually impossible to do so. In any case, the reality is that they do not operate in isolation: they are intertwined, the interconnections between countries are obvious and at the same time obscure and their consequences, cumulative.

With the benefit of hindsight it will be possible to determine whether the Asian economic crisis will prove to be a mere blip on a long-term trend or of more lasting significance. Fortunately, there are signs that the worst may be over and that recovery may be starting to occur. In fact, Francesco Frangialli, Secretary-General of the World Tourism Organisation, indicated that: "[t]he Asia-Pacific region was once again the star of world tourism in 1999, reaching a growth rate of 7.5 per cent and a new record total of 94 million international tourists" (*The Globe and Mail*, 16 February 2000). Regardless, the changing circumstances will ensure that future tourism will not be the same as in the past. Thus, both time and circumstances combine to make it appropriate to re-examine the past, present and future of tourism in Southeast Asia.

The regional context

Although other papers have mentioned the topic, it is reasonable to reflect upon the magnitude and limitations of the area under consideration in this book. In other words, what and where is Southeast Asia? The diversity of Southeast Asia creates the possibility of defining the region in different ways and, at the same time, leads to variability in the regions that are so designated by different individuals and organisations.

Geographers usually acknowledge the existence of two types of region: formal or homogeneous regions and functional or nodal regions. A third type of region, a composite region in which both physical and human phenomena combine to give an area distinctive characteristics, has long been discredited as a useful concept for the boundaries of such phenomena rarely are coterminous and the notion smacks of environmental determinism (Whittlesey, 1954).

Formal regions are areas with common characteristics, such as rainfall within a specified range or the majority of people espousing a particular religion. They are homogeneous in the sense that all areas within the region exhibit the common specified characteristic that distinguishes it from other areas. Functional regions, on the other hand, exhibit a core area with ties that often tend to diminish in strength with increasing distance from the central node. Examples are cities and their hinterlands and ports and the areas from which they draw products for shipment. Of course, one should not expect formal and functional regions to be identical in location, extent or boundaries.

It is reasonable to question the applicability of these concepts to Southeast Asia either as a whole or with respect to specific parts. Clearly, both Asia and Southeast Asia are extremely diverse with respect to both physical and human phenomena. In fact, this is an attraction of the area for tourists. There are large land masses and archipelagos; mountains, plains and coasts; wet and dry areas; tropical forest and xerophytic scrublands; major cities and remote rural areas; and agricultural and livelihood systems of many different kinds. There is great cultural diversity, including languages, religions and architectural styles, as well as considerable variations in levels of development. Countries of the region have varied sizes, wealth and colonial histories. From a functional perspective, there are important nodes, such as Singapore and Bangkok, but not a single core, which unites the whole region. Thus, it is perhaps misleading to consider Southeast Asia as a region in the strict formal or functional senses.

Geographers now tend to regard regions as human constructs rather than tangible phenomena. They are used to assist in the organisation of knowledge about places, and their areas and boundaries may vary depending upon the purposes for which they are being constructed and used. Thus regions are tools rather than artefacts. In this chapter, following Teo and Chang (1998), Southeast Asia is viewed as comprising 10 countries: Brunei, Cambodia, Indonesia, Laos, Malaysia, Myanmar, the Philippines, Singapore, Thailand and Vietnam. The main criteria for grouping them together are proximity, convention and convenience.

Tourism, by definition, is an open system – it involves the movement of people as well as their expenditures, and often sources of investment, across boundaries. The definition of such boundaries influences the numbers and types of tourists and their expenditures that are recorded. From the perspective of tourism, there is obviously great variation within Southeast Asia in the scale, manifestations and degree of dependence upon tourism. Tourism is not evenly distributed throughout the region but tends to be concentrated in capital cities and in resort areas which are well endowed with natural or cultural resources and which have managed to acquire the capital to develop the infrastructure required by all forms of tourism except those which are extremely small in scale. Furthermore, both Southeast Asia and tourism are open rather than closed systems. Tourists both originate within the region and come from elsewhere, and some leave the region to become tourists in other parts of the world. Thus, there are incoming and outgoing flows of people, goods and capital as well as ideas and political influence.

Trends

Having argued that Southeast Asia is largely an artificial construct, attention now turns to a brief discussion of tourism trends in the region. The data which will be employed, with their advantages of accessibility and disadvantages of inconsistent definitions and changing regional boundaries, are taken predominantly from publications of the World Tourism Organisation, especially the WTO Commission for East Asia and the Pacific (1998) report on tourism market trends. In some cases, they have been recalculated to better meet present purposes.

Although the data are incomplete and selective, in unveiling the trends, two things are apparent: (i) the volume of movement of tourists within the Southeast Asian region is growing and the commodification of differences in physical features, culture and history support the notion of the region as being socially constructed; (ii) at the same time, the attractiveness of the region to international tourists promotes collaboration and cooperation and highlights interconnections within and outside the region which can be harnessed. The trends are:

- Global tourism has grown extremely rapidly as indicated by the numbers of international travellers and, especially, their expenditures. In 1986, globally, 339 million international tourists were enumerated. By 1996, this figure had risen to 594 million. This constitutes a growth of 75.2 per cent in a decade. The money spent by these travellers, partially fuelled by inflation, grew at an even faster rate: from US$142 billion in 1986 to US$423 billion for a growth of 197.7 per cent.
- Southeast Asian arrivals and receipts have grown at substantially greater rates than the global averages, at least until the recent Asian economic crisis and this is probably only a temporary setback. Between 1986 and 1995, international arrivals in Southeast Asia increased from 11.1 million to 30.5 million, i.e. 174.6 per cent. At the same time, receipts grew 438.6 per cent from US$5.5 million to US$29.5

million. Thus, tourism has grown more rapidly in Southeast Asia than the substantial global rates of growth with the result that Southeast Asia has hosted a growing proportion of both global arrivals (13.3 per cent in 1996 compared to 9.8 per cent in 1987) and global tourism receipts (15.5 per cent in 1996 and 10.0 per cent in 1987).

- The regional market has grown even more rapidly than the long-haul market. At the same time as the number of international tourists and their expenditures increased, the origins of international visitors also changed substantially. In 1986, 45.5 per cent of international tourists in Southeast Asia originated from other countries in the region, 23.2 per cent from elsewhere in East Asia and the Pacific, and 31.3 per cent came from other locations, i.e. long-haul travellers. By 1995, these figures had changed to 38.6 per cent, 33.9 per cent and 27.5 per cent respectively. Growth occurred in all of these markets but it was particularly marked in the broader regional market (especially Japan but also Taiwan and Hong Kong) with a decline in the *proportion* of the latter, long-haul, group. The implications of these changing distributions deserve to receive more attention than they have been given to date (Wall, 1997a). Not only do these trends suggest changes in the cultures, interests and behaviours of the mix of visitors but, at the risk of over-simplification, the long-haul visitors often have longer lengths of stay but tend to choose cheaper accommodation than many international travellers from within the region. They also may be less likely to travel on packaged tours. All of these differences have implications for expenditure patterns and, hence, the profitability of the various components of the tourism industry. Also, as suggested above, the Asian economic crisis particularly affected demand from those segments of the market that had previously been growing most rapidly.

- Tourism infrastructure has grown enormously in Southeast Asia in recent years. Reception of the growing number of tourists was only possible with the identification and marketing of attractions and the construction of supporting infrastructure of all kinds, including airports, roads, accommodation and restaurants. For example, in Asia and the Pacific in 1980, there was an accommodation capacity of 762,000 beds, i.e. 4.7 per cent of the global total. By 1995, this had risen to 3.5 million beds or 14.4 per cent, suggesting that the rate of expansion of supply was even greater than the growth of demand, with negative consequences for profitability.

- Southeast Asia has expanded as a supplier of international tourists and the Southeast Asian outbound market, especially the long-haul component, has grown at a faster rate than the inbound. It is natural that a study on tourism in Southeast Asia should concentrate on the attributes of tourism within the region. However, it is worth noting that Southeast Asia is a generator as well as a recipient of tourists and that growth in the number of international tourists who are permanent residents of Southeast Asian countries has also occurred. In 1996, East Asia and the Pacific generated 94 million tourist arrivals world-wide: 23.1 per cent to other parts of Southeast Asia and 26.4 per cent long-haul. The number of residents of Southeast Asia visiting long-haul destinations increased by 14.5 per cent in 1994, 16.5 per cent in 1995 and 9.7 per cent in 1996. This shows that travellers from Southeast Asia have been increasingly leaving the region and have become a growing market for destinations in distant parts of the world.

- The growth of tourism is unevenly distributed both nationally and intra-nationally. It is important to recognise that regional and national statistics mask considerable national and sub-national variations in tourism phenomena and that, in fact, tourism is highly concentrated within a region. For example, in Indonesia, approximately half of all 'starred' accommodation is shared between Jakarta and Bali (Wall, 1997b). The remainder is scattered across the immense Indonesian archipelago, either in cities where they cater to business traffic or in resort clusters developed by combinations of public and private investors under the guidance of tourism development corporations, often using the Nusa Dua, Bali integrated resort example as a model (Inskeep and Kallenberger, 1992). The impacts of tourism, whether one is examining economic, environmental or socio-cultural dimensions, are highly localised although there are few countries that are not touched by their consequences.
- Tourism has grown as a source of foreign exchange in Southeast Asia. It is commonplace to read that tourism is the fastest growing industry in the world and many countries in the region have identified tourism as a growth sector in their economic plans. Certainly, while tourism has grown very quickly, it is likely that some sectors, such as computers and information technology, have expanded even more rapidly. Of course, the tourism industry is a user of such technologies and a disseminator of information.

Other important topics concerning trends such as impacts and policies have not been dealt with. Some have been discussed elsewhere in this volume, usually on a national or local scale as well as at the scale of the region as a whole. What the trends do point out is that many factors, both internal to Southeast Asia and external to the region, underpin their development. The substantial increase in supply of tourism spots and facilities has already been noted. In addition, until recently, there has been growth in discretionary incomes, especially in the broader regional market. As has been pointed out, it is the growing middle classes of the major Asian cities that have particularly fuelled the growth of tourism in Southeast Asia, at least until the recent economic downturn. Increased incomes have contributed to a decline in the real costs of travel. At the same time, many countries in the region have placed increased emphasis on tourism in their national development plans; have done more to promote themselves as destinations through enhanced marketing budgets and initiatives such as 'international tourism years'; and have reduced travel formalities making access easier. All of these initiatives were taken to boost national tourism or regional tourism.

Global and local phenomena

Tourism is a global phenomenon. In fact, tourism constitutes the largest movement of people in human history, albeit that the majority return to their place of departure. In addition to people, it involves massive movements of capital and other resources as well as the exchange of ideas among diverse peoples and the transformation of the destinations which are visited. This leads some to see tourism as an homogenising force and as a form of globalisation (Relph, 1976). Globalisation is a process by which people from all over the world are drawn into world-wide networks through the deployment of communication and transportation technologies and the development of increasing flows and exchanges of commodities, information, ideas, knowledge and images.

However, global forces impinge upon local situations where they are not merely received, rather they are reformulated. Tourism is very unevenly distributed and is concentrated in specific locations such as major cities, coastal resorts and historic sites. These destinations have their own economic, environmental and cultural attributes which transform the global forces into unique local experiences, and seemingly small but distinctive characteristics of places and peoples are accorded special status and marketed accordingly (Harvey, 1989).

Thus, tourism is, at the same time, a homogenising and a differentiating phenomenon as global forces are mediated by local conditions and even small local differences may become causes for celebration and turned into tourist attractions. The combination of global and local may be termed 'glocal' to signify that both forces operate at the same time in ways which are difficult to separate. While tourists can have far-reaching consequences for the places they visit, local authorities and communities compete for international tourists and investors, often applauding their economic successes but also resenting the changes in lifestyles associated with tourism development. Thus, tourism should not be viewed simply as an external force which impinges upon destinations for it is also sought and manipulated. The resulting manifestations are derived from a combination of external and internal phenomena. The influence of tourism has become so pervasive in some societies, such as Bali, that it is impossible, and perhaps even unhelpful, to view them as being separate from tourism (Picard, 1997).

The broad global–local relationships are underpinned by a variety of tensions. Building upon the work of Swain (1989; 1993), these are identified as authenticity versus commoditization (see e.g. Teo and Yeoh and Cohen in this volume), economic development versus cultural preservation (see e.g. Parnwell, this volume), cultural evolution versus commodification (see e.g. Cartier, Ooi and Sofield, this volume), ethnic autonomy versus state regulation (see e.g. Black and Wall and Grundy-Warr and Perry, this volume), and mass tourism development versus sustainable tourism (e.g. Markwell and Wong. in this volume). Brief comments will be made on each of these dichotomies although they are not, in fact distinct, but overlap in many ways.

Authenticity is a relative rather than an absolute term and, like beauty, is in the eye of the beholder. Cohen (1988) argued that authenticity is a socially constructed concept and its social connotation is not given but is 'negotiable'. Authenticity and falseness are not a dichotomous pair of concepts and authenticity may be judged differently in association with varying types of visitor profiles (Wang, 1999). Commodification is usually used to refer to situations in which a price is placed on artefacts or experiences which were previously not for sale so that cultural expressions become marketable tourism products. The commodification of tourism has long been criticised as the 'bastardisation' and 'pollution' of previously authentic ethnic cultures for the purpose of touristic display (Wood, 1997). While this may seem to be unfortunate, it should be acknowledged that if tourism is to contribute to economic growth through jobs and incomes, then tourists must be charged for their experiences. Failure to do so would result in a situation where hosts receive most of the costs and few of the benefits.

Tourism is usually desired by host nations and destination areas because of the foreign exchange, jobs and incomes it may bring. In fact, participants in tourism usually want change and see tourism bringing benefits as well as costs (Wall, 1996a). However, where expressions of local culture are part of the attraction, it is likely that they will be commodified and even made into spectacles. Who should decide which changes are acceptable and which are not? Vibrant cultures are unlikely to be static but may evolve in response to both internal and external stimuli. Not only may attempts to 'freeze' culture be doomed to failure in the face of global forces of change, such approaches would frustrate the legitimate desires of resident populations to seek improvements in their well-being.

With respect to local autonomy and state regulation, tourism has become a political tool. In many of the multi-ethnic societies of Southeast Asia, symbols of society have become both tourist attractions and icons of nationalism promoted for both internal and external consumption: symbols of national identity and pride for domestic consumption and means of international differentiation for the foreign tourism market. Yet, what is in the interests of the nation may not always be what minority groups would desire. Thus, cultural diversity may be an advantage for attracting tourists but may be an impediment to national solidarity and nation-building. Few would deny that national and regional governments have important roles to play in tourism, but there is often no agreement on what the specific responsibilities should be.

The rhetoric of sustainable development has been embraced in Southeast Asia but, as in other parts of the world, the contributions which tourism can and should make to the sustainable development agenda continue to be unclear and contested (Butler, 1993; Wall, 1997c).

While the availability of statistical data on aspects of tourism in Southeast Asia is improving slowly, the research agenda has widened to embrace evaluation of the meaning and significance of tourism in the region. These are questions that are not readily answered using conventional tourism statistics and that require the use of qualitative as well as quantitative research techniques for their resolution. The research questions which are being asked, and the means adopted for their exploration, have broadened immensely during the last decade of the last century. The exploration of Swain's paradoxes provides a rich opportunity for tourism researchers in many disciplines and is raising a plethora of new questions in the region, including the role of intermediaries, such as guidebooks (Connell, 1993; McGregor, 2000) and guides, whether licensed or 'wild' (Bras, 2000), the importance of entrepreneurship (Dahles and Bras, 1999), the part to be played by the informal sector (Timothy and Wall, 1997) and the distribution of power, including gender relationships (Cukier, Norris and Wall, 1996). Given the diversity of the region, one might expect locational differences in the research findings and their potential applications.

Opportunities and challenges associated with diversity

Diversity is both an asset and a challenge. Diversity provides the opportunity to develop distinctive tourism products and to cater to specialised market niches. At the same time, it creates challenges for the development of strong national identities and, if taken to the extreme, can lead to fragmentation and political dissension.

Tourism thrives on the identification, celebration and commodification of differences. The diversity of natural and cultural phenomena, both within the region as a whole and at national and local levels which has been noted above, should afford an unparalleled opportunity to develop distinctive tourism products. A rich supply of sea, sun and sand, and vibrant cities backed by hinterlands with diverse cultures, including amazing historical relics, as well as places with exceptional biodiversity should enable the region to cater to a wide range of different market segments. Unfortunately, current levels of development (including lack of infrastructure) which may in themselves be attractions to some emerging market niches such as ecotourists and adventure tourists, frustrate the expansion of tourism in the very places which could most benefit from visitor expenditures (provided that associated negative consequences can be mitigated).

Unfortunately, the very diversity which is attractive to tourists may be viewed as a threat by host governments that are striving to forge national identities in multicultural situations. In many cases, countries in the region have not long won their independence from colonial powers and the arrival of large numbers of foreigners may be viewed as a mixed blessing. Celebration of the manifestations of cultures living in peripheral locations may be viewed as encouraging regionalism. Symbols of tradition may be interpreted as being signs of backwardness in places which are striving to modernise, albeit on their own terms. It is a paradox that, through tourism, societies are encouraged to retain and share their traditions so that they can improve their life opportunities. In other words, they should be traditional so that they can modernise, i.e. remain unchanged so that they can change! Clearly, there are many difficult questions associated with striving for a balance between authenticity, however determined, and commodification; and between the interests of the tourist industry, whether locally or externally controlled, national governments and ethnic minorities.

Regional responses

It is my impression from travelling widely in the region that, in spite of the impressive growth of visitor and expenditure statistics, responses to the opportunities and challenges afforded by tourism have been mixed. For example, in spite of its diversity, Southeast Asian nations have tended to present an unnecessarily homogeneous tourism product based on largely undifferentiated tourism plans. There appears to have been an emphasis on the provision of accommodation to the relative neglect of other aspects of the tourists' experiences. To draw upon a Chinese proverb, it appears that there has been a strong belief in the saying: "Build the nest, and the birds will come!" My retort is that people do not usually wish to spend money simply to sleep in a bed that perhaps thousands of other people have slept in before. There are usually other reasons for visiting a place. Successful tourism requires the careful integration of all those factors which contribute to the tourism experience – attractions, transportation, food and beverage provision, service quality, safety etc. – for deficiencies in any one of these will reduce visitor satisfaction and undermine the tourism product. Burns in this section of the volume clearly states that there must be coalescence between national agendas and local level planning so that problems such as this will not occur. Likewise, Cohen's chapter and Nuryanti's chapter point out the dangers of homogenisation and of trickling-down effects not taking place as anticipated.

While the scale and quality of some tourism developments have done much to enhance the reputation of some Southeast Asian tourism destinations, this approach has often resulted in developments which are out of scale with the resource base on which successful and sustainable tourism ultimately depends. In places like Kuta, Bali, where the number of small establishments has proliferated to such an extent that a tourist city has developed, complete with traffic congestion, air and noise pollution and one-way streets (Wall, 1996b), or Melaka, Malaysia, where high-rise hotels now dwarf some of the heritage buildings, the developments are out of scale with the natural and cultural resources on which tourism ultimately depends. The environments of many destination areas in Asia are reeling from the consequences of tourism with eroded beaches, inadequate sewage disposal and groundwater contaminated by salt-water intrusion (Knight, Mitchell and Wall, 1997). Western tourists walk around with bottled water not only because of the tropical climate, but because they are afraid to drink the local water as well as to eat much local food. Perhaps as many as one-third suffer from some medical discomfort on their holidays in Southeast Asia. If tourism is to contribute to sustainable development, then environmental quality must be ensured. This could contribute to the well-being of local people as well as tourists.

Concentration on the provision of 'starred' hotels and resorts to the relative neglect of alternative forms of development has resulted in the supply of an unnecessarily homogeneous tourism product and dependence on external investors. It has also caused increased competition in mature markets to the relative neglect of emerging markets. There is an over-supply of visitor accommodation in many locations in the region with associated low occupancy rates and cut-throat pricing strategies. Furthermore, reliance on outside investments has often ensured that there are only limited opportunities for local people to become involved in the formal tourism industry; they are often displaced, disadvantaged or try to survive on the margins of the industry in the informal sector (Wall, 1996c). This, in turn, exacerbates regional and social inequities.

Conclusions

This book, as well as the conference on which it is based, come at a critical time for tourism in Southeast Asia. A period of rapid growth has stalled in the face of the Asian economic crises and, when coupled with the millennium which provides a timely excuse to reflect upon the past and to contemplate the future, these events provide an appropriate context in which to undertake an assessment of tourism in the region, to examine what is and what is not known, and to chart a new course if it is decided that is necessary.

The great natural and cultural diversity of the region provides considerable opportunities for the further development of tourism if this is treated in appropriate ways. At the same time, tourism provides many challenges for governments facing major development needs in post-colonial societies and searching for national cohesion in multi-ethnic situations. It has been suggested that, in an international world which some regard as becoming increasingly homogeneous, small differences are increasingly important. As the tourists become more discerning, new avenues must be sought to sustain the flows of tourism. The opportunities are limitless and can be as creative as danger-zone tourism as suggested by Adams in this section of the book. If harnessed appropriately, diversity can be an asset and, as in natural systems where biodiversity promotes resilience to perturbations, increased product differentiation for an increasingly segmented market could provide a means by which tourism can contribute towards sustainable development in Southeast Asia.

References

Bras, K. (2000) *Image-Building and Guiding on Lombok: The Social Construction of a Tourist Destination*. Amsterdam: K. Bras.

Butler, R. (1993) 'Tourism – an evolutionary perspective', in J.G. Nelson, R. Butler and G. Wall (eds.) *Tourism and Sustainable Development: Monitoring, Planning, Managing*, Department of Geography Publication Series No. 37. Waterloo: University of Waterloo, 27–43.

Cohen, E. (1988) 'Authenticity and commoditization in tourism'. *Annals of Tourism Research*, 15(3), 371–86.

Connell, J. (1993) 'Bali revisited: Death, rejuvenation and the tourist cycle'. *Environment and Planning D: Society and Space*, 11(6), 641–61.

Cukier, J., Norris, J and Wall, G. (1996) 'The involvement of women in the tourism industry of Bali, Indonesia'. *The Journal of Development Studies*, 33(2), 248–70.

Dahles, H. and Bras, K. (1999) 'Entrepreneurs in romance'. *Annals of Tourism Research*, 26(2), 267–93.

Globe and Mail, The (2000) 'Asia, Middle East hot as tourism expands', 16 February, Toronto.

Harvey, D. (1989) *The Condition of Postmodernity: An Enquiry into the Origins of Cultural Change*. Cambridge, Mass.: Blackwell.

Knight, D., Mitchell, B. and Wall, G. (1997) 'Bali: Sustainable development, tourism and coastal management'. *Ambio*, 26(2), 90–6.

Inskeep, E. and Kallenberger, M. (1992) *An Integrated Approach to Resort Development*. Madrid: World Tourism Organisation (WTO).

McGregor, A. (2000) 'Dynamic texts and tourist gaze: Death, bones and buffalo'. *Annals of Tourism Research*, 27(1), 27–50.

Olsen, D.H. and Timothy, D.J. (1999) 'Tourism 2000: Selling the Millennium'. *Tourism Management*, 20(4), 389–92.

Picard, M. (1997) 'Cultural tourism, nation-building, and regional culture: The making of a Balinese identity', in M. Picard and R.E. Wood (eds.) *Tourism, Ethnicity and the State in Asian and Pacific Societies*. Honolulu: University of Hawaii Press, 181–214.

Relph, E. (1976) *Place and Placelessness*. London: Pion.

Sunday Morning Post Magazine (2000) 'Paradise postponed', 9 April, Hong Kong, 22–5.

Swain, M. (1989) 'Developing ethnic tourism in Yunnan, China: Shilin Sani'. *Tourism Recreation Research*, 14(1), 33–9.

Swain, M. (1993) 'Women producers of ethnic arts'. *Annals of Tourism Research,* 20(1), 32–51.

Teo, P. and Chang, T.C. (1998) 'Critical issues in a critical era: Tourism in Southeast Asia'. *Singapore Journal of Tropical Geography,* 19(2), 119–29.

Timothy, D. and Wall, G. (1997) 'Selling to tourists: Indonesian street vendors'. *Annals of Tourism Research,* 24(2), 322–40.

Wall, G.(1996a) 'Ecotourism: Change, impacts and opportunities', in J.A. Miller and E. Malek-Zadeh (eds.) *The Ecotourism Equation: Measuring the Impacts,* Bulletin Series 99. New Haven: Yale School of Forestry and Environmental Studies, 108–17.

Wall, G. (1996b) 'One name, two destinations: Planned and unplanned coastal resorts in Indonesia', in L.C. Harrison and W. Husbands (eds.) *Practicing Responsible Tourism: Case Studies in Tourism Planning, Policy and Development.* New York: Wiley, 41–57.

Wall, G. (1996c) 'People outside the plans', in W. Nuryanti (ed.) *Tourism and Culture: Global Civilization in Change, Proceedings of the Indonesia–Swiss Forum on Culture and International Tourism, Yogyakarta, 1995.* Yogyakarta: Gadjah Mada University Press, 130–37.

Wall, G. (1997a) 'Types of travellers and the implications for planning: Consumption and production of tourism experiences'. *Histoire et Anthropologie,* 15, 55–62.

Wall, G. (1997b) 'Indonesia: The impact of regionalization', in F. Go and C. Jenkins (eds.) *Tourism and Development in Asia and Australasia.* London: Cassell, 138–49.

Wall, G. (1997c) 'Sustainable tourism – unsustainable development', in J. Pigram and S. Wahab (eds.) *Tourism Development and Growth: The Challenge of Sustainability.* London: Routledge, 33–49.

Wall, G. (1998a) 'Reflections upon the state of Asian tourism'. *Singapore Journal of Tropical Geography,* 19(2), 232–37.

Wall, G. (1998b) 'Indonesian tourism: Crises, response and recovery', in M. Gunawan (ed.) *Pariwisata Indonesia: Menuju Keputusan Yang Lebih Baik* (Indonesian Tourism: Recovery and Improvement). Bandung: Pusat Penelitan Kepariwisataan, Institute of Technology, Bandung, 6–14.

Wang, N. (1999) 'Rethinking authenticity in tourism experience'. *Annals of Tourism Research,* 26(2), 349–70.

Whittlesey, D. (1954) 'The regional concept and the regional method' in P.E. James and C.F. Jones, (eds.) *American Geography: Inventory and Prospect.* Syracuse: Association of American Geographers and Syracuse University Press, 19–68.

Wood, R. (1997) 'Tourism and the state: Ethnic options and constructions of others', in M. Picard and R. Wood (eds.) *Tourism, Ethnicity, and the State in Asian and Pacific Societies.* Honolulu: University of Hawaii Press, 1–34.

World Tourism Organisation Commission for East Asia and the Pacific (1998) *Tourism Market Trends East Asia and the Pacific 1986–1996.* Madrid: WTO.

Author Index

Note: this index contains only personal names. Corporate organisations and institutions are included in the *Subject Index*. An 'n' prefix indicates a note, e.g. 278n.4 refers to note 4 on page 278.

Subject Index

Note: a) all personal names are included in the Name Index, b) an 'n' prefix indicates a note, e.g. 278n.7 refers to note 7 on page 278.